Economic Justice

Economic Justice

The Market Socialist Vision

JAMES A. YUNKER

ROWMAN & LITTLEFIELD PUBLISHERS, INC.
Lanham • New York • Boulder • Oxford

ROWMAN & LITTLEFIELD PUBLISHERS, INC.

Published in the United States of America
by Rowman & Littlefield Publishers, Inc.
4720 Boston Way, Lanham, Maryland 20706

12 Hid's Copse Road
Cummor Hill, Oxford OX2 9JJ, England

British Library Cataloguing in Publication Information Available

Yunker, James A.
    Economic justice : the market socialist vision / James A. Yunker.
    p.   cm.
    Includes bibliographical references (p.   ) and index.
    ISBN 0–8476–8476–8 (cloth : alk. paper). — ISBN 0–8476–8477–6
(pbk. : alk. paper)
    1. Marxian economics. 2. Mixed economy. 3. Socialism.
    4. Capitalism. I. Title.
HB97.5.Y864   1997
335.4—dc21   96–51869
                                                        CIP

ISBN 0–8476–8476–8 (cloth : alk. paper)
ISBN 0–8476–8477–6 (pbk. : alk. paper)

Printed in the United States of America

⊖™ The paper used in this publication meets the minimum requirements of American
National Standard for Information Sciences—Permanence of Paper for Printed Library
Materials, ANSI Z39.48–1984.

to my parents,

JAMES A. YUNKER
MARGARET F. YUNKER

for not being unduly
concerned by their eldest
son's deviations from orthodoxy

CONTENTS

PREFACE

Can we have economic justice *and* economic efficiency? According to majority opinion at the present time, the answer is no—if by "economic justice" is meant a more equal and equitable distribution of capital property income (dividends, interest, and so on) than that which is currently prevalent in the United States and the other leading capitalist nations of the world. The extravagant inequality which presently prevails in these nations in the distribution of capital wealth and capital property income is widely believed to be a vital determinant of good economic performance, both in the near term and in the long term. Inequality in capital wealth is alleged to be essential to provide adequate incentives to entrepreneurship, enterprise, risk-taking, and other critical inputs to economic success. Extreme inequality in capital wealth ownership is regrettable but unavoidable. It is, in short, a necessary evil.

This book issues a challenge to majority opinion on this matter. The challenge is based on the market socialist alternative to contemporary capitalism. A market socialist economy of the sort proposed in this book would combine public ownership of large, established corporations with a high degree of reliance on free market mechanisms: such as the determination of prices by supply and demand, decentralization of economic decision-making authority, operation of business firms on the basis of profit-maximization, and consumer sovereignty. Such an economy, in its everyday operations, would appear almost identical to the market capitalist economy of today. There would, however, be one critical difference: profits and interest generated by publicly owned corporations would be distributed to the general public as a social dividend supplement to labor income, instead of being paid out in proportion to financial asset ownership. Owing to the extravagant inequality presently prevailing in the ownership of financial assets, this one small change would put significantly more income into the pockets of well over 90 percent of the population.

To say that this is a controversial proposal might seem an almost ludicrous understatement. During the twentieth century the idea of socialism has been a major factor in bringing about a series of extremely violent revolutions and civil wars. Moreover, during the Stalinist era in the

U.S.S.R. and the Maoist era in China, socialism was an integral component of an horrific totalitarian system. Many people have concluded, in light of this sobering history, that socialism is simply too dangerous and too incendiary an idea to be worthy of further consideration. These people have enthusiastically welcomed the recent collapse of Soviet Communism, and they sincerely hope that this dramatic development augurs the final and definitive termination of this particular tragic aberration in human history.

There is certainly no doubt that the collapse of Soviet Communism was an immensely positive and optimistic development in human history. It liberated the Soviet people from an oppressive and stultifying political and economic system. Even more importantly, it liberated all of humanity from the dire peril of a catastrophic nuclear holocaust. There is no doubt that we should all be giving thanks at this time. But at the same time, we should not throw out the baby with the bathwater. What corrupted Soviet Communism was not socialism, but rather its undemocratic, totalitarian political system, and (to a much lesser extent) its excessively ambitious system of central economic planning. The economic and political system that prevailed in the ex-U.S.S.R. and its Eastern European satellites, as well as similar systems still prevailing in the remaining Communist nations of the world, has nothing in common with the economic and political system proposed in this book—aside from the basic socialist principle of public ownership of capital.

To many individuals at the present time, the collapse of Soviet Communism is a welcome harbinger of the final extinction of socialism in any way, shape, or form whatever. But in one important respect, the collapse of Soviet Communism has actually assisted the cause of socialism in the world. The elimination from contention of the undemocratic Soviet model of central planning socialism has cleared the decks for consideration of potentially efficient and democratic forms of socialism—forms which could overcome the problem of excessive inequality of capital wealth ownership under contemporary capitalism without jeopardizing either economic efficiency or political democracy.

Starting with the seminal contribution of Oskar Lange in the 1930s, there has gradually developed a substantial economic literature on market socialism. From the beginning, the market socialist model has been perceived as a more promising socialist alternative to the centrally planned socialist model in the Soviet Union and elsewhere in the Communist world. There are several distinct variants of the basic idea currently being debated among economists. This is not to say that the idea is being *widely* debated within the profession of economics at the present time. Just as only a small minority of the general population is presently disposed toward sympathetic interest in socialism, so too only a small minority of the population of professional economists is so disposed. But it is safe to say that as the literature on market socialism grows and develops, this small minority is gradually increasing. Whether the number of economists with a sympathetic interest in market socialism will ever attain adequate dimensions to imply a serious threat to the continuation of the capitalist status quo is uncertain—and at this point it certainly appears to be highly dubious. But occasionally in human history, remarkable transitions occur in remarkably short periods of time.

This book is based on the premise that the time has come for a broader range of the public to be made aware of the market socialist idea. Up to this point, the literature on market socialism has been entirely professional in nature—written by economists for economists. Of course, economists are renowned for their reluctance to reach firm, operational conclusions. In fairness to economists, they are given some difficult problems to chew on. It is not surprising, then, that their analyses of these problems should often result in ambiguous conclusions. It is frequently found that two slightly different sets of intuitively appealing assumptions yield very different conclusions. When this happens, the economist has to go back to the noneconomist and simply say: "OK, which of these two slightly different sets of intuitively appealing assumptions do *you* think is the more plausible?"

The potential performance of a market socialist economy, as one might expect, is an *extremely* difficult problem, simply because no economic system of this type has ever before been implemented in the real world. On the basis of more than 20 years of research and writing on market socialism, I deem it highly unlikely that professional economics will achieve any truly compelling evidence on the question of the potential performance of market socialism within the next several generations of humanity. The economic analysis is helpful in a general way in the illumination of specific problems and issues bearing on the basic question. But in the end, it comes down to subjective judgments based on each individual's personal perceptions of the world.

This book endeavors to provide an introduction to the idea of market socialism, and of its development in the economic literature, which is understandable and accessible to the general reader. There are no mathematical models, no tables full of numbers, no figures or diagrams, and comparatively little usage of advanced economic concepts. When such concepts do occur in the course of the discussion, the reader is provided with brief explanations. The scholarly apparatus is modest, consisting only of a section of "Reference Notes" at the end of the book. The purpose has been to boil down the contents of the economic literature on market socialism to digestible terms which the average noneconomist can readily grasp and appreciate.

No pretense has been made that this is an objective, third-party appraisal of market socialism. This book is quite obviously a full-fledged advocacy of market socialism. However, a sincere effort has been made throughout to fairly represent the case *against* market socialism. Moreover, it is explicitly conceded at the outset that the case against market socialism *may* be valid. That is to say, it is explicitly conceded that in practice market socialism may not work as well as hoped. If that happens, then we could, should, and no doubt would make haste to restore the capitalist status quo ante. What is being proposed in this book, therefore, is merely a *tentative and provisional* implementation of market socialism, with the intention of observing its performance for a reasonable period prior to deeming the change to be permanent. Only an actual experiment with market socialism would provide truly definitive evidence on its economic performance.

James A. Yunker
February, 1997

1

HAS SOCIALISM FAILED?

Throughout its career of nearly two hundred years, the idea of socialism has been a potently divisive force in human affairs. At one extreme, it has aroused emotions of intense enthusiasm and exaltation among various progressives inspired by visions of a more just and equitable human society. At the other extreme, it has aroused equally intense emotions of fear and loathing among various conservatives concerned that the egalitarian thrust of socialism would produce a mediocre and stagnant society. Throughout the nineteenth century the idea of socialism was responsible for a great deal of intellectual controversy and dispute, but was a relatively minor contributor to civil unrest. The Russian Revolution of 1917 initiated a turbulent twentieth century era in which the idea of socialism has been implicated in extremely violent revolutions and civil wars, and has also been a major contributor to international tension and hostility. If at the height of the Cold War during the second half of the twentieth century, a nuclear war among the superpowers had devastated human civilization, controversy over the idea of socialism could have been plausibly cited as the single most important root contributor to the catastrophe.

As we approach the dawn of the third millennium, the idea of socialism appears to be in full retreat. The recent collapse of Soviet Communism in the U.S.S.R. deprived socialism of the support of one of the largest and most powerful nation-states in the contemporary world. Although the emergence of an unalloyed democratic market capitalist social system in Russia and the other republics of the ex-U.S.S.R. seems to be taking an uncomfortably long period of time, still, at this stage it is difficult to imagine that traditional hard-line communism will ever again become dominant in Russia and cause a resumption of the Cold War. Apart from the collapse of the U.S.S.R., there have been other significant signs of the disintegration and dissipation of the socialist movement in the contemporary era: especially the worldwide trends toward privatization of public enterprises and reduction of various social benefits associated with the welfare state.

In view of socialism's tortured history, it is understandable that so many people around the world have concluded that the idea of socialism has been a perverse and malevolent factor in human affairs over the last two centuries. It is understandable that these people are pleased with the various signs of socialism's impending demise, and that they should be eagerly anticipating the final, definitive, and irrevocable extinction of socialism as a significant force in human affairs.

Nevertheless, these people are making a serious mistake. The fact remains that there is a core of genuine value in the socialist idea. This core of genuine value has been deeply obscured by various adverse and unfortunate developments in the real-world history of socialism. Of these developments, by far the most serious has been the association of socialism with an undemocratic and totalitarian political system: Soviet Communism as it developed during the period of Stalin's dictatorship. In addition, the development of Soviet Communism saddled the idea and image of socialism with another unfortunate connotation: central planning of the economy. Finally, as a result both of Communistic socialism as practiced in the Soviet Union and elsewhere, and revisionist socialism as practiced by various social democratic governments in several Western European nations throughout the twentieth century (most notably in the Scandinavian nations), socialism has become associated with extreme and excessive implementations of egalitarianism, welfarism, and paternalism. But the fact remains that these associations are not *necessary* elements of socialism.

This book will argue that the core idea of socialism involves nothing more nor less than public ownership of large, established corporations. The "nothing more" part of this statement implies that neither undemocratic political systems, nor central planning of economic production and distribution, nor unhealthy excesses of egalitarianism, welfarism, and paternalism are *necessarily* associated with socialism. It will be argued that the empirical association of these adverse principles and conditions with socialism has been in the nature of an historical accident rather than the inexorable outcome of cause and effect.

Animating this book is a desire to redefine and rehabilitate the idea of socialism among all humanity—but with special immediate emphasis on the educated middle class of the leading capitalist nations of North America and Western Europe. This, of course, is a category of the world population among which the present opinion of socialism is particularly low. The thrust of the argument is that promising *democratic market so-cialist* possibilities exist in principle, which have not as yet been implemented in the real world. A system of democratic market socialism would incorporate three critical characteristics: (1) ownership of large, established corporations would reside with the public as a whole, with the key implication that the profits and interest earned by such corporations would be distributed among the general public in some relatively equitable manner; (2) economic decision-making and activity would be highly decentralized, meaning that primary reliance would be placed on free market forces in the ordinary and on-going operations and functions of the economy; (3) the political system would be authentically democratic, meaning that provisions for regular election of key government positions would be complemented by full and unrestricted rights of speech, press, and political organization.

There is no avoiding the fact that no full-scale, unalloyed social system of democratic market socialism has as yet appeared anywhere in the real world at any time in human history. Following the strict dictionary definition of "socialism" as involving public ownership of the preponderance of the capital stock (in other words, leaving aside the revisionist "social democratic" definition of socialism), only the Communist nations of the twentieth century, including the Soviet Union, Red China, and their smaller allies (Cuba, Vietnam, etc.), have practiced socialism. At the same time, without any important exceptions, these nations have been characterized by oligarchic political systems rather than democratic political systems, by planning-oriented economic systems rather than market-oriented economic systems, and by overdevelopment of the principles of egalitarianism, welfarism, and paternalism.

In light of this, some individuals—especially individuals who are somewhat lacking in mental flexibility and social vision—will conclude that the concept of democratic market socialism has always been, is now, and always will be a utopian delusion, a futile aspiration, an impossible dream (in the literal sense). These people are probably wrong. But it is necessary to concede that there is no way—short of an actual experiment—to *prove* that these people are wrong.

One of the principal themes of this book is that the potential performance of democratic market socialism is *an empirical question and not a theoretical question.* That is to say, it is not a question which may be resolved by means of syllogistic deductions from universally recognized and accepted realities. Thus the preferability of democratic market socialism over contemporary capitalism cannot be established by a priori logic. (Neither may the opposed proposition.) Moreover, the various available empirical evidence which bears on the relative performance question is all more or less indirect and circumstantial, which means that this evidence is far from conclusive in any sort of strict, scientific sense. Thus the preferability of democratic market socialism over contemporary capitalism cannot be established by means of an overwhelming preponderance of compelling evidence. (Once again, neither may the opposed proposition.)

It must be strongly emphasized from the outset, therefore, that the proposal set forth in this book for a social system of democratic market socialism is intended to be *tentative and provisional*. This means more than simply that the specific institutional forms proposed here are meant to be suggestive, are only intended to provide a basis for discussion, and are subject to revision upon further study and deliberation.

In addition to that, the proposal for democratic market socialism put forward herein is founded upon the clear and explicit recognition that there is a non-negligible possibility that the system would in actual practice prove *inferior* to the democratic market capitalist status quo with which we are presently familiar. Should that prove to be the case—after a fair test in the order of 10 to 15 years—then the democratic market capitalist system with which we are presently familiar should be reinstated as quickly and completely as possible. Strictly speaking, what is being proposed in this book is not a "for all time," irrevocable implementation of democratic market socialism. Rather what is being proposed is a *tentative and provisional* implementation of democratic market socialism for a sufficiently extended period of time to provide strong evidence on the performance of the new system relative to that currently witnessed under democratic market capitalism.

Of course, it goes without saying that in the judgment of the present author, the weight of the existing evidence strongly (if not compellingly) supports the preferability of democratic market socialism over democratic market capitalism. Consequently this evidence is seen as strongly supportive of the desirability of an actual experiment with democratic market socialism in order to establish this preferability to a high level of certitude.

As for the lack of real-world precedents for democratic market socialism, that is an inherently unimportant point in light of the gradual but persistent record of social progress throughout human history. Not so very long ago, during the heyday of absolute monarchy in Western Europe, a political system of representative democracy, such as is successfully practiced in the United States at the present time, would have seemed veritably inconceivable. Confident predictions would have been made that any political system incorporating universal suffrage and open election of high legislative and executive officials would quickly degenerate into civil war as the privileged classes resisted the leveling policies of demagogues elected by the rabble. These predictions are analogous to predictions made by anti-socialists today that a socialist economic system would necessarily, through the destruction of material incentives to effort, result in a lamentable condition of economic stagnation and decay. Experience to date has proved that universal suffrage does not necessarily lead to anarchic civil war. Future experience may also prove that the greater equity of a socialist economic system need not necessarily be attained through the sacrifice of economic efficiency and dynamism.

On the other hand, future experience may show no such thing—simply because democratic market socialism may never be given the opportunity to prove itself. A tremendous amount of resistance against the idea of socialism has gradually accumulated within the human population. No doubt the single most compelling argument against socialism remains the extravagantly totalitarian social system which arose in the Soviet Union during the ascendency of Stalin—a system which excused all of its terrible excesses, evils, and liabilities on grounds that these were merely necessary means to the glorious end of "socialism."

Aside from that, there have been numerous errors and omissions made by proponents of socialism in their presentation and advocacy of the idea. A primary example of this is Karl Marx. This is not to deny the intellectual power and substance of Marx's nineteenth century codification of the socialist critique of capitalism. Quite obviously, the present author fully subscribes to Marx's fundamental insight that modern capitalism perpetuates a serious economic injustice which should be rectified by means of the implementation of an appropriate socialist alternative. But it has not helped the cause of socialism since the time of Marx that so many adherents to this cause have tended to make Marx a demi-god whose every pronouncement must be treated as revealed truth.

One of Marx's most damaging proclamations was that socialism not only *should* succeed capitalism—it *would* succeed capitalism. Socialism is not put forward in Marx's work as a prescription or a recommendation, but rather as an unavoidable, inexorable inevitability. To Marx's mind, the superiority of socialism over the capitalistic status quo is so clear, obvious, and self-evident that eventually it *must* be implemented. There is something inherently presumptuous and off-putting in confident predictions regarding the future course of human history. While some adherents to the cause of socialism may have been inspired by the belief that their goal would one day certainly be achieved, many other people, no doubt, were strongly alienated by Marx's pseudo-scientific fortune-telling, and made it their business to help ensure that Marx's prediction did *not* come to pass.

Most sensible scholars and writers eschew predictions because so few of them are borne out by actual developments. The past evolution of human civilization on planet earth has been an immensely complicated process of which our current understanding is highly incomplete and imperfect. Future developments will be no less complex than past developments. Just as past developments are difficult to comprehend, so too future developments are difficult to foresee. More than 100 years have passed since the death of Karl Marx, and if anything the advent of socialism within worldwide human society seems even less likely now than it did at the time of Marx's death. As much as this author hopes that Marx will eventually be vindicated, and that socialism will in fact be widely implemented, any predictions to that effect are explicitly disavowed. Socialism (of the democratic market socialist variety) is being put forward herein merely as a recommendation. There is no certainty that humanity will perceive the validity of the case for democratic market socialism put forward herein, and will act favorably upon the recommendation advanced. In fact, realism dictates the acknowledgment that at the present time, the likelihood of this eventuality seems quite low (although perhaps not quite so low as is widely presumed).

AN OUTLINE OF THE ARGUMENT

The fundamental proposition advanced in this book is that while various real-world implementations of socialism have obviously failed (by far the most dramatic example of failure being the Soviet Union), the idea of socialism as a *general* concept and aspiration has *not* failed, because the specific reasons for the failure of the real-world implementations have had little or nothing to do with the basic socialist principle of public ownership of large, established corporations. Three subsidiary propositions are necessary to support this general proposition. First, it is necessary to show that secondary characteristics of the failed social systems were in fact responsible for the systems' weaknesses, and not socialism per se. Second, it is necessary to show that contemporary capitalism is

subject to serious problems which could conceivably be effectively resolved by socialism. Finally, it is necessary to show that alternative socialist systems are possible which would not be subject to the various
weaknesses which brought about the downfall of the failed implementations.

The first chapter of the book ("Has Socialism Failed?") is concerned
with the first of these subsidiary propositions: that it was not socialism,
in and of itself, which caused the weakness and failure of social systems
which have been widely associated with socialism. Prior to tackling this
question, however, some critical commentary is offered on excessively
negative interpretations of the real-world history of socialism. The intertwined propositions that "socialism has failed" and "socialism is dead"
have been given a tremendous boost in the 1990s as a result of the collapse of Soviet Communism and the dissolution of the Soviet Union. But
these propositions were in fact widely bandied about prior to the collapse
of Soviet Communism, at a time when they were more generally recognized as serious oversimplifications. Despite the collapse of Soviet Communism, these propositions remain serious oversimplifications.

In fact, there is one widely customary interpretation of the term "socialism" according to which it would have to be acknowledged that socialism has been a resounding success. This is the "revisionist" or "social
democratic" interpretation which defines socialism not in terms of public
ownership of the preponderance of capital stock and natural resources,
but rather in terms of government regulation of business, progressive
taxation, and welfare entitlements. These kinds of policies and programs
are ubiquitous throughout the world, and are well-entrenched even in
such self-righteously "capitalistic" nations as the United States and Australia. The fact is, however, that the self-evident success of "social democratic socialism" throughout the world cannot be utilized herein as
evidence that "socialism has not failed" because "social democratic socialism" is not accepted herein as "true socialism."

For purposes of this book, "socialism" is defined exclusively in terms
of public ownership of the preponderance of the stock of nonhuman factors of production: capital and natural resources. In this strict sense, only
the communist nations of the twentieth century (the U.S.S.R., the P.R.C.,
etc.) are properly characterized as "socialist." Therefore, in assessing
whether or not socialism has failed, we must look only to these nations.

The recent collapse of the U.S.S.R. has provided a spectacular example of what conservatives are fond of describing as the "failure of socialism." But there are two key considerations to keep in mind while ponder-

ing the history of the Soviet Union and its ultimate collapse. First, while the Soviet Union never achieved a level of economic performance comparable to that of the leading capitalist nations of North America and Western Europe, it did in fact achieve quite an impressive level of performance. It was not a true economic crisis which brought the system down, but rather a crisis of confidence among the top leadership owing to the system's inability to match the performance of the leading capitalist nations. The second key consideration is that many factors having nothing at all to do with public ownership of capital and natural resources contributed heavily to the weakness and eventual downfall of the Soviet Union. These factors ranged from the undemocratic political system through to the heavy military burden imposed on the economy by the U.S.S.R.'s involvement, throughout most of its history, in an all-out arms competition with the West. To emphasize the multiplicity of these factors, an even dozen such factors will be discussed—no doubt still more could be taken into account in a truly exhaustive enumeration.

Conservatives throughout the world are so busy gloating over the recent demise of the U.S.S.R. that they pay little attention to the fact that as of the present time, the *second* great socialist nation in the world, the People's Republic of China, has *not* collapsed, and as a matter of fact boasts one of the more dynamically progressive economies in the world today. In some ways, the economic system of the P.R.C. provides a model for market socialism as it might one day be practiced in the industrially advanced capitalist nations such as the U.S., the U.K., and so on. It would not be appropriate, however, to place too much emphasis on Red China as a potential model for the rest of the world. In the first place, the political system of the P.R.C. is still hopelessly undemocratic. In the second place, the P.R.C. is still a fundamentally agrarian, Third World nation laboring under a heavy burden of overpopulation. While the economic condition of the general population in the P.R.C. might be somewhat superior to that of the general population of *comparable* capitalist nations (especially India), the economic condition of the general population in the P.R.C. is so hugely inferior to that of the general population of *advanced* capitalist nations such as the U.S. and the U.K.—and will no doubt remain so into the foreseeable future—that the P.R.C. is never likely to provide really impressive evidence in favor of the potential economic performance of market socialism.

Of course it is not possible to arrive at a final conclusion on the question of whether socialism has failed on the basis of the assets and liabilities of Communistic socialism as practiced in the U.S.S.R., the P.R.C., and a variety of other nations during the twentieth century. Even conceding that the liabilities of real-world Communistic socialism probably exceed the assets and that none of these nations provide an example which the rest of the world would sensibly wish to emulate, there are still two central questions to be considered. First, is contemporary capitalism so thoroughly and completely revised and reformed, relative to the harsh early industrial era capitalism on which Karl Marx and other nineteenth-century socialists based their criticism of capitalism as a general concept, that there is no sensible contribution left to be made by socialism in the public ownership sense? Second, granting for the sake of argument that contemporary capitalism is subject to certain seemingly endemic and permanent equity problems which *in principle* are curable through socialism, one must ask whether there exists a *practical* socialist alternative through which these problems could be eliminated without weakening incentives to effort in the economy to such an extent that serious efficiency problems are incurred?

The first question is addressed in the second chapter of the book ("Is Capitalism Best?"), while the second question is addressed in the following two chapters ("The Market Socialist Idea" and "The Current Debate"), which describe, develop, and defend a specific institutional proposal for democratic market socialism, the economic component of which is designated "profit-oriented market socialism." The final chapter of the book ("A New Beginning?") summarizes and concludes the argument.

Even the most ardent defenders of contemporary capitalism will typically concede—if pressed on the issue—that the extremely unequal distributions of capital wealth and property income under the present system constitute an apparent equity problem. It simply does not seem fair that such a large proportion of the population should hold very little capital wealth and receive very little property income, while at the same time such a tiny proportion of the population should hold so much capital wealth, and receive so much property income.

This is especially the case in view of the fact that property income does not *seem* to be earned. Dividends, interest, capital gains, and other forms of capital property income *seem* to accrue naturally to the owners of capital wealth without need of the same kind of obvious toil and effort required to earn the wages and salaries (labor income) on which the vast majority of the population are dependent for their livelihood. The unfairness and inequity of this situation is magnified by the fact that inheritance is clearly an important factor in determining the distribution of capital wealth. Thus, not only is little or no *current* effort required to obtain property income on capital wealth, but for the large number of wealthy capital owners, whose wealth was based on inheritance rather than effort and achievement, little or no *past* effort was required either. In view of the apparently unearned nature of capital property income, one might well speculate that the extremely unequal distribution of this income under contemporary capitalism is not at all necessary for the maintenance of economic efficiency and high productivity, and that a socialist alternative involving public ownership of capital and a more equitable distribution of income produced by capital would in fact be preferable.

Defenders of the capitalist status quo have two fundamental responses to this socialist challenge. The first of these is that the equity problems of capitalism perceived by proponents of socialism are greatly exaggerated. The second is that whatever may or may not be the equity problems of capitalism, the capitalist system is nevertheless fully justified on the basis of its very high level of efficiency and productivity.

The well-known term "people's capitalism" is a convenient descriptor for a complexus of apologetic arguments to the effect that *when properly interpreted*, the distributions of capital wealth and property income under contemporary capitalism are *not* sufficiently unequal to form a legitimate basis for concern. Much of Chapter 2 is devoted to refuting various strands of the people's capitalism thesis. There is an imposing body of evidence, ranging from casual empiricism through to social scientific studies of the transfer of wealth through inheritance, that: (1) whether the distributions of capital wealth and income are taken in current terms or in lifetime terms, they are in fact extremely stable and extremely unequal; (2) the two most important factors in explaining the limited amount of capital wealth mobility which *does* exist are inheritance and random chance—factors which, of course, have nothing whatever to do with the hard work and productive entrepreneurship stressed by apologists for capitalism.

In addition, some attention is devoted in Chapter 2 to a related argument: whatever might be the degree of inequality in the present-day distribution of after-tax capital property income, the distribution of after-tax capital property income, at least in principle, *could be* sufficiently equalized by progressive taxation under capitalism as to constitute "virtual socialism through taxation." Thus the fundamental socialist aspiration of greater equity in the distribution of capital property income *could be* achieved without incurring the cumbersome and probably inefficient device of public ownership of capital. It will be argued that this is actually a thoroughly impractical suggestion and that its frequent invocation by defenders of the capitalist status quo represents a disingenuous effort to confuse the opposition rather than a sincere proposal toward the significant reform of this status quo.

The second fundamental response to the socialist challenge relies upon the efficiency consideration. This is the position that whatever might be the equity advantages of socialism over capitalism in principle, in practice capitalism has such a large efficiency advantage over socialism as to be clearly preferable. In other words, even though the pie under capitalism is divided up very unequally, the absolute size of the pie is so much larger under capitalism that the vast majority of people get a larger amount under capitalism than they would get under socialism. There are two conceptually distinct but closely intertwined arguments through which this general proposition may be explicated and amplified. The first lies in simply denying the pro-socialist proposition that capital property income is unearned. The second lies in asserting that no conceivable socialist system is possible which would equalize the distribution of capital property income without at the same time encountering such serious efficiency problems that the living standards of the great majority of the population would be significantly lowered. These arguments are actually two sides of the same coin, in that allegations of the inefficiency of specific socialist alternatives to capitalism necessarily rely basically on allegations that under contemporary capitalism, capital property income recognizes and rewards some legitimate economic contribution (such as saving and/or entrepreneurship) and is earned income in a sense—if not the *same* sense in which it may be said that labor income (wages and salaries) is earned income.

The two chapters following Chapter 2, as a body, address this central issue. Chapter 3 traces the origins and development of market socialist thought and provides a detailed democratic market socialist proposal put forward as a viable and attractive alternative to the contemporary capitalist status quo. Chapter 4 then critiques the allegation that under contemporary capitalism, such capital property income categories as dividends, interest, and capital gains are justifiable as earned returns to legitimate economic contributions such as saving and/or entrepreneurship. This order of presentation is based on the belief that a much more focused and reliable judgment may be made on the abstract proposition that (in the pro-socialist view) capital property income under contemporary capitalism is mostly if not entirely an unearned, rentier-type income by a reader who has a clear understanding of precisely what kind of a socialist system is being proposed as an alternative to capitalism. This is particularly true since the proposed system is very much different from conventional conceptions of "socialism."

Chapter 3 provides a history of the idea of market socialism, along with a description of various market socialist alternatives which have been put forward in the literature on economic systems. The idea of market socialism gained a foothold in mainstream Western economics owing to the seminal contribution of Oskar Lange (1904-1965) in the 1930s. Due credit must certainly be given to Lange for almost single-handedly winning a modicum of acceptance for the idea among mainstream economists. Prior to Lange, the term "market socialism," had it been used at all, would have been considered by almost all of these economists to be no more than a nonsensical oxymoron. But at the same time, it must also be recognized that Lange's specific market socialist proposal is too much informed and influenced by the theoretical economics of the 1930s—and that is probably a major part of the reason why it has never been taken seriously by Western economics as a *practical* alternative to capitalism. While the consensus view in Western economics is that Lange's market socialist system might well perform more efficiently and effectively in practice than a centrally planned socialist economy such as that of the Soviet Union, nevertheless it would remain decidedly inferior to market capitalism as exemplified by the economies of the United States, the United Kingdom, and so on.

Since the time of Lange, market socialism has been a minor but persistent factor in the study of comparative economic systems, and over the years a substantial amount of literature has gradually accumulated on the subject. With this literature there has also gradually accumulated greater awareness that the study of market socialism does not stop with Oskar Lange's rather unappealing, theoretically based proposal of the 1930s. Aside from what might be termed "Langian market socialism," there are at least two other major categories of market socialism: "cooperative market socialism" and "profit-oriented market socialism." Most contemporary mainstream economists would deem both of these alternatives to be more practical and promising than Lange's original market socialist proposal.

"Cooperative market socialism" is also designated by such terms as "self-management" and "labor management." This system does not involve public ownership in the usual sense, but rather employee ownership. The basic idea of self-management is that the employees of the corporation, as a group, would hold either all, or at least a majority share, of the voting stock of the corporation. Thus the top managers of the corporation would be fundamentally and primarily responsible to the employees: the employees and only the employees would be in a position to hire and fire the corporation's top managers. Employee ownership, of course, is already an accepted concept under contemporary capitalism, and in fact is one of the many ideas and concepts interwoven into the overall fabric of "people's capitalism." Nevertheless, it would be a major step from the current situation, in which employee ownership plays an extremely limited and peripheral role in the economy, to a potential market socialist situation in which most firms would be legally required to be employee owned.

Such a step would not be supported by many economists, at least at the present time. The concept of cooperative market socialism (under various designations of which "employee ownership" is relatively recent) has been extant in socialist thought for a very long time, predating even Karl Marx. During that extended period of time and up to the present day, orthodox, mainstream economists (i.e., the vast majority of economists) have tended to be skeptical of the production cooperative. The suspicion has always been, and continues to be, that a firm whose managers are democratically elected by the employees would be as unsuccessful in business competition as an army whose officers are democratically elected by the rank and file soldiers would presumably be in battle.

This common prejudice against cooperative market socialism is in fact shared by the author of this book, although the "new synthesis" market socialist proposal discussed herein does in fact incorporate the central tenet of cooperative production: that the top managers be responsible to the rank and file employees through elections. On the other hand, in the "new synthesis" proposal, these managers would *also* be responsible to representatives of an outside ownership interest, and these representatives would *also* be armed with explicit powers of dismissal. These representatives would be agents of a public ownership authority whose primary interest would be in the profitable operation of publicly owned business enterprises under socialism.

Such a public ownership authority is the central institutional feature within any particular profit-oriented plan of market socialism. To date, three such plans have been put forward in the economic systems literature: (1) pragmatic market socialism (by James A. Yunker); (2) municipal ownership market socialism (by Leland G. Stauber); (3) bank-centric market socialism (by John E. Roemer). These three plans exemplify the basic notion that under market socialism the publicly owned business enterprises would be both instructed and motivated to maximize the long-term rate of profit achieved on their operations. Managers of publicly owned firms would be induced to pursue profits not only by making their salaries and bonuses dependent on achieved profits, but also by threatening their job security. Managers of firms making inadequate profits would be subject to dismissal—to use the colloquial term, to being fired.

Profit-oriented market socialism represents a fundamental departure from nineteenth-century Marxist orthodoxy. According to this orthodoxy, it is the *process* of profit-seeking which is inherently perverse and exploitative. In the alternative view proposed herein, the process of profitseeking in the business sector is *not* inherently perverse and exploitative—on the grounds that there exists a sufficient degree of competition among firms for markets and employees, and a sufficient degree of governmental regulation of business activity to prevent this. The fatal flaw of contemporary capitalism is perceived to lie not in the process of profit-seeking by business enterprises, but rather in the maldistribution of these profits among the private households *after* they have been earned by the business enterprises. This distribution is perceived to be excessively unequal owing to the high level of concentration of capital wealth ownership in the contemporary capitalist economy.

The practical implication of this alternative view is direct and dramatic: under profit-oriented market socialism, the publicly owned business firms—far from being forbidden to maximize their profits—would instead be required, encouraged, and induced to maximize their profits. Higher profits in the publicly owned business enterprise sector would mean more social dividend income in the pockets of the citizen owners. The fund of social dividend income available for distribution to the population would be based mostly on the profits earned by the publicly owned business enterprise sector. Every employed citizen under the proposal for market socialism put forward herein would have an entitlement to social dividend income—although it would not be an equal entitlement. The entitlement of each individual to social dividend income would rather be in direct proportion to that individual's earned labor income (wages and salaries): people receiving more wage and salary income would be entitled to more social dividend income than people receiving less wage and salary income.

As with the proposal that business processes under market socialism be guided by profit maximization, the proposal for distribution of social

dividend income in proportion to labor income rather than equally probably will not appeal to many of those who subscribe to what might be
termed "classical socialist" viewpoints. There are other such aspects of
the current proposal which probably will not appeal. For example, this
proposal envisions a substantial role for privately owned business. Private ownership would be retained not only for small businesses in farming, retail trade, and professional services, but also for entrepreneurial
businesses—of whatever scale and level of financial success achieved.
An entrepreneurial business is defined as a business which is still being
personally managed by the original founder-owner. Under the proposal
put forward herein, all such firms would remain in private ownership so
long as they remain legitimately entrepreneurial; that is to say, so long as
they are still being personally managed by their founder-owners.

That many traditionally oriented socialists would object to such provisions as these is not a matter of any great concern to this author. The
reason is simply that traditional socialism no longer commands sufficient
interest or respect among the world's population. Traditional socialism
has been rejected by the majority of the intelligentsia and by the majority
of the people as a whole. Either socialism will be redesigned along such
lines as are advanced herein, or socialism really will be finished. At least
this will be the case insofar as "pure" socialism is concerned—that is to
say, socialism in the public ownership sense.

The concluding section of Chapter 3 sets forth a discussion of an
original institutional proposal for market socialism. This proposal, based
on various concepts and proposals from the prior literatures on cooperative market socialism and profit-oriented market socialism, endeavors to
amalgamate some of the best features of the earlier market socialist proposals. The issue of transition is considered, with special attention to the
critical question of compensation of private owners of socialized capital
property. Various exceptions to socialization are specified in the areas of
small business and entrepreneurial business. Much of the discussion relates to the three new public ownership agencies envisioned by the proposal. The primary purpose of the Bureau of Ownership (BPO) would be
to establish a strong incentive toward profit maximization among the
high executives of publicly owned business corporations. The primary
purpose of the National Investment Banking System (NIBS) would be to
assist the existing financial intermediary sector in the capital investment
process. The primary purpose of the National Entrepreneurial Investment
Board (NEIB) would be to assist private entrepreneurs in the establishment of viable new firms.

In its presentation of a concrete proposal for democratic market socialism (the economic component of which is labeled "profit-oriented market socialism"), Chapter 3 indirectly addresses questions of the feasibility and potential performance of such a system. Using the proposal of Chapter 3 as the basis for discussion, Chapter 4 addresses these questions directly. Having a specific socialist proposal as a reference point enables a far more focused and explicit treatment of the numerous difficult issues involved. The chapter offers a rebuttal to both the major economic argument and the major political argument against socialism—as they would be applied to the "new synthesis" market socialist system proposed at the end of Chapter 3.

The major economic argument against market socialism is based on the proposition that capital property income under contemporary capitalism is legitimately earned by capital owners through the provision of genuine factors of production. Under socialism, the providers of these factors would not be paid enough to generate an adequate amount of them, with the result that economic efficiency and output would—rapidly or gradually as the case may be—sink to abysmal levels. The two factors of production in question are capital management effort and saving. In the apologetics of capitalism, property income is represented both as an earned return to capital management effort, and as an earned return to saving. Saving is familiar to all of us, but "capital management effort" needs a bit of explanation. As used herein, capital management effort is a very general term referring to any and all active behavior by capital owners or managers (since under socialism, the capital managers would not be legal owners) which is designed to increase the rate of return on capital. This includes corporate supervision such as provided by members of boards of directors, investment analysis such as provided by loan officers of financial intermediaries or private investors, and entrepreneurship such as provided by the founder of a new business enterprise.

The major political argument against socialism is that the combination of economic and political power under socialism poses a threat to freedom and democracy. According to the argument, if the state directly controls all economic power as well as all political power (as it would under socialism), then it would constitute an irresistible force toward the suppression and elimination of all vestiges of political opposition. What this means in practice is that the incumbent party in power under socialism would continue in power for a very long period of time—perhaps forever. Unchallengeable by an organized political opposition, its dominion would become steadily more despotic.

Both the economic argument against socialism and the political argument against socialism are very serious arguments which need to be carefully studied and addressed. One of the major weaknesses in the socialist movement throughout its history is that proponents of socialism have been so busy castigating capitalism that they have not devoted adequate effort to responding to the criticisms of socialism offered by defenders of capitalism. Of course, the multitudinous potential problems and shortcomings of socialism have become infinitely more compelling now that Soviet history during the Stalinist period has clearly demonstrated the depths to which a social system which incorporates public ownership socialism might sink.

Since this book is in fact an advocacy of democratic market socialism, it is to be expected that the various arguments against socialism considered herein, whether economic or political, will all be found wanting in the final analysis. But these arguments are given their due, and it is conceded that they possess sufficient weight and plausibility so that the superiority of democratic market socialism over democratic market capitalism cannot be assumed. Thus to reiterate a key point, the proposal of this book is for a *tentative and provisional* implementation of democratic market socialism, with the intention of returning to capitalism should severe economic and political problems emerge under socialism. The idea is that we would let objective experience settle the question of whether democratic market capitalism or democratic market socialism is the superior social system.

The final Chapter 5 summarizes the arguments and recommendations put forward in the book, and offers some thoughts on the question of implementation. As of the time of writing, a majority of the world's population favors the retention of capitalism over the implementation of public ownership socialism, and as far as the advanced industrial nations are concerned, this majority must be described as "overwhelming." In light of the tremendous consensus in favor of capitalism which presently exists, one might well question whether it makes any difference that untried democratic market socialist alternatives exist which might well perform better than the capitalistic status quo. Perhaps the weight of public opinion is so heavy—even though the public's judgment on the issue might well be incorrect—that it will never be altered.

This pessimistic proposition is challenged in the final chapter. It is argued that there is an existent, consequential possibility that socialism can actually be rehabilitated and the socialist movement revitalized. But this argument depends critically on an operational redefinition of the term "socialism" to better fit the proposal put forward in this book. Socialism must be revised and modernized. To begin with, it is obvious that socialism must distance itself from the oligarchic political regimes of the Communist nations both past and present. But it must also distance itself completely from the idea of central planning of the economy. Finally, in order to be a political possibility, the proposed socialist system must incorporate a relatively conservative and cautiously judicious approach to egalitarianism, welfarism, and paternalism. It cannot be a "welfare state," as that term is normally interpreted. This particular point is elucidated in the following section, which attempts to clarify the important distinction between social democracy and socialism.

SOCIAL DEMOCRACY VERSUS SOCIALISM

In the spirit of giving the devil his due, even the most adamant antisocialist of today may well concede that there was at least one positive consequence of the life and work of Karl Marx: it contributed to the reformation and humanization of the capitalist economic and social system. At the beginning of the nineteenth century, the condition of the urban proletariat in the industrializing nations of Britain, France, and Germany was, by modern standards, horrific. Wages were pitifully low, hours were interminably long, and the typical factory worker enjoyed no security whatsoever against loss of employment through incapacitation, business depression, or simply the infirmities of old age. For these workers and their families, life was hard, precarious, and unrewarding.

At the same time, however, the technological and industrial revolutions of this period were laying the basis for a level of efficiency and abundance which could not have been imagined at earlier times in human history. Dramatic advances in productive capabilities were creating opportunities for major upgrades in living standards, not merely among the elite of society but among a broad range of the population. Human society had always been hierarchical and class-oriented, and whatever economic progress had been made in earlier times had been very gradual and highly uncertain. In light of history and tradition, it could not have been an easy matter to gain wide acceptance for the proposition that significant progress could and should be made with respect to the living standards of the "masses." At least part of the reason why this proposition eventually *did* become a standard viewpoint is the possibility of violent social revolution as preached by Karl Marx and other radical socialists of the nineteenth century. It is plausibly arguable that while technological

progress created the *opportunity* of significantly raising the living standards of the rank and file of society throughout the nineteenth century, it
was the threat of socialist revolution that induced the social leadership to
take *full advantage* of this opportunity.

As a matter of fact, the idea of enlightened capitalism well predated
Marx. For example, the idea found full expression in the life and work of
Robert Owen (1771-1858), the Welsh businessman and social reformer
of the early nineteenth century. Owen tried to persuade his fellow industrialists that generous payment and compassionate treatment of the factory workforce was not only morally proper but commercially viable. It
was commercially viable because of the dramatically higher productivity
of a workforce which is well fed, well rested, secure, and content. On the
whole, Owen's peers remained dubious that all this generosity and com-
passion was affordable, and the pessimists gloated over the bankruptcy
of New Lanark, Owen's effort to create a new model factory/community,
during the depression of the early 1820s. But as the nineteenth century
progressed, Owen's ideas became steadily more influential among factory owners, industrialists, businessmen and capitalists.

Marx's judgment on Owen was dismissive: Owen was categorized as
a "utopian socialist," along with individuals such as Charles Fourier
(1772-1837)—with his plan for a society composed entirely of serene
and largely self-sufficient little communities called "phalanxes." According to Marx, Fourier's plan was impractical because it failed to recognize
the dominant role to be played by huge factories in the future economy.
Such factories were certain to supplant small-scale handicraft production
because of their overwhelming efficiency advantage. Also according to
Marx, Owen's prescription for "enlightened capitalism" was equally impractical because of the inevitably ruthless competition among capitalists. Any capitalist unwise enough to pay the workforce more than a
"subsistence wage" would quickly be driven out of business by other
capitalists running their factories according to the accepted commercial
principles of the day.

Karl Marx (1818-1883) perceived the evil essence of industrial capitalism in the formulaic proposition: production has been socialized, while
ownership remains privatized. In earlier times of less efficient handicraft
production, it was practical for the individual worker to personally own
his or her own set of tools. But in the modern era, the "tools of production" have become large, complicated machines housed in cavernous factories. These machines cannot be used independently to create the
product; rather dozens or even hundreds of them cooperate in creating

the product, each machine devoted to one small stage of the overall production process. The totality of capital equipment in the factory is utilized by a large labor force in an interdependent, cooperative, "socialized"
production process. In such a production environment, private ownership
of particular pieces of capital by particular workers is impractical both
administratively and financially. Production could not be coordinated efficiently if individual contracts had to be drawn up with each one of dozens or even hundreds of worker-owners of specific machines. In any
event, the machines are so large and complicated that the acquisition of
even a single one of them would be beyond the means of even the most
prosperous worker.

Personal ownership rights over capital may have been appropriate in
the era of handicraft production, but, according to Marx, the retention of
such rights in the modern era of factory production is perverse and dysfunctional. The concentration of physical capital in large factories tends
to be paralleled by a concentration of financial capital in large fortunes.
This means that the great majority of the population ends up with little or
no capital wealth, while a small minority ends up with large accumulations of capital wealth. Marx, of course, did not think highly of the
"small minority" of wealthy capitalists. Far from being the courageous
entrepreneurs described by defenders of capitalism, Marx argued that
they were for the most part merely unusually rapacious, dishonest, and/or
simply lucky in their business activities.

The solution of the problem, in the view of Marx, lay in the abroga-
tion of private property with respect to capital—especially capital which
is utilized in large-scale factory production. As is well known, Marx devoted almost all of his time and energy to critical analysis of capitalism,
with the result that he had very little left over for describing the socialist
system which would succeed capitalism. Thus even very basic questions
about socialism cannot be unequivocally answered on the basis of
Marx's work, voluminous though that work may be. One such question
is whether social ownership should hold at the factory level or the firm
level or the economy level. For example, ownership of a particular factory might be exercised by those employed in the factory. Alternatively,
ownership of a multi-factory firm might be exercised by those employed
in the firm. Alternatively, ownership of all of the firms in an economy
might be exercised by all those employed in the economy. It is this last
formulation which seems to be the most common understanding of the
term "socialism," as it is normally defined in contemporary dictionaries.
This will be the usual meaning of "socialism" throughout this book.

For those who favor socialism in the public ownership sense, such as this author, it is a relatively minor but still irritating hurdle, in trying to put forward the case for public ownership socialism, that there exists a competitor understanding of "socialism" which does *not* involve public ownership. This is the "revisionist" or "social democratic" definition of socialism. As of the late nineteenth century, the revisionist offshoot of the overall socialist movement—which by that time had become pre-dominantly Marxist—proposed the abandonment of two basic proposi-tions from classical Marxism: (1) that the transition from capitalism to socialism must be accomplished by violent revolution; (2) that a neces-sary condition to the achievement of the goals of socialism is public ownership of capital.

During Marx's formative years, the French Revolution was yester-day—a stunning event in recent history which was widely perceived as heralding a new era in human civilization. Throwing off the dominion of the hereditary aristocracy was not accomplished easily, and violence and the threat of violence played a pivotal role in events throughout the criti-cal years following the fall of the Bastille in 1789: the execution of Louis XVI and Marie Antoinette, the Terror, and finally unrestricted warfare between revolutionary France and her traditionalist neighbors. Marx con-cluded from this record that major social transitions cannot be accom-plished peacefully: just as violence had been necessary to throw off the dominion of the landed aristocracy, so too violence would be necessary to throw off the dominion of the capitalist class.

Violence would be necessary, in Marx's view, because of the impos-sibility of significant reform of an existing regime so long as property rights and relationships remain unchanged. The landed aristocracy, confi-dent that its ownership of land endowed it with unchallengeable political power, saw no need to submit to demands for reform. They failed to per-ceive that the rising class of nonaristocratic but wealthy industrialists, merchants, and financiers, with their property rights over capital rather than land, had become—owing to the technical development of the econ-omy (capital was becoming as important as land, if not more important, in the economic system)—a competitor power center. It therefore re-quired a violent revolution to curb the power and arrogance of the land-owning nobility. The same would be necessary, according to Marx, to curb the power and arrogance of the "capital-owning nobility."

By the latter part of the nineteenth century, it was becoming quite clear, even to enthusiastic Marxists, that conditions were not evolving exactly as foreseen by the Master, either in a political sense or an economic sense. In the political sphere, there was definitely a trend toward universal suffrage in the advanced capitalist nations as exemplified by Britain, France, and the United States. Earlier in the nineteenth century, even in the most democratic polities, the citizen needed to possess a substantial amount of property in order to vote. Property restrictions on voting were gradually being reduced, it was being found from experience that the newly enfranchised voters were not excessively radical in their political preferences, and in due course it seemed inevitable that all adult citizens would be allowed to vote, even if they were virtually indigent. Of course, political empowerment of the propertyless did not fit very well with Marx's pronouncement of total capitalist class control over the state.

In the economic sphere, there was a definite trend toward significant improvement in the living standards of the general population (the so-called "masses"). Some of the improvement was the result of direct government intervention in the economy. The earlier dominance of laissez faire was giving way to apparent realities. Governments restricted the length of the working day, imposed holidays, set health and safety standards, forbade the employment of child labor. Social insurance and pension programs were implemented, so that disabled and retired workers would not become indigent and dependent upon their children or private charity. Earlier legislation forbidding or restricting unions was revised or repealed so that collective bargaining could play a larger role in the determination of wages and benefits.

It was not simply a matter of state officials continually having to force a recalcitrant capitalist class to comply with social standards. Among the capitalists themselves, an enlightened, humanitarian spirit was spreading. Not every wage and benefit increase for the workforce had to be wrested from unwilling, obstructionist employers (though a great many did). Whether in response to rational Owenian calculations regarding the productivity of a well-paid, satisfied workforce, or to fear of a possible socialist revolution, or to the exhortations of Christian humanists, or to inner needs of morality and self-respect, the capitalist class gradually accepted the idea that *all* strata of society, and not merely the elite, should share in economic well-being and progress. A necessary precondition for this attitudinal transformation, of course, was the technological progress which continued throughout the nineteenth century and into the twentieth. This progress made possible a significant improvement in working class living conditions. Attitudinal transformation made the merely possible into existent reality.

Under the intellectual leadership of figures such as Eduard Bernstein (1858-1932), whose seminal work *Evolutionary Socialism* was published in 1899, an influential revisionist wing emerged within the world socialist movement. As indicated above, the revised program of Bernstein and like-minded socialists excised the revolutionary component. Whatever form or shape socialism might take in the future, it was to be achieved peacefully via democratic voting. Bloody revolution was no longer necessary in view of the rise of democracy. It also excised public ownership—at least as an immediate objective. Public ownership of land and capital might be attained in the long run, but in the short run the emphasis was to be on the implementation of progressive income taxation, social regulation of business, and various welfare and social insurance programs for the direct alleviation of poverty. Through such means the traditional socialist goals of social equity and working-class security and prosperity could be achieved without raising the explosive issue of public ownership of the means of production.

Disputes between the revisionists and the classical Marxists were bitter. The classical Marxists accused the revisionists of watered-down reformism and crass opportunism, of proposing to sell out the proletariat's birthright for a few crumbs off capitalism's table. The revisionists accused the classical Marxists of mental rigidity and utopian idealism, of proposing to spurn significant gains in the here and now in favor of pursuing a dubious millennial order which may or may not be achieved in the remote future—long after everyone presently alive has gone to their eternal reward. The split gradually hardened, and both wings of the socialist movement went on to achieve notable successes in the twentieth century.

The Russian Revolution of 1917 installed hardline classical Marxists as leaders of an important nation-state. By the mid-twentieth century, following the communizations of China, the Eastern European nations, and several others in the wake of World War II, approximately one-fourth of the human population lived in nations whose governments espoused hardline Marxism-Leninism. At that time, it seemed well within the bounds of possibility that Soviet totalitarianism might succeed where Nazi totalitarianism had failed—it might one day rule the world. This prospect was regarded with varying degrees of apprehension and horror by the populations of non-Communist nations. As of the end of the twentieth century, the threat of worldwide communization under Soviet hegemony has greatly receded, to the great relief of these populations.

Meanwhile, a number of social democratic political parties whose historical roots lay in revisionist Marxism, for example the British Labor Party, came into power at various times and places throughout the twentieth century. During their tenures in power, these parties busied themselves with the passage of various types of social legislation. While the legislation was under consideration, the conservative opposition tended to howl in protest, asserting that the passage of these laws and the implementation of these policies augured the end of civilization as we know it. By and large, however, it was found from experience that once these laws and policies were in place, their effects on the overall economic and social systems were relatively minor and arguably benign, so that when the conservative parties later regained power, they were usually content to leave them alone.

The crystallization and codification of socialist thought by Karl Marx in the nineteenth century was so massive, systematic, and intellectually compelling that following Marx's work the term "socialism" was *defined* in terms of public ownership of the means of production. This definition of socialism remains the dominant primary definition to this day, as may be verified from the great majority of dictionaries. In fact, most dictionaries do not include the social democratic understanding of socialism (egalitarian social legislation in the absence of public ownership of land and capital) even as a secondary definition of the term. Even though the revisionist social democrats had eliminated public ownership from their program of immediate goals, so that their actual objective could be more sensibly and properly described as "reformed capitalism," they had too much of a traditional and emotional stake in the term "socialism" to abandon it. Therefore they simply redefined the term to mean "reformed capitalism."

As a result, to this day we have the phenomenon of plutocratic capitalists who feel quite unthreatened by—and who are indeed quite sympathetic toward and actively supportive of—political parties which describe themselves as "socialist" and their objectives as "socialism." Such plutocratic capitalists (a definite minority among plutocratic capitalists as a whole) are properly enlightened and fully cognizant of the critical distinction between public ownership socialism and social democratic socialism. They know that should the projects of the social democrats to assist the poorest elements in society be put into practice, these projects will be financed mostly by taxes on the middle class and not the upper class. In other words, their own personal living standards, obscenely lavish though they might be, will probably not be affected significantly.

Obviously it is necessary for language to be flexible, which means that sometimes the same term will have quite different definitions, each one of which is well understood and widely accepted. Nevertheless, as a proponent of socialism in its correct and proper public ownership sense (defining "correct and proper" in terms of the primary dictionary definition of the term), I myself find it irksome that social democrats insist on describing their goals and projects as "socialism." This misuse of the term contributes heavily to the confusion and misunderstanding which surrounds socialism, and which makes sensible, focused, goal-oriented discussion and consideration of the subject so very difficult. Without this misuse, it would not be necessary to devote significant time and effort, for example, to dispelling the misunderstanding that "democratic market socialism," as set forth in this book, is *not* in fact "what they have in Scandinavia."

My problem with social democracy goes beyond an objection to misuse of the term "socialism." In addition, I believe that the social democratic attitude tends to be excessively idealistic and egalitarian, so that many if not most social democratic plans and projects are impractical and/or dysfunctional. Idealism and egalitarianism are fine principles in and of themselves, and one of the hallmarks of enlightened humanity is relentless pursuit of them. But just as with most other positive principles, they are capable of being pushed too far—and that, in my judgment, is what social democrats tend to do. In fact, although I cringe to use a derisory term favored by individuals whom I consider "benighted conservatives," many social democrats do indeed seem to be accurately described as "knee-jerk liberals."

Rather than properly concentrating on the needless and unjustified financial privileges of wealthy capitalists—such privileges as would indeed be terminated by socialism properly defined—instead they expend most of their energies lamenting and bemoaning the condition of the relatively small minority of extremely poor and disadvantaged people in society. Owing to their excessively idealistic and naive view of human nature, they systematically underestimate the costs of alleviating the plight of this minority. Moreover, owing to their inadequate appreciation of the salient distinction between the unearned capital property income of the very wealthy and the earned wage and salary income of the middle class, social democrats normally propose that the costs of alleviating the plight of the extremely poor and disadvantaged be borne equally by the middle class as by the very wealthy. The extent of their radicalism with respect to taxation of the wealthy is normally confined to such trivial matters as whether or not expensive restaurant lunches should be tax-deductible as business expenses.

Moreover, social democrats normally are not interested particularly in fundamental socioeconomic policy, either because it is inherently boring, or because they believe that no important changes are possible in this area. They rather utilize most of their time, energy, and resources in pushing the left-wing position on a variety of issues more or less divorced from the fundamental socioeconomic system: issues such as the environment, abortion, discrimination, crime control, international affairs, and so on and so forth.

These comments are not intended to disparage the historical role of social democracy. One may be skeptical of the contemporary version of a sociopolitical attitude and movement, and yet feel that this attitude and movement made a significant beneficial contribution in the past. Social democracy has been quite likely an indispensable element in the evolution of the democratic market capitalist social system within the advanced industrial nations to a stage at which only the most closed-minded and doctrinaire mentality can fail to appreciate its great strength and commendable virtues. The level of material prosperity, artistic culture, and humane civilization presently existing in the United States, the nations of Western Europe, and several other localities around the world, far exceeds anything heretofore witnessed in human history.

The transition from democratic market capitalism to democratic market socialism proposed in this book, should it be accomplished, would be a matter of fine-tuning a fully viable and impressively successful system. The gain from such fine-tuning would be appreciable and worthwhile, but hardly overwhelming. The revised socioeconomic system would clearly not be ideal or utopian by any stretch of the imagination. Just as it is necessary to give contemporary capitalism its due, so also it is necessary to give social democracy its due in the historical development of contemporary capitalism.

SOCIALISM IN THE U.S.S.R.

By the early twentieth century, social democracy was rapidly becoming the dominant force within the worldwide socialist movement. Public ownership socialism, that is to say, socialism in its hardline classical Marxist incarnation, might have faded out of the picture altogether if it had not been for the Russian Revolution of 1917. Although it was a complex event, the ultimate significance of the Russian Revolution of 1917 was that it eventually installed hardline Marxists as the leaders of a large, populous and important nation-state. In so doing, it gave public owner-ship socialism a new lease on life.

It is one of the numerous ironies of socialist history that the social up-heaval which resurrected hardline Marxism as a force to contend with in human affairs was drastically dissimilar to events as forecast by Marx himself. Instead of occurring in an advanced industrial nation such as Britain or France, it occurred in Russia, still a predominantly agricultural nation with a relatively embryonic industrial sector. Instead of being pre-cipitated by a devastating business depression, it was precipitated by a costly war of attrition which imposed terrible hardships, both physical and psychological, on the Russian population. Along with most of Europe, in 1914 tsarist Russia had become embroiled in World War I. The war did not go well for Russia, and its heavy burden gradually crys-tallized the population's resentment and hostility toward an absolutist re-gime that was regarded—both inside and outside Russia—as the most reactionary and unprogressive in Europe.

Moreover, although events viewed in retrospect often have an inexo-rable appearance, the emergence of the Bolsheviks as the rulers of Russia in the wake of revolution and civil war seems almost as remarkable today as it did at the time. The Bolsheviks, after all, were only one seemingly minor component of a complex prerevolutionary brew in which Russian capitalists, anxious to emulate the notable successes of their counterparts in Western Europe, were no doubt the most important factor, at least as far as raw finances are concerned. Under the brilliant and resourceful leadership of Vladimir Lenin, however, what might have been dismissed as a contemptible little band of extremist misfits, taking full advantage of the drastically disturbed conditions produced by Russia's unsuccessful participation in World War I, argued, exhorted, maneuvered, and fought their way into secure control of the Russian nation and its various periph-eral territories.

Proclaiming as they did the desirability, necessity, and even inevita-bility of worldwide socialist revolution, the Communist Party leaders of the U.S.S.R. immediately found themselves in potentially deadly opposi-tion to the leaders of the capitalist nations. For more than 20 years, until the cataclysm of World War II presented it with some allied nations, the Soviet Union stood alone, in precarious isolation and virulent hostility, against all the other nations of the world. Luckily for the Communist leadership of the Soviet Union, the prevalent attitude toward Soviet Communism throughout the capitalist world during this period was com-placently tolerant, even condescending, rather than fearful. Many anti-socialists found solace in the thought that the Soviet Union was providing the world with an object lesson on the impracticality and perversity of socialism. By the time the Soviet Union, in the aftermath of World War II, was widely perceived as constituting a serious threat to the worldwide capitalist status quo, it had become far too strong to be easily conquered militarily, so that its Communist leadership could be overthrown and replaced by conservatives—as had earlier been the case with revolutionary France following the defeat of Napoleon and, according to the terms of the Treaty of Vienna of 1815, the restoration of the Bourbon monarchy.

Among the first official actions taken by the Communist government of the Soviet Union in early 1918 was the total dispossession, without any compensation whatsoever, of both the landed aristocracy and the nascent capitalist class in Russia and its peripheral republics. Total public ownership of land and capital was implemented immediately, without ceremony, and without apology. Wholesale socialization galvanized the conservative resistance to the Communist regime and led to almost four years of bitter civil war. When it was over, most of the internal opponents of the regime were either dead or in exile. The civil war thus challenged the authority of the Soviet Communist leadership, but the failure of that war confirmed it. The socialization of Russia, naturally, greatly concerned the more conservative elements in other countries. Among others, Winston Churchill argued that military intervention should be mounted at once to crush the Bolshevik threat. Luckily for the Bolsheviks, the capitalist nations could not muster the resolution for more than a small-scale and ineffectual effort at military intervention. The combination of war weariness in the wake of the catastrophic World War I and the general consensus that socialism was thoroughly impractical—a fact which the Soviet Union would presumably soon discover, precluded a full-scale invasion of the fledgling Soviet Union by Western European and American forces.

Throughout most of the twentieth century, the Soviet Union has been engaged in a virulent, propagandistic controversy with the capitalist nations over the relative virtues and vices of capitalism versus socialism. Owing to the seriousness of the issue and the intensity of the controversy, the normal standards of objective inquiry and rational discussion have been drastically degraded. Both sides have taken an excessively negative view of the other side and an excessively positive view of their own side. It has been very difficult for thoughtful and sincere people on both sides to see through the miasma of vociferous vituperation to whatever elements of truth might underlie the other side's proclamations and assertions. But now, at the threshold of the twenty-first century, as we look back on twentieth-century Soviet history in calmer retrospect, what basic conclusions seem valid and legitimate?

A very large consensus is now possible, a consensus fully shared by many if not most citizens of the ex-U.S.S.R., that the Soviet socio-economic system during the era of Communist Party rule was deeply flawed. The inherent propensities in a basically undemocratic and oligar-chic political system toward unrestrained totalitarianism were dramati-cally demonstrated by the Stalinist purgatory of the 1930s. In terms of the everyday living standards of the Soviet population, despite decades of sustained effort, they never seriously challenged the living standards achieved by the advanced capitalist nations such as the United States, the nations of Western Europe, and so on.

On the other hand, it will also be acknowledged by most fair-minded individuals that the Soviet Union achieved an impressive level of per-formance under very difficult circumstances. As to the political system, although hierarchical and authoritarian in its structure and procedures, at least it was relatively open at its base. Membership in the Communist Party was open to most if not all citizens, and once in the Party, upward progress was governed largely by genuine merit and accomplishments. True, the aspirant to high rank had to please his or her superiors; but mat-ters were perhaps not so much different in substance from matters under representative democracy as practiced in the West. After all, under repre-sentative democracy, an aspirant to high elective rank must please the in-cumbent political activists and financial supporters in order first to be nominated and then to obtain the necessary resources to mount an effec-tive campaign for a high-level elective office.

As to the living standards of the Soviet population, they rose far be-yond the subsistence levels prevalent within most Third World nations which continue to abide by the private ownership principle of capitalism. As of the 1980s, living standards in the Soviet Union were comparable to those in such capitalist nations as Turkey and Argentina—although Tur-key and Argentina, of course, did not have to endure a withering barrage of scorn and ridicule on account of the paltry living standards of their populations. Turkey and Argentina, after all, were not making explicit threats to bury the capitalist socioeconomic system. It should also be ap-preciated that the relatively respectable living standards of the Soviet population were achieved in the face of a crushing military burden. Throughout almost its entire history, the Soviet Union was involved in an arms competition with the capitalist world. With the development of thermonuclear bombs and ballistic missile delivery systems, this competition became unprecedentedly intense and perilous in the Cold War period following World War II. Although the Soviet Union never produced quite as much guns and butter (to use a favorite example from principles of economics courses) as did the United States during the Cold War, it did in fact produce quite a lot of both guns and butter. In the final analysis, the economic system of the Soviet Union performed quite impressively by many standards.

Whatever might be said for or against the Soviet Union, few would dispute the statement that it was a socialist nation. Whatever it achieved, it achieved without the assistance of capitalism or capitalists. To the extent that one is impressed by what the Soviet Union did accomplish, doubts must arise in one's mind as to how necessary capitalism and capitalists actually are to the continued economic success of the Western non-Communist nations. On the other hand, whatever flaws and shortcomings characterized the Soviet Union, the absence of capitalism and capitalists *might* have contributed to them.

The argument advanced here is that, contrary to a widespread misapprehension, there is no substantial evidence to suggest that the actual flaws and shortcomings of Soviet Communism were to any significant extent the consequence of socialism in and of itself. These various flaws and shortcomings are plausibly attributed to factors quite unrelated to the socialist public ownership principle. In fact, when the multiplicity of factors which impeded the performance of the Soviet Union throughout its history is fully appreciated, one is drawn naturally toward the conclusion that socialism, in and of itself, tends to be a fully viable and highly efficient economic principle—otherwise the Soviet system would not have done nearly as well as it actually did.

To emphasize the multiplicity of these negative factors, unrelated to socialism per se, which adversely affected Soviet performance and achievement, the following discussion will be organized around an even dozen such factors. Admittedly, some of these factors are closely interrelated with others. On the other hand, each of them is well documented as a separate factor in the economic and political literature produced in the West on the Soviet Union. Several additional factors could no doubt be invoked if the list were to be made fully comprehensive. A summary listing of the twelve factors is as follows: (1) the psychological burden of protracted conflict with the capitalist world; (2) the military burden of continuous participation in an arms competition with the capitalist world;

(3) inadequate participation in the world economy; (4) the stultifying effect on society of pervasive Communist Party control; (5) the guidance of investment decisions by political rather than economic criteria; (6) the inflexibility imposed on enterprises by the central planning system; (7) the guidance of enterprise decision-making largely according to the goal of plan fulfillment rather than profitability; (8) reluctance to allow bankruptcy of inefficient firms; (9) excessive job security among the workforce; (10) excessive egalitarianism in the determination of wages and salaries; (11) weaknesses in the agricultural sector; (12) resentment and hostility among national minorities within the Soviet Union.

Psychological burden of protracted conflict with the capitalist world. Although a great deal of nonsense has appeared, in the wake of the recent Soviet collapse, which argues that this collapse was inevitable and predictable, the fact remains that no tangible, objective factor seems to have been the precipitating element. Rather it was a *psychological* crisis of confidence among the high leadership of the Communist Party which opened the doors to a tide of change which eventually, to the consternation of these same leaders, swept the Communist Party out of power. At the time of Gorbachev's accession to power in 1985, the condition of the Soviet economy was undynamic, even stagnant, but far from critical or disastrous. The people were relatively comfortable, and the military was being adequately supplied with armaments and other equipment.

The basic problem, however, was the long-term inability of the Communist Party leadership to make good on its promises to the Soviet people. For decades the leadership had been promising higher living standards than those in the West. For decades they had been promising that revolutionary movements abroad would dislodge capitalism in the West and make the world safer and less hostile to Soviet socialism. Neither promise was being realized: the populations of the advanced capitalist nations continued to be more prosperous than the Soviet population, and the governments of those same nations continued to be serenely untroubled by the prospect of any sort of socialist transformation, whether democratic or revolutionary. In the meantime, the Soviet people continued to live in the middle of a gigantic nuclear bull's-eye drawn on the Soviet Union by the United States and its allies. Nuclear war, should it have occurred, would have completely devastated the Soviet Union, along with much of the rest of the world. As much as the Soviet people had been indoctrinated in their moral duty to support socialist revolution throughout the world, they could not totally avoid recognizing the fact that as the effective aggressor in the conflict between capitalism and socialism, theirs was the larger share of the moral responsibility for the persistence of the Cold War and its concomitant threat of wholesale destruction.

Military burden of continuous participation in an arms competition with the capitalist world. The burden of the Cold War was hardly confined to apprehensions caused by the possibility of nuclear holocaust. There was also a tangible economic cost as the military machine continued to claim not only a large proportion of the physical resources and output of the national economy, but also the best and the brightest among the nation's human resources. A considerable amount of economic literature statistically documents the intuitively appealing proposition that a heavy military burden not only substantially reduces current living standards among the civilian population, but also substantially reduces the achieved rate of economic growth. From the beginning, the Communist Party leadership has considered it obligatory to keep the Soviet Union heavily armed. Early apprehensions concerning invasion by a hostile capitalist outer world were eventually vindicated when, on Hitler's orders, the Nazi military machine invaded the Soviet Union in June 1941. Only Germany experienced more death and destruction during World War II than did the Soviet Union. This epic struggle had an enormous impact upon the Soviet nation, both physically and psychologically. In light of what had occurred on the eastern front from 1941 through 1945, the overweening need for a strong military was little questioned by the Soviet people throughout most of the Cold War era.

Inadequate participation in the world economy. Free participation in international trade is without doubt an extremely important contributor to the economic success of a nation. For all the caveats and modifications which have been appended to it over its long history, the mutual advantages to be gained from trade between nations is still one of the most compelling propositions of economic thought. Owing to ideological isolation and military exigencies, the Soviet Union never derived much benefit from interaction with the international economy. While the Communist Party leadership never categorically rejected trade with the capitalist world, their paranoiac suspicion of capitalist trading partners and their pathological dread of becoming dependent on capitalist nations for either military requirements or the necessities of life precluded any significant amount of trade. Even after the Soviet Union, in the aftermath of World War II, gained some ideological allies in Eastern Europe and Asia, trading with other Communist nations was still fenced about with a plethora of regulations and restrictions. Thus the Soviet Union forwent the benefits of obtaining some commodities more cheaply from abroad than from domestic production, and it also lost the efficiency benefits that would have necessarily accrued if it had been forced to produce its export commodities up to competitive world standards. A related point which is worthy of mention is that Russia's intransigence with respect to its forcibly Communized Eastern European satellites after World War II denied it any participation in the Marshall Plan largesse provided by the United States, which greatly accelerated the postwar economic recovery of the Western European nations.

Stultifying effect on society of pervasive Communist Party control. Even those historians who view Soviet history and society very negatively will usually acknowledge that the prerevolutionary Russian political system had been neither open nor democratic. As of the 1917 revolution, the Russian state was as close an approximation to an absolute monarchy along seventeenth-century lines as existed anywhere in the world. Taking this oligarchic tradition into account along with the fierce internal and external opposition to the Soviet state aroused by its twin policies of radical, uncompensated socialization at home and open support for socialist revolution abroad, it is not surprising that the Communist Party leadership regarded political democracy along American and Western European lines as an unaffordable luxury. Throughout its history, the Soviet state regarded itself as being under siege by a host of deadly enemies. Obviously the acrid political debates and leisurely government decisionmaking of Western democracy are disruptive and debilitating in the short run—their valid defense is that they are a safeguard against the kind of oligarchy and arbitrary, unresponsive government which is even *more* disruptive and debilitating in the long run. But among the Soviet leadership, concern for their short-run survival abrogated contemplation of the long-run benefits of Western-style political democracy.

The economic costs of political oligarchy are difficult to pinpoint and quantify, but they are quite possibly extremely significant nonetheless. Some of the economic costs are encompassed by the various sources of economic weakness detailed below, in that some of the policies responsible for these weaknesses probably would not have been pursued had they been subject to the intellectual checks and balances entailed in free and open discussion pursuant to democratic decisionmaking. Among the more obvious additional points is that since Communist Party membership was the sole route to power and (relative) wealth, and since advancement in the Party depended primarily on slavish obedience to one's immediate superiors, the political system tended to siphon off a large proportion of the most capable and ambitious members of society and then mold them into quasi-robots devoid of originality and spontaneity.

Beyond this lies a still more speculative and intangible—but nevertheless potentially extremely important—factor: the overall psychological demoralization of a society which knows in its heart that it is on the wrong side of a portentous ideological confrontation. Soviet ideologists were put into a virtually impossible situation by the assaults on "Soviet tyranny" of Western anti-Communists. It is to the credit of the Soviet Communist ideological system that it never openly and explicitly rejected democratic ideas and ideals—as did the fascist ideological system of Nazi Germany and its allies. Western democracy was assailed by Soviet ideologues not on grounds that democratic governance was inherently dilatory, vacillating, and weak, but rather on grounds that the effective political domination of the capitalist class (achieved through financial support only of acceptably anti-socialistic candidates for elective office, suppression of favorable discussion of socialism by the privately owned media of communication, and so on) made a mockery of genuine democracy. By the same token, Soviet ideologues adamantly insisted, in the face of scorn and ridicule from the West, that the Soviet political system was indeed genuinely democratic, citing the regularly scheduled elections for important government positions (albeit there being only one Communist Party-approved candidate for each position), the free availability of Communist Party membership to all citizens, and the alleged fact that in a classless society from which the capitalist exploiters had been eliminated, there was no longer any purpose or point in acrid political controversy between independently organized political parties.

Despite their best efforts at self-persuasion, the Soviet ideologues responsible for defending Soviet democracy probably sensed that they were on the losing side of the argument. It was simply too much of a strain on logic, rationality, and common sense to have to accept that democracy is a beneficial political principle, and at the same time to argue that freedom of speech, press, and political organization are not necessary institutions to the achievement of genuine democracy. As the tide of change initiated by Gorbachev's perestroika and glasnost initiatives rolled out of control in the Soviet Union, the reform movement focused itself primarily on political change rather than economic change. As of the time of writing, several years following the overthrow of Communist Party dominion and the dissolution of the U.S.S.R., the economic system in Russia and the peripheral republics is far less radically changed than the political system. In particular, public ownership of large-scale industrial enterprises is still very much the rule rather than the exception. The drastic revision of the political system which has taken place demonstrates the Soviet people's lack of faith in the old system, a lack of faith which no doubt contributed indirectly to the economic weakness of the overall social system.

Guidance of investment decisions by political rather than economic criteria. Throughout the history of the Soviet Union, major economic decisions have been based on perceived political necessity rather than economic grounds of immediate efficiency and/or social welfare. The single most dramatic example of this was the gigantic internally financed and generated industrialization effort commenced in the late 1920s and continued throughout the 1930s and thereafter. The living standards of the Soviet population were cut to bare subsistence in order that economic resources could be principally allocated to a crash campaign to build up economic infrastructure and industrial capacity. An effort was made to keep up the spirits of the people by telling them that the purpose of industrialization and modernization was to lay a basis for a lavish consumer society in the near future. The current sacrifices, it was promised, will bear fruit in the very near future.

In actual fact, the majority of the Soviet population during the 1930s (that part of it which survived the crucible of World War II) were well into middle or old age by the time the industrialization campaign began to moderate in the late 1950s and 1960s. It seems highly improbable that had the Soviet people exercised democratic control over the government in the 1930s, the Communist Party would have remained in power. Such extremely severe short-term sacrifices as were imposed on the people at that time almost certainly would not have been undertaken voluntarily, even presuming that the leadership had utilized the most intensive exhortation imaginable to persuade the people that destiny was at hand and that these sacrifices were to their own long-term advantage. As a matter of fact, it was *not* the material prosperity of the general population which was uppermost in the Communist Party leadership's collective mind when they proclaimed and implemented the industrialization campaign. Rather it was the security of the Soviet state—that is to say, their own security. The industrialization campaign was motivated by fear of invasion by a hostile capitalistic outer world: its basic purpose was to develop a modern, industrial economy capable of producing an abundance of up-to-date weaponry: guns, tanks, airplanes, and so on. Only a modern armaments industry could provide a secure deterrent against potential invaders both attracted by the Soviet Union's ample living space and abundant natural resources, and fearful of the sparks of worldwide socialist revolution harbored within the Soviet Union. As it turned out, growing Soviet military power did not deter Nazi Germany from an effort at conquest, but it was no doubt instrumental in the defeat of that effort between 1941 and 1945.

Throughout most of its history, the Soviet government has been far more concerned with developing military capacity than with developing consumer goods capacity. Even within the Communist Party itself, however, questions have been raised as to the wisdom and necessity of this policy. The wave of intra-Party dissent generated by the extremely intensive industrialization program of the 1930s was harshly suppressed by means of a devastating purge which executed or exiled millions of people, many of whom had previously been highly placed officials of the Communist Party. The Stalinist tyranny of this period dwarfed the Terror of the French Revolution, and constituted by far the most difficult and tragic period in all of Russian history. It also, of course, severely tarnished the image of socialism in human thinking—perhaps doing irreparable harm to the prospects of ever achieving a benign and humane socialist society in the real world.

Inflexibility imposed on enterprises by the central planning system. Long before the slowdown in Soviet economic growth in the 1970s and 1980s, Western economists specializing in the study of comparative economic systems had busied themselves drawing up lists of "reasons for Soviet economic weakness." At or near the top of every such list was the central planning system. Comprehensive economic planning commenced in the Soviet Union with the First Five-Year Plan (1928-33), and by the mid-1930s the centralization of economic decision-making authority in the hands of the State Planning Committee (Gosplan) and several other bureaucracies headquartered in Moscow had reached heights unprecedented in the economic history of human civilization. The annual plan specified in minute detail exactly how and how much each one of thousands of enterprises was to produce each one of hundreds of thousands of commodities. It specified the exact prices at which the millions of transactions between enterprises were to be carried out. It specified exactly how all investment resources were to be allocated among enterprises. Since many months elapsed between the drawing up of the plan and its actual implementation, and since the information on which the planning process was based was usually inaccurate or out of date anyway, on top of which the whole gigantic task was undertaken with "paper and pencil" methods (since the powerful computers which we now take for granted had not yet been invented), it is not surprising that central planning in the Soviet Union was exceedingly clumsy, unwieldy, and inefficient.

Be that as it may, Soviet central planning as implemented and developed during the Stalinist era should be given its proper due. Central planning was an integral part of the crash industrialization effort undertaken in order to build up a modern armaments industry capable of deterring (or defeating) supposedly rapacious capitalist nations with both ideological and imperialistic motivations for invading and conquering the Soviet Union. No such attempt at rapid industrialization "by the bootstraps" (i.e., in the absence of any appreciable investment by or trade with the outer world) had ever before been witnessed in human history. That at least a respectable amount of success had been achieved was made clear by the successful resistance by Russia against the Nazi war machine in World War II. While lend-lease assistance received from the United States was an instrumental factor in the survival of the U.S.S.R. during this period, so also was the impressive productivity of its own domestic armaments industry.

In fact, it has been widely conceded, even outside the Soviet Union, that Stalinist era central planning was basically successful: its objective was to ensure the physical survival of the Soviet state in a hostile world, and that objective was achieved. It also has to be recognized that the Soviet central planning system was designed in the absence of any prior historical experience with such an economic system, and also without benefit of any appreciable input from Karl Marx—to the works of whom the Communist Party leaders looked for inspiration and guidance as devote Christians look to the Bible. Marx's thunderous denunciations of the "anarchy of the market" under capitalism naturally suggested that some sort of comprehensive social coordination would be appropriate under socialism, but Marx himself never provided anything remotely approaching a "blueprint" for a socialist economy. Perhaps if Marx had lived to see Soviet central planning, he would have deemed it overambitious and excessively centralized—just as the vast majority of Western economists have.

Guidance of enterprise decisionmaking largely according to the goal of plan fulfillment rather than profitability. Even at the height of the Stalinist era industrialization campaign, Soviet central planning was never a "pure" planning system in the sense that the plan completely and absolutely supplanted the market. In a pure planning system, there would be no need for monetary exchange of any sort, and commodities would be unpriced. Such an economic system, in the judgment of most economists, would quickly become horribly inefficient, and would probably collapse entirely within a short period of time. Fortunately for the Soviet Union, the Soviet economists of the 1920s who designed the central planning system were neither so naive nor so radical as to propose the abolition of money and prices—and hence of the economic market itself. The planning system was regarded as a coordinating overlay on the market rather than a replacement of the market—a heavy overlay, to be sure, but still merely an overlay.

Similarly, the designers of the central planning system did not propose to abrogate the traditional "capitalist" categories of profit and interest. Therefore the annual plan envisioned that each productive enterprise would be financially solvent and even profitable, and indeed, because the plan called for the enterprise to earn a profit, its managers were to some extent evaluated on the basis of profitability. Profitability, therefore, could hardly be "ignored" by the managers. On the other hand, by far the single most important goal of the plan was the quantity of physical output of commodities. An enterprise which was producing the specified number of goods might be forgiven for not achieving the specified amount of profit—but the converse was definitely *not* true.

In orthodox Western economics, which presumes that for the great majority of industries the "perfect competition" specification is an adequate approximation to reality, and further that "external effects" (e.g., pollution) are relatively minor (possibly owing to the observance of socially imposed regulations), the pursuit of profits by firms is seen as the great engine which drives the whole economic system in a generally beneficial direction. Profit maximization by firms under competitive conditions is regarded as the great natural force which ensures that consumers are provided with the commodities they desire at reasonable prices, that is to say, that the appropriate commodities are produced effectively and efficiently. Profit maximization is perceived not only as the instrumental factor in the attainment of static (current period) efficiency in production and marketing, but also as the instrumental factor in the achievement of dynamic (long-term) progressiveness through investment and innovation. Innovations in commodities and production processes are introduced, and investment funds are allocated toward the objective of earning high profits in the future. While it is recognized that some social constraints may have to be placed on the pursuit of profit by business enterprises in order to keep it within proper bounds, this pursuit is regarded as basically healthy and indeed vital to the good performance of the economy now and in the future.

Thus Western economics has identified as an important contributor to Soviet economic weakness the fact that Soviet enterprise managers were evaluated first and foremost in terms of their success in meeting the physical output goals specified in the annual plan, and only secondarily and to a minor extent on the basis of the profitability of their enterprises. Heavy emphasis upon physical quantity rather than quality led to erosion of quality standards, while relatively minor emphasis on profitability eroded incentives toward the efficient production of goods.

Reluctance to allow bankruptcy of inefficient firms. The Soviet economic system was heavily influenced by Karl Marx's critique of the capitalist economy. According to this critique, bankruptcy of any particular business enterprise is a manifestation of the socially perverse "anarchy of the market" under capitalism. Most bankruptcies occur during the needless economic depressions imposed on society by capitalism. But even the minority of bankruptcies which occur during periods of prosperity would be easily avoidable if there were some degree of coordinative control over the economy to avoid overproduction of particular commodities, and to facilitate the smooth transfer of productive resources from declining commodities to rising commodities. Marx's view completely rejects the orthodox perception of bankruptcy as a regrettable but necessary disciplinary device which induces both workers and managers to adhere to high performance standards lest bankruptcy of the firm project them into a highly disagreeable condition of unemployment.

The reluctance of Soviet economic planners to allow enterprises to cease operations owing to financial bankruptcy translated into what has been termed in Western economics the "soft budget constraint." The soft budget constraint means that enterprises are not required to be profitable, that any losses which they might incur are covered by subsidies from the state financial authorities. Thus insulated from the threat of bankruptcy, both the managers and the workers of enterprises become relatively careless, lax, and indolent. While the Western perception of the soft budget constraint probably somewhat exaggerates the ease with which managers of losing enterprises were able to obtain financial subsidies with which to continue operations, nevertheless there is quite likely a considerable measure of truth in the scenario.

Excessive job security among the workforce. Just as Karl Marx's perception of bankruptcy as a "capitalist problem" led to the soft budget constraint of Soviet enterprises, so too Marx's perception of dismissals and unemployment as a "capitalist problem" led to excessive job security among the Soviet workforce. According to Marx's ideologically loaded view of economic reality, the dismissal of a particular employee almost never occurred as a consequence of the incompetence or uncooperativeness of that employee—rather it usually occurred owing to the exigencies of capitalistic business depression, though on some occasions it might simply manifest the arbitrary and capricious cruelty of capitalist employers unconstrained by any moral, legal, or social responsibilities toward their workers. Aside from Marx's preconceptions, there was the fact that the Soviet industrialization effort placed an enormous strain on the Soviet population—living standards were cut to the bare subsistence level in order that more economic resources could be allocated to capital investment. The Communist Party leadership may well have been concerned that if, in addition to the hardship and scarcity imposed by extreme austerity, the Soviet workforce had also had to endure the job uncertainties and anxieties associated with the free market economy, that workforce might have become so demoralized and dispirited as to constitute a serious threat to the stability of the Soviet state. As a result, employees of Soviet firms could not be dismissed for anything short of the most egregious and flagrant inactivity or obstructionism. This also contributed to low productivity and economic weakness.

Excessive egalitarianism in wages and salaries. In the propaganda war which waged between the Soviet Union and the non-Communist world during the perilous Cold War era, much was made on the non-Communist side of the "nomenklatura"—the system by which special privileges were accorded to those, most of them high officials within the Communist Party of the U.S.S.R., on the list (nomenklatura) of those entitled to such privileges. For example, only nomenklatura individuals were permitted to purchase goods at special stores well stocked with luxuries which were either unattainable or prohibitively expensive to the ordinary population. Thus the egalitarian ideals preached by Soviet ideology were being hypocritically ignored in the actual operations of Soviet society—the Communist Party elite in effect constituted a "new class" which inherited the unjustified privileges of the capitalist class which Soviet ideologues loudly proclaimed to have been abolished. As irritating as these privileges undoubtedly were to many ordinary Russian citizens, they ought to be put into proper perspective. Even with these privileges, Russian society was indeed exceptionally egalitarian by Western standards. Even among the highest Party officials, living standards were actually quite modest relative to the customary "lifestyles of the rich and famous" in the non-Communist world.

As a matter of fact, excessive, ideologically imposed egalitarianism was almost surely an important constraint on the performance of the Soviet economy. Differences in wages between different levels of skilled labor were significantly less than in the West, as were income differentials between managers and professionals relative to blue-collar laborers. Although Western economics may perhaps be prone to exaggerate the effectiveness of material incentives to effort, such incentives are without doubt highly important. Economic equality is desirable in terms of psychological serenity and social harmony, but unfortunately it does have a significant price in terms of lower incentives to effort. In terms of overall socioeconomic performance, there is a happy medium on the spectrum between very high economic equality and very high economic inequality. Almost certainly the Soviet Union erred on the side of too much economic equality.

Weaknesses in the agricultural sector. There were two principal components of the crash modernization effort initiated in the U.S.S.R. in the late 1920s and early 1930s: the collectivization of agriculture and rapid industrialization financed by state investment. One of the principal reasons why the effort imposed far more hardship on the population than had been anticipated was the gross exaggeration of the benefits of collectivization. The Communist Party planners had expected agricultural productivity to soar owing to the introduction of "factory methods" on farms. The tremendous agricultural surplus which would supposedly be generated by the planned mechanization and modernization of agriculture was expected to keep the employees of the growing industrial sector as well as the farmers well fed, and at the same time provide a source of foreign exchange from the export of foodstuffs. These hopes were badly disappointed, and the failure of agriculture to perform up to prior expectations enormously increased the burden of the industrialization campaign on the people.

Somewhat over a decade had elapsed between the great land redistribution immediately following the 1917 Russian Revolution and the commencement of the great collectivization effort of the late 1920s and early 1930s. The postrevolutionary land redistribution broke up the large estates of the nobility into a huge number of small parcels of land which were more or less independently farmed by family groups. These families did not own the land in a legal sense: for example, they could not sell their land allocations, nor choose to leave them fallow. On the other hand, they worked the land with a minimum of supervision from above, and they were allowed to dispose of the majority of the produce of the land at their own discretion, consuming some of it directly and marketing the rest to obtain monetary income. Under these arrangements, Soviet agriculture did quite well throughout most of the 1920s. The rural population was generally well fed and prosperous (recall that the U.S.S.R. was an agrarian nation, so that a large majority of the population was in fact rural), and the agricultural surplus available to support the urban population and export trade was growing slowly.

Unfortunately this slow rate of growth in the agricultural surplus was not satisfactory to the Party planners. They were convinced that the same kind of specialization and division of labor utilized in urban factories could be applied to rural agriculture and would generate dramatic increases in agricultural productivity. They were also influenced by the grumblings of less successful farmers against their more prosperous neighbors. Owing to differences in effort and luck, substantial inequality in living standards was emerging in the countryside, and this did not seem sufficiently "socialist" to many. When collectivization was initiated, however, it turned out that a very large number—if not a substantial majority—of farmers strongly preferred the system of the 1920s. They opposed collectivization fiercely—sometimes by force but usually with non-cooperation and passive resistance. Matters degenerated to the point of serious civil disturbances which threatened to re-ignite the civil war of 10 years earlier. Millions of farmers were relocated forcibly, and numerous concentration camps were established and filled up rapidly (the beginning of the infamous "gulag archipelago").

There were two principal reasons for the inferiority of the collective farming system over the earlier independent farming system in the eyes of many if not most farmers. First, under the old system farmers were allowed to either consume personally or sell on local free markets the great majority of their produce, while under the new system, the great majority of the collective's output went to fulfill mandatory deliveries to government collection centers—and these collection centers paid prices which were a small fraction of what could be obtained for the same produce on local free markets. The mandatory delivery system at submarket prices greatly diminished the aggregate income of the agricultural workforce. Second, the collective farms tended to follow extremely egalitarian policies in the distribution of what scanty revenues they did receive from the government collection centers. Since every collective employee received the same amount regardless of personal effort, the effort level of all employees in the collective tended to subside toward the lowest common denominator level established by the least energetic and/or conscientious employees.

What the planners had failed to foresee was the devastating impact on the morale and productivity of the agricultural workforce of being herded together in large collectives which followed extremely egalitarian policies in the distribution of revenues, and which moreover received aggregate revenues which were a small fraction of the combined former incomes of the employees owing to the newly imposed mandatory delivery system. The collapse of workforce morale fully overshadowed the modest improvements in agricultural technology attained through increased mechanization and more intensive utilization of fertilizers and pesticides. As a consequence, the agricultural sector has been a weak link in the economic chain of production throughout most of Soviet history. Later modifications in agricultural policy eased the condition of the rural population and improved its morale and productivity. Nevertheless, the disastrous impact of the Stalinist-era collective farm system on Soviet agriculture was never entirely overcome.

Resentment and hostility among national minorities within the Soviet Union. The Soviet Union was a federation of thirteen republics of which the Russian republic was dominant in terms of land area, population, and political control. As most of the peripheral republics had been components of the Russian empire for centuries prior to the Russian Revolution, as Marxist ideology has always been commendably tolerant and internationalist in viewpoint, and as many representatives of national minorities within the U.S.S.R. were observed in the highest state and Party positions (for example, Stalin was a Georgian), it was widely assumed that national distinctions within the Soviet Union had become almost entirely obsolescent and irrelevant, and that the Soviet population as a whole had been thoroughly homogenized and made highly oblivious to distinctions of nationality. Recent events have demonstrated how thoroughly false this previously widespread conception was. As stunning as the Soviet people's unmitigated denunciation and renunciation of the Communist Party's previously unchallenged "social leadership" was, perhaps even more unexpected was the simultaneous dissolution of the Soviet state into a weak confederation. It now appears that in the judgment of many if not most citizens of the peripheral republics, the Soviet Union in reality was largely an evil and perverse instrument of Russian domination and oppression.

Just as it would be difficult to precisely specify and quantify the adverse effects on the Soviet economy of the political domination of society by an authoritarian Communist Party apparatus, so too it would be

44   *Economic Justice*

difficult to precisely specify and quantify the adverse economic effects of nationalistically based dissatisfaction and disaffection. But just as the economic costs of political authoritarianism might all the same have been very substantial, so too the economic costs of nationalistic disharmony might have been very substantial. Individuals who consider themselves downtrodden—whether they are or not—are not likely to be energetic and productive contributors to economic processes.

Whatever may have been the past economic costs of discontent among the national minorities, the present costs are approaching the catastrophic level. The Soviet national economy was planned from the beginning to be highly interdependent, with different areas specializing in different commodities. The reconstitution of the republics as virtually independent and autonomous nations within a weak confederation has drastically disrupted the smooth interchange of commodities within the ex-U.S.S.R. Regulation and restriction of interrepublic trade has blossomed as officials of the newly independent republics, in the glow of their newfound chauvinistic xenophobia, decide that more and more goods are better off being consumed at home rather than being shipped off to be enjoyed by unworthy "foreigners" in other republics of the ex-U.S.S.R.—especially those in the Russian republic. In their enthusiastic pursuit of the narrow, short-term self-interest of their own citizens, they tend to overlook how dependent they themselves actually are on commodities imported from the other republics—especially the Russian republic. As a cause of disruption and low productivity in the ex-U.S.S.R., the curtailment of internal trade is probably second only to sheer confusion and disagreement over the locus of economic authority and the correct specification of enterprise goals.

With this I conclude this brief exposition of twelve clearcut and conceptually distinct sources of Soviet economic weakness which are *not* either logically or causationally related to the fundamental socialist principle of public ownership of the nonhuman factors of production. Obviously an array of serious problems and difficulties of this magnitude might be capable of bringing about the drastic transformation of a social system of the sort which has just been witnessed in the collapse of the Soviet Union. Therefore it was not socialism, in and of itself, which first weakened and eventually destroyed the Soviet Union.

Of course there are those whose antisocialist preconceptions are so overpowering that they perceive connections between public ownership of capital and a whole range of socioeconomic vices and evils, some of which have been cited in the foregoing as sources of Soviet weakness.

Two of the better known examples of such alleged connections are that public ownership "tends naturally" to produce central planning of the economy, and that public ownership "tends naturally" to the suppression of democracy and the establishment of oligarchic rule. Such propositions as these will be refuted at appropriate points in what follows. At this point I will merely state that all such propositions are purely conjectural at this time—and they are almost certainly the inventions of propagandistic myth rather than legitimate rational conclusions from the facts as we presently know them.

SOCIALISM IN CHINA

In the aftermath of World War II, Soviet-style Communistic socialism was externally imposed on several Eastern European nations (Poland, Hungary, Czechoslovakia, and so on). Although there had been a few adherents to Soviet Communism among the populations of these nations during the interwar period, they would never have come to power, even in the wake of a devastating war, had it not been for direct force of arms applied by the occupying Red Army. Apprehension and indignation in the West over the externally forced communizations of the Eastern European nations was the principal immediate impetus to the Cold War, but another factor was the communization of several other nations in which the Red Army was not directly resident. Among these other nations, by far the largest and most important was China.

China had been deeply mired in civil war and social turmoil ever since the overthrow of the Manchu dynasty in 1912. The epic struggle between the Nationalists under Chiang Kai-shek and the Communists under Mao Tse-tung left much of the country in a state of anarchy presided over by an array of competing "war-lords." The scenario was then complicated by the Japanese invasion of 1937. An uneasy alliance between the Nationalists and the Communists was maintained until the defeat of Japan in 1945. To the consternation of the West, Chiang Kai-shek's Nationalists were then outfought on the battlefield and outmaneuvered in the propaganda struggle for the allegiance of the population, with the result that in 1949 a second great nation was added to the Communist bloc of nations: the People's Republic of China (P.R.C.).

The non-Communist world soon observed, to its relief, that nationalistic distinctions tended to override the universalistic ideals of Marxist ideology. The Eastern European nations were very restive under Soviet dominion, which is hardly surprising in that Communism had been externally imposed on them in the aftermath of World War II. But even aside from Eastern Europe, Russia's other ideological allies, especially China, were disinclined to slavishly follow the Soviet Union's prescriptions and preferences. As did the United States during the same period, the Soviet Union found that being the senior partner of a military alliance did not completely insulate it from substantial criticism and opposition from junior partners of the alliance.

In the earliest period of Sino-Soviet disharmony, the major controversy revolved around the proper nature and pace of revolutionary social transformation both domestically and internationally—the Chinese accused the Soviets of being inadequately determined on both fronts. The Sino-Soviet conflict was never quite as dire as depicted by some Western propagandists searching anxiously for signs of weakness in Communism. There was never any serious likelihood of a war between the U.S.S.R. and the P.R.C. However, the conflict was serious enough to preclude close cooperation and friendship between the two nations. The tide of radical social egalitarianism crested in the P.R.C. in the Cultural Revolution of 1966-69, nearly 20 years after Mao Tse-tung's accession to power. This turbulent period was followed by a more or less inevitable "Thermidorean reaction," during which the P.R.C. reconciled itself to a certain amount of social distinction and economic inequality.

China's effort to follow the teachings and practices of Marx, Lenin and Stalin was influenced importantly both by its salient national characteristics and its international environment. China is of course smaller in territory than the Soviet Union and much more densely populated. It is a nation with a very long history and a very complex cultural tradition. At the time of the Communist victory in 1949, its industrial sector was even less developed than the Russian industrial sector had been at the time of the Bolshevik victory in 1917. China followed the Soviet lead in the collectivization of agriculture and also in the initiation of a modernization and industrialization campaign in which central planning of the economy played an important role. However, central planning was never as comprehensive and detailed in China as it was in the Soviet Union. There is at least one good reason for this: industrialization for purposes of self-defense was never as urgent in China as it had been earlier in the Soviet Union. Unlike the Soviet Union, Red China never had to stand alone against a hostile capitalist outer world. Following its socialist revolution, it was able to take shelter under the nuclear umbrella provided by the Soviet Union. In addition, Red China was to some extent able to learn from the mistakes of its predecessor in socialism. Thus for example, when its collective farm sector performed disappointingly, the Chinese government fundamentally revised the structure of agricultural production by means of the well-known "responsibility system."

Just as the revolutionary transformation of the Russian empire in 1917 led eventually to the totalitarian dictatorship of Joseph Stalin, so too the revolutionary transformation of China in 1949 led eventually to the totalitarian dictatorship of Mao Tse-tung. And just as the demise of Stalin in 1953 led to an era of reform in which socioeconomic policy moderated, so too the demise of Mao in 1973 led to an analogous era of reform. In both cases, emphasis was placed on decentralization of economic decision-making authority and increased reliance on market forces and individual incentives in the functioning of the economy. Western economists soon became rather scornful of the perennial Soviet economic reform efforts. A succession of well-publicized reform programs were commenced over the years, and one after another they were judged to have "failed" by Western economists as not having had a significant impact on the actual functioning of the planned Soviet economy. Western economists spoke of the Soviet economy as being on a "treadmill of reforms"—much effort, but little progress. Of course the legendary stability of the Soviet system came to an abrupt end in the early 1990s. The political system was indeed radically transformed within a short period of time by the elimination of direct Communist Party control over the state apparatus and the dissolution of the U.S.S.R. Several years after this dramatic political transformation, the economic system remains in a state of confusion and disarray. To this point, the substantive institutional changes in the system have by no means been fundamental. The Soviet Union is still a very long way from being a reasonable facsimile of the industrialized democratic market capitalist nations of the West. It is conceivable that the world may be witnessing yet another "failure" of economic reform in the ex-U.S.S.R.

Similar efforts of decentralizing economic reform have been undertaken in the People's Republic of China, and perhaps because the economic system there had never been as thoroughly centralized as it had been in the Soviet Union, these reforms are widely viewed in the West as having been more successful. Although there have been changes in both heavy and light industry, by far the single most important change has been in agriculture, which remains the dominant sector in the Chinese economy. The "responsibility system" effectively abolished the system of communal farming which had been the prevailing standard in the Communist world ever since the collectivization of Soviet agriculture in the early 1930s. Chinese agriculture has blossomed mightily under the responsibility system, and its success in generating a surplus of food has laid the basis for the development of all types of industry, heavy and light, domestically oriented and internationally oriented.

The responsibility system in Chinese agriculture is often characterized as being equivalent to private ownership agriculture as practiced in the West: the land allocations of the Chinese farmer being regarded as fully analogous to the privately owned small family farms which are widely prevalent in Western agriculture. This is a serious misrepresentation of the actual situation, and given the purpose of this book, it is a misrepresentation which requires correction.

A Chinese farm family working under the responsibility system does *not* own the land assigned to it. The land is owned by the local commune, which in effect leases the land to the family under a long-term, open-ended contract at a very modest rental rate. In contrast to ownership rights to land in the West, the family assigned a plot of land in China may not choose to allow that plot to remain fallow, it may not sell the plot or sublet it to another family, and if unknown assets are discovered in the land (e.g., mineral deposits), the family has no right to any part of the revenue derived from the sale of those assets. The rights of the family under the responsibility system are limited to the value of agricultural commodities obtained from the land through the family's own personal labor. So long as the family is engaged in good faith tillage of the land, it is subject to a bare minimum of outside intervention in and direction of its production and marketing efforts. The family exercises full control over the great majority of its produce: this produce may, at the family's discretion, be consumed at home or sold on local markets at free market prices. The relatively modest rental charge for use of land imposed by the commune means that the great majority of revenues received by the family are retained by the family, and enjoyed by the family through consumption and/or saving. The nearest equivalent to Western practices might be a situation of tenant farming in which the landlord is a close relative who requires only a nominal rental payment.

The responsibility system in Chinese agriculture has invigorated not only agricultural production but the economy as a whole, and the Chinese economy has become one of the fastest-growing economies in the world. Living standards in China have risen dramatically since the initiation of the responsibility system. This success provides important circumstantial evidence for the economic practicality of market socialism as proposed in this book. The system demonstrates that powerful incentives to effort can be achieved in the absence of legal ownership. It is not necessary that the Chinese farmer own his/her land to induce hard work and careful, conscientious management of the land. Rather it is simply necessary that the farmer possess an entitlement, based solely on personal labor currently applied, to the preponderance of the current output from the land.

Under Western capitalism, a powerful mystique attaches to the concept of private ownership of capital. The same sort of a priori legitimacy of ownership rights which exists with respect to items of personal property such as books and clothing, or to the small tools used by a craftsman such as a carpenter, is supposed to also apply to monetary earnings derived from financial capital instruments such as stocks and bonds. There are of course important distinctions between different types of private property. Unlike books and clothing, stocks and bonds are not directly consumed by the owner. Unlike small tools used by a craftsman, stocks and bonds do not require labor on the part of the owner to produce value. But these distinctions between capital property and other types of property tend to be minimized, if not ignored altogether, by the mystique attaching to private ownership in and of itself. An important practical upshot of the mystique is that private ownership of the business enterprise is deemed essential to the effectiveness of the business enterprise. Supposedly only private ownership of a business enterprise can imbue those responsible for its management with the necessary effort incentives to make the enterprise efficient and successful.

That the private ownership mystique is a myth, and that this particular practical upshot is specious and invalid, is strongly suggested by the success of the Chinese agricultural sector under the responsibility system. The land allotment of the typical Chinese farm family is run as a long-term business enterprise by the family. The solid performance of the Chinese economy demonstrates clearly that it is run well as such. This occurs in the absence of any legal ownership right on the part of the typical Chinese farm family to the land allotment. This evidence suggests that it is not land ownership per se which is important, but rather that the agricultural worker possess an entitlement to the produce of the land obtained directly from that same worker's personal effort. This clear-cut lesson from the recent experience of Chinese agriculture under the responsibility system possesses dire implications concerning the legitimacy (or the absence thereof) of modern capitalism. Whether these implications will ever be recognized, appreciated, and acted upon by the citizens of the capitalist nations is, of course, another question.

A major hindrance to proper appreciation in the West of the circumstantial support for the potential effectiveness of market socialism currently being provided by the Chinese experience is the unfortunate fact that, despite the recent improvements, the living standards of the Chinese population are still relatively spartan. The people of China are somewhat better fed and more prosperous than their counterparts in, say, India—but this may not be very impressive in the eyes of the typical middle-class citizen of the United States or the United Kingdom, whose standard of living would be considered almost unimaginably luxurious in China. China's fundamental economic problem is its huge population in relation to limited land area and scarce natural resources. Given the overabundance of humanity relative to the available capital and natural resources, the impact of the systemic factor (capitalism versus socialism) is relatively minor. Whether it subscribes to capitalism or to socialism, China is fated to be a poor nation both at the present time and, even under the most optimistic scenario, for a very long time into the future.

Of course, the population explosion is a world problem—not just a Third World problem. Even those nations which are today the richest and most powerful will eventually be reduced to weakness and poverty unless the present tendencies toward exponential population growth are eliminated. Even if the rate of exponential growth is very low, the numerical power of the exponential function is so great that eventually it produces gigantic numbers. In fact, it is a virtual certainty that within at most a few hundred years (a very short time span in the overall history of humanity), the present tendency toward exponential population growth *will* be eliminated. The questions pertain to the circumstances and mechanisms of its elimination. Will it be by voluntary private choice or social intervention under conditions of prosperity? Or will it be owing to famine and disease under conditions of desperate poverty?

Returning to the here and now, there is no doubt that population pressure is the single most formidable obstacle confronted by Third World nations such as China in their efforts to increase the living standards of their people toward the high levels enjoyed in the First World nations. Although the long-term population problem is a world problem, clearly in the short run the problem is most acute in the Third World nations of Africa, Asia, and Latin America. Proper appreciation of the threat to human welfare implicit in the rapidly increasing world population began emerging around the middle of the twentieth century—at about the same time that the development of nuclear weapons and delivery systems were exposing humanity to the possibility of nuclear armageddon. It could be that exposure to the more obvious and dramatic nuclear threat somewhat deadened the response to the population threat. After all, if the entire population stands a good chance of being annihilated in the near future by means of a nuclear holocaust, does it really matter how large that population is? The Communist regime came to power in China at about the same time that both the nuclear threat and the population threat were being established in human consciousness. It was China's misfortune that a perverse ideological attitude traditionally associated with Marxism substantially postponed the Communist government's full appreciation of the drag of rapid population growth on Chinese economic development under Communistic socialism.

Marxists had traditionally scorned Malthusian concerns about excessive population growth as an exclusively "capitalist problem." Supposedly the revolutionary transformation of capitalism into socialism would so unchain the productive forces of society that abundance and prosperity would prevail regardless of the rate of population growth. In addition, China had the example of its predecessor in socialism, the Soviet Union. With a huge, well-endowed, and sparsely populated land area at its command, the Communist Party of the U.S.S.R. had never had any qualms about rapid population growth, and indeed encouraged it on grounds that it augmented the military strength and productive resources of the nation. In contrast to the Soviet Union, of course, China did *not* have a huge, well-endowed, and sparsely populated land area with which to work. Therefore, the pursuit of pro-natalist policies by the People's Republic of China for the first twenty years or so of its existence contributed strongly to its disappointing economic performance—at least in the area of individual living standards. By the time the Chinese Communist Party leaders realized that population problems were not necessarily confined to capitalism, and radically revised social policy to inhibit fertility among the population, a great deal of damage had already been done. Even now, after decades of anti-natalist policy, the Chinese population is still growing briskly. It seems that confronted with the raw power of the human reproductive propensity, there are highly restrictive constraints on the power of even the most totalitarian states.

Moreover, population pressure is certainly not the only constraint on Chinese economic performance. Most of the potential "reasons for Soviet weakness" (other than socialism) discussed in the previous section have also applied at various times to the People's Republic of China, if—in the case of some of them—not to the same extent. Of these reasons, the absence of democratic governance, even if its direct economic impact may not be as important as that of some of the others, is no doubt the single most important reason why proponents of democratic market socialism, such as the author, are unable to hold up the P.R.C. proudly as a model for emulation. In China as in Russia, the radical transformation of society required by Marxist ideology elicited enormous internal resistance—and this resistance was put down by force. The current "human rights violations" in China about which the Western governments ritualistically complain are minuscule in comparison with the mass deportations, incarcerations, and executions of the revolutionary period. As Chairman Mao once put it so memorably, "A revolution is not a dinner party." In China as in Russia, the combination of internal dissension with external peril made democracy an unaffordable luxury in the eyes of the Communist Party leadership.

It could well be that China will one day follow the lead of the former Soviet Union, throw off the dominion of the Communist Party, and commence building a democratic political system. But there is no telling when that day will come. In the meantime, the political flaws of Communistic socialism as practiced in China supplement its lackluster performance in terms of individual living standards. Therefore, both political and economic weaknesses severely constrain the usefulness of the People's Republic of China as evidence supporting the desirability of democratic market socialism.

SOCIALISM HAS NOT FAILED

As unpalatable as it may be to proponents of democratic market socialism, there is no escaping the fact that socialism as practiced in the Communist nations of the twentieth century has been deeply disappointing and extremely sobering. The economic performance of the U.S.S.R., the P.R.C., and their smaller allies in the Communist camp has been at most respectable—but hardly impressive. And of course the political performance of these nations has been even worse than their economic performance. Until the very recent past, they were, one and all, undemocratic polities characterized by greater or lesser degrees of totalitarianism depending on the time period. Recently, the republics of the former Soviet Union, as well as the nations of Eastern Europe formerly incorporated in the Warsaw Pact, have thrown off the total domination of their political and social systems by their respective Communist Parties. Since then there have been several elections in these nations characterized by an unprecedented degree of openness. It is still too early to predict whether

Western-style democracy will become fully viable and accepted in these nations, but auspices seem favorable and there are certainly grounds for guarded optimism.

Proponents of democratic market socialism may console themselves with the thought that the experience of humanity with Communistic socialism throughout the twentieth century, as unfortunate and disappointing as it may have been, does not constitute a definitive and irrefutable condemnation of the socialist idea and ideal. In the first place, neither the economic nor the political performance of the Communist nations has been totally negative. In the second place, the deficiencies in the economic and political performance of the Communist nations may be plausibly attributed to a large number of factors having nothing to do with socialism in and of itself.

As to the political performance of the Communist nations, while it must be conceded that all of these nations went through periods of severe totalitarianism in the wake of radical revolutionary transformation, their political systems became much more moderate and tolerant after these periods had finally been transcended. None of the Communist nations descended to the depths of social depravity witnessed in Nazi Germany throughout its brief but terrible history. Relative to fascism, Marxism is a social philosophy of commendable toleration, rationality, and progressiveness. It is to the credit of Communism that its leaders were never really comfortable with political oligarchy, and that they strove to present an appearance at least of freedom and democracy. They never went to the extreme of rejecting the ideal of democracy, but merely argued that Western democratic forms were impractical under conditions of internal and external resistance to revolutionary transformation. The plan for democratic market socialism being put forward in this book is relatively mild and evolutionary in nature, so that its implementation would not result in the polarization of society and the threat of civil war. To begin with, the plan envisions reasonable compensation paid to owners of surrendered capital property. Compensation was never envisioned in the radical socializations carried out following the ascent of Communist Parties to power.

Economically, the standards of living achieved under Communistic socialism have been comparable to those in all but a handful of the most advanced industrial capitalist nations. These respectable living standards were achieved in the face of a crushing military burden, as well as many other adverse economic conditions and practices. In the case of the Soviet economy, its performance has been hamstrung, among other things, by an excessively centralized planning system. In the case of the Chinese economy, it is inevitably struggling under a crushing burden of overpopulation. In light of the many serious obstacles and adversities against which they have had to contend, the socialist economies of the Communist nations have performed quite respectably. Their performance indeed provides strong testimony to the potential efficiency and effectiveness of a potential socialist economy operating under more favorable conditions.

In sum, therefore, it is a drastic and unacceptable oversimplification to hold that "socialism has failed." Untried democratic market socialist possibilities exist which would not be subject to the liabilities and disabilities of Communistic socialism. Furthermore, contemporary capitalism is marred by serious equity problems for which some appropriate form of democratic market socialism might offer a plausible and appealing solution. It is worthwhile, therefore, to take a careful new look at both capitalism and socialism—a look not excessively influenced and prejudiced by the misfortunes and errors of the past.

2

Is Capitalism Best?

The central problem with contemporary capitalism is that it perpetuates an extremely unequal distribution of unearned capital property return. It is necessary to the efficiency of the economic system that business enterprises, government agencies, and other entities pay out various forms of capital property return (dividends, interest, etc.) for the use of financial capital. But these disbursements should be made to a public ownership agency which would redistribute this income flow as a fair and equitable social dividend supplement to the wage and salary income of the working population. The capitalist principle of distributing this income to the individual owners of financial assets creates a situation in which the great majority of hardworking contributors to the economic process receive little or no capital property return, while a tiny fraction of the population, owing mainly to the workings of inheritance and chance, receives the largest share of it. Wealthy capitalists are rewarded far out of proportion to their actual economic contributions, while the vast majority of working-class and middle-class people are underrewarded for their contributions. Allegations that this problem is "a necessary evil" and that "the cure would be worse than the disease" are false. A simple and appealing solution to this problem does in fact exist: the solution is democratic market socialism.

The proposition that contemporary capitalism "perpetuates the inequity of highly unequal distribution of unearned capital property return" may seem to some people a rather abstract, convoluted, and undramatic accusation. It doesn't have the same intuitively obvious, highly emotional impact as statements to the effect that capitalism "constitutes robbery of the poor by the rich," or that capitalism "creates hunger and oppression." These latter kinds of statements will be studiously avoided herein. In an effort to attract attention and arouse indignation, many advocates of socialism in the past have indulged in passionate, overheated rhetoric. Such rhetoric might possibly be effective among desperate individuals trapped in the lowest conditions of abject poverty. But if the audience to be reached and persuaded consists mostly of people in comfortable economic circumstances—and people who are, moreover, inclined toward skepticism of socialism—then this type of rhetoric is ineffective and even counterproductive. Such agitated rhetoric seems out of touch with reality and seems to promise more than socialism can possibly deliver. Therefore it further discredits socialism among the majority and makes its implementation in the real world still less likely. There is a risk, of course, that the restrained rhetoric and level-headed tone adopted herein will fail to excite the imagination, to fire the spirit—that far from inspiring the reader to go forth and work toward the realization of socialism, it will put the reader to sleep. That risk will have to be taken. The greater risk is that an excessively strong and assertive tone will alienate those readers who, while cautious and skeptical, possess basically open minds on the subject of socialism. These are the kind of readers who have to be reached if there is to be any significant hope of resurrecting socialism.

While the argument advanced in this book is necessarily careful, and while the tone is necessarily restrained, let there be no mistake about it: the vast majority of the population under contemporary capitalism are in fact being deprived of sums of money sufficiently large that *if they were aware* that they were being unjustly deprived of these sums of money, they would most certainly experience a very strong emotional reaction. The social dividend supplement to wage and salary income under the market socialist system proposed herein would probably be in the range from 5 to 10 percent of the household's wage and salary income. For example, if a household's total wage and salary income was $40,000, and the rate of social dividend payment was 7.5 percent, the household's social dividend income under market socialism would be $3,000.

Now the *net* income gain to the household might be less than this, since under socialism there would be no dividends, interest, or other forms of property return received on the household's financial wealth. But the vast majority of households with an annual income of $40,000 possess very little financial wealth (stocks, bonds, savings accounts, etc.)—most of their wealth is in nonfinancial forms such as residential property (homes), personal property (automobiles, furniture, clothes, etc.), and pension fund accumulations. The distinction between financial and nonfinancial wealth is that only the former produces explicit, tangible income flows. For the vast majority of households with an annual labor income of $40,000 or less, most of their wealth is in nonfinancial forms, and the amount of capital property income received per year would be in the order of 1 percent or less of labor income. Deducting 1 percent from the 7.5 percent of labor income representing social dividend income leaves 6.5 percent of labor income—or $2,600 as the net annual income increase as between market socialism and capitalism.

One can imagine the indignation of a person who, once a year, lost $2,600 in a street mugging. Or who lost $2,600 per year in uninsured property to a burglar. Or who lost $2,600 per year through participation in a game of chance which was later found to be rigged in such a way that the player never had any appreciable chance of winning. Or who had to pay $2,600 per year toward the support of welfare recipients who were perfectly capable of self-support but preferred to shirk their social responsibility to productive labor. Or who had to pay $2,600 per year toward the support of totally useless government bureaucrats who make absolutely no worthwhile contribution to society. The fact is that under the contemporary capitalist status quo, our hypothetical household is in effect paying $2,600 per year mainly toward the support of a tiny minority of wealthy capitalists whose obscenely luxurious personal living standards are outrageously disproportionate to the economic contributions they make to society.

For most of the people presently reading this book, the actual amount involved probably considerably exceeds $2,600. This is a very conservative figure. Whatever the actual amount, under the contemporary capitalist status quo it is money out the window, down the drain, into the ozone. It is money that you could have had, you should have had, and which possibly someday you *will* have—*if* enough people can see through the self-protective web of propagandistic distortion and misrepresentation which capitalism has spun around itself—if they can see though this web to their own genuine, personal, financial self-interest.

These comments are not intended as rabble-rousing calls to action against individual wealthy capitalists. It is one of humanity's most negative and dangerous traits to want to blame *individuals* for social problems. These problems cause us pain, discomfort, and frustration—it is blissfully satisfying to *punish* those individuals responsible for these unsatisfactory conditions. Unfortunately, instances in which punishment of individuals is appropriate are relatively rare. Given the constraints confronting human civilization (mortality, limited knowledge, limited resources, etc.), it is impossible to achieve bliss in everyone, and it is also impossible to avoid circumstances which are advantageous to some individuals in society at the same time that they are disadvantageous to other individuals. Thus, it is sometimes necessary for some people in society to accept a certain amount of pain, discomfort, and frustration in order that others in society will reap benefits which are proportionately greater. It is understandable that those in one particular category might be prone to miscalculating the relative costs and benefits to their own advantage. Thus those who will benefit from a certain condition are likely to exaggerate its aggregate social benefits, while those who will lose from it are likely to exaggerate its aggregate social losses. But these errors in judgment are normally not intentional and calculated; they do not usually proceed from a malevolent, purposeful decision to place individual self-interest above the larger social interest.

With respect to the question under consideration here, the maintenance of the capitalist status quo is in fact advantageous only to a very small minority of very wealthy capitalists. The large majority of the population would be materially and significantly benefited by the implementation of democratic market socialism. At the present moment, however, only a very small fraction of this large majority is aware of this fact. A case might be made that wealthy capitalists are in fact more likely than is the general population to be aware of the fact that capital property income is unearned—after all, they know from direct personal experience that the capital property return which they receive is not a return to noble entrepreneurial endeavor, to risk-taking, or to any other economically and ethically worthy endeavor. However, no such argument will be made here—on the presumption that the inherent tendency in all human individuals toward the rationalization of self-interest is too strong for there to be any appreciable amount of conscious hypocrisy and malevolent intent in the support among wealthy capitalists for the continuation of the capitalistic status quo.

As for the support among the large noncapitalist majority for the continuation of the capitalistic status quo, this support stems from the widespread misperception of reality and self-interest among this majority. This is an "honest error" rather than the result of crafty manipulation of public opinion by a capitalist minority which is fully cognizant of the fact that its financial privileges are neither economically nor ethically legitimate. Even if the capitalist minority *were* so cognizant (they are almost certainly not), there are limits to what can be accomplished by means of "crafty manipulation of public opinion." Thus the sensible proponent of socialism should try to suppress any sense of personal animus against wealthy capitalists and should studiously avoid trying to arouse any personal hostility toward capitalists among noncapitalists. The persistence of capitalism is not the result of culpable, unethical activity on anyone's part—it is rather the consequence of a particular misperception of reality which is extremely prevalent at *all* levels of society.

The point just made involves a distinction between "capitalists" and "noncapitalists." This is a convenient point at which to clarify this distinction—which is, of course, an extremely important distinction for present purposes. The definition of "capitalist" utilized throughout this book is an individual who owns sufficient financial capital wealth (stocks, bonds, etc.) that the property return on that wealth (dividends, interest, capital gains, etc.) is *by itself* adequate to support at least a comfortable standard of living. Thus a capitalist is an individual who is not obliged to work in order to earn a living. *Non*capitalists are those who do *not* receive enough capital property income on which to live comfortably—they are individuals who are obliged to find gainful employment in order to earn a living. This distinction applies to those of working age. As to retired individuals, capitalists and noncapitalists may be distinguished as follows: capitalists are those whose retirement income is mainly derived from financial capital wealth which remains intact upon the death of the owner and is passed along (less estate taxes and legal fees) to a new owner or owners via inheritance; while noncapitalists are those whose retirement income is mainly derived from pension fund entitlements which are terminated either upon the death of the owner or upon the deaths of both the owner and his/her spouse. By this definition, capitalists clearly constitute a very small proportion of both the working population and the retired population—probably less than 5 percent.

Although working-age capitalists are by definition not obliged to work in order to earn a living, certain data exist (to be described below) which suggest that as a matter of fact most capitalists of working age *do* work—even very wealthy capitalists. Most psychologists would agree that people "need" work. Whether internally implanted by evolutionary natural selection, or externally imposed by familial and educational socialization, most people abhor inactivity as nature abhors a vacuum. In the absence of continuous, systematic, purposeful activity, most people experience strong feelings of boredom and discontent. Therefore even the wealthiest capitalists are usually gainfully employed—even though their labor income, while substantial in an absolute sense (normally earned in high-level professional work), is only a small fraction of their capital property income. It is to the credit of wealthy capitalists that the great majority of them refrain from becoming obviously parasitical playboys and playgirls. As we will see below in Chapter 4, however, the fact that most wealthy capitalists are gainfully employed in responsible career work undercuts the argument that capital property income is an earned return to effort expended in investment analysis (a form of capital management). It rather suggests that this type of income is a pure rental return which accrues to the owner of financial capital wealth regardless of whether he or she does or does not engage in serious, full-time study of various investment options.

An understanding and appreciation of the distinction between the tiny minority of capitalists and the overwhelming majority of noncapitalists is pivotal to the refutation of the first of capitalism's three main lines of defense: the people's capitalism line. (The second line is the contention that there are legitimate *economic* purposes served by the capitalist system; while the third line is that there are legitimate *noneconomic* purposes served by the capitalist system.) The essence of the people's capitalism first line of defense is to blur the distinction between the status of capitalist and that of noncapitalist: preferably to delude the noncapitalist into believing that he or she *is already* a capitalist, but failing that, to delude the noncapitalist into believing that he or she *will probably become* a capitalist in the future. If either of these delusions can be successfully inculcated in the noncapitalist, then he or she is unlikely to perceive anything unfair or inequitable in the present distribution of capital property return under contemporary capitalism.

Capitalism's three lines of defense may be understood in relation to the fundamental contemporary socialist objection to capitalism: that capitalism perpetuates the inequity of highly unequal distribution of unearned capital property return. The first line (people's capitalism) denies that there is anything inequitable in the distribution of capital property return under capitalism: either, in the first place, this distribution is not unduly unequal, or, in the second place, there is sufficient equality of financial opportunity under capitalism that the existing degree of inequality—whatever it might consist of—is not ethically offensive. The second and third lines both deny that capital property income is "unearned" in the sense of "having no purpose or justification." The second line finds these purposes and justifications in economic considerations: it contends that capital property return is indeed directly earned by its recipients through their positive economic contributions to society: entrepreneurship, risk-taking, corporate supervision, investment analysis, saving, and so on. The third line finds these purposes and justifications in various noneconomic considerations: political, psychological, and/or philosophical. The capitalist economic system, it is alleged, constitutes a bulwark of political democracy and/or personal freedom, it provides individuals with necessary opportunities for self-realization and/or self-fulfillment, and it has the sanction of religious and/or ethical criteria.

To some extent the three lines are interrelated in that they tend to blend into one another at the edges. But from a logical point of view, they are clearly separate, and an effort will be made to deal with them systematically herein. My intent in this book is to provide a critique and refutation of each one of capitalism's three lines of defense—but with the primary emphasis on the second line: the position that considerations of economic efficiency justify contemporary capitalism. To some extent this emphasis is dictated by my area of professional expertise in economics. But aside from that—and allowing for the possibility that my perceptions might be influenced by my professional specialization—it is the second line which appears to me by far the strongest and most plausible. That is to say, *if* an intellectually compelling case is to be made for capitalism, it must almost certainly be based on the proposition that various static and dynamic economic efficiency considerations justify the high level of inequality in capital wealth and property income under contemporary capitalism—that capital property income is in some meaningful sense economically earned by its recipients.

The first line of defense—that the distribution of capital wealth and property income is *not* unduly unequal—will be addressed primarily in this chapter through a critical analysis of the people's capitalism thesis. This is done because it is the high level of inequality in capital wealth and property income which raises the initial question concerning the legitimacy of capitalism. There is no point in even considering socialism if capitalism is in fact acceptably egalitarian with respect to capital wealth and property income. But once it has been accepted that there *is* a high level of inequality in the distribution of capital wealth and property income, the possible preferability of a socialist alternative becomes evident. However, then the question becomes: Is any possible socialist alternative *actually* preferable to capitalism? That is to say: Could it be that the high level of inequality under capitalism is justified by the fact that, owing to various economic and noneconomic considerations (the second and third lines of defense), there exists no practical socialist alternative to capitalism which would yield a higher level of overall social welfare? In other words, is capitalism "a necessary evil" owing to the fact that "the socialist cure would be worse than the capitalist disease"?

Of course, discussions of this latter question are hopelessly loaded against socialism if the worst characteristics which have been historically associated with real-world socialism (e.g., Stalinist tyranny in the U.S.S.R.) are taken as inevitably applying to any possible socialist alternative to capitalism. But aside from this, over the long history of the socialist movement numerous conceptual blueprints for "socialism" have been put forward by a host of advocates and sympathizers. Thus, even if no clearly tendentious definitions of socialism are involved in the discussion (e.g., socialism equals Stalinist tyranny), the discussion may still be hopelessly unfocused and circular owing to confusion and uncertainty as to precisely which institutional socialist alternative to capitalism is actually under consideration. To avoid this problem, the principal discussion herein of the second and third lines of defense of capitalism will be postponed until after a specific and detailed democratic market socialist proposal has been set forth. The proposal will be developed in Chapter 3. Chapter 4 will then respond to the fundamental objection that owing to various economic and non-economic considerations, the contemporary capitalist status quo is preferable to the democratic market socialist alternative put forward in Chapter 3.

THE SOCIALIST CRITIQUE IN PERSPECTIVE

Over the nearly two centuries which have passed since the development of an intellectually cohesive socialist critique of capitalism, worldwide human civilization has evolved at an extraordinary rate. As between the early part of the nineteenth century, when socialism came into being as an organized movement, and the turn of the twenty-first century, human society has undergone massive, fundamental changes. According to opponents of socialism, these changes have completely eliminated the relevance of the traditional socialist critique of capitalism. Many of these opponents will concede that the socialist critique may have played a useful historical role in inducing the capitalist system to reform itself, to excise from itself those dysfunctional features against which Marx and the other early socialists railed. But now that these dysfunctional features have indeed been completely eliminated, there remains no purpose or validity in socialism. The socialist movement therefore *should* expire, and it probably *will* expire in short order—especially now that the Communist nations are apparently coming to their senses and preparing to rejoin the capitalistic world mainstream.

If one takes a worldview of contemporary capitalism, celebrations of its "triumph" are especially dubious. Most of the population of the Third

World live in nations in which private ownership of capital is the rule rather than the exception: in nations, therefore, which may be characterized as capitalist. Although there have been some hopeful signs of progress over the last few decades, it remains a fact that conditions in these nations are roughly comparable to those which prevailed in the advanced capitalist nations as of the early 1800s. Most of the population live amid conditions of desperate poverty and little hope, while a tiny handful enjoys opulent luxury. However, this point will not be dwelt upon herein. The woes of the Third World nations may be plausibly attributed to factors other than the basic capitalist institution of private ownership of the means of production. The present condition of the Third World seems mainly the consequence of a population explosion occurring within traditional societies in which neither the economic, political, nor cultural characteristics of democratic market capitalism, as currently practiced in the United States and Western Europe, have taken firm hold.

Looking to the First World nations in which democratic market capitalism has reached its highest expression, any sensible proponent of socialism ought to be be prepared to concede that the combination of technological progress with social democratic reforms which has occurred in these nations since the time of Marx and Engels has indeed dramatically improved and humanized them. No longer is the great majority of the working-class population in these nations mired in poverty and hopelessness. No longer is there a dramatic gulf between rich and poor—that gulf has been filled in by an extremely populous middle class. Obscene luxury among the wealthiest has been curbed by various forms of progressive taxation, while abject misery among the poorest has been eased by a variety of welfare programs. Not only must it be conceded that contemporary capitalism in the First World nations is fully viable into the foreseeable future—it must also be conceded that both the average standard of life, and the degree of economic equality among the population, far exceeds anything hitherto witnessed in the entire history of human civilization.

This is all quite true. Nevertheless, it does not alter the fact that what is good sometimes *can* be made better—and sometimes *should* be made better. One must indeed give some credence to the ancient folk wisdom: "If it isn't broken, don't fix it." But at the same time one cannot allow this particular wisdom to predetermine every decision which needs to be made about the proper form of human society. To do so would halt the continuous flow of progress which so much benefits humanity. Change was necessary in the past to bring the unsatisfactory human society of the early nineteenth century to its present level of development. Further change will be necessary in the future to bring it to an even higher level. To properly understand why it is that democratic market socialism would be an improvement over democratic market capitalism—even granting that the reformed and enlightened capitalism of today is a marvelous advance beyond the harsh early industrial era capitalism of Karl Marx's time—it is necessary to look at the socialist critique of capitalism in historical perspective. What aspects of this critique have indeed been rendered irrelevant by the passage of time? But what central element of this critique remains valid even in the present day? And what are the practical institutional reforms that might be carried out to eliminate the relevance of this central element?

Two key factors were especially instrumental in the germination of the socialist critique of capitalism in the early nineteenth century. The first was what Karl Marx described as the "bourgeois revolution": the long-term social upheaval, of which the French Revolution of 1789 was the single most dramatic milestone, during which the well-to-do but mostly nonaristocratic merchants, industrialists, and bankers (Marx's "bourgeoisie") succeeded in drastically curbing the traditional political and economic rights of the hereditary aristocracy whose personal property was mostly concentrated in land. These rights had their historical roots in the medieval period of European history, but their original utilitarian purposes had been greatly eroded by the passage of time, and as of the Enlightenment period which immediately preceded the revolutionary period, they were widely regarded among the nonaristocratic gentry and intelligentsia as "unjustified privileges." Once the notion that there were "unjustified privileges" afoot in the world had become widely accepted, some left-wing intellectuals and revolutionaries began perceiving them in places where the right-wing and middle-of-the-road intellectuals and revolutionaries had not. Thus it was that the well-to-do merchants, industrialists, and bankers, who delighted in railing against the unjustified privileges of the landed aristocracy, were eventually discomfited to find that a left-wing socialist faction had arisen which was railing against *them* as possessors of unjustified privileges.

The second key factor was the intensive industrialization and urbanization trend which coincided with the period of bourgeois revolution. This created a great mass of people whom Marx termed "proletarians": urban factory workers and their families who led extremely impoverished and precarious lives. The early socialists found their principal inspiration in the plight of these people. Of course, it is not really possible today to assess the condition of the urban proletariat of the early nineteenth century relative to that of the agrarian population at the same period. No doubt most factory workers of today transported back to those times would immediately become enraged revolutionaries. But that the terms and conditions of factory work in the early nineteenth century would be unacceptable to a factory worker in the late twentieth century does not necessarily imply revolutionary propensities among the population of that time. Presumably those who left the land to seek employment in urban factories mostly did so voluntarily, which suggests that the economic condition of the urban proletariat was not, on the whole, inferior to that of the agrarian population. Perhaps the sting of poverty in the crowded, impersonal cities was greater than its sting in the countryside. Certainly the concentration of poverty in the cities made it more visible, and this concentration also facilitated the organization of political activity toward the reform of society and the amelioration of poverty.

There were thus two key inputs into the socialist critique of capitalism so powerfully formulated by Karl Marx (1818-1883) in the nineteenth century: (1) the condition of a substantial proportion of the population, the urban proletariat, was considered wholly unsatisfactory; (2) the improvement of society by revolutionary means was considered not only possible but desirable—just as the capital-owning bourgeoisie had successfully overthrown the landed aristocracy, so too the proletarians could successfully overthrow the capital-owing bourgeoisie. Marx perceived the fundamental ailment of modern capitalism to reside in the maintenance of the anachronistic private ownership principle with respect to capital means of production which are used in what had become an essentially social production process. According to Marx, private ownership of capital is fully appropriate for handicraft production by independent craftsmen who personally complete each stage of the production of a certain commodity. But in the context of factory production, in which a large group of workers use complicated machinery in an interdependent and cooperative production process, the exercise of private ownership rights over the plant and machinery of the factory by a single owner, or a small group of owners, creates an extremely adverse outcome for everyone except the owners.

Marx utilized the labor theory of value, a standard and well-accepted concept from the classical economics of his day, as the foundation stone on which to base a theory of surplus value exploitation. According to the surplus value theory, the private ownership rights of the employing owners puts them into an unassailable bargaining position with respect to the workers. The workers can produce little or nothing unless they have access to capital plant and machinery—but the owners have the legal power to deny the workers access to these tools of production. As a result, the owners only have to pay the workers enough to support a subsistence standard of living (anything less and the labor force would die off, leaving the capitalists with useless equipment). The amount of value created by labor's efforts, over and above the amount needed to pay a subsistence wage, is termed "surplus value" and it is appropriated entirely by the capitalist owners. In practice, this surplus value is a substantial proportion of total value, anywhere from 25 to 50 percent.

The surplus value exploitation mechanism renders modern capitalism morally unworthy, but, according to Marx, it is not this moral unworthiness which will eventually bring down the capitalist system. The instrumentality of capitalism's ultimate collapse will rather be the increasing severity of business depressions. Surplus value exploitation puts large sums of money into the hands of wealthy capitalists. Despite their heroic efforts to do so, they are not able to spend all of this money on personal consumption. Instead they reinvest a large proportion of it into their businesses. But the payment of subsistence wages to labor tends to restrict the purchasing power mustered by the mass of impoverished proletarians. Thus the demand for commodities does not keep pace with potential production. The unprofitability of investment eventually brings about panic, crisis, and depression. During the depths of depressions, some capitalists are destroyed by bankruptcy, leading to further concentration of capital wealth in the hands of an increasingly tiny minority of plutocratic capitalists. Eventually, after a series of depressions of steadily increasing severity, conditions will become so horrendous as to spark a socialist revolution.

In the 150 years which have passed since Karl Marx formulated this bleak vision of capitalism in *Das Kapital*, a great deal has occurred which casts doubt upon it. First and foremost, the material condition of the great mass of working-class people (in the advanced capitalist nations) has neither stagnated nor deteriorated—it has improved. The conditions of life of the proletariat can no longer be sensibly described by the term "subsistence." The economic polarization of society into a large and ever-increasing majority of impoverished workers and a small and ever-shrinking minority of wealthy capitalists has not occurred. Instead, a large and prosperous middle class has evolved between the very rich and the very poor. As for business depressions, Marx was well ahead of his time in recognizing that these would be a serious and persistent problem for a large and complex industrial economy. But there is little evidence of "steadily increasing severity," and moreover, none of the numerous depressions which have occurred throughout the nineteenth and twentieth centuries have been nearly severe enough to ignite a socialist revolution. The Great Depression of the 1930s stands out as by far the worst economic calamity in the history of modern capitalism, but even it was not adequate to bring forth a socialist revolution in any capitalist nation of the time. In the wake of the Great Depression, guided by the innovative macroeconomic concepts of the most influential economist of the twentieth century, John Maynard Keynes, the governments of most capitalist nations have explicitly accepted responsibility for implementing any such anticyclical policy measures as may be needed to avert the development of a minor business recession into a major business depression. In the nearly 50 years which have passed since the so-called "Keynesian revolution" in economics and public policy, the problem of business recessions, while continuing to be persistent, has been significantly mitigated in terms of severity.

In retrospect, all but the most idolatrous Marxists can clearly perceive the presumptuousness and fallibility of "the Master." Under the influence of some half-digested nineteenth-century science, Marx was deluded into thinking that the future of human civilization could be predicted as fully and accurately as the future positions of the planetary bodies. Therefore he could not resist the temptation to proclaim himself not merely a social visionary but a social prophet. He was not merely suggesting what future human society *should be*—he was rather describing what it *would be*. Beyond this personal egomania, Marx also displayed profound contempt for his adversaries, the capitalists. The means by which they could avert their own destruction were implicit in Marx's own theory. By voluntarily paying their workers a larger proportion of their revenues, they could avert the constriction of effective demand which would eventually bring on the maelstrom of business depression. Failing voluntary action, the state (presumably controlled by the capitalists as a class) could intervene to enforce upon individual capitalists what was in their own collective self-interest: shorter working hours, higher wages, and social insurance to keep the workers physically healthy, psychologically content, politically quiescent, and capable of generating sufficient effective demand to avert catastrophic depressions. Marx supposed that the capitalist class, congenitally stupid and complacent, would ignore the warning he was so energetically broadcasting, and would thereby go to its doom amidst a violent socialist revolution. This is a clear-cut case of seriously underestimating the opposition.

Despite Marx's grievous errors of omission and commission, there remains a kernel of value and validity in his critique of capitalism. Back in the nineteenth century, he correctly perceived in capitalism a condition which remains fully relevant at the threshold of the twenty-first century: capitalists receive more income than they have an economic and moral right to. Marx used the term "exploiter" to characterize the representative capitalist. This term is inappropriate, because it implies an active and conscious process of exploitation through which the capitalist knowingly deprives the workers of value which the latter have produced. Reading Marx's work, one derives the impression that the capitalists work very, very hard and conscientiously at exploiting the labor force. However, the term which far more accurately and descriptively describes the representative capitalist of the late twentieth century is "rentier." The evolution of the economic system has rendered the private capital owner, considered as owner, a useless appendage, a supernumerary, a parasite. He or she, as an owner of capital, makes a negligible contribution to the economic process. The process by which the capitalist class appropriates capital property return has become automatic and self-sustaining. It requires no conscious thought, effort, or activity on the part of individual capitalists. As capital owners, they are not the busy and active exploiters envisioned by Karl Marx, but are rather inert and passive rentiers.

It is to the credit of most real-world capitalists, as human beings and members of society, that they resist the temptation to live lives consisting of unalloyed and uninterrupted consumption. Most capitalists are in fact actively employed, usually in responsible professional work. They are doctors and scientists, lawyers and professors, executives and administrators. The labor incomes which they earn from being doctors, scientists, lawyers, professors, executives, and administrators are fully and legitimately earned incomes. But the same cannot be said of the far larger amounts they receive from dividends, interest, and capital gains on their financial wealth. This income flows into their bank accounts without need of meaningful effort or intervention—it is unearned, rentier income which accrues to them from economic processes to which they make no significant contribution. Marx, furthermore, was basically correct in perceiving as the fundamental reason for this inequity the maintenance of private property rights over the capital means of production in an era in which the evolution of production techniques has endowed the production process for most commodities with a social character rather than an individual character.

Socialism, defined as public ownership of the nonhuman factors of production (capital and natural resources), was perceived by Marx as the natural and appropriate antidote to the problems caused by private ownership of such factors utilized in a social production process. In light of history, we now know that these problems are far less severe than they were perceived to be by Marx. Private ownership of the nonhuman factors of production does not necessarily cause the large majority of the population to subsist in desperate poverty, it does not necessarily cause the economy to be recurrently prostrated by severe business depression, it does not necessarily create conditions in which social revolution becomes inevitable. However, while the private ownership principle applied to the nonhuman factors of production does not create intolerable conditions, it does create undesirable conditions. Highly unequal distribution among the population of a substantial flow of capital property return, which is essentially unearned by human beings, constitutes an offense against the currently prevailing standards of justice and concepts of equity. This is an offense with which we do *not* have to live. A significant improvement in social welfare could be achieved through the implementation of an appropriate form of democratic market socialism: an economic system which would substantially equalize the distribution of unearned capital property return without entailing any appreciable efficiency losses of either a static or dynamic nature.

But once again, it is very important that this particular improvement not be overstated and exaggerated. Over the course of time, advocates of socialism, in an effort to attract interest and broaden support, have claimed all sorts of benefits from socialism above and beyond the elimination of extreme inequality in the distribution of capital property return. In general, these benefits are quite dubious, and the considerable emphasis placed upon them by past advocates of socialism has probably done much to discredit the concept of socialism by making its proponents appear to be hopelessly naive enthusiasts. For example, the implementation of democratic market socialism as proposed herein probably would not, in and of itself, significantly alleviate the persistent business recessions which periodically beset the economy. It probably would not, in and of itself, eliminate various pockets of hard-core poverty in the economy. It probably would not, in and of itself, do very much toward the alleviation of a whole range of what might be termed "derivative" or "higher-order" social problems: problems such as imperialism, militarism, crime, alienation, racism, sexism, and environmental degradation.

With respect to these latter kinds of problems, over time various proponents of socialism have come up with a wide variety of arguments to the effect that these problems are either created by, or at least exacerbated by, the social institutions and/or mental attitudes of capitalism. For example, nineteenth-century European imperialism in Africa and elsewhere in the world has been attributed to the lust among capitalists for new markets in which to sell their wares, and for ensured sources of raw material supply. Militarism has been attributed to war-mongering among armaments industry capitalists desirous of selling weapons. Crime has been attributed to the grinding poverty imposed by capitalism on the masses, together with the envious resentment aroused among the masses by the luxurious living standards of the capitalistic elite. Psychological alienation is generated by the fact that workers do not possess full and direct ownership rights over the commodities which they produce—these commodities rather belong to the capitalist owners. Racism is fostered by capitalists wanting to hire the labor of the oppressed racial group at submarket wages. Sexism is fostered for the same reason, and also because the obsession under capitalism with possession extends to relationships between men and women. Environmental degradation is intensified under capitalism because pollution is profitable.

The most serious problem with these kinds of arguments is that the conditions to which they pertain, without exception, were recognized as serious problems of human civilization long before the rise of modern capitalism. This fact flatly contradicts the position that modern capitalism *created* these problems. Moreover, arguments that these problems have been *aggravated* (as opposed to created) by modern capitalism are inherently speculative. To begin with, we do not have quantitative measures of the prevalence of these problems in the precapitalist era, so that there is no meaningful way to compare these problems now with what they were in the past. Aside from the issue of measurement, each one of the various arguments put forward to the effect that capitalism is implicated in various social problems involves highly dubious and/or speculative propositions. With respect to crime, for example, it is clearly untrue that modern capitalism has imposed grinding poverty on the masses. Aside from that, there is not necessarily a linear relationship between the level of material welfare and propensities toward crime: the crime rate in the United States, one of the richest nations in the world, greatly exceeds that in many less prosperous nations. (Of course, it could be that this merely reflects measurement error—the crime rate might be underreported in poorer nations.) As to racism and sexism, it could be argued that modern capitalism tends to ameliorate rather than exacerbate these problems. The presumed obsession among capitalists with bottom-line profitability might blind them to the race or sex of their employees, on top of which the higher educational attainment and personal wealth of capitalists, relative to the general population, might endow them with greater openness and toleration—virtues not so easily afforded by poorer people.

This is not to deny that they may be a *modest* amount of applicability of *some* of the arguments to the effect that a transition from capitalism to socialism might have beneficial effects beyond the relative equalization achieved in the distribution of capital property return. As a matter of fact, two subsidiary arguments for democratic market socialism will be put forward in the following discussion: an economic argument and a political argument. According to the economic argument, there are grounds for expecting at least a slight increase in the efficiency and dynamism of the economy. According to the political argument, the equalization of capital property return will to some extent equalize the distribution of effective political power and influence and thereby achieve a somewhat more genuine form of democracy. But it is extremely important not to endanger the credibility of the basic argument for socialism by enumerating a large number of subsidiary arguments for socialism and by placing excessive emphasis on these subsidiary arguments. In the contemporary climate of opinion, it is all too easy for proponents of socialism to be casually dismissed as naive idealists who expect socialism to bring forth utopian conditions throughout the world.

Of course it is not true that democratic market socialism is capable of bringing forth utopian conditions around the world. But it is most certainly capable of bringing forth *improved* conditions throughout the world. The modern concept of progress is evolutionary, incrementalist—progress is seen as a succession of small forward steps, each one of which might seem inconsequential in and of itself. Democratic market socialism would be one of these small forward steps. Highly unequal distribution of unearned capital property return is an apparently permanent, integral part of contemporary capitalism. Eliminating this inequity by means of democratic market socialism would bring about a modest but significant improvement both in the material living standards of the vast majority of noncapitalists in the population, and in the overall moral quality of human civilization. This might not be the millennial advance envisioned by Karl Marx and other nineteenth-century socialists, but it would be a worthwhile advance which we ought to make.

VARIATIONS ON PEOPLE'S CAPITALISM

The term "people's capitalism" was invented in the 1950s by the U.S. Advertising Council as its contribution to the propaganda battle being waged by the capitalist nations against the worldwide Communist menace. The thrust of people's capitalism is that the "rank and file" of society either have already become the owners of the capital means of production—or, alternatively, will soon become the owners of the capital means of production presuming present trends continue a while longer. In other words, the capitalist class is being absorbed into the general population; it no longer stands isolated as a small minority whose financial characteristics and interests are substantively and permanently different from those of the large majority of the population. Therefore the fundamental basis for the socialist critique of capitalism is rapidly eroding into irrelevance. Evidence for this historic transformation of capitalism was found by the Ad Council in the spread of common stock ownership among the population: as of the 1950s, a larger proportion of U.S. households owned common stock than had been the case in the 1940s and 1930s.

Of course, if one goes back to the late 1920s, when the American public succumbed to a veritable mania of stock market speculation, common stock ownership was comparable to what it was in the 1950s. Most of the 1920s small-scale investors in the stock market had their savings wiped out by the crash of 1929 and the subsequent prolonged depression of the 1930s. What happened on a grand scale in that era continues to transpire on small scale to this day: as a rule, small-scale investors in the stock market lose money. In fact, it can probably be said that the stock market is and remains a highly effective institution for the continuous transfer of capital wealth from low- and medium-income noncapitalistic households to high-income capitalistic households. Small-scale investors do not have sufficient capital with which to adequately diversify their investment portfolios; also, they are far too conscious of the hard work which went into the slow and painful accumulation of their small hoard of savings. As a result, they are anxious and skittish investors. Time and time again, they panic, sell out, and take a loss. Meanwhile, the large-scale capitalistic investors, with widely diversified portfolios worth tens of millions of dollars, calmly wait out most temporary downturns in the values of specific assets, and normally refrain from selling assets unless and until they can make a good profit on the sale. This same pattern holds for the entire range of investment assets, although it is most pronounced in the case of common stock. Thus, owing to the workings of the stock market, the wealth of small-scale investors is diminished while that of large-scale investors is augmented. Far from being a harbinger of "people's capitalism" in any meaningful sense, increased participation by working-class and middle-class households in the stock market is probably a sign that the concentration of capital wealth in the hands of the wealthy capitalistic minority is about to increase.

But as a matter of fact, in a larger sense modern capitalism has displayed, and continues to display, an extremely high level of stability in the distribution of capital wealth. Stability has persisted throughout the twentieth century, but it has become especially evident during the second half of the twentieth century (since World War II). The percentage of households owning some common stock has fluctuated within a fairly narrow band, and so also have the overall level of inequality in common stock ownership in particular and capital wealth ownership in general. For as long as we have had systematic statistical data on capital wealth ownership, the distribution of capital wealth has been fairly and accurately describable as "extremely unequal." Despite occasional upward swings in common stock ownership, such as the one which inspired the Ad Council to come up with the memorable term "people's capitalism," there is no verifiable long-term trend toward significant equalization of capital wealth. Furthermore, there is no verifiable long-term trend toward the reduction of capital property income as a proportion of national income. Thus, there is no basis for speculating that the problem of maldistribution of capital property income will eventually "cure itself" if we merely wait long enough.

The essence of people's capitalism, as a defensive tactic, is to obscure the hard and unpalatable fact of extreme inequality in capital property income distribution under contemporary capitalism. This is accomplished by various forms of misinterpretation and misrepresentation aimed at diminishing the awareness among the noncapitalist majority that they are not now, nor probably ever will be, members of the tiny capitalist minority. These misinterpretations and misrepresentations fall into three general categories, each one of which may be understood in terms of a general proposition concerning the distribution of a certain concept of capital wealth under capitalism, or, alternatively, in terms of a specific proposition concerning the typical individual under capitalism. First, there is the proposition that the distribution of *current* capital wealth is relatively equal, which implies that the typical individual *probably already is* a capitalist. Second, there is the proposition that the distribution of *lifetime* capital wealth is relatively equal, which implies that the typical individual *is likely to become* a capitalist as he or she grows older. Third, there is the proposition that the distribution of *expected lifetime* capital wealth (in the sense of statistical expectation) is relatively equal, which implies that there *is a substantial probability* that the typical individual could become a capitalist at any time, regardless of his or her age. These are the three principal variations on the people's capitalism theme.

Current capital wealth refers to a person's capital wealth at the present point in time, as opposed to average wealth over the person's lifetime including the working period and the retirement period (lifetime capital wealth), and expected capital wealth on the basis of various determinants of capital wealth mobility other than the accumulation of pension fund assets for purposes of providing retirement income (expected lifetime capital wealth). The illusion of relatively high equality in current capital wealth is achieved by blurring the distinction between capital wealth and noncapital wealth such as residential real estate and consumer durables. As a matter of fact, under contemporary capitalism many if not most forms of noncapital wealth are far more equally distributed than capital wealth forms. What this means is that the typical household will own an amount of noncapital wealth much closer to the average amount of noncapital wealth than is the case with respect to capital wealth. For example, if, hypothetically, the average amount of noncapital wealth over all households in the economy is $100,000 per household, and the average amount of capital wealth is also $100,000, a certain household which owns, say, $50,000 worth of noncapital wealth (50 percent of the average), is likely to own only $5,000 worth of capital wealth (5 percent of the average).

The distinction between capital wealth and noncapital wealth is very clear and important. Capital wealth consists of financial instruments such as stocks and bonds which yield tangible property income in terms of dividends and interests, and which are capable of yielding further capital gains income upon sale. Noncapital wealth consists of material goods such as homes and gardens, appliances and furnishings, books and pictures, clothes and jewelry, automobiles and other transportation equipment, stockpiles of food and medicine, and so forth. These are all valuable commodities which *may* be sold at a profit (yielding what the tax code deems a "capital gain"), but which definitely *do not* yield a tangible income flow of any kind. A person could own $10 million worth of noncapital wealth, but if that person chooses neither to work nor to sell any of the property, then that person would soon starve to death. On the other hand, a person who owns $10 million worth of capital wealth could choose not to work and also not to sell any of the property, and that person could nevertheless live quite comfortably on the property income (dividends, interest, etc.) generated by the capital wealth (stocks, bonds, etc.).

Thanks to the widespread success of that very basic form of people's capitalism misrepresentation which simply lumps together capital and noncapital wealth into one homogeneous mass of "property," there are uncountable millions of impoverished and quasi-impoverished people living in the capitalist nations, who own not one dollar worth of legitimate capital property, but who are nevertheless convinced that they themselves are "capitalists" whose personal prosperity would be threatened by socialism. They believe this because they own various types of downscale noncapital property: a dilapidated shack on a weedy half-acre, a rusty pickup truck with flat tires, a moth-eaten wardrobe, a broken watch. It might be humorous if it were not so pathetic.

A strong propensity to blend together capital wealth and noncapital wealth into "wealth" pure and simple is not confined to the hopelessly ignorant and/or naive. Educated economists, for example, like to talk about the "implicit income" of owners of residential property—if a house owner did not own the house, he or she would be forced to pay rent for a dwelling place, and this "what if" amount can be considered the owner's "implicit income." The obvious shortcoming of this bit of intellectual legerdemain is that a person could be receiving millions of dollars a month in implicit income, but if that person had no other form of income, that person would be starving. The idea simply does not square with a commonsense understanding of the term "income." For another example, the government statisticians responsible for reporting information on "wealth" concentrate almost entirely on "total wealth" or "aggregate wealth" rather than capital wealth. In other words, most of the information which they provide pertains to the sum of capital and noncapital wealth. Since noncapital wealth is much more equally distributed than is capital wealth, this approach diminishes the apparent degree of "wealth inequality" in society and diverts attention from the extremely high level of inequality with respect to capital wealth.

There could be an "innocent" explanation for this sort of thing. It does not necessarily proceed from a conscious and malicious effort at misrepresentation of the facts. Psychologists agree that with respect to unpleasant realities about which nothing can be done (e.g., death, taxes, dental problems), a mentally well-adjusted person will, as much as possible, put these realities out of his or her mind. Brooding contemplation of unpleasant but unavoidable realities generates depression, melancholia, unhappiness. So if you can't beat it, and you also can't escape it—then ignore it. This bit of psychological wisdom is certainly unquestionable as far as it goes. The problem, of course, is that if one does not contemplate unpleasant realities at least to some extent, then one might never recognize that some of them are not, after all, unavoidable.

The implicit assumption which rules much if not most contemporary thinking about anything to do with capitalism and socialism is that, for a variety of reasons, capitalism is inevitably superior to socialism. That is to say, any effort to cure the problems of capitalism by means of socialism will generate new problems of even greater magnitude. The extraordinary inequality of financial capital wealth and capital property income under contemporary capitalism is therefore regarded as an unpleasant but unavoidable reality. According to the "good mental health principle" just described, this inequality should be, to the greatest extent possible, put out of one's mind, minimized, diminished, ignored, forgotten. Thus economists come up with "implicit income" as a means of blurring the important distinction between capital wealth and noncapital wealth. Thus government statisticians report information on total wealth rather than breaking the information down into capital and noncapital components. But according to the argument being put forward herein, viable and attractive democratic market socialist alternatives do in fact exist to contemporary capitalism. Therefore it is neither necessary nor sensible to avert our eyes from that large wart on contemporary capitalism's face: maldistribution of capital wealth and property income.

That the distribution of capital wealth is highly unequal has been "common knowledge" for a long time. For example, it was a basic presumption made by Karl Marx in his nineteenth-century critique of capitalism—and while Marx's many critics have discerned numerous errors and omissions in his work, by and large they have not challenged this particular presumption. Apparently the evidence from casual empiricism has been compelling: people living in lonely mansions on the hill tend to possess lots of stocks and bonds; people living in modest frame houses down in the town tend to possess very little of this sort of thing. But we are living today in an age of quantitative, numerical science, and if we are to contemplate something so seemingly drastic as a transition from capitalism to socialism (albeit the transition to the specific type of socialism proposed herein would not be nearly so drastic as commonly supposed), then we would want to have as precise an idea as possible of those conditions which determine the relative degree of desirability of the transition. One of these conditions is the distribution of financial capital wealth under contemporary capitalism. Just exactly how unequal is it? And what are the implications of this inequality in terms of a potential transition to market socialism?

Of all the advanced capitalist nations today, the amount of available information on the financial condition of the population is probably greatest for the United States. The following discussion pertains to the United States, but roughly the same situation holds for the other advanced capitalist nations: Canada, Australia, New Zealand, and the nations of Western Europe.

The most extensive and reliable information on the financial circumstances of U.S. households comes from tax returns. Since the imposition of individual income taxation by the federal government in 1916, a tremendous amount of information has flowed into Washington on income distribution. Owing to fairly stiff penalties for misreporting income, and to fairly active enforcement of the tax rules, this information is reasonably reliable. For several decades, the federal government has made a respectable effort to organize this information and make it available to the general public in the form of the annual series of Internal Revenue Service publications: *Statistics of Income: Individual Income Tax Returns.* From this source, for example, we may ascertain that at low- to medium-income levels, capital property income (primarily dividends, interest, capital gains) is a very small component of total household income, while at very high income levels, capital property income becomes a very substantial component of total household income. From this information on the flow of capital property income it is evident that ownership of the stock of financial capital is highly unequal—although this information does not provide direct and precise evidence on inequality of capital wealth ownership itself.

If the federal government imposed taxes on household wealth, we would have far better information on wealth distribution than we do at present. There is no annual tax on household wealth comparable to the annual income tax, but taxation of wealth does occur at the time of the owner's death, in the form of estate taxes. This type of taxation is approximately as old as individual income taxation. Information on U.S. wealth distribution based on estate tax returns has not been provided to the public in as great a degree of detail, and for as long a period of time, as has been the case for U.S. income distribution based on income tax returns. But the Internal Revenue Service has since the 1960s been issuing an intermittent publication entitled *Supplemental Statistics of Income: Personal Wealth Estimated from Estate Tax Returns*. This publication verifies a high degree of inequality in the distribution of total wealth, including both capital forms and noncapital forms. The information is not as precise as would be desirable for present purposes, both because of the emphasis on total wealth rather than capital wealth, and because of the inadequate degree of detail provided concerning households in the highest wealth brackets. Information from estate tax returns has been used by economists such as Robert J. Lampman and James D. Smith to assess changes in U.S. wealth distribution over time. Through such contributions, it has been established beyond reasonable doubt that the distribution of total wealth (and by implication of capital wealth) has been both highly unequal and highly stable throughout the twentieth century. U.S. wealth distribution has been especially stable since the end of the Second World War.

Since the 1960s another very important source of information on U.S. income and wealth distribution has appeared: periodic surveys conducted by the Federal Reserve Board (FRB). The collection of financial information through surveys has certain strengths and weaknesses relative to its collection through tax returns. Since the information is not being provided for tax purposes, there is not an automatic incentive toward underreporting. Also, the survey questionnaires go into far more detail than do tax forms. On the other hand, since there is no incentive for responding to the surveys other than general public spiritedness, and since there is no legal penalty for providing incorrect information, either by accident or by intention, the surveys also have serious limitations as sources of financial information.

The first of the FRB's surveys was called the *Survey of Financial Characteristics of Consumers (SFCC)*; succeeding surveys have been called *Surveys of Consumer Finances (SCF)*. The *SFCC*, conducted in 1963, was quite unique in terms of the quantity of hard information made available to the public in accessible printed form. A 166-page statistical report carrying the title of the survey, authored by Dorothy S. Projector and Gertrude S. Weiss, was issued by the Board of Governors of the Federal Reserve Board in August 1966. Two years later, in November 1968, another 321-page statistical report, authored by Projector alone, was issued on the 1964 follow-up survey of respondents to the 1963 survey: *Survey of Changes in Family Finances*. The nearly 500 pages of tabular data issued on these two related surveys remains to this day the most abundant and accessible single source of information on U.S. wealth and income distribution.

Considerably less information has been provided on the more recent *Surveys of Consumer Finances*. A limited amount of very general information derived from these surveys has been published in the FRB's monthly, the *Federal Reserve Bulletin*. For example, the three articles in the *Federal Reserve Bulletin* pertaining to the 1983 *SCF* amounted to only 45 pages. The Federal Reserve Board offers magnetic data tapes of the raw information from its various surveys for sale to researchers, but the demand for these tapes is not exactly brisk. Aside from the cost, only experienced programmers with access to advanced computer equipment have any hope of extracting understandable information from these tapes. And the incentive for doing so is not great in that the resulting information is not highly publishable—both because it is "uninteresting" (since it is already wellknown that capital wealth is very unequally distributed), and because it is "irrelevant" (since it is also wellknown that no viable cure exists for inequality in capital wealth ownership). As to the FRB's motivations in failing to provide detailed printed information on the more recent *SCF*s comparable to that provided on the 1963 *SFCC*, no doubt it would cite "lack of interest and need." But it is perhaps significant that the well-known anti-establishment writer Ferdinand Lundberg, in his Vietnam-era diatribe against maldistribution of wealth in the United States entitled *The Rich and the Super-Rich* (1968), cited the voluminous printed reports on the early 1960s *SFCC* very extensively. Whatever ammunition might exist in the more recent *SCF*s against the capitalistic status quo has been a lot more difficult for anti-establishment writers to get their hands on.

As to the speculation that the degree of inequality in U.S. capital wealth distribution is considerably lower in the latter 1990s than it was in the early 1960s, this speculation has been convincingly refuted by a small but significant amount of careful study utilizing the FRB's various data tapes. For example, definitive research by Edward N. Wolff published in the *Review of Income and Wealth* indicates significantly *greater* capital wealth inequality as of the 1990s relative to the 1960s. This finding is not altogether unexpected, in view of the conservative counter-revolution against progressive taxation, public expenditure, and the welfare state which peaked during the 12-year Republican incumbency in the U.S. presidency from 1980 to 1992 (encompassing the administrations of Ronald Reagan and George Bush).

The present author has utilized the printed data in the 1966 *Survey of Financial Characteristics of Consumers* in a considerable amount of published writing comprising three professional journal articles and two books. The numbers derived from the 1966 *SFCC* report authored by Projector and Weiss are eye-opening to say the least. Here is one example. According to the report, the average amount of investment assets owned by all 57.9 million U.S. households in 1962 was $7,013. At the same time, the richest .1 million households (i.e., 100,000 households) owned an average amount of investment assets of $1,264,653. Thus the richest 100,000 households owned 180 times the average amount of investment assets in the economy. One implication of this is that the richest .17 percent of households (i.e., less than two-tenths of 1 percent) owned a full 31.14 percent of total investment assets owned by all U.S. households. There is no way one can reasonably soften or explain away this amount of inequality—this is truly *obscene* inequality.

Another indicator is the Gini coefficient of inequality, widely utilized in economics and other social sciences to provide a single number indicating the degree of inequality over the entire range of income or wealth. The higher the value of the Gini coefficient, the greater the degree of inequality. A value of this coefficient for a population in which a certain type of wealth or income was completely equal would be 0, while the value of the coefficient for a population in which that type of wealth or income was completely unequal (i.e., one household possessed all of it while all the other households possessed none of it) would be 1. The Gini coefficient for the U.S. capital wealth distribution based on the 1966 *SFCC* report is calculated as .86. This is an extremely high Gini coefficient. Estimated Gini coefficients for U.S. labor income tend to be in the range from .30 to .40, while for U.S. total income these coefficients tend to be in the range from .40 to .50.

Figures such as these might be regarded by many people as excessively abstract, as devoid of any appreciable impact or immediacy, as irrelevant and meaningless. Numerical statistical data is often regarded as such, even by people who are professionally accustomed to examining this kind of data. But it so happens that these particular figures do in fact possess tangible importance to many if not most of the people reading this book. What these figures mean is that the annual incomes of the vast majority of people reading this book would in all probability be significantly higher under democratic market socialism than they are presently under capitalism. This is because the social dividend payment to the vast majority of individuals under democratic market socialism would be significantly higher than the amount they are currently receiving under capitalism in the form of capital property income.

There are two central implications inherent in the extreme inequality of capital wealth ownership under contemporary capitalism: (1) the large majority of the population would receive more social dividend income under market socialism than they currently receive capital property income under capitalism; (2) the large majority of the population would receive a numerically significant amount of social dividend income under market socialism. It must be conceded, of course, that there is a very important caveat to be added to this statement: the truth of these propositions depends on the level of overall economic efficiency under market socialism being at least comparable to that under capitalism. According to the various arguments that capital property income is earned income (as a return to entrepreneurship, risk-taking, corporate supervision, saving, etc.), the social dividend principle of distributing the capital return generated by the operations of business enterprises would either drastically attenuate or completely eliminate the incentive to these economically vital activities, leading ultimately—more quickly or less quickly as the case may be—to economic inefficiency and loss of output. These arguments, to be addressed in considerable detail below, are *probably* invalid, but they cannot be *proven* invalid short of actual experiment with market socialism.

On the other hand, it is fully possible, for reasons to be discussed below, that market socialism might prove somewhat *more* efficient in practice than contemporary capitalism. But the efficiency gain—if there is one—would probably be modest. Still, even a modest gain in efficiency would translate into a still larger percentage of the population benefited by social dividend distribution of capital property return, and a still larger amount of annual social dividend income paid to each household. The estimates which I have made of the percentage of the U.S. population benefited by social dividend distribution, on the basis of the assumption of *equal* economic efficiency as between market socialism and capitalism, are very high. Applying two different estimation methods to the data provided in the Federal Reserve Board's *Survey of Financial Characteristics of Consumers* yielded 94.4 percent for the first method, and 94.2 percent for the second method. A conservative conclusion from these estimates is that assuming comparable economic efficiency as between market socialism and contemporary capitalism, over 90 percent of the U.S. population would receive more social dividend under market socialism than they currently receive capital property income under the capitalist system.

As to the actual amount of social dividend income to be received by each household under market socialism, that cannot be estimated to the degree of precision which we would prefer. As to the absolute amount, that would depend, in the first place, on the household's earned labor income (wages and salaries): the absolute amount of social dividend income would be determined by the application of some percentage to the household's labor income. Since the labor incomes of various households vary over a wide range, so too would the social dividend payments. As for the percentage of labor income to be paid in social dividend under market socialism, for a variety of reasons this is difficult to estimate exactly. The safest answer is that it would probably fall into the range from 5 percent to 10 percent of labor income. A very conservative estimate of the potential annual U.S. social dividend fund, which I made in a paper published in 1977, indicated 6.75 percent of annual U.S. wage and salary income. Accepting this 6.75 percent for purposes of illustration, it would mean that a household with $10,000 annual labor income would receive $675 in social dividend, while a household with $100,000 annual labor income would receive $6,750 in social dividend. It can reasonably be said that to a family with $10,000 in annual earned income, $675 represents a significant amount of money, and similarly, to a family with $100,000 in annual earned income, $6,750 represents a significant amount of money.

To summarize the key implications of the highly unequal distributions under contemporary capitalism of current financial capital wealth and current capital property income, this inequality implies that the large majority of the population would receive more social dividend income under market socialism than they currently receive capital property income under capitalism, and also that the amount of social dividend income paid to each household under market socialism would be a significant amount of money. The essence of the people's capitalism defense of capitalism is to obscure and obfuscate these realities. Normally this is accomplished by means of the typical person's unawareness of such information as has been provided in the FRB's *Survey of Financial Characteristics of Consumers*. Even if the person is in fact dimly aware of this type of information, he or she is unlikely to understand and appreciate its practical significance in terms of the relative desirability of contemporary capitalism and market socialism.

But even if we imagine a person who is not only fully aware of the available information on current capital wealth distribution, but is also fully conscious of the practical significance of this information, the purveyors of people's capitalism have two further opportunities to confuse that person and to blind him or her to his or her true interests. The key, from the purveyors' point of view, is to get the person to believe that the relevant distribution of capital wealth is something other than the current distribution, and that this relevant distribution is in fact much more equal than the current distribution. This being the case, a much smaller percentage of the population would be benefited by social dividend distribution of capital property return, and there would be a much larger probability that any given person, taken at random, would *not* be in the percentage benefited. The two alternative distributions adduced by the respective variations on the people's capitalism theme are: (1) the distribution of *lifetime* capital wealth; (2) the distribution of *expected lifetime* capital wealth.

With respect to lifetime capital wealth distribution, this variant of people's capitalism relies on blurring the distinction between capital wealth and retirement benefits (often called "pension fund benefits"). The concept of "life cycle saving" refers to the accumulation of assets over the individual's working career for the purpose of providing retirement income to the individual and his/her dependent spouse. The U.S. Social Security system provides subsistence payment to retired individuals, but most individuals supplement Social Security with other retirement provisions, often pension plans provided by their employer. The basis of all such provisions involves the individual making regular payments into the system throughout the working career, followed by the receipt of regular income payments throughout the retirement period. The key characteristic of pension-type rights, that which distinguishes them from true capital property, is that the benefits are terminated upon the death of the recipient and the dependent spouse.

Wealth in the form of retirement benefits (i.e., the cash surrender value of such benefits, or their present discounted value) follows the "inverted-V" pattern over the life of the individual: it rises gradually to a peak at the time of retirement, followed by relatively rapid decline toward the value of zero at the expected age of death. If we take the entire population at a given point in time, younger people have a small amount of this type of wealth, while older people have a relatively large amount. But clearly, inequality in this type of wealth evens out over the lifespan of the individual: today's younger people are tomorrow's older people. If we take the average amount of this type of wealth which each person can expect to hold over his/her lifetime, this lifetime distribution would be relatively equal. That is, it would be comparable to the distribution of total income—which is far more equal that of financial capital wealth. One variant on the theme of people's capitalism, therefore, consists of the allegation that observed capital wealth inequality at each point in time is due mostly to life-cycle saving—by and large, poorer people are younger people, while wealthy people are older people. Obviously this type of inequality is innocuous: in fact, if it were *not* allowed, then how would people make provision for their retirement years?

Under market socialism, the vast majority of people would make provision for their retirement years in exactly the same manner they do under capitalism: they would participate in various types of pension plans. The number of people under capitalism who make provision for retirement income by means of the accumulation of income-producing stocks and bonds is extremely small—this number would be comparable to the number of capitalists, properly defined, in the population. As indicated above, a capitalist is herein defined to be an individual who owns a sufficient amount of capital wealth that the property income on the wealth is by itself adequate to support at least a comfortable level of life. The percentage of the working-age population in this category is extremely small: probably about 1 percent—certainly no larger than 5 percent. Furthermore, the percentage of the retirement-age population in this category is not much larger. The fact is that retirement benefits are qualitatively different from capital wealth. The average amount of retirement benefits held by the retirement-age population is quite small relative to the amount of capital wealth held by this segment of the population. But the distribution of capital wealth *within* the retirement age population—in contrast to that of retirement benefits—is practically as grotesquely unequal as it is among the general population.

While it is true that life-cycle saving does in fact make some contribution to capital wealth inequality, this contribution is extremely small. We know this to be the case from a variety of separate sources. Simulation models of life-cycle saving generate a level of inequality in retirement benefits which is only a small fraction of that observed with respect to capital wealth. Information provided in the *Survey of Financial Characteristics of Consumers* on the distribution of capital wealth by age bracket shows that the distribution of capital wealth is practically as unequal within each age bracket (including the elderly age brackets) as it is for the entire population (i.e., over all age brackets). Information from estate tax returns shows that the value of capital wealth, in contrast to that of retirement benefits, does not decline with the individual's age: this data shows that capital wealth at the time of the wealth-holder's death is comparable to that at retirement age. This provides fuel for the engine of inheritance, which will be examined in the next section.

With respect to life-cycle saving and the accumulation and decumulation of retirement benefits over the lifespan, suffice it to say in conclusion that these factors have little to do with the observed distribution of financial capital wealth under contemporary capitalism, and that they in no way suffice to provide either an economic or a moral justification for the extreme degree of inequality in this latter distribution. These factors do not significantly diminish the percentage of the population that would be benefited by social dividend distribution of capital property return under market socialism, nor do they significantly diminish the total amount of social dividend income that would be paid out to the typical individual over his/her lifespan.

INHERITANCE AND CHANCE

The third variant of people's capitalism—that which alleges the relative equality of *expected lifetime* capital wealth—is in many ways the most sophisticated of the three variants with which we have been concerned. It does not rely upon deluding noncapitalists that they are capitalists right now because they own houses, automobiles, and/or a few thousand dollars worth of stock. It does not rely upon deluding noncapitalists into thinking that they will become capitalists as they approach retirement because they are making provision for retirement income—for example, by making monthly payments into a pension fund. The kind of information that would be necessary to definitively refute this variant of people's capitalism, namely data on the capital wealth ownership of each one of a large number of individuals during each and every year of his/her lifespan, is not presently available, nor is it likely to become available in the future. Furthermore, a basic component of this variant of people's capitalism—that a possibility exists that even very poor people might become wealthy capitalists in the future—is both empirically true and widely known. From earliest childhood, people are indoctrinated in Horatio Alger stories of rapid rise from rags to riches. The moral of these stories is straightforward: "You too might easily become a wealthy capitalist—wealth could be right around the corner!"

There are two points at which the implications of this type of message diverge from reality: (1) for the vast majority of people, the actual probability of becoming a wealthy capitalist in the future is much smaller than is suggested; (2) the two most important determinants of significant upward capital wealth mobility are not the suggested hard work and courage, but rather inheritance and chance. Therefore this third variant of people's capitalism misrepresents reality both with respect to the actual *degree* of upward capital wealth mobility, and with respect to the usual *means* of upward capital wealth mobility.

Let us consider the population of "wealthy capitalists," defined, for example, as all those individuals possessing net capital wealth of $5 million or greater. If we had reliable information on the sources of this capital wealth for all such individuals, what would we find? According to exponents of people's capitalism, among wealthy capitalists we would mostly find successful entrepreneurs who started their careers with little or no inherited capital wealth, and who by virtue of courage, intelligence, perspicacity, determination, and hard work, built large-scale business enterprises which make a significant, undeniable contribution to economic prosperity and human welfare. From a population of hundreds of millions of individuals, it is certainly possible to find individuals—in historical times and in our own—who fit this image: Cyrus McCormick, Andrew Carnegie, Henry Ford, Ray Kroc, Sam Walton, Steven Jobs, Bill Gates. The question is, however, what proportion of wealthy capitalists of the present day are legitimately characterized as self-made entrepreneurs? And what proportion are, on the other hand, legitimately characterized as inheriting rentiers? The proposition which will be argued here is that under the mature capitalism we know today, the vast majority of wealthy capitalists are more legitimately described as inheriting rentiers than as self-made entrepreneurs, and that using the virtues and contributions of a tiny handful of entrepreneurs to justify the financial privileges of the entire class of wealthy capitalists is illegitimate and invalid.

Of course, socialists are routinely accused of being oblivious to the paramount economic value of risk-taking and entrepreneurship. It is alleged that in their misguided lust for economic equality, socialists propose to abrogate the incentive to entrepreneurial endeavor and thus lay the basis for long-term economic stagnation and collapse. It is no doubt true that some proponents of socialism do not properly appreciate the important role of inequality in maintaining incentives to effort—just as it is also true that many proponents of capitalism do not properly appreciate the extraordinary degree of capital wealth inequality which exists under contemporary capitalism. The problem is to devise an economic system which achieves an optimal compromise between the competing objectives of economic efficiency and social equity. A very important component of the market socialist compromise proposed herein is the exclusion of genuine entrepreneurial enterprise from public ownership. So long as the founder-owner of a business enterprise under market socialism remains personally involved in its management, the firm would remain under private ownership, regardless of how large and profitable it becomes. What this means is that any successful entrepreneur capable of amassing a personal fortune under capitalism would be equally capable of amassing a personal fortune under market socialism. Under both systems, there would in fact be a tiny minority of individuals owning large financial fortunes derived from successful entrepreneurial endeavors. It is certainly possible that owing to other aspects of the economic system under market socialism, the personal fortunes of successful entrepreneurs might not be as large: perhaps only 100 million dollars rather than a billion. In addition, under socialism personally owned financial wealth would not produce property income: therefore a successful entrepreneur owning 100 million dollars could spend only 100 million dollars—not the property income derived from that 100 million, which over an extended period of time could amount to many times the original 100 million dollars. Be this as it may, the financial incentive to personal entrepreneurship would be extremely strong under the market socialist system proposed herein.

According to the working proposition underlying this discussion, the exclusion of entrepreneurial firms from public ownership would divert into private income only a very small amount of what would otherwise have become social dividend income. According to the exponents of people's capitalism, on the other hand, to whom successful entrepreneurship is the overwhelmingly dominant factor in upward capital wealth mobility and overall capital wealth inequality, this exclusion will result in the diversion of most, or at least a large part, of property return generated by business enterprise into the hands of private entrepreneurs, i.e., capitalists. What would *actually* happen, of course, may only be reliably ascertained by experimentation with market socialism. The stated provision for private ownership of entrepreneurial enterprise *ought* to render such experimentation innocuous to those who *sincerely* believe in this particular tenet of people's capitalism. One might have grounds for suspecting the sincerity of those who express opposition to market socialist proposals, even though these proposals involve the retention of private ownership of entrepreneurial firms. At a minimum, such opponents must have important objections to socialism apart from the stated qualms about the suppression of incentives to entrepreneurship.

Within the realm of capitalist apologetics, the term "entrepreneur" has a profound, mystical, and quasi-religious significance. The anointed priests of the cult of entrepreneurship include writers and editors of the business press, as well as adherents to certain conservative academic schools of thought such as the Austrian. Entrepreneurs are proclaimed by these priests veritable demigods among humanity, whose magnificent contributions to human welfare are so glorious that they fully and completely merit the reward of enormous personal financial wealth. Entrepreneurs are the vital geniuses upon whose courage and vision depends the forward progress not merely of the economy but of human civilization itself. And so on and so forth. The idea of getting rich while at the same time being a socioeconomic hero has appealed to uncounted hordes of aspirants to the exalted status of entrepreneur. In their thousands, their hopes buoyed up by the seemingly endless tales of success recounted in the business press, they launch their little rafts of enterprise upon the stormy business seas. The vast majority of these efforts quickly founder and sink, leaving the aspirant entrepreneur with heavy burdens both financial and psychological, and far more conscious of the numerical significance and human meaning of the grim bankruptcy statistics which are so studiously ignored by the business press.

A far more reliable path to large-scale capital wealth than entrepreneurship is the path of inheritance. Of all those individuals who at the present moment in time may be categorized as "wealthy capitalists" by virtue of personal ownership of, say, 5 million dollars or more in net capital wealth, quite probably at least 80 percent received, at some point in their lives, inheritances worth $500,000 or more. Unfortunately, a precise empirical proposition of this sort cannot be firmly pinned down by means of reliable, objective evidence. Exponents of people's capitalism. of course, would stridently deny this proposition. They can point, however, to no meaningful, systematic evidence to support their own contention that inheritance is *not* in fact an extremely important determinant of large-scale capital wealth. The tiny handful of self-made entrepreneurial multimillionaires whom the business press extols do not constitute such evidence—this kind of evidence is too anecdotal, too selective. After all, the fact that there exists a tiny handful of winners of multimillion-dollar jackpots in various state lotteries within the United States does not demonstrate that the purchase of lottery tickets is a reliable path to large-scale wealth. When it comes to serious, systematic, social scientific evidence, this evidence powerfully suggests the paramount role of inheritance in the acquisition of large-scale financial capital wealth.

One important source of evidence on inheritance consists of financial surveys of the population. Some of these surveys ask questions about receipt of inheritances. For example, the *Survey of Financial Character-*

istics of Consumers conducted by the Federal Reserve Board in the early 1960s (discussed above) contained an item pertaining to inheritance. According to Table A31 of the 1966 report, 59 percent of households in the highest wealth bracket ($500,000 and over in net wealth) reported having received some inheritance. This number is not inconsequential in and of itself, but it is important to recognize that in all probability it is an underestimate of the true figure. Wealthy capitalists whose fortunes are based on passive inheritance rather than glorious entrepreneurship are, for obvious reasons, not proud of the fact. Confronting a survey item on inheritance, they are more than likely to grunt something along the lines of "none of their damn business," and to either leave the item blank or check the "no inheritance" box. Aside from the possibility of underreporting, there is the fact that the highest wealth bracket reported in Table A31 is not all that high. A net wealth figure of $500,000 in the early 1960s would represent a far greater amount in today's terms, but still the amount would be well short of the $5 million which we are using as a benchmark to represent a "wealthy capitalist" today. Data given in Table A31 show that the proportion of households in each bracket reporting inheritances steadily increases with the wealth level, which means that for households with significantly greater than $500,000 in wealth at the time of the FRB *SFCC*, significantly more than 59 percent were the recipients of inheritances.

Another important source of objective information on inheritance has the important advantage of not depending on the possibly faulty memories and uncertain reliability of survey respondents. It has the disadvantages, however, of providing indirect rather than direct information on inheritance, and also of being extremely laborious to implement. This is the probate court record technique, pioneered in the 1920s by Josiah Wedgwood, and more recently applied by scholars such as Colin D. Harbury in the United Kingdom and Paul L. Menchik in the United States. The technique utilizes records kept by probate courts on the wealth of decedents subject to estate taxation, and compares the recorded wealth at the time of death of a sample of individuals with the recorded wealth at the time of death either of those individuals' children or those individuals' parents. The information obtained is not quite what one would prefer: one would prefer to compare the wealth at the time of death of a particular individual with inheritances received by that same individual. This is because there is always the possibility that if a case is found of a parent who died leaving great wealth, and that parent had a child who also died leaving great wealth, the wealth of the child might not be directly based on the wealth of the parent—it could be that the inheritance was first frittered away, and then after that the child became serious and accumulated another fortune on his or her own. Of course, common sense suggests that such cases are rare, and that if a case is found of a parent and a child who both died wealthy, most likely the child's wealth is directly attributable to inheritances received from the parent.

What is very definitely demonstrated by this type of research is a very high level of correlation between the wealth of one generation and the wealth of the next. In particular, children who die wealthy are very likely to have parents who died wealthy. For example, one research project by Colin Harbury started with a sample of men who died in the 1950s leaving estates of £100,000 or more, which put them into the top one-tenth of 1 percent of wealth-holders in Britain at that time. Harbury then sought the probate court records on the fathers of these men, most of whom had died in the 1920s. Some 71 percent of the men dying in the 1950s had fathers who died leaving estates of £5,000 or more, which by the standards of the 1920s put them into the top 1.625 percent of wealth-holders in Britain. This suggests that of every ten very wealthy people in Britain, seven come from very wealthy parentage. Menchik finds similar results for the United States.

Clearly, there are serious shortcomings of probate court records as a source of information on inheritance. The fact that a parent left leaving a large fortune does not mean that the children received large inheritances: bequests might have been made to charity or to other relatives. The samples tend to be very small owing to the difficulty of matching up records of parents and children. Moreover, the samples are subject to serious biases. Owing to name changes of female children who marry, the samples are oriented to male parents and male children. Another bias comes from the fact that most of the matches between parent and child are obtained when both the parent and child die in the same locality. It is very difficult to obtain a match when the child leaves the locality in which the parent died—and of course the increasing mobility of the population in the modern era means that a great many individuals who die leaving estates in a certain locality have neither parents nor children whose estates can be located.

Nevertheless, this kind of evidence is worthy of considerable respect. It is serious, systematic, statistical, social scientific evidence. It is far more worthy of attention and consideration than the carefully selected success stories about self-made millionaires featured in the business press. The fact that a tiny handful of extraordinarily capable and/or fortunate individuals have managed to reach the highest ranks of wealth without the assistance of inheritance is not serious evidence that inheritance is a minor contributor to wealth inequality. One cannot conclude that there is a respectable probability of winning a multimillion dollar jackpot in a state lottery from the fact that "dozens and dozens" of people have won such jackpots in the past. Probabilities are inferred by looking at the denominator as well as the numerator. In this case, when the denominator consists of millions and millions of people, the fact that there exist dozens and dozens of self-made millionaires in the world does not necessarily indicate that there is a respectable probability that any given person—who does *not* expect to receive a substantial inheritance—will nevertheless achieve a substantial capital fortune. It is not simply a matter of there not being much room at the top (i.e., the fact that wealthy capitalists are a tiny minority of the general population). It is also a matter that most of the room at the top is occupied by people who started with the unfair advantage of a substantial inheritance (i.e., the high incidence of inheritance among wealthy capitalists).

There is an important qualitative difference between a large inheritance, of sufficient magnitude for the property income on it to provide at least a comfortable standard of life, and the usual modest inheritance, of the sort which many people receive at some point in their lives, which can only yield an inconsequential amount of property income and which is therefore almost immediately plowed into household finances or some specific short-term project (a new roof on the house, a European vacation, a college education for a child). Those individuals lucky enough to receive the former type of inheritance do not generally fritter it away in a short-term spending spree. Ordinarily, they immediately adopt that ruling principle among the wealthy: "Spend only the income—never touch the capital." This is indeed a very sensible principle. If conscientiously adhered to, the consumption obtained from a given amount of capital wealth, over a protracted period of time, could amount to many times the initial value of the wealth. With any luck, a substantial inheritance will last a lifetime and provide the basis for bequests to grateful offspring.

Particularly when capital wealth is held in the form of common stock, the rate of appreciation in its value tends to exceed the rate of inflation because of the practice among business firms of retaining a proportion of profits which would otherwise have been disbursed as dividends to common stock shareholders. These retained earnings are reinvested in business capital, which adds to the book value of a given share of common stock. Of course, the relationship between book value and market value of common stock shares is very loose and unstable. But over a sufficient period of time, and over a sufficiently large number of firms, there is in fact a positive statistical correlation. The tendency toward appreciation at a rate higher than inflation is stronger for capital property than for other types of property commonly considered to represent "wealth": especially the categories of residential property, consumer durables, and luxuries such as master paintings and fur coats. Although there have indeed been some dramatic cases of rapid rises in the value of these kinds of assets (e.g., the rise in house prices in the United States during the 1970s, the rise in the prices of Impressionist paintings between the late nineteenth century and the mid-twentieth century), in general these kinds of assets only increase in value at the rate of general inflation. Therefore a sensible investor with a very large amount of money to invest will not concentrate it in fine homes and/or master paintings; rather he or she will put it mostly into common stock. Very large capital fortunes are in fact mostly concentrated in common stock, on which the rate of appreciation, in a statistical sense, is the greatest.

As a result, substantial capital fortunes tend to appreciate in value at a rate higher than the rate of inflation, meaning that the real value of the capital tends to rise. An initial inheritance of $500,000, invested in an array of common stocks, might be worth, for example, $2 million some 20 or 30 years later (which would represent $1 million in real value, if the rate of inflation during the entire period has been 100 percent). On the other hand, 20 or 30 years later, if the investor is exceptionally unlucky, the stocks and bonds acquired with the inheritance might be worth nothing at all. Values of capital assets are notoriously volatile: they often fluctuate violently for no obvious reason. Even the bluest of blue chip stocks sometimes experience sustained drops in value. Although the principle of cause and effect tells us that nothing happens without a reason, the reasons for these fluctuations in the value of specific capital assets are so obscure and unfathomable that no mortal human being is truly capable of understanding them. The term "random" is used to describe events which cannot be predicted in advance owing to the limitations of human knowledge. Fluctuations in capital asset values fall into this category: they are random fluctuations.

Some investors experience dramatic rises in the value of their capital wealth; while others experience dramatic falls. By far the most important factor in determining these changes is random fluctuation (i.e., chance). The former investors are simply lucky investors; while the latter investors are simply unlucky investors. This, of course, is a very controversial proposition. Owing to its potent ideological implications, it tends to be stridently rejected by all those who are absolutely convinced that capitalism represents the best of all possible economic worlds. In this category, one tends to find adherents to the conservative Austrian school of socioeconomic thought, writers and editors for the business press, purveyors of investment information and advice, and wealthy capitalists. According to these people, the reason some investors are successful and others are unsuccessful is that the former are more wise, intelligent, informed, perspicacious, judicious, and generally worthy than the latter. It would not do to concede that very large capital wealth fortunes are largely the result of chance—that might call contemporary capitalism itself into question. Preferably large capital wealth fortunes are to be attributed to the active and noble process of entrepreneurship. But even if it conceded that as a matter of fact a great many wealthy capitalists of the present day have no personal experience in the founding and operation of a new business firm, it can still be alleged that their wealth is mainly attributable to their exceptional ability and brilliant vision in selecting investments.

Very few investors select their investments completely at random. Typically they engage in at least a little bit of personal research and study prior to making purchases of capital assets. At a minimum, they are likely to take the advice of an investment counselor reputed to have a "good track record" in picking investments. In other words, they do have reasons for selecting particular investments. Having made at least a modest effort to obtain these reasons, they are understandably reluctant to accept that the performance of their portfolio is almost entirely determined by pure chance. To the extent that they are successful, their confidence grows proportionately that their success is due to wise decisions rather than good luck. To the extent that they are less successful, they are more inclined to accept the reality that investment outcomes are determined almost entirely by chance.

It is necessary to concede that it is not possible to prove, in a scientifically or logically conclusive manner, that chance is the principal determinant of different rates of appreciation among large-scale capital wealth fortunes. There is inevitably an important element of subjective judgment here. However, there are some powerfully suggestive pieces of "circumstantial evidence," so to speak. To begin with, there is the extravagant level of inequality in capital wealth ownership, which drastically exceeds the level of inequality in measured human capabilities such as intelligence. If it were differences in human capabilities which largely determined differences in capital wealth ownership, then we would expect far less inequality in capital wealth ownership than we actually observe. As a matter of fact, the distribution of labor income (wages and salaries) is much more equal than that of capital wealth and much more closely approaches the distribution of human capabilities. And so it makes more sense to attribute differences in labor income to differences in human capabilities. A related point is that of the discontinuities in the rate of appreciation of capital wealth over the careers of particular capitalists. If the observed differences in rate of appreciation were mainly the result of differences in investment ability, then the more able investors should show a rate *consistently* higher than that of the less able investors. But it has long been noted that the genesis of most very large capital fortunes tends to lie in a very rapid spurt of growth over an abbreviated period of time, rather than in a somewhat above-average rate of growth over a protracted period of time. These rapid spurts in value over a short period of time are more consistent with the chance hypothesis than the investment ability hypothesis.

According to the principle of Ockham's Razor, which is regarded as a generally sensible principle among investigators of various kinds, simple explanations of phenomena are preferable to complicated explanations—so long as the simple explanations do as good a job of explaining reality as the complicated explanations. It so happens that pure chance provides a very simple explanation for the development of inequality in capital wealth ownership. Although chance is commonly regarded as the "great equalizer" (anyone at all can be either lucky or unlucky), the fact is that among students of wealth and income distribution, chance is regarded as a source of inequality rather than of equality. This principle is known as Gibrat's Law: it states that if a group of individuals start from a position of complete equality (each individual has the same amount), the workings of chance will produce inequality. When one thinks about it, this is intuitively apparent. If random fluctuations occur, some will go up while others will go down, leading to inequality. It is possible to write simple computer programs which clearly demonstrate Gibrat's Law. For example, if the rate of growth applying to the capital wealth of a particular individual at a particular period of time is a normally distributed random variable with a particular mean and variance, then starting from an initial condition of full equality, the workings of chance will quickly produce unequal capital wealth over a group of individuals. The larger the variance of the rate of growth, the larger will be the asymptotic degree of inequality which the capital wealth distribution approaches over time.

Now as a matter of fact, Gibrat's Law is only one of several contributing factors to the existing capital wealth inequality under contemporary capitalism. Gibrat's Law envisions growth from an initial condition of complete equality, plus a random growth factor which is the same for all individuals in the population. Neither of these conditions is accurately descriptive of the real world. First, the capital wealth endowments of individuals in the real world do not start from equality: in fact, a tiny fraction of the population receives substantial inheritances which it uses to commence capital wealth fortunes whose growth over time is thereafter determined by chance. Second, the random variation governing the appreciation of capital wealth is not constant over all individuals: it rather varies according to the absolute value of the individual's capital wealth-holding. The wealthier the individual, the higher the rate of return received on capital, and the smaller the variance of the return.

It was mentioned earlier in this chapter that the stock market in particular, and the capital markets in general, are extremely efficient mechanisms for transferring wealth from low- and medium-income households dependent almost entirely on labor income to high-income, wealthy capitalistic households who derive their income mostly from capital wealth. The problem is caused basically by the inadequate diversification of small-scale investment portfolios. If only a small amount of money is involved (anything less than, say, $100,000 would have to be considered small), transactions costs prevent a significant amount of diversification. As a result, the small investor is highly vulnerable to losses in value of specific assets. This vulnerability is magnified by psychological considerations: the small investor is far too conscious of the hard work and effort which went into the accumulation of the investment portfolio. As a result, its value is carefully monitored, and this practice leads, time and time again, to premature sales of assets whose values have declined. A wealthy investor who inherited, say, $5 million in capital wealth, might be able to take a more relaxed attitude along the lines of "que sera, sera" or "easy come, easy go." This attitude tends to safeguard such an investor from the self-destructive act of premature selling of capital assets.

A large fortune may be adequately diversified over a substantial number of assets. A few investments in a large and diversified portfolio might go sour, but the law of averages is a strong guarantee that the aggregate value of the portfolio will not suffer a severe decline. This diversification allows the wealthy investor to invest a larger proportion of his or her assets in the more volatile assets carrying a higher rate of return: common stock is the archetype of such investments. Therefore large-scale portfolios show a higher percentage of assets in common stock than small- and medium-scale portfolios. Because they are concentrated in higher rate of return securities, larger portfolios show a higher rate of return, and in addition, because of their greater degree of diversification, they show a lower variance—a lower risk factor. Thus the random factor determining the rate of appreciation of a particular capital fortune is a function of the size of the fortune. Appreciation of any particular capital fortune is still random, but the larger the fortune, the larger is the expected rate of appreciation, and the smaller is the probability of a substantial decline in value.

This situation tends to aggravate capital wealth inequality. It implies both good news and bad news—but the good news is entirely to the present possessors of large-scale capital wealth, while the bad news is to the vast majority of the population which does *not* presently possess large-scale capital wealth. The good news is that once an individual has achieved a high level of capital wealth, that wealth is relatively insulated against substantial declines in value. The probability of going from "riches to rags" is correspondingly decreased. The bad news is that it is even harder to go from no capital wealth or little capital wealth to large-scale capital wealth than it would have been had random variation in capital wealth been constant over all levels of wealth. It is even harder to go from "rags to riches" than previously thought; the greased flagpole to the financial promised land has even more grease on it than would otherwise have been the case.

Considered simply as propaganda, "people's capitalism" has been remarkably successful. The information adduced above is hardly a "state secret" of any sort. Most of the population is at least dimly aware of this information. But at the same time, the great majority of the population seems fully oblivious to the significance of this information is terms of their own personal prospects of getting rich (i.e., of becoming a wealthy capitalist). They cannot conceive of how extravagantly the odds are stacked against them. They continue to buy into the falsehood that "with a lot of hard work and a little bit of luck, I too could become a wealthy capitalist." The fact is that hard work has extremely little to do with it: most people work as hard as they possibly can throughout their lives, and never come within miles of being a wealthy capitalist. The fact is also that luck has everything to do with it: to have any appreciable chance of becoming a wealthy capitalist, you must be lucky enough to receive a substantial inheritance, or (if you do *not* receive an inheritance) you must be prodigiously, extraordinarily, and unbelievably lucky in the capital markets. As noted above, good mental health requires ignoring uncongenial realities about which nothing can possibly be done. Perhaps the widespread inability to recognize and appreciate the uncongenial truth about contemporary capitalism is basically due to the equally widespread misconception that there exists no viable, practical, attractive alternative to contemporary capitalism. Perhaps if people can be made properly aware of the fact that there *is* such an alternative—the democratic market socialist alternative—they will be able to perceive "people's capitalism" as the grossly distorted misrepresentation of reality which it actually is.

In summary, hard work, entrepreneurship, risk-taking, and other worthy and worthwhile human endeavors have very little to do with the rise of that tiny handful of the population which achieves the financially exalted status of wealthy capitalist. Upward capital wealth mobility is dominated by inheritance and chance. The great majority of large capital fortunes were founded on inheritances. Whether inherited fortunes then expand or contract is determined almost entirely by random chance. The probability that a given individual, who does *not* anticipate a substantial inheritance, will nevertheless become a wealthy capitalist, is vestigial, almost nonexistent—nor is this probability significantly enhanced by such worthy and worthwhile human endeavors as hard work, entrepreneurship, and risk-taking. Therefore, most people could and would do far better under market socialism.

VIRTUAL SOCIALISM THROUGH TAXATION

Contemporary capitalism is characterized by extreme inequality in capital wealth and property income. Most of the population receives little or nothing in the way of dividends, capital gains, and other components of property income, while at the same time a tiny minority of the population enjoys an extravagantly luxurious lifestyle financed with property income. This situation is even more objectionable owing to the fact that the technological and institutional evolution of contemporary capitalism has made property income into unearned, rental-type income, and also to the fact that inheritance and chance, rather than entrepreneurship and risk-taking, are the most important contributors to the unequal distribution of unearned property return. The principal objective of market socialism is therefore to rectify this economic injustice, to spread property income around more equitably over the entire population, to achieve a more equal distribution of unearned property income. The emphasis is merely on rectifying the extremely unequal distribution of capital property income; it is not on changing the functioning of the economy in deeper and more fundamental respects. In the advanced industrial nations, the economic system is characterized by an enviably high level of efficiency and dynamism. No harm in intended to these desirable qualities. The basic idea of market socialism is simply to capture significant equity benefits at minimum risk to the efficiency and dynamism of the economy.

This emphasis on efficiency rather than equity tends to elicit the idea that public ownership is not necessary to the intended purpose, that the benefits envisioned by market socialism could just as easily be attained by an appropriate expansion of the tax system. It is not necessary (so it is held) to have a public ownership agency collecting property return as it is disbursed by business enterprises; rather the same effect could be achieved through confiscatory taxation of property return as and when it is received by owning households. One could thereby attain "virtual socialism through taxation"—the elimination of maldistribution of capital property income, but without incurring the possible serious economic and political disadvantages of public ownership of business enterprises. In some respects, this idea represents the ultimate extension of the social democratic concept of "socialism." Social democratic "socialists" have long argued that public ownership is irrelevant, because the objective of bettering the individual human condition through social action does not necessarily require public ownership of capital and natural resources. (The quote marks are needed here because public ownership of the non-human factors of production is the operative definition of "socialism" used throughout this book.)

No doubt the possibility of virtual socialism through taxation is sometimes broached by individuals who are genuinely sympathetic to socialism, and who actually believe that it would be a good idea from the point of view of political practicality. They see it as a possible means of achieving the fundamental socialist objective of eliminating the maldistribution of capital property income—without incurring the "socialistic bugaboo" of public ownership of property. More commonly, however, this possibility is raised by opponents of socialism as a red herring with which to confuse the opposition. In this more common context, virtual socialism through taxation is simply a debater's tactic designed to discredit proponents of socialism by making them appear to be so obsessively fixated on public ownership that they fail to perceive obvious alternatives to public ownership for achieving the same ends. Those who invoke virtual socialism through taxation with this intention in mind are opposed to making any fundamental change in the distribution of capital wealth and property income, whether by means of public ownership of capital, confiscatory taxation of property income, or anything else.

It is important to be clear about what is meant by "virtual socialism through taxation" so as to avoid becoming entangled in extraneous matters. One such issue is what would be done with property return once it has been taken by the government, whether by means of collection from enterprises by a public ownership agency as per the proposal for democratic market socialism advanced herein, or by means of taxation of property income of households according to the methods already employed by the U.S. Internal Revenue Service for the taxation of general income. It makes a big difference whether this type of government revenue is plowed into general government expenditures on public goods and services (as is the case with most tax revenue today), or rather is turned around and redistributed directly to the public as a transfer payment. In order to compare as closely and fairly as possible the market socialist proposal put forward herein with virtual socialism through taxation, let us assume that the latter system would be exactly analogous to the former system both with respect to the proportion of property return taken by the government for social use, and with respect to the specific use made of these funds. According to the market socialist proposal, approximately 95 percent of total property return taken from enterprises by the public ownership agency would be immediately returned to the public in the form of a social dividend payment directly proportional to the household's wage and salary income. Therefore, let us define as virtual socialism through taxation a system under which 95 percent of property income received by households would be taxed away by the tax agency, and that the proceeds from this tax would *not* be plowed into general government expenditures, but would rather be immediately returned to the general public as a social dividend payment directly proportional to the household's wage and salary income. Such a system would indeed achieve through the use of taxation exactly the same equity objective intended by public ownership under market socialism. No doubt it would indeed be a major improvement over the present status quo. But as an alternative to standard public ownership socialism, it has some important problems.

To begin with, virtual socialism through taxation is not really a meaningful alternative to public ownership market socialism from the standpoint of political practicality. Although public ownership of capital is not part of the virtual socialism plan, still it would hardly be possible to "slip this by" the alert watchdogs of the capitalistic status quo. A proposed revision of the tax system of the necessary direction and magnitude would be instantly recognized by these watchdogs for what it is—namely an effort to achieve "socialism under another name." Most of the same objections to standard public ownership socialism, including all of the sensible ones, no doubt could and would be mustered against virtual socialism through taxation. In addition, the proponents of the new tax system could be plausibly characterized as dishonest and deceitful, as attempting to trick the people into accepting socialism through crude semantic subterfuge. Far from being a clever way of sidestepping the public's objections to socialism, any effort to implement confiscatory taxation of property income would become a public relations disaster. There is no way around the public's objections to socialism; they must be met head-on. The public must be persuaded that these objections are invalid. The public must itself reject these objections, and must understand clearly that its interests lie with democratic market socialism.

The fact is that if circumstances were to emerge under which confiscatory taxation of property income were to be a genuine political possibility, then those same circumstances would make public ownership socialism a genuine political possibility. Hopefully these circumstances will indeed emerge before too many more decades have gone by. Let us cast our minds forward to a period in time in which a substantial proportion of the population has come to recognize and appreciate the fact of maldistribution of capital wealth and property income under contemporary capitalism, and that social dividend distribution of property return is a viable alternative to the status quo, an alternative under which they personally would be significantly benefited in a basic financial sense. Two alternatives are being considered for the collection of property return for redistribution as social dividend income: (1) a public ownership agency which would collect property return as it emerges from business enterprises and redistribute 95 percent of it; (2) a tax agency such as the IRS which would take 95 percent of property income once it has been received by those households which do receive it, for purposes of redistribution. What reasons are these for deeming the first alternative to be the preferable alternative?

One consideration is the administrative costs of collection. It could be argued that we already have an Internal Revenue Service in place which is in annual contact with the vast majority of households, wheras a public ownership agency does not exist and would have to be established. On the other hand, if established, the public ownership agency would collect only from the relatively small number of business enterprises—not from the relatively huge number of households. As a matter of fact, if one is really concerned with the issue of administrative costs of collection, one might think seriously about eliminating personal income taxation of households altogether and collecting all tax revenues from enterprises, for example, through a value added tax of sufficient magnitude. The fact that we collect tax revenues as we do—and that we have done so for a long time prior to the development of modern computers and communications—suggests that the administrative costs of collection are not really that consequential after all. Aside from the direct costs of collection, there are psychological morale factors to be considered. When a household receives income—and then has to immediately turn over a large proportion of that income to the government—the people in that household have natural tendencies toward frustration, resentment, and hostility. Managers and employees of a business enterprise might have a more philosophical and tolerant attitude toward the payment of taxes, deeming them simply part of the costs of doing business. At the workplace level, the flow of income is "communal" in the sense that no one individual has a personal possession right to it. Therefore, the allocation of some of this business income to taxes does not have the same mentally painful effect as does the payment of personal income taxes. Since business enterprises are less disposed to tax evasion than private households, the costs of enforcement are less.

Questions about the administrative costs of collection pale into insignificance, however, when we consider the incentive implications of virtual socialism through taxation with respect to corporation executives. Even under the present system in which owners of capital wealth get the bulk of property income accruing to them (taxation of property income being essentially equivalent to taxation of labor income), the phenomenon of separation of ownership and control has created a situation in which the controls and constraints operative upon the corporate elite are seriously inadequate. The implementation of virtual socialism through taxation would make these controls and constraints even weaker and more inadequate. It is vitally necessary to the efficiency and dynamism of market socialism that there exist a public ownership agency armed with the power of dismissal over those corporation executives whose profit performance is very seriously substandard. The public ownership agency must be ready, willing, and able to utilize its power of dismissal freely and vigorously.

The separation of ownership and control (alternatively known as the separation of ownership and management) will be a recurrent term throughout this book owing to its absolutely central importance to the issue of the potential performance of market socialism. This separation is by far the most important single piece of circumstantial evidence suggesting that capital property return is not a return to capital management effort, and is indeed an unearned, rental-type return. It is essential not only to the argument that property income is unearned income, but also to the argument that quite conceivably democratic market socialism would actually achieve a *higher* level of efficiency than that currently achieved by capitalism. True, the primary objective of market socialism is a gain in equity, not a gain in efficiency. But the equity gain only becomes the operative consideration if the market socialist system is likely to achieve basically the same level of efficiency. Therefore, the efficiency consideration is vital, and in fact, the bulk of the analysis and argumentation in this book relates directly to the efficiency issue rather than to the equity issue. It is essential to defend the potential efficiency of market socialism. On the basis of the principle that often the best defense is a good offense, if it can be established that there is a good chance that market socialism would be *more efficient* than capitalism, then the case is won that market socialism would be *as efficient* as capitalism. At the same time, it is important that the potential efficiency gain not be exaggerated and overemphasized, since the equity gain is both more assured and clearly more important as a reason for implementing socialism.

As the separation of ownership and control will come up again in the course of our analysis of the potential efficiency of market socialism, its bearing on the possibility of virtual socialism through taxation will be very briefly described here. The separation of ownership and control is the term used to describe the typical circumstance of the large modern corporation: (1) the top executives of the corporation own a very small proportion of the total voting stock, the great majority of it being held by individuals with no direct involvement with the corporation either as an employee or a manager; (2) the great majority of voting stock held by individuals outside the corporation is highly atomized over a very large number of stockholders, each one of whom exercises only a small proportion of the total voting rights in the corporation. This situation significantly diminishes the pressure on the corporation's top executives to achieve a high rate of profitability, because it is very difficult for the stockholders to get themselves sufficiently organized to oust the top executives on grounds of poor performance. If one of the numerous outside stockholders in the corporation decides that the incumbent top managers are incompetent and should be replaced, there is little which he or she personally can do to implement this view. It would be necessary to contact other stockholders and argue them over to the same view with the intention of electing a new board of directors at the next annual stockholders' meeting, which would then dismiss the incumbent executives and find new ones. Such a course of action is in fact highly impractical for the individual stockholder. In practice, most stockholders in a given corporation who decide that the top managers of the corporation are incompetent make no effort whatsoever to have those managers ousted. Instead, they merely sell their stock shares in that corporation and invest the proceeds elsewhere. As a result, the performance of the typical corporation has to become truly abysmal before the board of directors becomes sufficiently galvanized to dismiss its top managers.

In theory, the selling of stock shares by dissatisfied stockholders puts pressure on the managers to improve profitability. Such sales reduce the prices of the company's securities in the capital markets, and thereby increase the cost of additional capital for investment and expansion. Ultimately, the added cost of capital could prove disastrous for the firm. Unable to replace worn-out equipment or to expand into new markets, in the long run it will lose its competitive edge and suffer bankruptcy. However, this theoretical mechanism seems very roundabout and leisurely when compared to a pink slip in the here and now. The premature termination of an executive's career with a corporation, by virtue of dismissal by the board of directors, is bound to have a much more immediate impact than gradual declines in stock share prices from gradual sales of stock by dissatisfied stockholders. The fear of being fired in the short run is a far more potent incentive to effort for a high corporation executive than is the mild anxiety caused by the possibility of corporate bankruptcy at some unspecified time in the remote future.

If a firm has a single owner or a small group of owners who dispose of a majority of the common stock voting rights, the probability of dismissal for inadequate profitability is far more meaningful to the high executives. They cannot take refuge in the fact that the stockholders are dispersed, unorganized, and unable to bring strong and focused pressure on the board of directors. There are a variety of ways in which market socialism might organize the relationship between the typical publicly owned firm and the public ownership authority. The specific proposal put forward in this book envisions a high degree of concentration of the ownership rights over the typical firm in the hands of a small number of agents of the public ownership authority—possibly in the hands of a single agent. This would create the equivalent of the single-owner situation or small-group ownership situation. The practical implication of this concentration of ownership rights is that there would be a substantially larger probability of dismissal confronting the high executives of business enterprises than there is currently under contemporary capitalism. Market socialism would so organize the public ownership authority that the separation of ownership and control would to a considerable extent be offset.

Under virtual socialism through taxation, there would be no public ownership authority of the sort implied by standard public ownership socialism. As a result, virtual socialism through taxation would entail further amplification of the adverse effects of the separation of ownership and control. Already under contemporary capitalism, high corporation executives have become a super-privileged, super-protected class of individuals. Instead of being properly awed and intimidated by the formal authority of the boards of directors, typically the incumbent high executives manipulate these boards like marionettes, treating them as casually as if they were mere employees of the corporation. They know that unless profitability becomes absolutely atrocious, they will be protected by the inertia built into the system by the separation of ownership and control. Thus high corporation executives with impunity award themselves exorbitant salaries which bear no relationship to their own economic contributions to the corporation. They *preside* over their corporations, with emphasis upon lunch breaks, pointless staff meetings, and lavish "entertainment," rather than *managing* them, with emphasis upon close study and rigorous analysis of tough business problems. The institutional flexibility of market socialism would provide the means by which society could tighten the reins on the corporate elite. This opportunity would be wasted if society were to go the route of virtual socialism through taxation. Therefore, virtual socialism through taxation must be rejected as a viable alternative to public ownership market socialism.

CAPITALISM IS NOT BEST

Even Karl Marx acknowledged that modern capitalism has achieved an impressive level of performance. What was true in Marx's time is even more dramatically evident today. Assisted by marvelous technological advances and ever more intensive utilization of the world's natural resource base, contemporary capitalism has achieved a standard of living in the industrially advanced nations that would have been deemed unbelievable even in Marx's time, to say nothing of earlier times. True, this standard of living is enjoyed only by a relatively small fraction of the earth's population. Capitalism has not performed so brilliantly in places like Brazil, to say nothing of India. This alerts us to the fact that there is nothing necessarily magical in capitalism in and of itself, defined as private ownership of the nonhuman factors of production (capital and natural resources). One needs more than private ownership of the means of production to achieve prosperity on a wide scale. On the other hand, it is also clear that socialism, in and of itself, is not necessarily a cure for poverty. After all, socialistic China is not very much better off, if at all, than capitalistic India.

Confining our attention to the rich nations (the United States, the nations of Western Europe, and a few others around the world), it must be recognized and acknowledged by all sensible proponents of socialism that capitalism in these nations has brought about an average standard of life qualitatively beyond anything ever witnessed in the entire prior history of human civilization. It is trite but true that even common people in these nations today enjoy living standards superior to those of exalted kings and queens in past eras. It must also be recognized and acknowledged that economic inequality under contemporary capitalism is significantly less than anything witnessed since the dawn of organized human civilization. The gap between the richest and poorest members of society is less now than it has ever been. But even granting all this, the fact remains that there are few things on this earth so good that they cannot possibly be improved upon. And in this very small category of the absolutely unimprovable—capitalism does *not* belong.

Any sensible person recognizes the need for a certain amount of inequality. One cannot rely entirely on innate tendencies toward goodness and duty, nor upon generalized public spiritedness, to elicit that individual effort upon which our prosperity depends. Material incentives to effort are important—even essential. It is fully appropriate that those who make more of a contribution should get more of a reward. We do in fact observe a substantial amount of inequality with respect to wage and salary income (i.e., labor income), and the proposal being advanced here for democratic market socialism involves nothing whatever in the way of public policy aimed at reducing inequality in labor income. The intent of the proposal is solely and exclusively to achieve a higher level of equality in the distribution of capital property return. This is because the level of inequality in this particular type of income under contemporary capitalism has achieved extraordinary proportions, and unlike inequality in

labor income, this degree of inequality is not necessary to the maintenance of adequate material incentives to effort. Unlike labor income,
capital property income is not earned income. Therefore, contemporary
capitalism, for all of its virtues, possesses one irredeemable vice: it perpetuates an extremely unequal distribution of unearned capital property
income. Since this situation is not required on grounds on economic efficiency, it constitutes an offense against social equity. In consequence,
democratic market socialism would be a superior alternative to the presently existing democratic market capitalism. Capitalism is not best.

Throughout this book a consistent effort is made to avoid rhetorical
exaggeration and overstatement of the case. In this spirit, a few comments need to be made here. The problem with contemporary capitalism
is not simply a matter of there being some people with very large wealth.
The purpose of market socialism is hardly to eliminate large fortunes, nor
to make the achievement of large fortunes in the future impossible. For
example, consider the kind of people whose living standards are show-
cased on the popular television series *Lifestyles of the Rich and Famous*.
Most of them are people who would be as wealthy under the proposed
system of market socialism as they are now under capitalism. Popular
culture superstars (Kevin Costner, Madonna, etc.) would receive the
same personal services incomes under market socialism as they do presently under capitalism, because these incomes, as astronomical as they
may seem to ordinary mortals, are in a technical sense labor incomes.
The same would be true of athletic superstars. Similarly, self-made entrepreneurs in the mold of Bill Gates, founder of Microsoft, would accumulate the same large fortunes under market socialism as they do under
capitalism, owing to the exception to the rule of social ownership of
business enterprise made for entrepreneurial firms.

The actual problem with contemporary capitalism is that most large
capital fortunes are owned by people who would never even be considered for *Lifestyles of the Rich and Famous* because they do not meet the
"famous" criterion. They did nothing to earn their fortunes, but rather
achieved them through a combination of inheritance and random appreciation. Even if the *Lifestyles* program did want to examine the living
standards of these people, no doubt they would decline to participate.
Unlike the handful of self-made superstars and entrepreneurs who are legitimately proud of the wealth they have achieved through their own efforts, these other wealthy capitalists are quite conscious of the fact that
they have never done anything in their lives that would justify the luxury
which they presently enjoy. They would much rather keep their living

standards to themselves and not flaunt them before the general public. After all, one cannot be too careful, and there are few wealthy capitalists so completely smug and complacent to dismiss the possibility of heavier taxation of the wealthy—to say nothing of the possibility of socialism itself. Among that small proportion of the population which may be legitimately characterized as wealthy capitalists, a far larger proportion consists of low-profile inheriting rentiers than the high-profile self-made superstars and entrepreneurs who populate *Lifestyles of the Rich and Famous.*

Some qualifications should be provided concerning inheritance—a term which often recurs in this discussion. One of these is to counter a possible impression that market socialism is totally opposed to inheritance, and that it intends to suppress inheritances entirely. No doubt it is true that dramatic equalization in capital wealth could be achieved simply by confiscatory taxation of personal inheritances, even in the absence of public ownership socialism. Much the same objection would apply to this option as applies to the full-scale "virtual socialism through taxation" discussed in the previous section. Specifically, under circumstances of separation of ownership and control, greater capital wealth equality would tend to enhance the already excessively privileged and protected status of the corporate elite. But beyond this is the fact that inheritance by itself is not necessarily a sufficient offense to social equity to require suppression. What makes inheritance under capitalism so objectionable is the fact that inherited capital wealth produces property income. The recipient of the inheritance therefore receives not only the original value of the inheritance, but a potentially perpetual source of income that over time could cumulate to many times the original value. If market socialism were to eliminate property income on financial wealth, so that an inheritance of, say, $1 million, would represent no more than $1 million worth of purchasing power, then quite possibly inheritance would be fully acceptable.

Another qualification may be needed to counteract a possible impression that advocates of market socialism necessarily make an excessive estimate of the persistence of capital wealth through successive generations of inheriting capitalists. Sensible socialists will recognize and acknowledge that even the very largest capital fortunes will not be perpetuated indefinitely through inheritance. The dissipative factors (such as multiplicity of heirs, spendthrift heirs, unlucky heirs, etc.) will eventually win out, and finally even the last remnants of the fortune will peter out. Nevertheless, between the initial accumulation and the final dispersal, several generations of inheriting capitalists, comprising dozens or even hundreds of individuals, will have enjoyed standards of living dramatically above anything they could have afforded on the basis of their own earnings. This is simply not right—it is not just. Especially when it is recognized that the income which purchases extravagant luxury for a handful of wealthy capitalists under capitalism could instead under market socialism be broadly distributed as social dividend income over the entire population, leading to a modest but appreciable gain in the living standards of many millions of deserving, hard-working people.

Admittedly, justice is a very subjective quality. Often, what seems just to a particular individual seems to depend not so much on the merits of the case itself, but on how the case is perceived by that individual. Most individuals today have it firmly fixed in their minds that socialism is unviable and unworkable, and that it would be so destructive of material incentives to effort as to cause economic efficiency and productivity to plummet to abysmal depths. Thus when they conclude that the capitalist system of distributing property return is indeed adequately just and equitable—despite the extraordinary amount of inequality in that distribution, and despite the protests lodged by socialists over almost two hundred years of dissent—they are in reality merely making a virtue out of perceived necessity. They rationalize the status quo, by means of swallowing blatant falsehoods about capital property income being mostly a legitimate return to noble entrepreneurial endeavor, quite simply because they can see no meaningful alternative to the status quo.

But there is no need to rationalize and accept this morally perverse, ethically illegitimate status quo. There is in fact a viable, workable, and fully attractive alternative to the capitalist status quo. This alternative is democratic market socialism. It is to this alternative that we now turn. Chapter 3 traces the development of the market socialist idea, reviews several market socialist options, and develops a specific market socialist proposal. Chapter 4 uses this specific proposal as a basis for analyzing the various arguments which may be advanced in favor of the capitalist status quo. In the light cast by the democratic market socialist alternative, the serious dysfunctionalism of contemporary capitalism may be clearly perceived.

3

THE MARKET SOCIALIST IDEA

The term "market socialism" is of recent origin, dating from the seminal work of the mainstream economist Oskar Lange (1904-1965) in the 1930s. Prior to Lange, it was generally assumed, both by pro-socialists and anti-socialists, that socialism and the market were contradictory, incompatible, and antithetical. Marx's famous phrase "anarchy of the market" epitomized the extremely negative attitude toward the free market which has been customary among traditional socialists. To Marx, private ownership of capital, the economic marketplace, and exploitation, were three inseparable and codependent facets of the capitalist socioeconomic system—thus, getting rid of one of them meant getting rid of all three.

For their part, orthodox, mainstream economists have tended to glorify the market as the operative mechanism of the famous "invisible hand," a powerful metaphor advanced in Adam Smith's *Wealth of Nations* (1776). The invisible hand guides the economy toward its benign consummation, ensuring that the pursuit of private self-interest by individuals promotes the social good (e.g., bakers advance their private prosperity by providing the bread needed by others for sustaining their own life, health, and happiness). Smith himself expressed his pro-laissez faire message in relatively restrained terms, citing a number of important caveats and qualifications—cases in which the unrestrained and unregulated pursuit of private self-interest would *not* have such beneficial social consequences. By the early nineteenth century, however, during Marx's intellectually formative period, enthusiasm for laissez faire among many influential mainstream economists had developed to such a point that the caveats and qualifications emphasized by Adam Smith were mostly ignored. Marx responded to this deification of the market by those he dubbed "vulgar economists" with an equally exaggerated and unrestrained vilification of the market.

The consensus mainstream attitude today toward the economic market is that it is indeed, just as Adam Smith argued, a powerful engine toward economic efficiency and social welfare—but also that this is an engine which requires a substantial amount of social intervention and control in order to achieve optimal performance. This general consensus was well established by the second half of the nineteenth century. Ever since then, the precise nature and degree of social intervention and control which is most desirable has remained a subject of perpetual, intensive debate between conservatives (favoring less intervention and control) and liberals (favoring more). Attitudes toward and judgments on the specific proposals for social intervention and control which come forward over time are largely determined by preconceptions regarding the usual consequences of government activity: in the view of liberals, healthy; in the view of conservatives, unhealthy. The primacy of preconceptions in determining judgment is owing to the fact that the available objective evidence concerning the probable impact of implementation of various proposals for social intervention and control is usually quite limited and inconclusive.

The continuum of social intervention and control is in fact a smooth and infinitely differentiated continuum, so that it is a matter of purely arbitrary semantics at which point social intervention and control becomes so comprehensive and extensive that the economy is no longer properly describable as a "market economy" but rather as a "regulated economy," "coordinated economy," "planned economy," or some such alternative term. Generally speaking, traditional socialists have considered that the achievement of "socialism," whether defined in the public ownership sense or the social democratic sense, would involve a sufficient amount of social intervention and control that the economy could not legitimately be referred to as a market economy. This judgment has normally been shared by anti-socialists. Particularly since the seminal work of Oskar Lange on market socialism in the 1930s, however, an increasing number of both pro-socialists and anti-socialists have adjusted their perceptions and usages in such a way that the term "market economy" properly applies over a larger range of the continuum of social intervention and control.

The overall continuum of social intervention and control is in fact composed of a number of important subsidiary continuums, of which some of the more important are as follows: (1) the proportion of the total stock of capital and natural resources (i.e., nonhuman factors of production) which is publicly rather than privately owned; (2) the proportion of aggregate income which is taxed away and devoted to provision of public goods (police and fire protection, roads, national defense, etc.); (3) the proportion of aggregate income which is taxed away and devoted to transfer payments (agricultural subsidies, social security, welfare benefits, etc.); (4) the degree of progressivity of the tax and welfare system, as measured by the relative inequality of pre-tax-and-benefit income and post-tax-and-benefit income; (5) the degree of regulation of private behavior; (6) the degree of regulation of business activity.

According to the strict public ownership interpretation of socialism which is being utilized throughout this book, only the first of these continuums would be the operative criterion for characterizing an economy as either "capitalist" or "socialist." For example, in the United States today, depending on how the "capital stock" is defined (using this term in the general sense as a proxy for the entire range of nonhuman factors of production), somewhere between 15 and 25 percent of this stock is publicly owned, and the U.S. economy is clearly a capitalist economy. Under the system of democratic market socialism proposed herein, since most large, established business enterprises would be publicly owned—which implies that somewhere between 70 and 80 percent of capital stock would be publicly owned, the U.S. economy would clearly be a socialist economy. But if there were an approximately equal mix of public and private enterprise, say 40 to 60 percent of the capital stock publicly owned, then it might not be so obvious whether the U.S. economy should be characterized as "capitalist" or "socialist." We might instead consider terming the economy "mixed" or "hybrid."

According to the social democratic interpretation of the term (*not* utilized herein), "socialism" is defined in terms of *general* social intervention and control, not in terms of the level of public ownership of capital. The level of public ownership of capital might be fairly low (the 15 to 25 percent currently prevalent in the United States), and yet an economy might be appropriately characterized as socialist if the position attained on the other continuums after the first listed above were sufficiently high (i.e., if a sufficient proportion of aggregate income were taxed away and devoted to public goods or transfer payments, if there were a sufficient degree of progressivity in the public revenue and expenditure system, if there were a sufficient degree of regulation of business activity). If we were to use this interpretation of socialism, it would make the determination of whether a nation were capitalist or socialist a very arbitrary and subjective matter.

The United States, for example, is characterized by a substantial proportion of aggregate income taxed away and devoted to public goods and transfer payments, by a substantial degree of progressivity in the public revenue and expenditure system, by a substantial degree of regulation of business activity. Is the United States therefore "capitalist" or "socialist"? Far right-wing conservatives are fond of affirming (with horror) that the United States is indeed "socialist"; while far left-wing liberals are adamant that the United States has a long way to go before it could be considered remotely socialist. Neither side has any meaningful, quantitative grounds for these statements. The social democratic interpretation of socialism, involving as it does some unspecified weighted average of positions on a variety of continuums of social intervention and control, is inherently vague and obscure. The question of whether the United States is capitalist or socialist would be far less muddled if the simple public ownership criterion were applied. In fact, this is the criterion utilized herein, and on this criterion it may be clearly and unambiguously stated that the United States is not presently a socialist nation.

The question of whether the United States has a market economy or a nonmarket economy is in principle just as obscure and muddled as whether the United States economy is capitalist or socialist in the social democratic sense. But the general consensus, which will certainly be followed here, is that the United States clearly has a market capitalist economy—the economy is capitalist rather than socialist, and is also market-oriented rather than nonmarket-oriented. Social intervention and control of the United States economy may be quite substantial, but it has not become so absolutely overwhelming and confining that the market basis of economic activity has been suppressed and obliterated. At least this would be the judgment of all those other than those same far right-wing conservatives who would also assert that the United States is a "socialist" nation.

The reason for this situation, no doubt, is that it would be completely impossible to suppress and obliterate the market basis of economic activity, particularly where large-scale human societies are concerned. Any serious effort to do so, even if made by a powerful totalitarian state, would cause an immense amount of confusion, dislocation, and inefficiency, and would almost certainly be doomed to ultimate failure. The market is an essential integrative and coordinative instrument for the economic processes of production and distribution within any large and populous polity. The essence of the market is the delegation of substantial economic decision-making authority to individuals within the context of monetary valuation and exchange of commodities. There must be a monetary unit of relatively stable value, all or most commodities must be freely exchangeable for the monetary unit (that is to say, commodities must be priced), and individuals making production and consumption decisions on the basis of these prices must be allowed a high degree of autonomy.

The typical understanding of "pure planning" among economists is an economic system which would have no money and no pricing of commodities, and in which all decisions on physical production, distribution, and consumption would be made within a single, hierarchically organized government agency. Nothing remotely approaching such a system has ever been witnessed throughout the entire history of human civilization. The most dramatic effort in modern history at centralization of economic authority and central planning of the economy was made in the Soviet Union during the Stalinist period. Soviet-style central planning involved a very significant degree of social intervention and control beyond what has been standard in the United States and the nations of Western Europe—but it still stopped well short of "pure planning." Under the Soviet system, money existed and was used, commodities were valued and exchanged according to monetary prices, households had considerable autonomy in deciding on where to work and how to spend their incomes, and managers of business firms had appreciable consultative input into the production and distribution decisions made by the central planners in Moscow. All these characteristics of the "centrally planned Soviet economy" are inconsistent with "pure planning" as commonly understood by economists.

The operative meaning of "centrally planned socialism," as opposed to "pure planning," was set by the planned economic system established in the U.S.S.R. in the late 1920s and early 1930s under the direction of the dictator Joseph Stalin, and which persisted, essentially unchanged, until the dissolution of the Soviet Union in the early 1990s. The heart of this system consisted of a very large and authoritative national government bureaucracy called Gosplan (the State Planning Agency). Each year all productive enterprises were required to prepare detailed plans for production and distribution of commodities during the following year. These plans were submitted to Gosplan, which integrated them all, made appropriate modifications, and then promulgated the revised plans back to the enterprises as strict requirements. Generally speaking, the revised plans called for unrealistically large increases in production of output commodities, given the input factors allowed to the enterprise. This characteristic of the system led to its being dubbed in the West the "taut planning" system. Performance of individual firm managers was largely evaluated on the basis of adherence to plan output goals. Penalties for nonfulfillment of output goals were severe—during the Stalinist period an unsuccessful firm manager might end up in a punitive labor camp in Siberia.

In terms of the continuums discussed above, Gosplan-directed central planning is most accurately conceived of as a very high setting on the continuum representing "regulation of business enterprise." In the market economy of the United States, regulation is confined to such things as the length of the working day, minimum wage specifications, safety conditions, effluent standards, certain business practices affecting the degree of competition in the market, and so on. Regulation does not extend to the specification of exactly how much of each output good is to be produced, nor to exactly how much of each input factor (types of labor and machinery) is to be utilized in their production. If we were to conceive of the continuum of governmental regulation of business as running from a theoretical minimum of 1 to a theoretical maximum of 100, then the contemporary United States economy might be represented by a number somewhere between 20 and 30, while the Soviet economy during the heyday of central planning from the 1930s through the 1950s might be represented by a number somewhere between 70 and 80. The same comparison applied to the continuum for public ownership of capital would show an even greater divergence: 15 to 25 percent public ownership in the United States, compared to 80 to 90 percent public ownership in the U.S.S.R.

The premise on which the market socialist idea is based is that there is a relatively high degree of *independence* between the various types of social intervention and control: that society possesses the option of setting itself at a relatively high level along one of the continuums mentioned above, while at the same time setting itself at a relatively low level along others. More specifically, that society possesses the option of setting itself at a relatively high level on the public ownership of capital continuum (a level as high as that witnessed in the Soviet Union throughout most of its history), and at the same time at relatively low levels on the other continuums (levels as low as those witnessed in the United States at the present time).

This premise could and would be contested by those located at opposite ends of the ideological judgment spectrum on socialism in the public ownership sense. It would be contested by far right-wing anti-socialists (e.g., Austrian school adherents) who would insist that an undesirably high setting on the public ownership of capital continuum leads naturally to undesirably high settings on most if not all of the other continuums of social intervention and control. It would also be contested by far left-wing pro-socialists (e.g., traditional hardline Marxists) who would insist that a desirably high setting on the public ownership of capital continuum "naturally implies" desirably high settings on most if not all of the other continuums. That both ends of this ideological spectrum are wrong on this matter is a fundamental argument of this book—an argument which is always implicit and frequently explicit throughout the entire discussion.

The notion that socialism and the free market are incompatible has deep roots in both the intellectual and the real-world history of socialism. As to intellectual history, an anti-market theme runs consistently through the work of Marx and the other founding fathers of socialism in the nineteenth century. This theme has been continued by numerous advocates of socialism down to the present day. This anti-market attitude is largely owing to the failure by these advocates to properly distinguish economic market processes in general from those specific economic market processes stemming directly from the highly concentrated private ownership of capital under modern capitalism. To some extent this failure stems from the generally low level of economic knowledge and understanding among past advocates of socialism. Another factor, possibly even more important, is the failure of almost all past advocates of socialism to think seriously about the socialist economy of the future. Following the lead of Marx, who declined to "write recipes for the social cooks of the future," they presumed that the economic institutions and processes of socialism would emerge naturally and spontaneously, and would not require serious forethought. Of course, had these advocates been armed with a sound knowledge of economics, and had they thought carefully about the economic workings of socialism, they might have realized the sensibility of maintaining much of the same economic market workings already familiar from capitalism.

When Lenin, Trotsky, and the other leaders of the Russian Revolution of 1917 gained control over the Russian empire previously ruled by the Romanov dynasty, they had little guidance from Karl Marx on which to rely for purposes of designing the practical institutions and operations of socialism. Nevertheless, they at least had sufficient sense to ignore those unhinged extremists, both within the Bolshevik party and within other radical parties of the time, who urged the abolition of money, prices, interest rates, profits, and all other economic concepts and categories associated with the market economy. In fact, as a means of recovering from the economic devastation caused by Russia's disastrous participation in

World War I and Russia's equally disastrous civil war following the 1917 Revolution, the ruling Communist Party of the U.S.S.R. promulgated the New Economic Policy (NEP) in the early 1920s, a policy which in its practical operations was remarkably similar to the market socialist proposal being advanced in this book. The fledgling U.S.S.R. flourished under the NEP, and made rapid progress toward reestablishing the prewar level of material welfare. Gosplan-directed central planning of the sort which later became associated with the U.S.S.R. did not commence until almost 10 years after the Bolsheviks first gained control of the country. And as already pointed out, this planning system, when it was finally established, did indeed retain monetary values, pricing systems, and many other central features of the capitalist market system. Just as Lenin and his associates had not been so foolish as to contemplate abrogating the market (despite Marx's proclamation of its "anarchic" nature), neither did Stalin and his associates.

The argument might be made that once the privately owned capital stock in Russia had been socialized in the early days of the Revolution, the emergence of Gosplan-style central planning was rendered inevitable—merely a matter of time. Once the state legally owns all or most business enterprises (so it could be argued), the natural temptation toward intrusive control of business enterprises by government agencies will eventually win out. Private ownership of capital creates legal, institutional, and cultural barriers to intrusive social control of business enterprise, and the elimination of private ownership removes these barriers. The ultimate result will be micromanagement by the state: business enterprises will eventually be issued strict instructions concerning exactly what to produce and exactly how to produce it.

This argument finds little support in the actual history of central planning in the U.S.S.R. The central planning system there did not emerge slowly and gradually—it was imposed very suddenly and comprehensively following an explicit decision by the ruling Communist Party hierarchy. Central planning was part of a gigantic three-pronged modernization campaign involving (1) collectivization of agriculture, (2) central planning of industry, and (3) forced-pace industrialization financed by a brutal austerity program. The purpose of the campaign was perceived as the preservation of the socialistic Soviet homeland, by means of building up a modern military machine supported by a technologically advanced armaments industry, from invasion by a fearful and extremely hostile capitalistic outer world. It was the perceived external threat, combined with the complete lack of democracy within the U.S.S.R., which explains the emergence of central planning there in the late 1920s and early 1930s. If we imagine a system of market socialism within a democratic polity not in undue fear of its military security, and if we imagine that that system of market socialism had deliberately been established as a conscious alternative to centrally planned socialism on the Soviet model, then there would be little danger of "creeping centralization of economic authority" simply owing to formal ownership of the capital stock by the state.

Turning to the history of social democratic socialism in the non-Communist world, we encounter another possible argument to the effect that a high level of public ownership of capital implies a high setting along all or most of the other continuums of social intervention and control. In the late nineteenth and early twentieth centuries, the revisionist social democrats abandoned two fundamental tenets of traditional Marxist socialism: the need for violent proletarian revolution in order to establish socialism, and the need for public ownership of capital as the defining characteristic of socialism. The first abandonment was a fully sensible reaction to the development of political democracy in the advanced capitalist nations—certainly if it were possible to effect fundamental social change by means of violent revolution, it would be much easier to effect that same change by winning elections. The second abandonment was motivated by the fact that socialists found from experience that it was much easier to implement reformist programs such as unemployment insurance, social security, and progressive income taxation, than it was to implement public ownership of capital. This is owing to the fact that private ownership of capital is the essential defining characteristic of capitalism, that characteristic which wealthy capitalists will defend to the last. Reformist social legislation might impinge noticeably upon the luxurious living standards of wealthy capitalists, but public ownership of capital would cut the taproot of those living standards.

Social democratic parties in Western Europe and elsewhere have been quite successful throughout the twentieth century, often sitting in the highest government offices and implementing a large proportion of the social programs contained in their platforms as of the beginning of the century. Once established, many of these programs soon became accepted parts of the status quo, so that when conservative parties eventually regained control of the government, the programs were retained rather than abrogated. Generally speaking, the far left wings of the social democratic parties have continued to maintain that the level of social programs achieved has not yet reached the level at which the respective nations could be described as fully and unambiguously "socialist." In the eyes of the more radical elements of social democracy, there is still too much economic injustice in society—the wealthy live too lavishly and the poor live too penuriously—for society to be legitimately socialist.

Let us consider the argument which might be extracted from the above-described situation by someone who believes that public ownership of capital will necessarily and significantly increase the level of social intervention and control of the economic market. It could be hypothesized that the real reason why left-wing social democrats are frustrated in their attempts to extend social programs to the point where even *they* would be satisfied that "socialism" had been achieved, is that the social democratic parties have never been able to achieve public ownership of the preponderance of capital stock. That is to say, private ownership of capital creates various tangible and intangible barriers to the extension and amplification of such social democratic programs as progressive income taxation, welfare benefits, and business regulation. Remove private ownership of capital, and these programs will proceed to grow without restraint, until they have assumed cancerous dimensions.

This argument is too farfetched to be taken very seriously. In all probability, what constrains the further growth of social democratic programs such as progressive income taxation and the like is not that public ownership socialism does not exist, but rather that these programs, for the most part, have already long since reached their approximately optimal levels. In fact, there is nothing logically contradictory in a given individual very much favoring democratic market socialism such as proposed herein, and yet believing that in most of the advanced capitalist nations, the welfare state and the regulatory state became somewhat overdeveloped in the 1960s and 1970s. Such an individual might even have approved of much of the policy of such conservative political leaders of the 1980s as Ronald Reagan in the U.S. and Margaret Thatcher in the U.K.—while of course disagreeing with the propensity of these same leaders toward veritable deification of the term "capitalism." What these leaders were pursuing was not the rebirth of capitalism (that institution had never been seriously challenged in their respective nations). Rather what they were pursuing (and to a large extent achieved) was the rebirth of the laissez faire, noninterventionist philosophy of government associated with the early nineteenth century.

The assumption of power and the rollback of interventionism by conservative political parties in the 1980s created opportunities for the social democratic parties—just as in physics, the swing of a pendulum toward the right sets up conditions for a counterswing toward the left. Thus the Democrat Bill Clinton brought the Republican Reagan-Bush era to an end with his election to the U.S. presidency in 1992. (The Democratic Party in the United States is analogous to the typical social democratic party in Europe, while the Republican Party is analogous to the typical conservative party.) In the larger view, the policy changes over which the conservative and social democratic parties have debated energetically over the last few decades are actually quite minor, amounting to a few small degrees either way over a 180-degree spectrum. The political and socio-economic status quo in the non-Communist world was remarkably stable throughout the Cold War period which extended over most of the second half of the twentieth century. The external threat no doubt overshadowed internal problems and issues, and dampened internal dissent against the status quo—such dissent being widely regarded as tending to give aid and comfort to a dangerous foreign enemy.

The paramount objective of social democratic parties, no less than of conservative parties, is to win elections and take office. Thus the recent swing toward a more conservative, pro-laissez faire attitude among both the intelligentsia and the general public has induced the social democratic parties to gravitate noticeably to the right. Meanwhile, the conservative parties have maintained their relative position a bit to the right of the social democrats. Both sides have learned that in order to win elections and take office, it is necessary to be a *little bit* different from one's political opponents—but not *too much* different. The social democrats have believed throughout the twentieth century that a serious effort at public ownership socialism on their part would preclude winning elections and taking office; thus no such effort has been made. On the other hand, they have found it possible to make considerable progress in the direction of social intervention and control along other continuums than the public ownership continuum. This fact effectively challenges the allegation that a high level of public ownership of capital would lead to a dramatic expansion of the welfare state and the regulatory state beyond what we know today.

Rather, what the history of twentieth-century social democracy strongly suggests is the *independence* of public ownership of capital from the other dimensions of social intervention and control. It has often been remarked that "practically everything" demanded by the early twentieth-century social democratic parties has, by the end of the century, been implemented. This happened despite any significant progress in the non-Communist world on the public ownership dimension. In fact, as far as programs specifically identified with the "welfare state" are concerned, in Western Europe these programs are not far short of those which were established in the Soviet Union. The "cradle to grave" welfare state in the Scandinavian nations is particularly well known—to some conservatives, particularly notorious. If there were any sort of direct correlation between the level of public ownership of capital and the size of the welfare state, then the welfare state in the non-Communist world would never have achieved the magnitude which it did achieve. The fact that a dramatic increase in the welfare state took place, without any appreciable increase in public ownership of capital, suggests that an increase in public ownership of capital can take place without an increase in the welfare state.

This is turn suggests the feasibility of market socialism: of an economic system which would display a high level of public ownership of capital, and yet a relatively low level of progressive income taxation, welfare programs, business regulation, and so on. In an industrially advanced economy, public ownership of almost all large, established (i.e., nonentrepreneurial) business enterprises would imply a minimum of from 70 to 80 percent of capital owned by the public ownership agency. But this high level of public ownership of capital could be combined with a welfare state no more extensive than that which is witnessed presently, a regulatory state no more extensive than that which is witnessed presently, and in general a level of social intervention and control on the other relevant continuums no more extensive than that which is witnessed presently.

The concept of market socialism is still fairly alien both to traditional pro-socialists, and to traditional anti-socialists. It represents a fundamentally new, fundamentally revised concept of socialism—even though it is a fully sensible concept of socialism and is indeed fully consistent with the primary definition of socialism to be found in almost every dictionary. At the beginning of the twentieth century, the term "market socialism" was unknown; but by the middle of the twentieth century the term was well established in Western thinking on comparative economic systems. What caused this important development in the intellectual history of socialism? By far the single most important figure was an individual by the name of Oskar Lange. It is to Lange's contribution that we now turn.

OSKAR LANGE: FATHER OF MARKET SOCIALISM

Oskar Lange was a young man in his early 30s when he published a lengthy essay titled "On the Economic Theory of Socialism" in two installments in the *Review of Economic Studies* (October 1936 and February 1937). This essay was the principal component of a book of the same name, published by the University of Minnesota Press in 1938, which also contained essays by Benjamin Lippincott (the volume editor) and Fred M. Taylor. Taylor's short essay ("The Guidance of Production in a Socialist State") had been his presidential address to the American Economic Association in 1928, and had appeared in the *American Economic Review* in March 1929. The Taylor essay speculated that efficient production might conceivably be possible under social ownership of capital, but the speculation was rather vague, and the principal role of Taylor's essay in the book version of "On the Economic Theory of Socialism" was simply to legitimize Lange's contribution, which went into the problem of efficient production under socialism in far greater detail. The University of Minnesota volume was reprinted in 1964 by McGraw-Hill, and it remained in print for a prolonged period thereafter.

The effect of Lange's essay on the economics profession was greatly magnified by Abram Bergson's article on "Socialist Economics," included in the American Economic Association's *A Survey of Contemporary Economics*, edited by Howard Ellis and published in 1948. Intended as a self-contained review of "all modern economics," the book contained survey articles on all the important branches of economics by such leading authorities as John Kenneth Galbraith and Paul Samuelson. For obvious reasons, it enjoyed very wide distribution among professional economists. At the time the book was planned, "socialist economics," owing largely to Lange's "On the Economic Theory of Socialism," was considered a sufficiently well-defined and professionally reputable area of economic inquiry to be included. Moreover, Bergson's appraisal of Lange was fairly positive. According to Bergson, Lange's market socialist proposal successfully responded to what had been, in the past, an extremely important line of criticism of socialism. On the other hand, Bergson perceived serious difficulties with Lange's proposal, and although he implied that it might well work better in practice than the centrally planned Soviet socialist system, he also expressed doubt that it would function as well in practice as the status quo economic system in the West: market capitalism. Bergson's final verdict on Lange's market socialist proposal came down essentially to: "interesting in theory—but unpromising in practice." This verdict has been adopted by the great majority of economists ever since Abram Bergson's 1948 article on "Socialist Economics."

Two key factors contributed to the very substantial impact of Lange's seminal work on market socialism within the economics profession: (1) the difficult situation confronting Western capitalism during the 1930s; (2) Lange's personal prestige as a brilliant mathematical economist.

With respect to the first factor, it must be recalled that the 1930s witnessed the greatest economic catastrophe ever to afflict modern capitalism: the Great Depression. Between the stock market crash of October 1929, and the trough of the Depression in 1933, the unemployment rate rose from 3.2 percent to 24.9 percent (an historic high). The Federal Reserve Board Index of Manufacturing Production in 1932 was only 52 percent of its value in 1929. Such a precipitous and calamitous economic decline had never been experienced before, and it has never been experienced since. As if the economic disaster were not enough in itself, during the early 1930s a painful contrast emerged between the capitalist world prostrated by the Great Depression, and the growing, vibrant socialist economy of the Soviet Union, then embarked on the first of its extraordinarily ambitious Five Year Plans. A mental projection of the existing trends in the early 1930s over an extended period would clearly suggest that socialism would eventually surpass capitalism. Quite a few people did in fact engage in this kind of mental projection. Both in the real world and the intellectual world, capitalism went on the defensive. Serious questions began to be raised in many quarters about the capitalistic status quo.

The "window of opportunity" created by the Great Depression for reinvigorating the socialist critique of capitalism did not remain open for very long. In the United States, the Depression bottomed out just as the voters elected the vigorous, confident Franklin D. Roosevelt to the presidency. The actual fiscal input into the economy involved in the multitude of Rooseveltian New Deal programs was actually fairly limited, and the rate of economic recovery was only minimally above what would have transpired had the laissez faire-oriented Herbert Hoover remained in office. But the impression of an activist, caring national government reassured the citizens and enabled them to better withstand the privation and uncertainties of widespread unemployment. As for the booming Soviet Union, the Moscow purge trials of the late 1930s severely discredited the economic achievements of the regime, giving credence to the arguments of conservatives that Soviet economic progress was being built on the blood and bones of a suffering population. As the 1930s drew to a close, concerns about a looming world war overrode social criticism. In any event, the last vestiges of the Great Depression were routed by the world-wide arms buildup inspired by the saber-rattling fascist powers of Germany, Italy, and Japan. When World War II finally descended upon hapless humanity, the various struggles for national survival eliminated any possibility for further development of the socialist critique of capitalism.

But by that time, Lange's contribution had had sufficient impact not to be entirely forgotten. The substantial impact of Lange depended not only on the disarray and ferment caused by the Great Depression, but also on Lange's considerable personal prestige as an economist. A native of Poland, Lange emigrated to England in the 1920s, and later went on to the United States. At that time, mathematical modes of inquiry were not as dominant in economics as they later became, but they were beginning to gain firm footholds throughout the discipline. Lange's education had included exposure to considerable higher mathematics, and he was well equipped to employ mathematical methods. Prior to writing "On the Economic Theory of Socialism," he had in fact published a large amount of "orthodox" research in economic theory and econometrics, and he was generally regarded as "one of our leading young economists." Lange's "orthodox" work was continued after the appearance of his seminal essay on market socialism, and he eventually achieved permanent status as an "important" figure, especially in the early development of econometrics.

Prior to Lange, there had been little in the way of meaningful communication and/or intellectual cross-fertilization between orthodox Western economists and proponents of socialism. Generally speaking, the economists and the socialists stood on opposite sides of the fence hurling accusations and imprecations at each other. The economists accused the socialists of rank ignorance and/or stupidity—because presumably if the socialists adequately understood such basic economic principles as the marginal productivity of capital, they would realize that payment of property return for the use of capital is vitally necessary to the maintenance of economic efficiency, and hence public ownership of capital (i.e., socialism), wherein no such payment would be made, would necessarily be inefficient. At the same time, the socialists accused the economists of being dishonest and venal—of manufacturing spurious rationalizations to try to mask the exploitative nature of capitalism.

Oskar Lange came as a veritable revelation to both sides. Here was an individual who was manifestly neither stupid nor ignorant of economic theory, yet who strongly and clearly advocated socialism in the strict public ownership sense. Lange's work demonstrated that orthodox economic theory is not necessarily sympathetic to capitalism and hostile to socialism. In historical perspective, the neutrality of economic theory with respect to the potential relative performance of socialism is perhaps not so surprising. After all, Karl Marx himself studied the economic theory of his day assiduously, and although he decried the typical "vulgar economist," he respected and admired such leading classical economists as Adam Smith (1723-1790) and David Ricardo (1772-1823). During Marx's intellectually formative period, the labor theory of value was considered "orthodox economics," and Marx's application of this theory as a moral bludgeon with which to chastise capitalism may have contributed to its demise in mainstream economics.

In the "neoclassical" theory of production and distribution, capital receives equal billing with labor as a source of value, and the determination of factor prices according to their "marginal productivity" adds an extra dimension of analytical complexity not known in classical economics. By the time neoclassical economic theory supplanted classical economic theory, Marx was an old man, too old to seriously study and assimilate these new ideas. Instead he dismissed neoclassical economics scornfully as transparent, spurious, pseudo-scientific capitalist apologetics manufactured by various vulgar economists who happened to be equipped with rudiments of higher mathematics. Lange helped to show that Marx's attitude toward neoclassical economics was unfair and unjustified. There is more to this body of thought than a shallow defense of the capitalistic status quo—in addition to which, neoclassical economics does *not* necessarily constitute a defense of capitalism.

The basic neoclassical principle that "capital earns its return through its marginal product contribution to output" only necessarily constitutes a defense of the basic capitalist principle of direct appropriation by private households of capital property return, if one simply ignores the clear and manifest distinction between capital itself (i.e., the inanimate instruments of production, and those human individuals designated as "capital owners" under capitalistic definitions of ownership). In a direct physical sense, it is the inanimate capital itself which contributes to production, and whose marginal product is recognized in the form of capital property return. Under modern industrial capitalism, the human capital owners are *not* clearly and directly involved in the production process. As the inanimate machines whose productivity provides property income to wealthy capitalists roar upon the factory floor, those human capital owners are likely to be a thousand miles away—playing croquet upon the lawns of their estates.

While contemporary capitalist apologetics prefers to simply ignore the distinction between inanimate capital itself and human capital owners, to blend these two separate categories together into one seamless intellectual construct—if pressed, it is certainly capable of producing reasons why the wealthy capitalists playing croquet upon their lawns do in fact, appearances to the contrary, make a worthy contribution to production, and are therefore economically and ethically entitled to the capital property income which they receive. The human capital owners are alleged to provide "capital management effort" in various forms—that form which is especially favored in capitalist apologetics being the noble activity of entrepreneurship. Besides that, the human capital owners provide the saving—at great personal cost to themselves—which is used to build the capital factories and machines which contribute directly to production. Finally, on top of it all, the capital owners are "risk-takers"—by investing their wealth instead of hoarding cash under their pillows, they are exposing themselves to dire risk of financial loss. For all of these reasons (and quite possibly many others—given sufficient time to fabricate them), the capitalist owner is held by capitalist apologetics to be fully worthy of his/her capital property income. The fact that intimate knowledge of neoclassical economic theory is *not* necessarily an obstacle to perceiving the invalidity of these specious justifications for capitalism was clearly demonstrated, once and for all, by Oskar Lange.

Interestingly enough, the immediate impetus to Lange's taking the time and trouble to put his thoughts on the potential institutions and processes of an economically efficient socialism into a coherent written essay was the publication of a book which endeavored to establish that an economically efficient socialism was a theoretical impossibility. *Collectivist Economic Planning: Critical Studies on the Possibilities of Socialism* (1935) was a somewhat heterogeneous collection of essays edited by the well-known Austrian school luminary Friedrich Hayek (1899-1992), who himself contributed two integrative papers to it ("The Nature and History of the Problem" and "The Present State of the Debate"). The volume was intended to counter the rising interest during the early 1930s among economists and other intellectuals (brought about by the glaring contrast between Depression-ridden Western capitalism and booming planned Soviet socialism) in government economic intervention in general, and Soviet planned industrialization in particular. As befits a production of Austrian economics, the book is not very crisp or focused by non-Austrian standards; however, the basic message is clear enough. That message is simply that public ownership socialism is inherently inefficient, and hence any socialist polity, whatever might be its short-term achievements, is bound to suffer economic stagnation and ultimate collapse in the long run. Aside from Hayek's contributions, two articles included in *Collectivist Economic Planning* are of special interest: "The Ministry of Production in the Collectivist State" by Enrico Barone (originally published in Italian in 1908), and "Economic Calculation in the Socialist Commonwealth" by Ludwig von Mises (originally published in German in 1920).

Enrico Barone (1859-1924), a mathematical economist and disciple of Vilfredo Pareto (1848-1923), of "Pareto optimality" renown in modern welfare economics, commenced his article with the observation that merely exposing the problems and shortcomings of Karl Marx's critique of capitalism does not necessarily imply that capitalism is an optimal economic system, and then posed the question of efficient production and distribution in a collectivist (i.e., socialist) economy. He proceeded to answer the question with a complicated mathematical exposition based upon what are known today as the "Pareto efficiency conditions" (e.g., for any two factors of production, the ratio of marginal products of the factors must be equal in all factories and firms). Barone's contribution demonstrates that there is nothing logically impossible about the achievement of efficient production and distribution under socialism.

But there remains the question of the *practical feasibility* of efficient production and distribution under socialism. Toward the end of "Ministry of Production," Barone argues forcefully that the problem, while solvable in principle, is unsolvable in practice. It is not merely a matter of the huge computational task of solving "millions of equations"—Barone stipulates that this task might conceivably be accomplished through the "arduous work" of an "army of officials." But Barone then delivers the verdict, on "a priori" grounds, that it would be impossible to obtain the vast quantity of numerical information (i.e., coefficients of firm production functions and household utility functions) necessary to numerically specify the efficiency conditions prior to solving them. This impossibility stems not only from the multiplicity of the coefficients, and from the fact that they are hidden in the myriad remote recesses of the economy, but also because these coefficients are constantly changing owing to the dynamic nature of economic conditions.

The contribution of Ludwig von Mises (1881-1973) to *Collectivist Economic Planning* ("Economic Calculation in the Socialist Common-

wealth"), originally published in 1920, argued that the calamitous economic conditions prevailing within the nascent Soviet Union at the time
of writing were the direct result of a misguided effort to accomplish what
Barone had shown to be a priori impossible—the attainment of efficient
economic production and distribution under public ownership socialism
through central planning of the economy. Of course, by the time Mises's
article was translated into English and published in *Collectivist Economic Planning* (1935), it was severely dated. By 1935, the Soviet Union
was booming in comparison with Depression-prostrated Western capitalism.

As of 1935, the Soviet Union was embarked on the third of three dis-
tinctly different periods in its early economic history. The first period,
from the Bolshevik Revolution of 1917 to the early 1920s, has been
dubbed "War Communism." During this period, the disruption and devastation caused by Russia's ill-fated participation in World War I was
compounded by a brutal civil war. "War Communism" was not a systematic effort at economic planning, but rather a desperate expedient by
which the various components of the Red Army roaming about the Soviet Union forcibly requisitioned whatever they needed to survive and
fight on. The hardship, famine, and death over which Mises gloated as
providing incontrovertible evidence of the perversity of socialism, is
more reasonably attributed to prolonged warfare than to the deficiencies
of socialism.

The second major phase of Soviet economic history, the New Economic Plan (NEP) period, persisted through most of the 1920s. Commenced just after the conclusion of the Civil War, the New Economic
Plan was remarkably similar to modern concepts of market socialism.
The Soviet economy prospered under the NEP and made rapid progress
toward recovery from the ravages of international and internal warfare.
But the Communist leadership, fearful of invasion from what it regarded
as a permanently hostile capitalist outer world, was dissatisfied with the
rate of industrialization being achieved under the NEP. Thus the initiation, in the late 1920s, of what has since been termed the "classical planning period." Classical central planning achieved impressive economic
growth in the Soviet Union for several decades—although at the cost of
spartan living standards for the Soviet people.

While living standards in the Soviet Union as of 1935 were quite low,
the desperate conditions of mass starvation associated with the War
Communism period were a distant memory. Therefore the proposition
put forward in Mises's article "Economic Calculation in the Socialist

Commonwealth," that socialism would *immediately* produce calamitous economic conditions, was already discredited upon its translation into English. However, if the proposition were simply revised to socialism *sooner or later* producing calamitous economic conditions, then it would not be in such obvious conflict with the reality of a viable, functioning Soviet socialist economy as of 1935. Such a revision was indeed specified by Hayek, a student and disciple of Mises, in his editor's contributions to *Collectivist Economic Planning*. The primary message put forward to the capitalist world by the book was along these lines: "Don't be discouraged by the Great Depression—and don't be fooled by the apparent success of Soviet socialism. Aside from the hardships being imposed on the Soviet people by the Communist leadership's obsession with rapid industrialization, it has been shown with mathematical logic (by Barone) and syllogistic logic (by Mises) that ultimately, in the long run, any effort at socialistic central planning of the economy is doomed to stagnation and collapse."

In the perspective of the mid-1990s, a perspective which has witnessed the spectacular collapse and dissolution of the Soviet Union, this message may well be perceived as more prescient and plausible than it was so perceived in the mid-1930s. But even if this message is indeed accepted as basically correct (though the "long run" referred to may be a *very* long run, encompassing several generations of humanity), this does not imply that socialism is necessarily inferior to capitalism. The message refers to "socialistic central planning"—not to socialism per se. Barone pointed out that poking holes in Marxist economics does not necessarily vindicate capitalism; it is equally true that poking holes in the concept of central planning does not necessarily vindicate capitalism. This is because central planning socialism is not the only possible form of socialism. There exists a whole range of market socialist possibilities—of socialist economies that would place primary reliance on the economic market (just as does capitalism) to arrive at a solution of the problem specified by Enrico Barone: the problem of economically efficient production and distribution.

To Oskar Lange belongs the honor of firmly establishing this point in the thinking of contemporary economics. In his essay "On the Economic Theory of Socialism," Lange argued cogently that the "millions of equations" implied in Barone's analysis of the problem of efficient production and distribution do not have to be explicitly solved by a central planning authority under socialism—any more than these "millions of equations" are solved by anyone (or any organization) under capitalism. Market decentralization of the economic problem may be implemented under public ownership socialism no less than it is under capitalism.

Central planning socialism implies that the managers of publicly owned firms are given detailed instructions on what to produce and how to produce it. Lange proposed that instead of these detailed instructions, managers of publicly owned firms be given two simple rules: (1) produce as much of each output commodity as is necessary to bring its marginal cost of production into equality with its price; (2) produce output commodities in such a way as to minimize the average cost of production. The first rule determines the quantity to be produced of each output commodity; while the second determines the quantities of input commodities (factors of production such as various types of capital and labor) to be purchased by the firm and applied to the production of each output commodity.

To be implemented, the marginal cost rule requires that firms know the prices of output commodities, while the average cost rule requires that firms know the prices of factors of production. Lange proposed that all prices be set by a Central Planning Board (CPB). (Given Lange's purpose of disassociating socialism from planning, "Central Planning Board" is an unfortunate choice of terminology.) The CPB would mimic the process by which the free market establishes prices of commodities: it would lower the prices of commodities which are in oversupply (production exceeds demand), and it would raise the prices of commodities which are in undersupply (demand exceeds production).

Finally, Lange proposed a system for the allocation of investment funds which would work analogously to the Marshallian free entry mechanism. Each industry would have an "authority" of some sort (this notion is uncomfortably close to the industry ministries of the planned Soviet economy) which would expand the number of factories and firms in the industry until the long-run marginal cost of production of each output commodity had been equated to the commodity's price.

Lange asserted that on the basis of both economic theory and apparent institutional realities, this proposed system of market socialism (which we will hereafter refer to as "Langian market socialism") would work not merely as well as—but actually better than—market capitalism. This particular argument advanced by Lange relied upon the very latest economic thinking of his day. One "hot topic" in 1930s economic thinking was the equivalence of marginal cost pricing to the Pareto efficiency conditions such as had been elaborated by Enrico Barone in "The Ministry of Production in the Collectivist State." Implementation of Lange's proposed rules throughout the economy would therefore presumably achieve Pareto efficiency. A second "hot topic" was that of imperfect competition (i.e., monopoly), the theory of which was codified and extended by work published during this period by Joan Robinson and Edward Chamberlin. A central result of imperfect competition theory is that the typical profit-maximizing firm will *not* equate the marginal cost of producing a given output commodity to its price, but rather to its marginal revenue. This result assaults the laissez faire ideology at its taproot. The laissez faire proposition that pursuit of profits by privately owned business firms will yield economically efficient production in the Pareto-Barone sense depends critically on the assumption of perfect competition. Then as now, the basic "story" of perfect competition (that firms have no control over price and consider it to be an exogenously determined parameter) does not seem to fit the facts very well except for a very small proportion of the economy (e.g., small-scale agriculture). Aside from a small handful of exceptions, the vast majority of firms in the modern economy behave as if output price *were* a decision variable (i.e., the marketing function is deemed fully as important as the production function)—and in so doing, proclaim themselves imperfect competitors in the strict economic theory sense.

According to Lange's argument, the imperfectly competitive nature of most of the contemporary capitalist economy means that this economy is inefficient by Pareto-Barone standards. There is no escape from this outcome under capitalism because the private ownership of firms guarantees that their guiding motivation will be toward the maximization of profit. In contrast, a market socialist economy could instruct firm managers not to maximize profits, but rather to follow the production rules (set marginal cost equal to price, and minimize average cost). Following these rules would indeed generate a pattern of production and distribution that would satisfy the efficiency conditions specified by Pareto and Barone.

Lange's essay "On the Economic Theory of Socialism" was sufficiently plausible and compelling—in conjunction with Lange's prior reputation as an extremely competent economic theorist—to have a significant and permanent impact on economic thinking about socialist economics. No longer could it be casually assumed that a socialist economy must inevitably doom itself to failure by attempting a direct, explicit solution of the "millions of equations" implied in Barone's exposition of efficient production and distribution. Many economists were forced to recognize that whatever level of success might be achieved by a centrally planned socialist economy on the Soviet model (a level of success which was not inconsiderable for many decades), it was quite probable that a market-oriented socialist economy would do even better.

Obviously, Lange's work did not inspire a mass conversion of orthodox economists to socialism. While it was recognized that in principle socialism might possibly perform more effectively than had previously been assumed, most economists took refuge in the belief that an optimally performing market capitalist economy would outperform an optimally performing market socialist economy. Lange himself gave skeptics a powerful phrase to use against his proposal when he expressed concerns about the possible "bureaucratization of economic life" under Langian market socialism. He went on to say that owing to the development of mass production by mega-corporations, economic life had already been significantly "bureaucratized," and that publicly controlled bureaucracies were superior to privately controlled bureaucracies. This amendment of the "bureaucratization" qualm has largely been ignored by later critics of Lange's proposal. In actual fact, the term "bureaucratization" could be—and has been—used to encompass a large number of objections to market socialism, both in the Langian form and other forms. These objections cover a wide spectrum from economic theory to institutional politics. In many cases, "bureaucratization" is not a particularly accurate descriptor of the perceived problem, but critics of socialism have long found the term to be quite effective as a rhetorical device, and they hasten to make use of it at every opportunity.

As far as focused, explicit criticism of Lange's market socialist proposal is concerned, a large proportion of it may be found clearly stated in two articles which appeared soon after Lange's contribution. Abram Bergson's 1948 article on "Socialist Economics" has already been mentioned. In addition, in 1940 Friedrich Hayek, editor of *Collectivist Economic Planning*, published a rebuttal article against Lange in the journal *Economica* ("Socialist Calculation: The 'Competitive Solution'"). Of the two, Hayek's critique is relatively strident, and it expends a disproportionate amount of energy attempting to show that price setting by the Central Planning Board would result in a sluggish and unresponsive price system (there are simply too many commodities to be priced). But as Bergson pointed out, the heart of the Langian market socialist proposal consists of the production rules, not the CPB pricing system. One could simply dispense with CPB pricing and allow the firms themselves to set the prices on the commodities they produce—thus easily evading the single most important of Hayek's objections.

Bergson's appraisal of Langian market socialism was certainly more judicious in tone than that of Hayek. According to Bergson, Lange had definitively answered the previously extremely influential objection to socialism that it would inevitably be strangled by the "millions of equations." Bergson agreed with Lange that these millions of equations need not be numerically specified and explicitly solved under socialism, any more than they had to be numerically specified and explicitly solved under capitalism. However, Bergson postulated that the critical stumbling block to effective performance of Langian market socialism was the absence of an "observable success criterion" by which to evaluate the managers of the publicly owned firms. Under market capitalism, the success of firm managers (or lack thereof) is measured by the profits earned by their firms. Profits are objective and externally visible. Lazy, ineffective firm managers are quickly and accurately identified by low profits. Such managers are either ousted by the firm's stockholders, or their firms will soon suffer bankruptcy in the competitive struggle with more efficient firms.

In contrast, there is no objective and externally visible measure by which the public authorities could identify those managers of publicly owned firms under Langian market socialism who were inadequately assiduous in implementing the Langian production rules (set marginal cost equal to price, and minimize average cost). To the extent that the managers are effectively implementing the rules, overall economic efficiency will be high—but there is no way to trace the contribution made to overall economic efficiency by any one firm. Knowing this, each manager may have an incentive to shirk, on the assumption that the slack caused by his/her lassitude will be picked up by others. But if all or most of the managers are behaving this way, then overall performance will decline significantly. Bergson considers the possibility of having the firms audited by external accountants, but to him this possibility elicits the same image of an "army of officials" which concerned Barone. He also considers the possibility of giving the firms a profit-maximization incentive. After all, if the firm is perfectly competitive, then the conditions for profit maximization are exactly the production rules specified by Lange. Thus assuming most publicly owned firms are perfectly competitive, profits would in effect be an indicator that the production rules are being followed. Bergson dismisses this possibility as contrary to the spirit of Lange's proposal—which assumes that most firms are *not* perfectly competitive. Under imperfect competition, a profit-maximizing firm will *not* follow the production rules, and the economy will thus suffer inefficiency in the Pareto-Barone sense.

It could well be that Bergson exaggerates the advantages of market capitalism in the matter of having an "observable success criterion" on which to evaluate managerial performance. As a matter of fact, profits are not as easily observable as Bergson implies. Under contemporary capitalism in which there has been a nearly complete separation of ownership from the corporate management function, a huge public accounting industry has become necessary to try to offset the natural tendencies among managers toward behavior which is contrary to the interests of the owners (i.e., stockholders, bondholders, and other external stakeholders): behavior such as misrepresentation of assets and profits, embezzlement, and looting of corporate assets. The "army of auditors" that would be required to enforce the production rules under Langian market socialism may not be any worse than the presently existing "army of auditors" which is manifestly required by contemporary capitalism. Moreover, even granting that properly calculated and reported profits may be an accurate measure of *corporate* performance, they are not necessarily an accurate measure of *managerial* performance. To some extent, profits are determined by external conditions such as changes in product demand and input costs over which the managers have no appreciable control. It requires considerable information and delicate judgment to evaluate whether a certain case of low profits is significantly attributable to inferior managerial performance.

Be that as it may, no effort will be made here to rehabilitate Langian market socialism. It so happens that this author fully shares the prevalent opinion among professional economists that any effort to implement Oskar Lange's market socialist proposal in the real world would quite likely rapidly lead to stagnation and decline. The basic problem is that the Lange proposal is too much informed and motivated by the textbook microeconomic theory of the single-product firm under perfect competition and complete certainty. The economic real world of today is dominated by imperfectly competitive large corporations which produce a wide range of products under conditions of uncertainty. The simplified decision rules of the microeconomic textbooks have no place in the real world of corporate decisionmaking. The real-world managers may have been exposed to these rules back in their student days, but they make no appreciable use of them in their present work. Any effort to impose these rules upon corporation executives as the primary guides to business decisionmaking could all too easily result in confusion, demoralization, and virtual paralysis among these executives. Langian market socialism would simply be too great a leap away from the way things are done in the present-day market capitalist economy.

The proposal for market socialism being put forward in this book is *profit-oriented*, which means that profits would remain the primary measure of corporate/managerial performance. Executives of publicly owned corporations would be well remunerated—perhaps not *quite* as well remunerated as they are under contemporary capitalism, but still *very* well remunerated. It is anticipated that the only group of people who would be earning more than high corporation executives under the proposed plan of market socialism would be superstars in the realm of sports and popular culture. This is so that the executives will be strongly motivated to retain their employment. Their primary means of guaranteeing retention of their employment will be through having their respective publicly owned corporations earning healthy rates of profit. Executives of publicly owned corporations which are *not* earning a healthy rate of profit would be at dire risk of dismissal by the public ownership agency. This situation would parallel the existing situation under capitalism, in which corporation executives of poorly performing corporations are at dire risk of dismissal by boards of directors representing the stockholders. Thus the plan of market socialism put forward herein is immune to Bergson's objection to Langian market socialism that the system lacks an "easily observable success criterion" on which to evaluate managerial performance.

It could well be that Langian market socialism would be taken more seriously today if Lange had further developed the plan and responded to the points raised by critics such as Friedrich Hayek, Abram Bergson, and others. However, for better or for worse, Lange never added anything to the market socialist proposal set forth in "Economic Theory of Socialism." After writing his famous essay, Lange occupied himself for several years with "orthodox" research, mostly in the area of econometrics. The Russian-sponsored Communist takeover of Poland in the aftermath of World War II presented Lange with a difficult personal decision. The establishment of Communism in Poland had turned his homeland into a full-fledged socialist state in the public ownership sense. As a proponent of socialism, Lange was happy about that. Unfortunately, the socialist system enforced upon Poland by the Red Army followed the Soviet central planning model. Lange elected to return to his homeland. His status as a leading economist in the West guaranteed him a high position in the Polish economic planning bureaucracy. No doubt he was hopeful that he might be able to influence the Polish socialist system toward greater market orientation.

Unfortunately, it did not work out that way. Lange's personal prestige and influence was not so great as to enable any significant deviation from the central planning orthodoxy imposed by the Russians. Instead, Lange himself became deeply enmeshed in the practical problems of central planning. Soviet-style central planning never concerned itself with the "millions of equations" involved in Barone's specification of the socialist planning problem. There was never any serious effort to represent the economy by a mathematical model composed of firm production functions and household utility functions, to numerically specify these functions, and to numerically solve the corresponding efficiency conditions. But although there were not "millions of equations" involved in the real-world central planning system, there certainly were "millions of numbers." While higher mathematics never entered the picture, there was indeed a tremendous amount of straightforward arithmetic involved in the process. The development of computers in the post-World War II period was of some assistance to the planners, but even with computers, the task was simply too great to be performed well. Along with the Soviet Union itself and the other Eastern European satellite states, Poland finally bowed to reality and definitively abandoned central planning in the 1990s. But by that time Lange had been dead for many years (he died in 1965, at the age of 61).

While the specific proposal for market socialism developed by Oskar Lange is too much influenced by elementary economic theory to be taken very seriously as a practical alternative to capitalism, Lange's work was in fact extremely influential in a larger sense: once and for all, it opened the minds of economists to the *possibility* of market socialism. Once this possibility had been recognized, the way was open to the development of other market socialist proposals of greater practicality. Such practical proposals for market socialism, in turn, have the potentiality of resurrecting the fundamental socialist critique of capitalism—of seriously challenging the capitalistic status quo which today seems so rock-solid and unassailable.

The market socialist proposal put forward in this book is a profit-oriented proposal based primarily on the ideas of James Yunker (the author), Leland Stauber, and John Roemer. But before developing this proposal, it is desirable that the reader have some notion of the potential range of market socialist alternatives. Profit-oriented market socialism is only one out of at least four major categories of market socialism (each of which could in turn be varied and modified into a number of sub-categories): (1) Langian market socialism; (2) service market socialism, a.k.a. the "nationalized industry model"; (3) cooperative market social-ism, a.k.a. "labor management"; and (4) profit-oriented market socialism. The latter three categories will be respectively described and discussed in the following three sections of this chapter.

THE NATIONALIZED INDUSTRY MODEL

Although social ownership of the preponderance of business enterprise had been excised from the social democratic platform (at least as an im-mediate objective) by the early 1900s, the more radical elements within the social democratic movement continued to push for socialization at least of "key industries" (the "commanding heights" of the industrial economy, as they were called by the American social democratic social-ist and perennial presidential candidate Norman Thomas). Dissatisfaction with the capitalistic status quo reached a sufficiently high level in the United Kingdom and other Western European nations during the devas-tating Great Depression of the 1930s, that following the conclusion of World War II this dissatisfaction was expressed in a wave of "nationali-zations" (this term being preferred to "socialization"). In Britain, for ex-ample, the coal, steel, railroad, airline, trucking, water, and electricity industries, among others, were taken into public ownership. In many na-tions (the United States not being one of them), there was a very signifi-cant expansion of the public enterprise sector during this period.

It is important to understand that the objectives of the postwar nation-alization movement, in Britain and elsewhere, were very much different from the objectives of profit-oriented market socialism as described herein. The purpose of nationalization, that is to say, the purpose of pub-lic enterprise generally when implemented in an economy which remains predominantly capitalistic, is to suppress the drive toward profit maximi-zation among the enterprises concerned, on grounds that special circum-stances exist in which profit maximization is economically and/or socially unhealthy. Economic theory specifies two such circumstances: (1) natural monopoly—a situation in which economies of scale are so important that a competitive market is either impossible or severely inef-ficient; (2) external effects—a situation in which the business decisions of one firm impact directly and significantly on other firms and house-holds in the economy. It is generally agreed among economists that un-der these special circumstances laissez faire is no longer an optimal policy, and that the appropriate response involves some form of social in-tervention, such as specially tailored taxation or subsidization, the imposition of external regulation by public agencies, or public ownership of the firms involved. Where the disagreement arises—and the disagreement is often intense—is in determining whether, in any particular case, the natural monopoly and/or external effects circumstances are sufficiently important to merit social intervention (keeping in mind that social intervention itself will be subject to problems).

Even in the United States, which is probably the most self-righteously capitalistic nation in the world (with the possible exception of Australia), the desirability of a significant amount of deviation from laissez faire is thoroughly accepted by the great majority of citizens. From the earliest days of the republic, municipalities have provided public libraries and schools, states have provided public universities, and the national government has operated a postal service. There has been a significant amount of public ownership in the electric power industry since its foundation (albeit by local governments rather than the national government), in addition to which privately owned electric utilities have, from the early days of the industry, been closely regulated by public agencies. From the experience of the Great Depression of the 1930s was taken the lesson that the national government should rapidly implement expansionary monetary and fiscal policy when the economy begins to slide into a major depression. Nevertheless, in comparison with many of the other leading industrial capitalist nations, deviations from laissez faire orthodoxy are relatively scarce in the United States. Specifically, there has never been any serious move toward nationalization of several important industries such as occurred in Britain following World War II.

Even so, the basic purpose of postwar British nationalization was comparable to that which underpins such longstanding and widely accepted American practices as subsidization of education and regulation of essential utilities. This purpose is essentially to override private profit maximization as the operative goal of the organizations involved. The primary purpose of nationalization, or more generally of any kind of public ownership in economies which remain primarily capitalistic (i.e., private ownership of business enterprise remains the rule rather than the exception), is *not* to effect a significant redistribution of capital property income among the households of the nation. This is demonstrated both by the fact that only a relatively small part of the economy is nationalized (though in the case of postwar Britain this part was quite large in an absolute sense), and also by the fact that the compensation paid to the erstwhile private owners of firms in these industries is both quite generous and in the form of interest-bearing government bonds. In general, cases of transition from private ownership to public ownership in the nationalized industry form have been characterized by such generous compensation that the practical effect is simply that the national government replaces the business enterprises involved as the private household's source of capital property income—and it often pays a higher rate of return than was being realized on the capital prior to nationalization. This has been especially true of nationalizations of declining industries, such as British rail and coal as of the time of their nationalizations. Wealthy British capitalists simply traded in their stock shares for government bonds and continued the lavish lifestyles to which they had always been accustomed. To them, nationalization presented no genuine threat.

The primary purpose of the profit-oriented market socialism proposed herein, on the other hand, is exactly to effect a significant redistribution of capital property income over the households of the nation by replacing the drastically unequal distribution pattern of today, according to which a tiny handful of wealthy capitalistic households takes the great majority of this type of income while the great majority of working class and middle class households receive little or nothing of it, with a more fair and equitable social dividend distribution system that would benefit the large majority of the population. At the same time, there is no intention in profit-oriented market socialism to deviate from profit maximization as the operative goal of the great preponderance of business enterprises. Although publicly owned, these business enterprises would seek to earn profits just as assiduously as they did when they were privately owned. Just as under contemporary capitalism, there would be a certain sector of the economy (involving, for example, postal services, education, essential utilities, and so on) in which profits would *not* be the major criterion of success. This particular sector would be no larger and no smaller than it is currently under capitalism. Enterprises within this sector would be the exception rather than the rule. *Most* publicly owned business enterprises would be primarily oriented to profit maximization.

No doubt the reader is well aware of the fact that at the present time, public enterprise under capitalism, both in the national ownership form and the municipal ownership form, is in rapid retreat. For example, during the Conservative Party ascendency in the U.K. under Prime Ministers Margaret Thatcher and John Major, most of the industries which had been nationalized after World War II were returned to private ownership. The British privatizations were symptomatic of a worldwide trend. Between the late 1940s and the 1970s and 1980s, the pendulum of public and professional opinion swung back toward the old nineteenth-century faith in the economic efficiency and social benevolence of laissez faire policies. Into sharp decline went the earlier concerns, which had been so greatly amplified by the Great Depression, about undesirable side effects of profit maximization caused by imperfect competition and external effects. At the same time, concerns about the problems of public ownership, including vague goals, dubious effort incentives of managers, and persistent needs for substantial subsidies from the public purse, came to the fore. Even where public ownership has been retained, the public enterprises have often been "commercialized" to a degree: their subsidies have been reduced, they have raised prices on the goods and services they produce, and in some cases they have changed from being claimants on public revenue to providers of public revenue. The public has ambivalent feelings about these transitions: as taxpayers they are relieved of some of their burdens, but as consumers they confront higher prices for certain goods and services.

Clearly there is a happy medium between the polar extremes of complete laissez faire and all-pervasive social control of business enterprise. But the determination of this happy medium is extremely difficult and controversial. It would be very easy to become entangled in this issue and to lose track of the central objective of this particular work. No such entanglement is contemplated. Quite frankly, this book will make to effort at all to contribute to this particular debate. For example, no opinion will be expressed (and, in fact, none is held by this author) regarding whether the postwar British nationalizations went too far in the direction of social control, or the recent British privatizations went too far in the direction of laissez faire.

In a practical sense (i.e., considering only those proposals which seem politically capable of implementation within the next five to ten years), the ongoing debate on the proper boundaries between private enterprise oriented principally toward profit, and public enterprise oriented more toward social service, involves a relatively small proportion of the economy. Enthusiastic conservatives might allow direct social intervention in 10 percent of the economy, while enthusiastic progressives might favor social intervention in 20 to 30 percent of the economy. In either case, it could be said that a "majority" of the economy would remain oriented to profit maximization. This situation implies that the present climate of opinion still subscribes to the general precept that with respect to the operations of productive organizations (i.e., organizations which produce saleable goods and services), laissez faire should be the rule and social intervention should be the exception. This precept will in no way, shape, or form be challenged herein. Since this precept is not a mathematical or scientific truth such as "2 + 2 = 4" or "$E = mc^2$" it may or may not actually be true. Whether it is true or not is fully irrelevant to the central question examined herein: the question of whether profit-oriented market socialism would or would not be a superior alternative to contemporary capitalism.

Although the present climate of opinion suggests that there is little likelihood that a market socialist system based on the social service objectives of nationalized industries could be seriously contemplated within the foreseeable future, the theoretical possibility of such a system exists. For the sake of providing a comprehensive survey of market socialist possibilities, the idea will be briefly discussed here.

How such a system would operate in practice would be importantly determined by whether all individual firms operating in a certain industry are gathered into one tightly organized administrative structure (the "industry monopoly" concept). Let us proceed on the assumption that this is *not* done, on grounds that it would create excessive monopoly power within the economy. Instead it is envisioned that approximately the same structure of administratively independent firms would remain as currently exists under market capitalism, and that these firms would derive all or a substantial part of their revenues from sales of goods and services to the public. Therefore these firms would effectively remain in competition with one another—even though the competition might be as much for government subsidies as it is for direct markets and sales.

The multiplicity of independently organized and separately evaluated publicly owned business enterprises would imply market operations and processes "basically" analogous to those of market capitalism and other forms of market socialism. The principal distinction of this system would be its explicit reliance on social welfare maximization as the operative goal of the typical publicly owned enterprise. The term "service market socialism" describes the fundamental idea: the central purpose of the typical firm is to provide "service" to its customers, as opposed, for example, to profits for its owners (whether they be private households, as under capitalism, or the public as a whole, under profit-oriented market socialism).

The major obstacle to the successful implementation of this idea is the same obstacle which Abram Bergson perceived with respect to Oskar Lange's market socialist proposal: the absence of a "clearly observable" success criterion by which to evaluate the performance of individual firms and their managers. Social welfare is an inherently vague, difficult-to-measure variable—and it could be a very subjective and unreliable matter to assess the specific contribution being made to overall social welfare by any one firm.

There is, however, one important possibility toward overcoming the fuzzy success criterion problem: revenue or output maximization subject to a minimum profit constraint. According to this approach, either the physical output of the firm which is sold to the public, or the amount of sales revenue derived from its sale, would be utilized as the major proxy for the firm's contribution to overall social welfare, and hence as the principal success criterion on which to evaluate the firm's performance. Output or revenue are at least as "easily observable" as are profits. A problem would exist, of course, if the firm were subject to no financial constraint of any sort. If the firm had virtually unlimited access to government subsidies with which to cover losses, very likely it could expand its output and revenue to very high levels. Therefore it is necessary to supplement the success criterion of output/revenue with a financial constraint: the firm must operate under a "minimum profit constraint." Normally the required minimum profit rate is some relatively low but positive level—enough to enable the firm to cover its capital depreciation, and at least part of its purchases of new capital. But in some instances in which there are important external effects (e.g., education), the "minimum profit rate" might actually be negative, in which case a more accurate phrase for the financial constraint might be "maximum loss constraint" or "maximum subsidy constraint."

It has been suggested that although the explicit, published mission statements of public enterprises under capitalism tend toward vague rhetorical invocations of "social service," in practice the principal operative goal is in fact none other than output (or revenue) maximization subject to a minimum profit constraint (or maximum loss constraint). If this is in fact the case, it suggests that much of the criticism of public enterprise efficiency has nothing to do with public ownership per se, but is based upon the presumption that the required minimum profit rate is too low, or the allowed maximum loss is too high. The path toward improving public enterprise efficiency is then clear: raise the required profit rate, or lower the allowed subsidy. (It should be recognized, however, that a rise in "efficiency" achieved through these means is likely to correspond to higher prices for the public enterprise's goods and services.)

Moreover, it has also been suggested that the contemporary real-world capitalist economy is in fact governed not so much by profit maximization as it is by revenue maximization subject to a minimum profit

constraint—albeit the "minimum acceptable profit rate" for a privately
owned firm is likely to be considerably higher than that for a publicly
owned firm. In response to the manifestly obvious separation of ownership and management under contemporary capitalism, a considerable
body of economic theory has been developed to try to provide a more realistic description of the typical firm than does the traditional profit-
maximization model. Several so-called "managerial" theories of the firm
have been proposed by various economists.

Probably the most important of these "alternatives to profit maximization" is the constrained revenue maximization model of William Baumol.
Baumol postulates that managers have an incentive toward maximization
of firm growth (in terms of sales revenue) owing to the institutional reality of a strong size-salary correlation. The larger the firm, the larger the
remuneration of its top executives. At the same time, the executives are
hardly in a position to ignore profits. Not only must they be wary of
bankruptcy (which means keeping up interest payments on bonds and
loans), but they must also pay the stockholders enough to keep them
happy, or at least happy enough not to sell their stock, or to cast their
votes for unfriendly board members desirous of ousting the incumbent
managers. Baumol speculates that for most large corporations in the
economy, for which stockholding has become highly atomized among a
large number of dispersed and unorganized stockholders, the minimum
rate of profit necessary to keep the stockholders content is significantly
below the maximum rate of profit which the firm would be able to earn if
it had to. If this is the case, then the economy will operate differently
from how it would have operated under unadulterated profit maximization. Just how much differently depends on the circumstances.

Not that this situation, if it really exists, is necessarily unhealthy. The
principle that profit maximization produces a higher level of economic
efficiency than constrained revenue maximization depends critically on
the perfect competition assumption. If, on the other hand, most of the
large-scale firms operating in the economy are imperfect competitors
rather than perfect competitors (not a wholly implausible assumption),
then constrained revenue maximization will likely yield higher economic
efficiency than profit maximization. In other words, constrained revenue
maximization might be a natural and healthy antidote to imperfect competition. On top of which, constrained revenue maximization is likely to
generate stronger incentives to innovation, investment, and growth than
are generated by profit maximization.

The notion of "production for use rather than production for profit" has a long history in socialist thought, and to those who have assimilated laissez faire ideology it seems a wholly impractical, idealistic, and utopian notion. No doubt it has been such in the form imagined by most of the socialists who have invoked this phrase in the past—socialists who have been inspired by woolly visions of warm, inviting little workshops in which craftsmen and artisans companionably manufacture the simple necessities of life for their families, friends, and neighbors. But the fact remains, as paradoxical as it may seem at first glance, that a full-scale, functioning industrial economy might actually be successfully undertaken which is based, fundamentally, on this principle: a service market socialist economy. Such an economy might indeed function very similarly to the market capitalist economy we know today—assuming that the Baumol constrained revenue maximization theory is a reasonable approximation to reality under contemporary capitalism.

For service market socialism to be practicable, it would almost certainly be necessary to install output or revenue maximization subject to a minimum profit constraint as the explicit and fully recognized principal objective of the typical publicly owned firm. It would also be necessary to establish a non-negligible minimum rate of profit for most firms. This rate might be *somewhat* less than the rate of profit necessary to keep the incumbent managers installed in their jobs under contemporary capitalism, but it probably could not be *substantially* less without running the risk of significant inefficiency.

While service market socialism, if properly implemented, may not be as impractical as it might seem at first glance, this system is not being recommended here, at least as a general principle for the entire economy. As in the case of Langian market socialism, it would seem to be too great a departure from the accustomed operations and processes of market capitalism. The initiation of socialism is a sufficiently large step to take at one time. We require a socialist system that would work—with the exception of a different system for distributing capital property return—as much as possible like present-day market capitalism.

COOPERATIVE MARKET SOCIALISM

Just as the notion of "production for use rather than for profit" has a long history in socialist thought, so too does the notion that "the workers should work for themselves and not for the owners." And just as this latter notion might at first appear completely woolly-minded and utopian, the fact remains there is a not inconsequential possibility that the basic idea could be put into practical operation throughout a large-scale industrial economy. Such a system might not bear much resemblance to the golden visions of the many socialists, past and present, who have invoked the phrase—but it could be a workable system, and it would incorporate the essence of the phrase.

The idea of the production cooperative, a firm in which the plant and machinery are collectively owned by the employees, goes back to before the time of Marx. The idea was assisted by Marx in that a rudimentary acquaintance with Marx's theory of exploitation would immediately suggest the production cooperative as a potential cure for the problem. According to the basic Marxian exploitation theory, a typical worker working ten hours a day produces ten hours of value. But he/she does not get to keep the ten hours of value—the wage will rather be the much smaller amount of value necessary to keep the worker alive and healthy (the subsistence wage). This might, for example, be only six hours of value per day. The four hours difference between the ten hours of labor produced, and the six hours going to the worker as a subsistence wage, is called "surplus value" and is appropriated by the capitalist owner of the firm. A straightforward deduction from this scenario is that if there were no capitalist owner of the firm, the worker would be able to retain the entire ten hours of value he/she produced that day, and all would be well.

Marx himself was not particularly impressed with the cooperative idea. From a more advanced theoretical standpoint, as developed in the Transformation Schema of Volume III of Marx's *Das Kapital*, surplus value is something which the capitalist class as a whole exploits from the working (or proletarian) class as a whole. Thus the amount of surplus value produced in a particular firm will not necessarily equal the amount of profit realized by the firm: the more capital-intensive firms will have profit amounts greater than their surplus value amounts. Thus if all the firms in the economy become production cooperatives, employees in the capital-intensive firms would receive more total income than they produce value, thus reproducing, albeit on a much smaller scale, the injustice of capitalism. Moreover, Marx saw the cooperative movement as diverting the workers' attention from the need for fundamental change through violent revolution. Many nonrevolutionary exponents of cooperative production were urging the workers to save their money with the objective of buying out the owners. Marx ridiculed this advice on grounds that the workers were too impoverished to ever accumulate enough funds to buy out the owners. In Marx's view, the only way to terminate capitalist exploitation was through the revolutionary transformation of society.

Despite Marx's jaundiced view of the production cooperative (he categorized it as one form of "utopian socialism"), the notion has continued to attract considerable attention and support, both under the "production cooperative" designation and a number of alternative designations ("labor management," "self-management," "employee ownership," "cooperative market socialism," and so on), right down to the present day. There has in fact been a significant amount of real-world experience accumulated with cooperative production—or quasi-cooperative production. For example, production cooperatives have been incorporated into numerous communalist efforts, many of them religiously inspired. The Israeli *kibbutz* is a contemporary embodiment of this particular approach. Employee ownership has been common among wood processing firms in the U.S. Pacific Northwest. Even among large-scale, successful U.S. corporations, there have been (and continue to be) a few instances of employee ownership, such as United Parcel Service and United Airlines. In the Basque region of Spain, the employee-owned Mondragon syndicate has become a large, diversified business operation.

In addition, considerable use has been made of the production cooperative throughout the history of the Communist nations. Collective farms comprised a large component of the agricultural sector in the former Soviet Union. Production cooperatives were mandated in *all* sectors of the economy in the former Yugoslavia. Prior to the "responsibility system," collective farms were standard in the People's Republic of China. It should be noted, however, that critics of Communist-sponsored production cooperatives maintain that owing to tight Communist Party control of these enterprises, they came nowhere near to the ideal embodied in the pure concept.

To its advocates, there are two primary, interrelated advantages of labor self-management: (1) it eliminates the inequity of inactive, parasitical outside owners appropriating the firm's profits; (2) inspired by the realization that they are "working for themselves rather than working for the owners," the workers will upgrade their productive effort, thus generating higher efficiency and greater output. The beguiling nature of these alleged advantages may be gauged from the fact that they (more especially, the second of the two) provide the rationale behind the flourishing ESOP movement (Employee Stock Ownership Plans). The ESOP concept is hailed by some conservative and business-oriented social commentators as the final solution to whatever lingering equity problems may remain within modern capitalism, and these plans are enthusiastically sponsored by numerous major corporations. Although workers today are certainly more prosperous than they were in Marx's time, they still do not possess anywhere near the very substantial resources that would be required to fully buy out the outside owners (except in cases where the firm is on the verge of bankruptcy and the owners are confronted with the possibility of complete loss of their investment). It is probable that the actual effect of the ESOP movement toward long-term equalization of capital wealth distribution has been negligible—and will remain negligible into the foreseeable future. As far as the corporations are concerned, ESOP is just another way of raising capital. As to the conservative social commentators who envision ESOP as a painless path toward eliminating gross inequality in capital wealth distribution under modern capitalism—they are simply indulging in wishful thinking.

The typical attitude of mainstream economists toward the notion of cooperative production, with a few notable exceptions, has been highly skeptical. The starting point for the typical economist is with the observation that while there have been a few isolated success stories in the history of cooperative production, on the whole these types of firms have a dismal record in competition with standard profit-maximizing firms with outside owners and hired labor. Normally the life cycles of cooperative firms are short and financially undistinguished. Economists have discerned a number of factors that tend to put cooperative firms at a competitive disadvantage. There may be problems of coordination and delay if there is too much in the way of general discussion and democratic decisionmaking, and too little delegation of authority to the managers with respect to ongoing business decisions. There may be a tendency toward excessive egalitarianism in the internal distribution of firm revenues among the members. There may be excessive reluctance to dismiss unproductive members, whether this unproductiveness stems from the personal deficiencies of the worker, or from adverse business conditions. The relatively low incomes of the working-class members of the cooperative, and consequently their short time horizons, may make it difficult to obtain adequate internal funding for capital replacement and improvement.

Advocates of cooperation have responded to these sorts of criticisms. They point to the fact that in a non-negligible number of cases, cooperative firms have indeed been financially successful over extended periods of time. Their principal explanation for the fact that, on the whole, cooperatives have been unsuccessful, is an alleged ideologically rooted prejudice against them among financial intermediaries. This makes it difficult for cooperatives to obtain both working capital and long-term investment capital. Another problem is that the organizers of many cooperatives have been overly idealistic and insufficiently realistic, so that there have been serious flaws in the structure and functioning of these ventures—a particularly common problem being inadequate delegation of authority to professional managers. According to their proponents, properly designed cooperative enterprises—which could bargain for financial capital from banks and other lenders on equal terms with conventional profit-maximizing firms—would have no difficulty in surviving and even prospering within a highly competitive business environment.

Serious scholarly study of cooperation is a much more involved and demanding task at the present time than it was, say, 50 years ago, owing to the extraordinary recent growth of a voluminous and dense literature produced by mathematically oriented economists on the economic theory of the cooperative enterprise. This theoretical literature was initiated by an article authored by Benjamin Ward and published in the *American Economic Review* in 1958: "The Firm in Illyria: Market Syndicalism." Ward's contribution demonstrated that it was possible to develop mathematical models of the cooperative firm using basically the same tools traditionally applied to professional study of the profit-maximizing firm. Economics being the sort of discipline it is, the discovery of this new area for the application of mathematical methods led to a tremendous outpouring of work in it. There are now many thousands of published pages in the literature, most of them packed with complicated equations, on the economic theory of the coop.

Most of this literature has been contributed by economists who were drawn to the subject not by any sort of sympathetic interest in cooperative production, but merely because it offered a new opportunity for the application of mathematical methods. More often than not, the primary purpose of the analysis is to highlight various theoretical problems of the coop relative to its "capitalist twin." The tone was set by Ward himself, the initiator of this literature, who derived the result from his pioneering model that the coop might possess a "perverse" supply curve of output. This means that under certain not-unlikely circumstances, a rise in the price of its output good will decrease, rather than increase (as would be the case with a profit-maximizing firm), the cooperative's quantity of output. Numerous analogous problems have been discerned by the many contributors to this literature following Ward. It is worth pointing out, however, that there have been a handful of notable dissents to the generally negative appraisal of cooperation to be found within the technical literature. For example, Jaroslav Vanek and Jacques Drèze are two highly competent and reputable mathematical economists who have written extensively and favorably about cooperation.

If we want to try to envision the potential performance of a cooperative market socialist economy (that is, an economy in which all or most business firms were production cooperatives in which the managers were mainly responsible to the employees), it is necessary to commence with an elementary, but very important, point: performance would depend largely on the specific institutional provisions and conditions which are implemented. One of the major complexities in thinking about cooperative market socialism is the diversity of possibilities for implementing the basic principle of employee control of the firm. It has to be said in this regard that a significant number of past advocates of the production cooperative seem to be seriously unrealistic in their expectations of how such a firm would or should operate in practice. These advocates seem to imagine that a business firm can be operated with little or no hierarchical organization, without any appreciable degree of authority and subordination, without imposed coordination and enforced discipline. They seem to imagine that business decisionmaking can typically be conducted along the same quaint lines as a New England town meeting, with full discussion of available options by all members of the firm, followed by policy determination by majority vote. Such a scenario could only possibly be workable in a very small firm producing technically unsophisticated goods and services.

But let us set aside those ideas about cooperative production which are more or less obviously impractical, and concentrate instead on a specific variant of cooperative market socialism which might be successfully implemented even in the large corporations which dominate the economic scene today. First of all, we postulate basically the same structure of firms as exists today: there would be no significant mergers of existing firms involved in the transition to cooperative market socialism, nor would there be any significant disaggregations of existing firms. Second, we postulate that all firms would retain their existing internal structures of hierarchically organized divisions and departments, and would also retain their existing policies and procedures, including those relating to supervision and discipline. Third, we postulate that the typical firm would have to be self-supporting. There would be no subsidization of firms, except (in a relatively few cases) on the same external effects grounds relevant under capitalism. Therefore, bankruptcy would be the normal means of terminating firms which are not self-supporting (i.e., whose revenues fail to cover their costs).

Employee management would be implemented through three key provisions. First, there would be no voting stock in the firm held by non-employees of the firm (recall that managers would also be considered "employees" of the firm). The firm would thus have to raise all capital from external sources through bonds and loan contracts: in other words, external holders of the firm's securities would have no voting authority over the firm's managers. Second, all employees of the firm would elect its chief executive in free and open elections at regular intervals of from four to six years. During his/her term in office, the incumbent chief executive might be dismissed in a no-confidence vote, but in such cases a very large majority of the firm's employees would have to vote against the incumbent. Third, any profits of the firm, after meeting wage and salary payments to employees and interest charges on external debt, would be either reinvested in the firm's plant and equipment or distributed to the employees—none of it would be paid to outside owners.

Provisions such as these might well produce an economy which would work in practice very similarly to the capitalist economy today—with the primary exception that the circumstance of outside ownership of the firm would be eliminated. Even though the top management would be periodically responsible to the employees in open elections, practical business operations and decisionmaking might not be much altered. There might be slightly more reluctance to dismiss unproductive employees than under capitalism, but not a great deal more reluctance. It is certainly true that rank-and-file employees are adverse to dismissals and that dismissals might cause problems for the incumbent management in the next managerial election—but typically the next election won't be until some months or years have elapsed, on top of which those who have been dismissed won't be around to vote in it. The need to avoid bankruptcy and to meet interest payments on outstanding bonds and loans will impose a significant degree of financial discipline on the firm, even though there would be no profit-interested outside owners adding to this discipline. Even under capitalism today, the discipline imposed by bond-holding external financial intermediaries interested in receiving their interest payments is to no significant degree more relaxed than the discipline imposed by external stockholders interested in receiving dividends and capital gains. In fact, arguably the former discipline is more intense. This is because a firm which does not meet its interest obligations must immediately either renegotiate the obligations or declare bankruptcy, while a firm which forgoes payment of dividends to stockholders faces no immediate penalties, and indeed, may go on doing so for several years before the ax falls.

At the same time, there might indeed be some significant morale advantages in having the employees of a firm elect their own chief executive, and of having such profits as remain after all expenses have been met (including wages, salaries, and obligatory interest expenses), distributed internally to the employees, rather than being paid out to inactive external owners who might reasonably be viewed as parasitical by the firm's employees. Obviously, working for an employee-owned corporation such as described above would not mean liberation from all supervisory restraint, doing what one wants freely and voluntarily, being "one's own boss" as the phrase is usually understood. It does not even involve the continual polling, consultations, and group discussions which some see as the central feature of cooperation—or at least there would be little more of this sort of thing than already exists under capitalism today. This would hardly constitute the hazy utopia imagined by the more woolly-minded proponents of cooperative production. But it might mean that the typical employee would indeed receive somewhat more income from his/her firm than is received under capitalism, and that this employee would indeed have a somewhat greater sense of worth and control knowing that he/she will have some voice in choosing the firm's chief executive officer in the next election. These benefits may constitute a marginal but appreciable improvement.

The same observation might be made about cooperative market socialism as was made earlier about service market socialism: in practice, the system might not work all that much differently from contemporary market capitalism—that is, in all significant respects other than the collection and distribution of capital property return. What this suggests, in turn, is that these varieties of market socialism might well implement a market economy which would be just as efficient as the market economy under contemporary capitalism, but with a distribution of capital property return that would be considerably more fair and equitable than that existing under contemporary capitalism.

While a careful and judicious consideration of a practically oriented service market socialism or cooperative market socialism suggests that their economic operations and level of efficiency could easily be closely comparable to those of capitalism, to date few individuals have indeed engaged in such careful and judicious consideration. Superficial thinking about such phrases as "production for use rather than production for profit" and "workers working for themselves rather than for the owners" suggests that they are unrealistic and idealistic. No effort will be expended herein trying to counter this impression, even though it may be inaccurate. The market socialist proposal put forward herein is a profit-oriented proposal intended to operate "almost exactly" like contemporary capitalism—except with respect to the collection and distribution of capital property return. It is the most conservative of the market socialist proposals: it envisions the minimum possible departure from the market capitalist economic status quo consistent with changing the legal-institutional basis for distributing capital property return. Therefore it is the least likely of the market socialist proposals to be susceptible to various incentive and operational problems which could adversely affect its economic efficiency.

PROFIT-ORIENTED MARKET SOCIALISM

The central characteristic of profit-oriented market socialism is that under this system, the acknowledged, recognized, explicit, primary objective of the typical publicly owned business enterprise would be the maximization of long-term profits. This exactly parallels what is generally regarded as the acknowledged, recognized, explicit, primary objective of the typical privately owned business enterprise under contemporary capitalism. The difference between capitalism and this type of market socialism would not be in how business firms operate. It would rather be in how the capital property return (profits, interest, and analogous categories of income), which is produced by the operations of business firms, is distributed among the population of private households. Under capitalism, each household receives capital property return in proportion to its financial capital wealth. Owing principally to the workings of inheritance and chance, the distribution of financial capital wealth is grotesquely unequal among households. Thus the distribution of capital property return is grotesquely unequal. Under profit-oriented market socialism, on the other hand, most of the capital property return produced by the publicly owned business firms would be converted into social dividend income and distributed to the private households on some other basis than financial wealth—a more fair, equitable, and egalitarian basis.

The specific recommendation put forward herein is for distribution of social dividend wholly or primarily on the basis of earned labor income of the households: each household would receive an amount of social dividend income determined by its earned labor income (i.e., wage and salary income). Households earning more labor income would receive more social dividend income. Earned income would beget social dividend income. By the same token, no earned income means no social dividend income. In other words, social dividend would not be a dole provided to households whether they do anything to earn it or not. This particular proposal is not wholly uncontroversial, and it will be explicated and defended at various appropriate locations in the following.

Profit-oriented market socialism is a recent development in the history of socialist thought, and no doubt many individuals indoctrinated in earlier socialist thought will find the idea strange and unattractive. But the fact of the matter is that profit-oriented market socialism fully embodies the essence of the socialist concept implied in its standard dictionary definition: a socioeconomic system in which the capital means of production are publicly owned. The concept of ownership implies, first and foremost, entitlement to benefit: the owner of something is entitled to appropriate benefits flowing from that thing, whether they be physical benefits (as in living in one's house, eating one's food, wearing one's clothes) or financial benefits (as in selling or renting one's property to others). Applied to business firms, the concept implies that the owners of the firms, whether they be private bondholders and stockholders as under capitalism, or the public at large as under socialism, are entitled to the benefits (i.e., profits, interest, and other forms of property return) produced by the firms' operations. A shift from private ownership capitalism to public ownership socialism implies a shift in the entitlement to the capital property return produced by business firms, from a relatively small minority of society, to the general population. (Under the specific proposal outlined herein for social dividend distribution according to earned labor income, it would be more accurate to say that under socialism it would be "that proportion of the general population" which is earning labor income which possesses an entitlement to capital property return in the form of social dividend. Of course, the vast majority of the general population *does* in fact earn labor income in some form or other.)

In traditional socialist thought, the perceived purpose of public ownership of capital (i.e., of business enterprises) is generally perceived to be "more" than simply altering the distribution of capital property return. The intention is clearly not to let business firms go on operating just as they have before, earning profits just as they have before—with the single innovation being that these profits would be more fairly distributed among the population than they were under capitalism. Rather the intention is to fundamentally revise the way in which firms operate—to eliminate exploitation and other socioeconomic perversities at the source.

Thus in traditional socialist thinking, business enterprises would most certainly *not* continue to profit-maximize. Instead, they might engage in "production for use instead of production for profit" (the social welfare maximization theme embodied in the service market socialist concept), or they might implement "workers working for themselves rather than for the owners" (the employee welfare maximization theme embodied in cooperative market socialism). Moreover, in traditional socialist thinking, not only profit-maximization but the market itself needs to be suppressed. A great deal of direct social intervention is typically envisioned: stringent regulation of production enterprises, steeply progressive taxation, massive welfare programs aimed at improving the lives of the poor, the disadvantaged, the needy. If and when a calm, logical, and reflective view of all this is taken, it becomes apparent that much of this program bears little or no relationship to the fundamental socialist principle of public ownership of the capital means of production. It does not just "go beyond" this fundamental principle, it departs entirely from it.

To some extent the low status of the term "socialism" in the contemporary world may be attributed to its association with the discredited Communistic social system, and also to some extent it may be attributed to the mass of sophistry produced by generations of clever and industrious defenders of capitalism. But at least some of the blame belongs to the socialists themselves. Far too many of them have been shallow in their thinking and irresponsible in their assertions and actions. It is a common human weakness to gripe, grumble, and complain about various unsatisfactory aspects of reality—but at the same time to have no clear, cogent, and sensible ideas about how to eliminate or even ameliorate these unsatisfactory aspects. This failing has been particularly pronounced among socialists. From Marx down to the present day, most of them expend the great majority of their time and energy criticizing the status quo, so that they have little left over with which to devise plausible means by which the status quo might be significantly improved. With very few exceptions (Oskar Lange being one of them), socialists since the time of Marx have remained blissfully ignorant of economics, both institutional and theoretical. Thus they find it especially difficult to formulate socialist blueprints which meet minimum standards of economic plausibility. If, in the past, individuals drawn to socialist ideals had had more familiarity with and respect for economic inquiry, quite likely the idea of profit-oriented market socialism would not have taken so long to come to the fore.

But there is no point in lamenting the past, in "crying over spilt milk." The fact is that profit-oriented market socialism is *now*, at last, coming to

the fore. The idea of profit-oriented market socialism is a natural response to evolving reality. The lackluster long-term economic performance of Soviet-style socialism clearly demonstrates the perils of overly
ambitious planning, of trying to attain too great a degree of central control over the economy. At the same time, the development of capitalism
in the United States and Western Europe has clearly demonstrated that it
is possible to cope satisfactorily with a wide range of economic problems, from poverty to business depression to environmental degradation,
without necessarily resorting to public ownership of business enterprise.
But, despite its success, a large wart persists on the otherwise beauteous
face of contemporary capitalism: the extraordinary degree of inequality
in the distribution of financial capital wealth. This feature of capitalism
seems permanent and immutable. It has persisted, essentially unchanged,
throughout the twentieth century, and it promises to persist, essentially
unchanged, into the remote and unforeseeable future. Market socialism
offers a potential reform by which the capitalistic wart could be excised
from the social countenance quickly, conveniently, and completely.

The level of success which has

The basic idea of profit-oriented market socialism dates back at least
to the 1940s. In his book *Socialism: An Economic and Sociological
Analysis*, the English translation of which was published in 1951, Ludwig von Mises, one of the leading Austrian school economists of the
twentieth century, discussed the proposal of "some of the younger socialists" for what he skeptically termed the "artificial market." This would be
a socialist economic system in which the managers of firms would be instructed to maximize profits just as they do under capitalism, the distinction from capitalism being that the resulting profits would belong to the
community as a whole rather than to private capitalists. Mises formulated

an argument against the practicality of this proposal, but his argument seems fully oblivious of the nature of the modern capital market, in which institutional investors are not merely active, but are dominant. The sensibility of Mises's argument against the "artificial market" depends on business enterprises obtaining investment capital entirely from issues of stocks and bonds to private capitalists. But in fact under contemporary capitalism, business firms obtain most of their investment capital from retained earnings and the issuance of securities to institutional investors such as investment banks, insurance companies, pension funds, mutual funds, and so on. The realities of modern capital markets—which are obviously dominated by various kinds of institutional investors—give the lie to the proposition that private investors are indispensable to the efficient operation of the investment mechanism.

In describing and criticizing the "artificial market," Mises did not name the "younger socialists" he had in mind, nor did he make reference to the published literature—which suggests that at that time the idea was part of what is known as the "oral tradition." Of course, if ideas are ever to have a significant impact on intellectual history, they must eventually graduate from the "oral tradition" to the published literature. At the present time, the idea of profit-oriented market socialism has indeed established a firm foothold in the published literature. Although the amount of published material on the concept is still relatively limited, the published material is growing at an accelerating rate. It may well be approaching that "critical mass" necessary to launch the subject of profit-oriented market socialism, within the near future, into intensive professional debate and public discussion.

To date there have been three separate, independently developed, clearly formulated proposals for profit-oriented market socialism put forward in the economic literature. My own article "Capital Management under Market Socialism," published in the *Review of Social Economy* in 1974, initiated the concept of "pragmatic market socialism." Since 1974 I have been intensively occupied with the development of the concept, and have published approximately 15 articles on it, as well as two books. An article by Leland G. Stauber titled "The Implications of Market Socialism in the United States," published in *Polity* in 1975, initiated a second variant of profit-oriented market socialism, which I designate (in the absence of any specific term suggested by Stauber himself) "municipal ownership market socialism." Finally, an article by John E. Roemer titled "Market Socialism: A Blueprint (How Such an Economy Might Work)," published in *Dissent* in 1991, initiated a third variant of profit-oriented market socialism, which I designate (in the absence of any specific term suggested by Roemer himself) "bank-centric market socialism." To date the volume of published writing on municipal ownership market socialism by Leland Stauber and on bank-centric market socialism by John Roemer is considerably less than that by myself on pragmatic market socialism. With respect to John Roemer, he has only recently commenced publishing on the subject of bank-centric market socialism, and there is every likelihood that he will be contributing a great deal more in the future. In contrast to myself and Roemer, professors of economics by profession, Leland Stauber is a professor of political science. Consequently, the economic theory content of his relatively limited published writing on municipal ownership market socialism is decidedly sparse. Nevertheless, speaking as a professional economist, I would have to say that Stauber seems to possess very sound economic instincts. His market socialist proposal is cogent, plausible, and in practice would probably mimic the market capitalist economy of today even more closely than the proposals of myself and John Roemer.

On the assumption that many if not most readers of this book are not specialists in the study of market socialism, I will forgo any effort at an evaluative analysis of the pros and cons of these three different varieties of profit-oriented market socialism. In actual fact, from a larger perspective their points of similarity are far more important than their points of dissimilarity. The discussion will be purely descriptive and will endeavor to impart some of the more important insights of each of these three authors on the problem of designing market socialist institutions capable of reproducing the level of economic efficiency currently achieved by the market capitalist economy.

It will be convenient to start with some aspects on which the three profit-oriented market socialist proposals are virtually identical. First, even though most large, established corporations would be publicly owned—meaning that the preponderance of the capital stock in advanced industrial nations would be publicly owned, there would remain a substantial role for private ownership in the economy. To begin with, almost any kind of business enterprise which falls under the "small business" rubric would remain under private ownership: this would include family farms, small retail stores, and professional proprietorships and partnerships in medicine, law, accounting, and so on. Nonprofit organizations and associations would remain privately owned. Last but hardly least, any sort of entrepreneurial business enterprise, whatever its size or level of profitability, would remain in private ownership. An "entrepreneurial business enterprise" is defined as one in which the founder-owner continues to be active in management. Of course, as we know from statistics on business formations and business failures, the vast majority of entrepreneurial business enterprises are relatively small operations in financially perilous circumstances. The bankruptcy rate among recently established businesses being managed by their founders is terrific.

But at the same time, there will always be a tiny handful of mega-successful entrepreneurial enterprises. For example, Microsoft Corporation, the computer software giant, which at the time of writing is still being personally managed by its founder Bill Gates, falls into this category. Under profit-oriented market socialism, Microsoft Corporation would remain privately owned so long as Bill Gates chose to stay on as its chief executive officer. Entrepreneurial enterprises would remain in private ownership so long as they remained genuinely entrepreneurial. Such firms would revert to public ownership only when their founder-owners choose voluntarily to depart from their management and sell their ownership interests. Typically the founder-owner would sell his/her ownership share to another publicly owned corporation, and therefore he/she would receive the full capitalized value of that ownership share. This means that large personal fortunes derived from genuine entrepreneurial endeavors (i.e., actual foundation of a productive enterprise—as opposed to mere financial speculation) could certainly be achieved under profit-oriented market socialism, no less than under contemporary capitalism. Although the odds against this happening under either economic system are something on the order of the odds against winning a million dollars in a lottery, it is generally regarded as a great strength of market capitalism that the possibility at least *exists*. Profit-oriented market socialism would possess this putative great strength to no less a degree than capitalism.

The profit-oriented market socialist proposals put forward by myself, Stauber, and Roemer all envision a level and intensity of competition among the publicly owned business firms at least comparable to the level and intensity among the privately owned firms under contemporary capitalism. The structure of firms would remain approximately what it is today: that is to say, there would be no mergers and amalgamations of independent firms into larger operations, nor would there be, as a general rule, any disaggregations of existing firms. It should be noted in this connection, however, that proponents of profit-oriented market socialism tend to be somewhat more sensitive to the potential costs imposed on the economy by imperfect competition than the typical economist today. In the past, a number of well-known authorities in the area of industrial organization have expressed considerable interest in a potentially extensive program of mandatory antitrust divestitures of very large firms in highly concentrated industries. Such disaggregations would be comparable to those imposed on Standard Oil and American Tobacco in 1911, toward the end of the "trust-busting" campaign initiated by President Theodore Roosevelt in the early 1900s. These authorities have argued persuasively that on the whole, disaggregations of this sort do not significantly endanger economies of scale—while at the same time they do significantly improve the long-term prospects for healthy competition in the business enterprise sector. In recent decades, the pendulum of political opinion has swung back to the right, thus eliminating the practical possibility of any such program of disaggregations. The fact remains that a better case can be made for such a program than most people realize. Perhaps the initiation of profit-oriented market socialism would sufficiently curtail the political influence of those wealthy conservatives excessively enamored of the status quo, to enable another look to be taken at this particular issue. However, any disaggregation program that might be undertaken at a later date has nothing to do with the basic nature of profit-oriented market socialism, and this type of market socialism implies that "as a rule" the structure of business enterprise would remain closely comparable to the present structure under capitalism.

Needless to emphasize, many critics of market socialism peremptorily dismiss the notion that there could be any appreciable degree of competition among a population of large-scale business firms most of which are owned by the government. It is quite true that under capitalism, in which the government is mostly kept out of business enterprise, we observe little behavior that is directly and obviously comparable to competition as witnessed in the business enterprise sector. Nevertheless, a closer inspection reveals quite a lot of competitive behavior. One does not have to be a military historian, for example, to be aware of "inter-service rivalry." What is true of the army, the navy and the air force is true of government divisions, agencies and organizations in general: they compete vigorously with one another for recognition, assignments, and budget appropriations. This occurs at the level of national government, and at lower levels as well. It so happens that this author is a professor of economics at a state university in Illinois. The competition between my university and other state universities in Illinois for student enrollment and state appropriations may not be explicit and acknowledged, but despite that it is none the less vigorous and intense in reality. At the same time, the public universities in the state of Illinois, taken as a whole, are in vigorous competition with the private universities, taken as a whole. Of course, education is not supposed to be a "business," and therefore it is not supposed to be characterized by "competition" as this term applies to business enterprise. But even if we consider the usual business sense of competition, there is at least a certain amount of competitive behavior by government agencies to be observed under capitalism today. For example, in the United States, Amtrak competes with the privately owned airlines for the patronage of travelers, and the U.S. Postal Service competes with such privately owned firms as United Parcel Service and Federal Express in the shipping market.

Critics of socialism often have great difficulty envisioning genuine competition among publicly owned business enterprises because they have an unrealistic conception of government as a totally unified and co-ordinated entity in which all personnel are energetically pursuing a common goal (the "antheap" perception). Of course, in reality, government authority in a democratic polity is very substantially decentralized and diversified. There is a division of powers both regionally (local, state, and national government agencies) and structurally (legislative, executive, and judicial branches of government). The "government" is far from being homogeneous and monolithic: it is actually a relatively loose conglomeration consisting of hundreds of separate divisions staffed by thousands of different individuals. Each one of that multitude of divisions and individuals is self-interested and self-motivated, and they all have their own separate and distinct ways of viewing their purpose and "serving the public interest" (and thereby, of course, their own interest).

Under profit-oriented market socialism, the tens of thousands of publicly owned large corporations would be "government agencies" only in the most general and abstract sense. They would bear no relationship whatsoever to "government agencies" as they are understood today under capitalism. The standard government agency, whether operating under capitalism or market socialism, depends for all or most of its revenue on appropriations from general government tax revenue, and is considered to be providing an essential public service so that it will be maintained permanently (though possibly at different levels of support depending on political conditions). In contrast, publicly owned business firms under profit-oriented market socialism would be financially self-sufficient, and no one of them would be deemed indispensable to the operations of the overall economy (since each type of commodity would normally be provided by dozens or even hundreds of different firms). The typical publicly owned business firm would receive no subsidies or financial support of any sort from the government. Rather the success of its managers would be evaluated on the basis of how much profit and interest the firm pays over to the public ownership agency. Managers of these firms would have to cope with two fundamental realities: (1) a firm whose costs exceed its revenues will soon succumb to bankruptcy, thereby throwing all of its employees, from top managers to janitors, out of work; (2) even if revenues are covering costs and bankruptcy is not an immediate threat, a firm which is producing an inadequate rate of profit, in light of profit rates of similar firms, will quite possibly have its chief executive officer dismissed by the public ownership agency.

Top corporate managers would be held strictly accountable for the success or lack of success of their firms, owing to the fact that they would be highly independent and autonomous in their business decision-making. Profit-oriented market socialism involves no planning or central coordination of business enterprise whatsoever. In fact, the public ownership agency would be strictly forbidden, in its organizational charter, from issuing any instructions whatever to the firm managers regarding the decision variables of business enterprise: quantities of production, product innovations, product prices, hiring and firing of labor, marketing expenditures, research and development, borrowing and capital investment, etc. The authority of the public ownership agency would be strictly confined to the retention or dismissal of high corporate executives on clearly defined, objective grounds of current and anticipated profitability. Assuming a particular corporation were earning a satisfactory rate of profit by legitimate means (i.e., was not in violation of environmental or safety regulations, was not engaging in conspiracies in restraint of trade or unfair business practices, was not misrepresenting its financial condition, and so on), then its top managers would be absolutely immune to any adverse actions, or threats of adverse actions, by the public ownership agency. The public ownership agency's interest in business enterprise would be confined, purely and simply, to bottomline profitability. Responsibility for deterring business firms from socially undesirable behavior would lie with other government agencies, agencies (in the United States) such as the Environmental Protection Agency, the Occupational Health and Safety Administration, the Food and Drug Administration, the Antitrust Division of the Department of Justice, the Federal Trade Commission, and so on.

Quite possibly the rate of dismissal of high corporation executives on grounds of inadequate profitability would be higher under profit-oriented market socialism than it is presently under capitalism. Under the real-world capitalism of the present day, top managers are well insulated against rigorous performance evaluation by the separation of ownership and control. Stock ownership in the typical large corporation under contemporary capitalism is so widely dispersed over so many heterogeneous, widely dispersed, and unorganized stockholders that it normally takes a prolonged period of time before poor profit performance elicits pink slips for the top management. Poor performance will motivate stockholders to divest themselves of their ownership interest in the corporation (i.e., to sell their stock, and this will drive the market price of the stock down). But it normally takes a very long time before declining prices of a firm's securities in the capital markets brings down the incumbent managers. The public ownership authority could be structured and organized in such a way as to accelerate this process, thus enforcing a more rigorous and effective discipline upon the corporate executive elite. As a matter of fact, it is easy to envision the public ownership authority becoming *too* severe and draconic in its relations with corporation executives. Aside from the possibility of debilitating morale problems among the top executives owing to excessive insecurity, they might become *excessively* assiduous in their pursuit of profits. They might be driven to trying to increase profits by illegitimate means, such as evading environmental and workplace safety regulations.

Another potential illicit avenue toward the raising of profits would be collusive behavior aimed at the suppression of competition. Firms in the same market might contemplate price-fixing or market-sharing agreements. Such agreements may be illegal (they certainly are in the United States), but if the managers are sufficiently desperate to try to increase profits even by illegal means, such agreements might become prevalent anyway. One might easily envision the public ownership agency under profit-oriented market socialism turning a blind eye on such collusive arrangements, and even doing what it could to foster them. After all, the basic measure of this agency's success would be the amount of social dividend income which it is able to distribute to the population, and this amount is in turn determined by the overall profitability of publicly owned business enterprise. Conceivably a pragmatic market socialist economy might display a very high rate of profit, but if this high rate was being achieved by means of the ubiquity throughout the economy of collusive arrangements to suppress competition, then this high rate of profit clearly would not be an indicator of a high level of efficiency. As in all other things, therefore, there is a happy medium with respect to the *intensity* of the profit motivation among corporate executives.

The potential problem of the public ownership agency under profit-oriented market socialism aiding and abetting collusive behavior among the publicly owned business firms, in the interest of raising the overall profit rate, is a serious problem, and it has been seriously considered by all three proposers of profit-oriented market socialist systems: myself, Stauber, and Roemer. All three proposals call for a very substantial degree of decentralization of the public ownership agency. Among other things, such decentralization would inhibit the ability of the public ownership agency to foster collusion among the publicly owned corporations. Of course, quite aside from this particular issue, it goes without saying that the organizational structure and internal procedures of the public ownership agency are absolutely central to the potential viability and performance of profit-oriented market socialism. To a large extent, the plausibility of any particular plan of profit-oriented market socialism is directly dependent on the plausibility of the proposed public ownership agency.

The public ownership agency under profit-oriented market socialism would take over the economic role of the class of private capital owners under contemporary capitalism: the role of instilling a healthy interest in profitability into the high executives who manage corporate business enterprise. According to the generally positive and optimistic view of profit maximization which is adopted herein, legitimate methods of raising profits (e.g., reducing costs of production, increasing demand by improvements in product quality, and so on) are economically beneficial. The nexus between the ownership interest and the corporation executives is the board of directors. The board of directors possesses continuing authority (although rarely utilized in practice) of dismissing the incumbent managers and replacing them with others. Under capitalism, the board of directors of any particular corporation is elected by private stockholders. It is therefore the interest of the private stockholders in profits which underlies the interest of corporation executives in profits, this latter interest being enforced by the board of directors. Under profit-oriented market socialism, the interest of the public ownership agency in profits would be transmitted to the corporation executives either through the board of directors mechanism or some highly analogous mechanism.

By far the most elaborate description of the potential institutions, mechanisms and processes of profit-oriented market socialism to be found in the published literature to date pertains to my own proposal for "pragmatic market socialism." This is merely a statement of fact, and by no means implies that these arrangements would be optimal. My writing on pragmatic market socialism has consistently emphasized the tentative and provisional nature of these proposed arrangements. My intention has been to provide just enough institutional detail to provide the reader with a clear impression of the nature and purposes of this type of market socialism. The objective has been to get people thinking about the concept, to lay a basis for further thought and discussion—not to firmly specify, once and for all, various institutional details.

With this proviso, I will first provide a brief summary of the public ownership agency under pragmatic market socialism, afterwards proceeding on to the corresponding proposals of Stauber and Roemer. To begin with, under pragmatic market socialism, there would not be one but rather three organizationally separate and independent components of the overall "public ownership authority": (1) a Bureau of Public Ownership (BPO) with direct authority to dismiss managers of large-scale, established (that is to say, nonentrepreneurial), publicly owned business enterprises; (2) a National Investment Banking System (NIBS) which would purchase bonds from and make investment capital loans to business enterprises (both publicly owned and privately owned), but would have no direct authority to dismiss managers; (3) a National Entrepreneurial Investment Board (NEIB) whose purpose would be to establish new publicly owned business firms, as well as to fund entrepreneurial business firms founded by private citizens. The BPO would be entirely self-supporting, and in fact it would disburse the great preponderance of the profits and interest paid over to it by the publicly owned firms within its jurisdiction to the citizen body as social dividend income. The NIBS and the NEIB would be financial intermediaries, and they would supplement (rather than replace) the existing financial intermediaries under capitalism (such as commercial banks, investment banks, insurance companies and pension funds), which under pragmatic market socialism would fall under the purview of the Bureau of Public Ownership. The NIBS and NEIB would not contribute to the social dividend fund, but would rather retain all net earnings for reinvestment. Quite possibly they would also receive from the national government continuing annual appropriations to augment the amount of investment capital available to the business enterprise sector.

All three agencies (BPO, NIBS, and NEIB) would be spatially decentralized and dispersed over a large number (at least several hundred) local offices in cities and towns across the nation. Each agency would have a central office in the national capital concerned with overall finances, staffing, and so on, but the effective decision-making authority in dealing with individual business enterprises would be exercised wholly by the local offices and not by the national office. In other words, the national office would appoint the directors of the local offices and would specify various general principles pertaining to their activities, but it would not make specific decisions such as whether to dismiss the chief executive officer of a publicly owned corporation which is experiencing low profitability, or whether to fund an investment project proposed by a particular publicly owned firm.

In their relations with their own "higher authority" (i.e., the national government), the public ownership agencies (BPO, NIBS, and NEIB) would be legally and administratively insulated against a high degree of direct control. The idea is to make them quasi-independent public corporations at least as autonomous as are such entities in the United States as the Federal Reserve Board and Amtrak. Their directors would be appointed by the president with the approval of Congress, and once appointed, they would be secure against dismissal except under conditions of severe incompetence or transgression of the public trust (as determined, in cases of dispute, by the Supreme Court). The direct authority of the national government over the Bureau of Public Ownership would be confined to two central principles: (1) the specification of a minimum rate of social dividend disbursement (i.e., social dividend payments as a proportion of labor income) below which there would be a prima facie case for the incompetence of the BPO's director; (2) the specification of the maximum amount of gross income received by the BPO, in the form of profit and interest payments from publicly owned business firms, which the BPO may retain internally for its administrative and incentive expenses.

Of course, one of the most time-honored and effective arguments against socialism is implied in the striking phrase of Oskar Lange (himself a proponent of market socialism): "bureaucratization of economic life." This basic idea, especially when applied to profit-oriented market socialism such as considered here, is crude, unfair and inaccurate—but that does not prevent it from being extremely effective as a rhetorical device against socialism. The terms "bureaucrat" and "bureaucracy" are strongly evocative and heavily loaded—they have the capacity of effectively shutting down the ordinary processes of rational thought, reflection, and deliberation. Throughout the protracted history of intellectual confrontation between capitalism and socialism, there is no telling how many minds have been swung against socialism by endless repetition of the hoary charge that under socialism, the brilliant, imaginative, courageous entrepreneurs we know under capitalism would be replaced by faceless, soulless "bureaucrats." Of course the typical person's conception of a "bureaucrat" is that of a minor official in the Internal Revenue Service: an unimaginative, unhelpful, unsympathetic personality, intellectually and emotionally limited, petty and obstructionist in outlook, an unsavory little would-be dictator whose main solace in life is in lording it over subordinates—and also over hard-working, reputable, innocent, blameless citizens who through no fault of their own run afoul of the byzantine rules and regulations of the IRS. Therefore, the image of "bureaucrats" running business enterprises under socialism is guaranteed to put socialism in a bad light.

If and when this image is examined seriously, one can perceive its tenuous roots in reality. In the first place, in sociological thought, "bureaucracy" is a neutral term and refers to any substantial, hierarchically organized human organization. Therefore it refers as much to General Motors Corporation, Harvard University, the United States Marine Corps, and the Audubon Society as it does to the Internal Revenue Service. From a sociological point of view, any individual with any sort of supervisory or administrative rank within a substantial organization is a "bureaucrat." Owing to the comprehensive nature of the sociological definition of "bureaucracy," there is no use in denying that the three public ownership agencies under pragmatic market socialism (the BPO, NIBS, and NEIB) would be bureaucracies. In fact, I have chosen to meet this particular challenge head-on in specifying as the name of the foremost of the three agencies the *Bureau* of Public Ownership (as opposed to the "Federal Holding Corporation," or some other more innocuous-sounding circumlocution). The fact is that these agencies would be as free of the usual pejorative connotations of the term "bureaucracy" as any other substantial human organization, of whatever nature or purpose. And the same would be true of the publicly owned business enterprises over which the BPO exercises the public ownership authority.

To begin with, the top managers of the publicly owned corporations would *not* be "bureaucrats" as the term is usually understood. The term is usually understood to refer to a civil servant who has made a career of employment with a government agency, and has gradually worked his/her way up through the ranks to the administrative level which in business is called "middle management." Such individuals are commonly viewed as excessively cautious and conservative, as lacking in initiative and imagination, and as obsessively preoccupied with abiding by formal rules and regulations. Needless to say, such individuals are generally regarded as highly unsuited to the demanding, challenging, ever-changing work of business management. With "bureaucrats" running business enterprises, we could expect only the worst—stagnation and decline. Without debating whether government civil servants are in reality as limited as presupposed in this argument, it must be emphasized, in the strongest terms, that this particular argument would be totally false and irrelevant as applied to corporation executives under pragmatic market socialism.

The chief executive officer of any given corporation will have spent his/her entire career in business enterprise, and will have risen through the ranks of a profit-oriented business enterprise according to the same principles and practices as hold today under capitalism. Among these principles and practices is the possibility of being dismissed, without ceremony, apology, or recourse, from a position of administrative authority—if one is perceived, for whatever reason, to be incompetent and/or ineffective by one's immediate superiors. The lack of job security in middle-level corporate administration is one of the most psychologically taxing aspects of this type of employment, and it is a principal reason why salaries must be generous to attract qualified individuals to these positions. The terms and conditions of corporate managerial employment under capitalism (especially the high salaries and low job security) are considered essential components of the economic success of the system. Exactly the same terms and conditions would hold under pragmatic market socialism—or, in general, under any variety of profit-oriented market socialism. Thus corporate executives under this system would most certainly *not* be "bureaucrats"—using the widespread pejorative meaning of this term. They *would* be bureaucrats using the neutral sociological meaning of the term—just as corporate executives under capitalism are bureaucrats using this meaning.

Of course, the corporate executives under pragmatic market socialism would be subject to dismissal by the personnel of the Bureau of Public Ownership. It might be argued that while the corporation executives themselves might personally be free of the odious and pernicious taint of bureaucracy, surely the personnel of the BPO would be "bureaucrats" in the nasty sense, and thereby the performance of the entire economic system would be called into question. One response to this is that even if we imagine the stereotypical stupid and malicious bureaucrat, such an individual might be able to successfully perform the essential function of the BPO, which is merely to dismiss the chief executives of corporations suffering from low profitability. How difficult can it be to look at the audited financial statements of a corporation, and conclude that its rate of profit is beneath that of comparable corporations? As for the stress of imposing the pain of dismissal on another human being, presumably stupid, malicious bureaucrats are better able to cope with this type of stress than is the common run of humanity.

Of course, just as it is inaccurate and unfair to characterize the typical civil servant of today as a stupid and malicious bureaucrat, so too it would be inaccurate and unfair to characterize the personnel of the Bureau of Public Ownership under pragmatic market socialism in such terms. But to make this point even stronger, I would propose that the BPO personnel to whom the actual effective authority to dismiss corporation executives is delegated *not* be permanent, career employees of the BPO. Rather these individuals would be called "BPO agents" (rather than "BPO employees"), and they would be employed as agents by the BPO only in their middle age, after they had personally achieved a high level of success as corporation executives. In other words, those called upon to pass judgment on corporation executives would themselves be corporate executives in terms of prior training and experience.

BPO agents would be selected at random from a roster of qualified individuals with substantial experience in upper level management for terms of from five to ten years. During that period of time, a BPO agent could be dismissed only on grounds of criminal activity or egregious incompetence. After serving one or two terms as a BPO agent, an individual could return to business management, although by that time most of them would have reached retirement age. The remuneration of BPO agents would be sufficiently generous that most of the high-level business executives tapped for service through the lottery mechanism would be happy to accept the appointment. Each BPO agent would be assigned ten to twenty publicly owned corporations to oversee. The BPO agent's primary responsibility would be to decide whether the chief executive officer (CEO) of a given publicly owned corporation, which is within the agent's sphere of authority, and which is also experiencing low profitability, should be dismissed (i.e., fired).

The dismissal of the top executive of a publicly owned corporation would of course be a rather drastic action (particularly from the point of view of the executive involved), and certain safeguards would be implemented to reduce the likelihood of arbitrary and capricious dismissals by BPO agents. The national office of the BPO would collect financial information from all of the publicly owned corporations in the economy. This information would be statistically processed for the purpose of determining the most likely rate of profit (i.e., expected rate of profit) of each particular publicly owned corporation. Using this as a base, two "critical" profit rates would be determined for each corporation. The "upper critical profit rate" would be a profit rate sufficiently high that the CEO of the corporation *could not be* dismissed under any circumstances. This means that the CEO of a corporation doing this well would be immune against being fired by the BPO agent of his/her corporation. The "lower critical profit rate" would be a profit rate sufficiently low that the CEO of the corporation *must be* dismissed whatever the circumstances. This means that the CEO of a corporation doing this poorly would have to be dismissed whatever extenuating conditions might exist—the BPO agent would have no discretion to be "merciful," so to speak. The BPO agent would only have discretionary authority to determine whether a certain CEO should stay or go when the profit rate of that CEO's corporation is *between* the "upper critical profit rate" and "lower critical profit rate" determined by objective statistical means. It is envisioned that at any given time, only two or three of the ten to twenty publicly owned corporations within any particular agent's sphere of authority would have profit rates in the range where dismissal of the CEO by the agent is an option. The BPO agent would have to study these particular corporations closely in order to decide whether their unsatisfactory profitability is at all attributable to the failings of their CEOs.

The specification of an "upper critical profit rate" would be the primary means by which corporation chief executive officers would be protected against arbitrary and capricious dismissals. Another means would be the review of dismissal decisions by a board consisting of other BPO agents. In addition, the replacement mechanism would be such that the BPO agent would have no incentive to fire a certain CEO as a means of creating a job opportunity for one of the agent's personal friends. Following dismissal of a corporate CEO, the successor would be chosen not by the BPO agent involved, but rather by a committee composed of the corporation's employees. The new CEO would have a grace period of at least two or three years before he/she could possibly become a candidate for dismissal.

While the power of dismissal is the most fundamental authority delegated to the BPO agent, the agent would also have a secondary authority of considerable consequence. This authority pertains to the remuneration and perquisites of the top executives of the publicly owned corporations within the agent's sphere of authority. Remuneration covers salary, bonuses, etc., while perquisites cover various nonpecuniary benefits such as company cars, office decor, etc. Principles and practices governing executive remuneration and perquisites would be designed by the executives themselves, but these principles and practices would then have to be approved by the corporation's BPO agent. A serious case may be made that owing to the separation of ownership and control under contemporary capitalism, executive benefits have become inflated, and considerably exceed the marginal productivity of these same executives. Certainly the extremely generous compensation of corporate CEOs under capitalism is a matter of continuing interest and concern. Quite possibly the implementation of pragmatic market socialism would witness a certain amount of scaling back of the benefits of the highest executives. However, it should be emphasized that owing to the critical importance of these executives in the economy, their remuneration would still be quite high, and would in all probability considerably exceed that of other high-level professionals such as doctors and lawyers (just as is the case under capitalism).

The principal work effort of the typical BPO agent would consist of careful study of those circumstances in which the dismissal of a corporate CEO is an available option. This means reading the financial statements of the company as well as its internal business plans and memoranda, interviewing employees, and studying the history and present status of the markets in which the company operates. The guiding question would be whether avoidable errors by the CEO contributed to the corporation's unsatisfactory level of profitability. Making the wrong decision could worsen the corporation's condition, possibly plunging it into bankruptcy. Basically the BPO agent would be engaging in performance evaluation, and anyone who has ever been involved in it knows that performance evaluation—if it is to be done well—is a subtle and difficult task.

The BPO agent's material incentive to perform fair and accurate performance evaluation of corporation CEOs lies in what will be termed herein the "retention coefficient." This refers to that proportion of the total amount of capital property return (profits and interest), paid over by the publicly owned corporations within his/her sphere of authority to the national office of the Bureau of Public Ownership, which the agent receives as personal income. In other words, a specified percentage of this total amount would be returned to the BPO agent as an incentive bonus. The personal income of the BPO agent would be dominated by this incentive bonus, because the flat salary of the position would be relatively modest. For example, a typical agent might receive $50,000 per year in salary, but could expect to receive 10 or 20 times that amount in the form of an incentive bonus proportional to the total amount of property income received by the BPO national office from that agent's corporations. The retention coefficient of the BPO agent might be in the range from .01 to .02 (i.e., 1 to 2 percent) of this total amount.

The BPO's retention coefficient as a whole might be on the order of 5 percent of capital property return produced by the publicly owned business sector. Of this amount, 1 to 2 percent would go directly to the agents as incentive bonuses, while the remainder would cover various administrative expenses. This implies that upwards of 95 percent of capital property income produced by the publicly owned business sector would be returned to the population in the form of a social dividend supplement to labor income (wages and salaries).

The corps of several thousand BPO agents would be dispersed over several hundred local BPO offices located in cities and towns across the nation. Human beings need peer companionship, and it is expected that this would be provided by other BPO agents, and supporting staff members, within the local office. Of course, a potential problem of the system being described is the natural incentive among BPO agents to foster collusive behavior among publicly owned corporations for the sake of augmenting profitability. Collusive behavior among corporation executives under U.S. capitalism is already illegal according to the antitrust statutes, and these statutes would of course apply also to BPO agents. Another means of helping BPO agents resist temptation is to have the corporations within the spheres of authority of the agents affiliated with one particular local office operating (for the most part) in different industries, so that these corporations would not be in direct competition with one another. In addition, agents affiliated with any one BPO local office would be strictly prohibited from contacts with agents at other BPO local offices. Penalties for any transgressions—of this and other rules regulating BPO agents—would be severe: including loss of employment, stiff fines, and lengthy terms of imprisonment.

The structure, operations, and regulations of the National Investment Banking System (NIBS) and National Entrepreneurial Investment Board (NEIB) would be roughly analogous to those just described for the Bureau of Public Ownership (BPO). In particular, these agencies would be decentralized over a large number of local offices, and their line personnel would retain as personal income some small proportion of the capital property return produced by the investments which they make.

Recall that the above-described public ownership authority pertains to my own proposal for "pragmatic market socialism." This set of tentative and provisional proposals is just one possibility out of a very wide range of possibilities. Let us turn now to the alternative possibilities put forward by Leland Stauber for "municipal ownership market socialism" and by John Roemer for "bank-centric market socialism."

Under Stauber's proposal, the public ownership authority would not be organized as a national agency with local offices—rather the "local offices," so to speak, would be entirely independent of one another, since they would be under the direct jurisdiction of various local government authorities which are entirely independent of one another. The public ownership authority would thus be decentralized among a large number (at least several hundred) fully autonomous regional investment funds, and these funds would operate very similarly to the pension funds and mutual funds with which we are familiar under capitalism. They would buy and sell stocks and bonds of corporations and would receive capital property income (including capital gains income) on their investments. Their income would be partly reinvested, partly contributed to the local municipality to help defray the costs of such public goods as roads and schools, and partly distributed as a social dividend income supplement to the population of the city (and surrounding region) in which the investment fund is located.

Private individuals would be excluded from the capital markets (except for individuals engaged in entrepreneurial enterprises), and therefore the business corporations could generally be described as "publicly owned." But even so, the circumstances of these corporations would be almost indistinguishable from the circumstances of corporations under capitalism. Each corporation would have its board of directors elected by stockholders. The only difference is that there would be no private individuals among the stockholders—voting stock would be held exclusively by institutional investors, including those existing already under capitalism (insurance companies, pension funds, etc.), plus the new municipal investment funds. Each corporation would obtain investment capital through loans taken from, or securities issued to, outside investors. The difference would be that the "outside investors" would include no private households—the role of private households in the capital markets would be entirely replaced by the municipal investment funds.

Stauber's plan for municipal ownership market socialism has two especially attractive features. First, of the three plans for profit-oriented market socialism currently available in the published literature, clearly it would mimic the institutions and operations of contemporary capitalism more closely than the other two plans (mine and Roemer's). Institutional investors have already become dominant in contemporary capital markets, which means that the subtraction from these markets of private households and the replacement of these private households by several hundred municipal investment funds would have a practically imperceptible effect on the operations of these markets, and hence on the economy as a whole. It is ironic in a way that a professor of political science should have produced a better mirror image of market capitalism than two professors of economics (myself and Roemer). All profit-oriented market socialist proposals aim at a close correspondence to market capitalism, but Stauber's municipal ownership market socialist plan achieves a virtually exact correspondence. To the extent that a close parallel to the economic status quo is reassuring, the Stauber plan is very plausible.

A second attractive feature of the Stauber plan is that it essentially eliminates the traditional objection to socialism that it constitutes a threat to democracy. According to this time-honored objection, socialism represents an unhealthy combination of political and economic power in the hands of national government officials. These high officials would utilize public ownership of all or most business enterprise as an instrumentality to ensure their own continuation in power. Political opponents would be punished by unwarranted dismissals from their employment, while political allies would be rewarded with lucrative managerial positions. Consequently, the capability of the political opposition to challenge the incumbent political party would be attenuated and even annihilated. This is of course a very serious charge against socialism, and it will be closely considered in the following chapter. But note at this point that this objection entirely collapses when confronted by Leland Stauber's proposal for municipal ownership market socialism. As the name implies, under this plan public ownership would not be exercised by the unified national government, but rather by a collectivity of local governments none of which possesses undue political power within the nation as a whole. This wide dispersion of the public ownership authority would render the system virtually immune to serious abuses by any one local government authority.

As is the case with any particular plan, there are some problems with Stauber's proposal. Many of these have been brought up and discussed by Stauber himself. For example, there is the possibility of misallocation of investment resources because the municipal investment funds will invest in local industries—even if they are not particularly profitable—in the interest of protecting local employment. Stauber proposes to handle this type of problem by regulations imposed by the national government on the municipal investment funds. One such regulation would be limitations on the proportion of fund capital which may be invested locally. Another possible problem is that random variation in capital asset values may gradually impoverish one municipal investment fund while it enriches another. If this persists for any length of time, a very substantial degree of inequality in social dividend income might emerge among the populations of the various localities. Stauber proposes to handle this by means of intermittent redistributions of assets among the funds in order to keep the long-run distribution of social dividend relatively equal among localities.

In my own view as a proponent of a competitor concept of profit-oriented market socialism, Stauber's plan is a very serious contender for consideration. I still have a preference for the Bureau of Public Ownership approach to the public ownership authority over the municipal investment fund approach—but it is hardly an intense preference. But if in reality the BPO approach *would* be better, the reason is that the BPO approach would, to a considerable degree, reverse the unhealthy effects of the separation of ownership and control under contemporary capitalism. Arguably, this separation has progressed to such a point that the top corporate executives form the weakest link in the economic chain. Unless the profitability of the typical large contemporary corporation becomes virtually disastrous, its top managers will face no serious challenge to their continued incumbency. The weak accountability of the top managers is manifested not only by the astronomical remuneration they award themselves, but also—even more harmfully—by inadequate effort toward corporate excellence. Many top executives "preside" over their companies rather than energetically "managing" them. If implemented, Stauber's plan would do nothing to rectify the separation of ownership and control—nothing to enhance the practical accountability of the highest corporation executives.

In contrast, my own BPO proposal directly addresses this issue. The concentration of all authority over one particular publicly owned corporation in the hands of one particular BPO agent is fully intentional: the objective could be described as a "one-person board of directors." In traditional economic thinking, the single owner situation represents the height of control and accountability, and hence the maximum incentive toward profitability among the top managers of a corporation. The BPO proposal would produce the analogue of a single owner situation for the full range of publicly owned business enterprise under market socialism.

This is an important reason why such a system might display not merely a level of economic performance *equivalent* to that of contemporary capitalism, but a level of economic performance *higher* than that of contemporary capitalism.

Turning finally to the plan of John Roemer for bank-centric market socialism, we find an institutional proposal for a public ownership authority somewhere between the Bureau of Public Ownership of pragmatic market socialism and the municipal investment funds of municipal ownership market socialism. This plan is inspired by the Japanese *keiretsu* system of investment banking, which has apparently worked quite well in practice, and which is often cited as an important contributor to the postwar "Japanese economic miracle."

Roemer envisions a network of several hundred public investment banks, nationally owned but operating quite independently in many different localities around the nation. He has not as yet provided a proper name for the public investment banks, but they would to some extent combine the functions of the Bureau of Public Ownership and the National Investment Banking System of my own proposal for pragmatic market socialism. Each publicly owned corporation would be assigned to one of the public investment banks in the system, and this bank would be known as the corporation's "main bank." The main bank would hold a controlling share of the voting stock in the corporation, and hence it would effectively possess the authority to dismiss the incumbent managers. The main bank would also be the principal source of new capital investment funding for the corporation. Each main bank would have at least several dozen publicly owned corporations within its sphere of responsibility. In order to evade the collusion possibility, these corporations would for the most part operate in different industries and not be in substantial direct competition with one another.

My own BPO proposal envisions no trading whatever in corporate securities among the BPO agents. Therefore a particular agent dissatisfied with the performance of one of the corporations within his/her sphere of responsibility would *not* possess the option of simply selling that corporation's securities to someone else. The Stauber proposal for municipal investment funds, on the other hand, envisions full trading in corporate securities among the funds. Thus a fund dissatisfied with the performance of a corporation in which it owns securities would simply sell those securities, either to another fund, or to some other type of financial intermediary (such as an insurance company or pension fund). The Roemer plan is midway between these two extremes: it does *not* envision the main banks trading among themselves in the securities of their corporations, but it *does* envision trading of corporate securities going on *within* the group of corporations assigned to a particular main bank.

While a majority of voting stock in a particular corporation within its group would be held by the main bank, a certain amount of voting stock (and also of other types of securities) would be held by the other corporations in the main bank's "family." These corporations would trade among themselves, and also with the main bank itself, in the securities of any particular member corporation. A signal that a particular corporation within the group was in trouble, therefore, would be a tendency among the other corporations within the group to want to divest themselves of that corporation's securities, leading to declines in the securities' prices and/or to a larger proportion of the corporation's securities held by the main bank itself. However, such tendencies toward divestiture would presumably not occur very often, owing to a program of mutual aid and assistance within the main bank group.

In the view of John Roemer, a special strength of bank-centric market socialism lies in its relatively sophisticated system of collective monitoring (i.e., performance evaluation) of corporations. The board of directors of any particular corporation within a main bank's group would typically include not only representatives of the main bank itself but also high-level managers of other corporations within the group. Such individuals would be capable of providing sound technical commentary and recommendations to a particular corporation which had gotten into difficulty, thus helping to restore it to financial health. And if at some point in the process of corporate recovery it were deemed necessary to replace the current top management group, there would be a greater likelihood that the dismissals were legitimately based on avoidable errors made by the dismissed managers. This system supposedly has helped make Japanese industry extremely competitive in the world market, and it could also, according to Roemer, make a major contribution to the success of profit-oriented market socialism.

Neither my own plan for pragmatic market socialism nor Stauber's plan for municipal ownership market socialism envisions the outside ownership interest in the typical publicly owned business corporation (in this case, the "outside owners" are the public at large) being represented by individuals who are managers of other publicly owned business corporations. Although it is a positive feature of Roemer's proposal that it would get technically well-qualified outside individuals involved in the evaluation of a particular corporation suffering from low profitability, the actual contribution made by these well-qualified outsiders may not be all that great. After all, running their own corporations would take all or most of their available time/energy resources, and their personal financial interest in the performance of some other publicly owned corporation in the group would be indirect and numerically slight.

Moreover, there could be a tendency for the system to dampen long-run competition. It is specified by Roemer that the member firms of a particular main bank group would not be in direct competition with one another. But two firms which are not presently in competition may enter into competition at some point in the future—for example, if they decide to enter the same market. Presumably common membership in a main bank group would deter any two corporations from contemplating simultaneous entry into the same market at some future date. Of course, as long as there is a sufficient number of main banks and a sufficient number of corporate groups in the economy, the unlikelihood that firms within the *same* group would enter into competition with one another may not have any appreciable effect on the overall level of competition.

As indicated above, it would certainly be premature at this point to enter into a detailed evaluation of the three existing proposals for profit-oriented market socialism (my own proposal for pragmatic market socialism, Leland Stauber's proposal for municipal ownership market socialism, and John Roemer's proposal for bank-centric market socialism). The similarities between the three proposals are far more important than the differences, and it is indeed quite striking that three separate individuals, working independently, should have developed such similar market socialist proposals. In the future, additional market socialist proposals, profit-oriented and otherwise, may well be added to the discussion. Sooner or later, if market socialism is ever to become a politically relevant possibility, some reasonable degree of consensus must be reached among advocates of the idea, so that the general public will know precisely what it is that is being proposed. On the other hand, all the minor details need not be specified in advance. Differences in minor details, after all, are not likely to be critical in determining the overall performance of the market socialist system.

TOWARD A NEW SYNTHESIS

At this point it should be evident that, even excluding Oskar Lange's original proposal for marginal cost pricing market socialism as manifestly impractical, there remains a very wide range of market socialist possibilities for which a good case may be made both intuitively and in terms of economic theory. While the emphasis herein has been, and will continue to be, on profit-oriented market socialism, the fact remains that neither the service market socialist possibility nor the cooperative market socialist possibility may be ruled out on a priori grounds. Although the more idealistic notions of these latter two forms are more or less obviously unrealistic and unworkable, practical versions of either one of them exist, and might well be established in a large-scale modern industrial economy with a reasonable expectation of economic success.

The following chapter will essay a serious, extended discussion of the potential performance of a market socialist economy relative to the market capitalist economy of today. While some of the issues discussed are sufficiently general to apply to almost any kind of market socialism, other issues are importantly affected by the specific type of market socialism under consideration. Therefore, in order to achieve a sharp focus in the next chapter, this chapter will be concluded with a brief specification of several key aspects pertaining to the proposed market socialist system. An effort will be made to combine certain elements from each of the three proposals for profit-oriented market socialism discussed in the previous section, as well as some elements from the idea of cooperative market socialism.

Compensation for socialized property. It should emphasized in this context that socialization would apply solely to *capital* wealth (stocks, bonds, etc.), and would not affect other types of wealth such as real estate, furnishings, automobiles, clothes, jewelry, and so on. The intention is not communalism but socialism (public ownership of *capital*). Financial compensation would be paid to the former owners of capital assets, but any such compensation would not be in the form of interest-bearing government bonds, as this would just perpetuate the distributional inequities of capitalism in a somewhat different form. Also, there would be no moral obligation to maintain wealthy capitalists in the luxurious circumstances to which they have become accustomed, since very large capital wealthholdings are typically the result of inheritance and/or random chance rather than the personal merit and productivity of the owner. Small- to medium-sized capital wealth holdings, up to perhaps $500,000 in value, would be compensated fully in cash. This would protect the vast majority of individuals holding a modest amount of capital wealth accumulated out of savings from personally earned labor income. Beyond that level, the percentage of capital wealth compensated by cash would be a diminishing function of the size of the capital wealth. Care would be taken not to unduly penalize elderly capitalists no longer capable of work. At a minimum, enough compensation would be paid to elderly capitalists to enable the purchase of an annuity sufficient to maintain at least a comfortable standard of life.

Exceptions to public ownership. The primary exceptions to public ownership of capital would include the following: (1) small businesses in agriculture, retail trade, professional service, etc.; (2) nonprofit organizations such as schools, hospitals, etc.; (3) any entrepreneurial enterprise. An "entrepreneurial enterprise" is defined as any business enterprise still being personally managed by its founder-owner. Upon leaving management, the founder-owner would be obliged to sell his/her interest in the firm, but the sale would be to a publicly owned business corporation at the full capitalized value of the ownership share. Thus any individual who achieves a substantial fortune under capitalism by genuine entrepreneurship (as opposed to ordinary financial speculation in which there is no managerial effort involved) would be equally capable of achieving this fortune under market socialism. In general, privately owned businesses would be subject to a "capital use tax" designed to appropriate the purely rental return on capital. This tax rate would be based on the average rate of return on capital in the economy, and would be assessed on the net value of the private owner's share of the business. Proceeds from the capital use tax would be added to the social dividend fund.

Social dividend. In general under market socialism, there would be no receipt of interest or other forms of capital property return on financial wealth. There would be no limitations on the *amount* of financial wealth held by the household, but no *return* would be received on this wealth: it would be purely a store of value, rather than a source of income. (There would be some minor exceptions to this rule. For example, pension funds would be allowed to pay compound interest on financial accumulations of individuals earmarked for the provision of retirement income.) The elimination of unearned capital property income might seem to some a disadvantage of socialism. It must be strongly emphasized, therefore, that this particular "disadvantage" would be directly counterbalanced by the advantage of social dividend. Under market socialism, households would receive a social dividend payment not received under capitalism. Owing to the extraordinary inequality of capital wealth ownership under contemporary capitalism, the vast majority of households would receive more social dividend income under market socialism than the amount of capital property income they presently receive under capitalism. The net revenues of the publicly owned business enterprise sector definitely *would not* be added to general government tax revenue to be spent on various public goods and services. Rather the net revenues of the publicly owned business enterprise sector would be distributed directly to the public in the form of social dividend income. This is so that the public will be able to properly distinguish and evaluate the benefits of public ownership of capital—these benefits would not be adequately perceptible to the public if the net revenues of the publicly owned business enterprise sector were simply "plowed into" general government revenues and used to lighten the tax burden. Social dividend payments to private individuals would be in proportion to earned labor income (wages and salaries), or (in the case of retired individuals) in proportion to pension income.

Publicly owned business corporations. The great majority of large-scale, established (i.e., nonentrepreneurial) business corporations would be publicly owned under market socialism. Under profit-oriented market socialism as described above, the central objective of the publicly owned firm—this objective being enforced by an outside authority representing the public ownership interest and armed with the power to dismiss the top managers—would be the maximization of long-term profitability. Under cooperative market socialism, the central objective of the typical employee-owned firm—this objective being enforced by the democratic accountability of the top managers to the employees in free and open elections—would be the maximization of employee welfare. It has been maintained, up to this point, that profit orientation is preferable to cooperative production because it would be a closer approach to the present market system under capitalism. On the other hand, it must be recognized that cooperative production has a long history, both in theory and in practice, and it enjoys the support of a relatively large group of people, many of whom are either professional economists or well acquainted with economics. In other words, cooperative production is a serious contender for consideration. As a matter of fact, it may be possible to achieve a reasonable compromise between the separate notions of profit-oriented production under market socialism and cooperative production under market socialism. The following proposal represents an exploratory effort to find a synergistic synthesis between profit-oriented production and cooperative production that would exploit the advantages of each type.

The idea is simply to make the top management responsible *both* to a board of directors representing the outside ownership interest, *and* to an employee council representing the employees. Periodic meetings would be held between the top management group (the chief executive officer and the vice-presidents) and the board of directors; and similarly, periodic meetings would be held between the top management group and the employee council. There might be six such meetings per year with each group, on a staggered schedule: in one month the top management would meet with the board of directors, and in the following month it would meet with the employee council. If at any such meeting, the board of directors or the employee council were to pass a motion of no confidence in the incumbent management, this would put the chief executive officer of the firm under notice of dismissal within a specified period of time. There might be a grace period of one year during which the no confidence motion could be rescinded, if the group which passed the motion (the board of directors or the employee council) feels that sufficient improvement has occurred. Under this arrangement, both the outside ownership interest and the employees would have ultimate authority over the incumbent management. The top managers would have to give due consideration to the concerns of both parties.

The board of directors would be a 5-10 person group consisting of representatives of one or more branches of the public ownership agency. Its interest would be in the profitability of the corporation: in the amount of profits and interest the corporation was paying over to the national office of the public ownership agency. The board of directors would operate under the constraint of a "lower critical profit rate" and "upper critical profit rate" as described above in the discussion of pragmatic market socialism. Using statistical data on all publicly owned corporations, the national office of the public ownership agency would compute for each publicly owned corporation a lower critical profit rate such that if the actual profit rate of the firm were below this level the board of directors would be obliged to pass a motion of no confidence, and also an upper critical profit rate such that if the actual profit rate of the firm were above this level the board of directors would not have the option of passing a motion of no confidence. Only when the profit rate of the corporation were between these two critical levels would the board of directors have discretion with respect to a no confidence motion.

The employee council would be a group of 10-20 employees democratically elected from various levels of the firm ranging from basic labor through to middle management. The concern of the employee council would be primarily with employee welfare, remuneration, benefits, and job satisfaction. Just as the authority of the board of directors to pass motions of no confidence (and thereby effectively to dismiss the CEO) would be subject to constraint (in the form of the critical upper and lower profit rates prescribed by the national office of the public ownership agency), so also would be the analogous authority of the employee council. A CEO subjected to a motion of no confidence would have the right to appeal the decision to an external review board which would decide whether there are sufficient substantive grounds for the motion to allow it to stand. This would provide some degree of safeguard against arbitrary and capricious dismissals of the CEO by the employee council.

This system of dual responsibility, of course, would appear to make the task of corporate management even more difficult and stressful than it is at the present time. Of course, there is a possibility that the system would not actually be so much different from the present system. While corporate executives under market capitalism may not be formally subjected to employee interests, they can hardly ignore these interests. The realities of the labor market, together with the need to maintain a reasonable level of internal morale, forces executives to take employee interests and concerns into continuous serious account. Be that as it may, conceivably the proposed system would be asking too much of the executives—would be placing too much strain on them. This is merely a tentative proposal, intended to stimulate thought and discussion. In the judgment of this author, the overall case for profit-oriented market socialism is somewhat more persuasive than the overall case for cooperative market socialism, which means that if the dismissal authority of one of the two groups (the board of directors or the employee council) is eliminated, then it should be that of the employee council.

Public ownership agency. The primary public ownership agency under market socialism would be the Bureau of Public Ownership (BPO) described above in the discussion of pragmatic market socialism—with certain modifications suggested by the alternative profit-oriented market socialist proposals of Leland Stauber and John Roemer. The "BPO agent" approach would be retained, but it would be revised to allow for the dispersion of the public ownership authority in any one publicly owned corporation over several BPO agents—rather than concentrating this authority in the hands of one single BPO agent. In addition, the revised proposal would allow trading in the voting stock shares of the publicly owned business corporations among the BPO agents.

As before, there would be several hundred local offices of the Bureau of Public Ownership located in cities and towns across the nation. Each office would be staffed by 10-12 BPO agents. The supervisor of each particular local office would not be appointed by the BPO national office, but rather by the municipal government of the city or town in which the office is located. The locally appointed supervisor would arrange the housing and support staff of the office, and would have some degree of authority over the selection of BPO agents for the office and whether specific agents will serve further terms after their first term. The municipal government's monetary incentive to appoint a competent supervisor would lie in its receipt of some small percentage (say 1 to 2 percent) of the total capital property income generated by the local office. Putting local office supervision under the authority of the municipal government to some extent incorporates Stauber's notion of regional dispersion of the public ownership authority. Note, however, that the vast majority of capital property return generated by each local office would go to the national office to be redistributed as social dividend income.

Another borrowing from Stauber's concept of profit-oriented market socialism is the provision for trading among BPO agents in the voting stock (and possibly other types of securities as well) of the publicly owned corporations. Just as the municipal investment funds envisioned by Stauber would buy and sell corporate securities in the capital markets, so too would the BPO agents. These capital markets would operate exactly as they do under capitalism, with the exception that private households would not take part in them. The capital markets are today generally regarded as critical to the efficiency of the capitalist economy, because movements of security prices in these markets are supposed to provide investors with relatively accurate information on the present condition and future prospects of the various corporations whose securities are being bought and sold. This current emphasis on the capital markets is a response to the obvious realities generated by the separation of ownership and control: in particular, the weak direct control of managers by stockholders owing to the atomization of stock ownership. Since the direct accountability of managers to their respective boards of directors has obviously been severely attenuated, consolation is sought in the proposition that movements of security prices in the capital markets impose adequate accountability. This may well be wishful thinking.

But it should be well noted that, regardless of how significant—or insignificant—they are to the maintenance of economic efficiency, capital markets would continue to play essentially the same role under profit-oriented market socialism that they do under capitalism. Even under the original pragmatic market socialist proposal in which BPO agents would not buy and sell stocks and other securities, there would be trading in securities among such financial intermediaries as insurance companies and pension funds. Such trading would create movements in security prices that might be taken as guides to the financial condition of a given corporation (although a more reliable guide would probably be the audited financial statements of that corporation). Under the revised proposal, BPO agents would simply add their presence to the already-existing population of buyers and sellers in the capital markets.

For various reasons, there would be some restrictions placed on the buy-sell privileges of BPO agents in the capital markets. To prevent excessive diversification of agent portfolios and consequent atomization of ownership rights in any one publicly owned corporation, the minimum stock share block in a given company would be 5 percent of voting stock, and a BPO agent could not own share blocks in more than 20 companies. Although this would not represent the equivalent of the sole-owner situation envisioned in the original BPO proposal, it would in fact entail a level of concentration of voting stock far above what is seen today under capitalism. This would dramatically augment the accountability of corporation executives relative to today. To protect against a soft budget constraint of local firms (a special Stauber concern), BPO agents could not buy stock share blocks in companies with large employment concentrations in the area of their local offices. Finally, to protect against tendencies toward collusion, agents affiliated with one local office (and therefore in daily contact) could not hold controlling investments (more than 50 percent ownership) in corporations in significant direct competition with one another.

The board of directors of each publicly owned corporation would consist of BPO agents from one or more local offices of the Bureau of Public Ownership. This departure from the "one-person board of directors" notion of the original BPO proposal would produce a board of directors similar to the board of directors specified by John Roemer's proposal for bank-centric market socialism. Roemer regards it as a special strength of bank-centric market socialism that it would put unto the board of directors of any one corporation individuals who are experienced high-level managers of other corporations. Such individuals are presumably capable of providing very fair and accurate performance evaluation of the first corporation. Recall that the BPO agents of the pragmatic market socialist proposal would be individuals with high-level experience in corporate management. While serving as BPO agents, these individuals would not be currently employed as corporation executives, but this absence of a major distraction means that they would be able to devote considerably more time and effort to evaluating corporate performance of firms included in their spheres of authority than would the directors envisioned by Roemer, who are supposed to be carrying on their duties as high-level executives while simultaneously serving on the boards of directors of other corporations. Roemer's idea may not be practical owing to the natural limitations on what can be accomplished by any one person.

Investment and entrepreneurship. Investment and entrepreneurship under the proposed plan of market socialism would be generated from three separate sources. First, there would be the existing large, established publicly owned business corporations operating under the aegis of the Bureau of Public Ownership (BPO). Although the mythology of capitalist apologetics apotheosizes the solitary entrepreneurial creator of new business firms, as a matter of fact in the contemporary market capitalist economy, long-established and firmly entrenched large corporations dominate investment and entrepreneurship, just as they do all other aspects of economic life. The typical corporation finances a substantial proportion of its capital investment from retained earnings, and it is constantly making exploratory forays into new markets (i.e., carrying on the entrepreneurial function). This well-established pattern would continue under market socialism.

The second source would be private initiative. An important exception to the rule of public ownership of capital would be entrepreneurial enterprise: any business firm being managed by its founder-owner would remain in private ownership so long as the founder-owner chooses to remain personally involved in management. Therefore, a certain amount of private household saving would be directly channeled into capital investment by individuals engaged in entrepreneurial endeavors. Similarly, at any point in time there would be a substantial number of privately owned entrepreneurial enterprises in operation in the economy.

Finally, additional support for capital investment and business entrepreneurship would be provided by two additional national government public ownership agencies supplementary to the Bureau of Public Ownership: the National Investment Banking System (NIBS), and the National Entrepreneurial Investment Board (NEIB). Both these agencies would be similar in structure and operations to the BPO: they would be divided into a large number of local offices (probably not quite so many as with the BPO) whose supervisors would be appointed by local government bodies. The line personnel of these agencies would be called "investment officers" rather than "agents." The NIBS would be closely analogous to ordinary financial intermediaries: their investment officers would seek to maximize the return on investments they make (i.e., loan issues and bond purchases). The principal difference is that the incentives of NIBS investment officers would be geared toward the rate of return achieved on their *recent* investments, rather than toward the rate of return received on *all past* investments. This is to avoid distortion of the pattern of investment caused by concerns for maintaining the profitability of "old" investments. The NEIB would be very similar to the NIBS except that it would make loans to, and purchase bonds from, entrepreneurial firms alone.

After paying incentive bonuses to their investment officers and meeting their administrative expenses, the NIBS and NEIB would retain their net revenues for reinvestment. In conjunction with private household saving channeled into capital investment by banks, pension funds, and other standard financial intermediaries, the capital investment flow of the NIBS/NEIB should provide an adequate sufficiency of investment resources for the economy. But if the national government were to regard these resources as insufficient, allocations to business capital investment could be made from the public revenues, these allocations to be channeled into the business sector through the NIBS and NEIB.

4

THE CURRENT DEBATE

Would democratic market socialism be economically, socially, and morally superior to the contemporary capitalist status quo? Clearly, this question is being answered in the affirmative by this book. But I do not wish to overstate the case, for fear of being labeled a zealot or an idealist. The proposition that democratic market socialism would be preferable to democratic market capitalism for the large majority of the population can hardly be proven in a scientifically rigorous sense, as if it were a mathematical theorem. The proposition is probably not even up to the standard of evidence applied in criminal law: "proof beyond a reasonable doubt." What may be reasonably asserted, however, is that the proposition is sufficiently plausible, in light of all available evidence, to merit at least an experimental implementation of democratic market socialism, with the intention of returning to capitalism should the performance of the system prove disappointing.

Of course, the notion of social experimentation on this large a scale will seem to some totally unrealistic. But this is because socialism is regarded by these people as a drastic divergence from the present economic system. Such a fundamental, revolutionary change, they reason, could only be undertaken by a population whose faith in socialism were transcendent, complete—without qualification and without reservation. The idea that socialism would be a radical departure from the accustomed status quo is partly the fault of overenthusiastic socialists, past and present, whose unrestrained rhetoric has suggested that they naively expect veritably paradisal conditions under socialism. And it is partly the fault of clever apologists for capitalism who have exploited the irresponsible rhetoric of the radical fringe of the socialist movement to manufacture a distorted, straw-man image of socialism.

Clearly, the democratic market socialist system put forward in this book bears no relationship whatever either to the feverish proclamations of overenthusiastic pro-socialists, or to the dark and dire jeremiads of overenthusiastic anti-socialists. In practice, the profit-oriented market socialist system proposed herein would work so similarly to the present market capitalist system that from the point of view of the ordinary daily life of the vast majority of the population, there would be no perceptible difference. This type of market socialist economy would most certainly not constitute a fundamental, revolutionary divergence from the current economic system.

Even though the close similarity of the present market socialist proposal to the market capitalist status quo renders the proposal immune against numerous objections directed against the more radical, uncompromising, and idealistic concepts of socialism, this is not to deny that a reasonably plausible case may be made against the proposal on both economic and political grounds. This chapter will carefully develop the case against profit-oriented democratic market socialism, and will offer a response to this case. Although the overall discussion will of course reflect the author's judgment that the preponderance of the evidence favors the preferability of profit-oriented market socialism over contemporary capitalism, a sincere effort will be made to state the pro-capitalism case carefully, comprehensively, and fairly. And it is hereby reiterated—hopefully to eliminate, once and for all, any possibility of misunderstanding—that it is *not* the argument of this book that the case for democratic market socialism (of the profit-oriented variety herein recommended) is so logically and empirically compelling as to overcome all rational doubts and reservations. Such doubts and reservations *may* be justified and legitimate, so that market socialism *would in fact* be a serious disappointment. If this were to occur, then we could, should, and would make haste to return to the capitalist economic system. Great Britain nationalized a substantial part of its industry in the 1940s, and then privatized (denationalized) it in the 1980s. What Britain did on a small scale in the past could be done on a large scale in the future by other nations—including the United States. There is a safety net, and we should not allow the erroneous notion that "there is no return from socialism" to deter us from a fair and unprejudiced consideration of the democratic market socialist alternative to capitalism.

The reader should be forewarned that much of what is presented in the following as the "case against market socialism" may seem totally unrelated to the "case against socialism" as he or she has hitherto understood it. Readers of a more skeptical bent may take this as evidence that the author is not fairly presenting the case against socialism. They might reason that surely important points against socialism are being ignored, and that the case against socialism is not being comprehensively and effectively stated. The reader should be assured at the outset that what is presented in the following pages is indeed a fair and comprehensive statement of the case against democratic market socialism *of the type proposed in this book.* It is not, on the other hand—nor is it intended to be—a fair and comprehensive statement of the case against socialism in all possible forms, including those forms actually experienced under various Communistic and social democratic regimes, as well as those idealized forms imagined by extremist elements within the socialist movement. The profit-oriented democratic market socialist system under discussion here bears little or no relationship to many concepts traditionally associated with the term "socialism." For example, it does not envision the tight central planning of the economy associated with Communism, nor does it envision radical redistribution of all types of income—including labor income—associated with social democracy.

There are, of course, numerous strands of the fundamental argument against profit-oriented market socialism that such a system is wholly impractical and totally infeasible. These arguments postulate that various dysfunctional elements associated with Communistic socialism and social democratic socialism (such as tight central planning of the economy and radical redistribution of all types of income) are inherent within the very nature of socialism, so that it is an impossibility to implement a real-world socialist economy free of some or all of these dysfunctional elements. Those enamored of this line of attack on socialism like to draw a distinction between "theory and practice." While a system of profit-oriented market socialism such as described here might be possible "in theory" (they would say), it is not possible "in practice." This argument may be, and in fact has been, presented in a formidable variety of apparently independent forms.

For example, one popular argument of this type is the proposition that the so-called "soft budget constraint" is an inevitable characteristic of any and all socialist systems. The "soft budget constraint," a term invented and popularized by Jànos Kornai, a Hungarian economist who has the unusual distinction of being affiliated simultaneously with the Hungarian Academy of Sciences and with Harvard University, refers to the situation in which a publicly owned firm is unconcerned about its costs exceeding its revenues, because it is assured of receiving subsidies from the state treasury to cover any and all losses incurred. According to Kornai, the soft budget constraint in fact applied continuously to Soviet-style socialism in the Soviet Union and Eastern Europe throughout its history, and this factor contributed heavily to the weakness and eventual downfall of the system. The adverse effects of the soft budget constraint were compounded by an "implicit contract" between the state and the rank-and-file workers which made it veritably impossible to fire these workers. The inability to dismiss unproductive workers tended to aggravate financial losses—which were then covered by state subsidies—with little or no questioning or penalizing of the managers involved. In contrast, the typical firm under market capitalism operates under a "hard budget constraint": if its revenues fail to cover its costs, it has no means of recourse, it confronts the imminent possibility of bankruptcy, and oftentimes the threat of bankruptcy rapidly becomes the reality of bankruptcy. Thus the typical firm under market capitalism is strongly motivated to avoid losses—to keep its revenues above its costs at all times. But in this effort it does at least have one important advantage over its socialist counterpart: the ability to cut costs by firing unproductive workers (whether the low productivity stems from poor external market conditions, or from poor abilities and/or attitudes among the fired workers) without encountering excessive administrative restraints or legal obstacles. The overriding need to avoid losses promotes efficiency—continuous assiduous effort is expended by the managers on keeping costs low, and also on improving product quality with an eye to enhancing sales revenue. A publicly owned firm operating under a soft budget constraint, on the other hand, has no overriding need to avoid losses, and hence has low incentives toward efficiency, whether attained through cost reduction or revenue enhancement.

The profit-oriented market socialist system proposed herein does of course envision the typical publicly owned business firm operating under a hard budget constraint: no subsidies would be paid to business firms to enable them to continue operating even though their costs exceeded their revenues. It is anticipated that the bankruptcy rate among publicly owned business firms under the proposed system would be approximately the same as it is currently among privately owned business firms under market capitalism. The possibility of bankruptcy would provide the same incentive toward firm efficiency that it does at present. According to the hypothesis of the *inevitable* soft budget constraint under socialism, bankruptcy could not possibly be as prevalent as it is under capitalism, and therefore it could not possibly play the same role in maintaining incentives among firm managers toward efficiency. This is because (it is alleged) it would be politically impossible for a socialist state to allow a substantial business firm to become bankrupt, thus depriving all or most of its workforce of their jobs and livelihood. Socialism inevitably entails an implicit political contract between the state and the citizen body according to which the involuntary loss of individual employment will not be tolerated—at least on a substantial scale.

Most arguments based on the notion of "inevitability" are invalid, and this particular argument is not an exception to the rule. The argument that the soft budget constraint is inevitable under any possible form of socialism, including profit-oriented market socialism, is an unwarranted generalization from the experience of the Communist nations. It has to be granted that under Communistic socialism there was indeed an extreme reluctance both to separate individual workers involuntarily from their employment and to allow substantial production enterprises to become extinct through bankruptcy. But this reluctance is not sensibly attributed to public ownership of capital stock in and of itself. To begin with (as many commentators have pointed out), employment security was an important tool by which the oligarchic Communist regime kept the general population politically quiescent and acquiescent. But there were other factors involved as well.

Probably the most important was an ideological repugnance, based on Marxist dictums, against both involuntary dismissals and enterprise bankruptcies. In traditional Marxist thinking, the threat of dismissal is the primary means by which the capitalist owners force the proletarian workers to accept wages which are below their productive contribution. Furthermore, bankruptcies are mainly associated with periods of depression in which the inherent "anarchy of the market" comes to a crisis point. The natural implication of this is that in a socialist system which has abrogated both capitalist exploitation of individual workers and capitalistic business depressions, both involuntary separations from employment and bankruptcies of business firms would be extremely rare. Employment security of the individual worker and the protection of ongoing production operations from bankruptcy thus became ideological symbols of social progress, of liberation from the shackles of capitalism. On top of this, planned Communistic socialism, owing to its misplaced confidence in the ubiquity and prevalence of economies of scale, went in for very large productive enterprises. Typically there would only be a handful of factories producing each type of commodity, and each of these factories would employ tens of thousands of workers. Under these circumstances, a production slowdown or interruption caused by the bankruptcy and reorganization of a particular enterprise would tend to have a serious disruptive impact on the entire economy.

The operative factors responsible for the soft budget constraint under Communistic socialism would not apply to the envisioned system of democratic profit-oriented market socialism under consideration here. Being democratically elected as opposed to oligarchically imposed, the government would possess greater legitimacy and would not have to "buy" the political acquiescence of the population through the maintenance of an excessive amount of individual employment security. The business sector would be far more diversified and decentralized than it was under Communistic socialism, meaning that the contribution of any one firm to overall production would not be so important as to constitute an important deterrent to bankruptcy should that particular firm incur financial losses.

Last but not least, the profit-oriented market socialist proposal is not unduly influenced by the fine details of Marxist thinking. In particular, it does not take such a jaundiced view of either individual dismissals or firm bankruptcies. These things, when they occur, are unfortunate and regrettable, and no doubt they should be kept to an acceptable minimum. For example, there should be legal and contractual guarantees against arbitrary and capricious dismissals, and there should be anticyclical monetary and fiscal policy to safeguard against business depressions in which bankruptcies become widespread owing to general market failure rather than to individual firm inefficiency. On the other hand, there should be appropriate restraints both on legal and contractual guarantees of employment, and on anticyclical policy. Excessive employment guarantees would protect lazy, uncooperative, and unproductive employees against dismissal, and excessive anticyclical pursuit of prosperity would produce an unacceptable rate of inflation. A reasonable threat of individual dismissal and a reasonable threat of firm bankruptcy are regarded—like dieting and exercise—as stressful but healthy. In the same way that Darwinian natural selection is a necessary instrument toward the improvement of the species, the possibility of individual dismissal and firm bankruptcy are vital to the preservation of incentives toward efficiency at respectively the individual level and the firm level.

On these grounds it is asserted that the "soft budget constraint," whatever may have been its role under Communistic socialism of the past, would not be a significant hindrance to the potential profit-oriented market socialism of the future. Under such a system of market socialism, unprofitable publicly owned business firms could and would be allowed to lapse into bankruptcy.

The soft budget constraint argument is only one out of a large variety of potential arguments against market socialism based on the proposition that socialism, in and of itself, necessarily involves various dysfunctional conditions. Among these dysfunctional conditions are: comprehensive central planning of the economy; the proliferation of intrusive social regulation of individual behavior and business enterprise; pervasive political intervention in the running of individual business enterprises; extreme social egalitarianism as implemented through highly progressive taxation and a massive welfare state. Some reference has been made, and will continue to be made, to these kinds of arguments at various appropriate points in the discussion. But the reader should try to appreciate that a truly comprehensive and fully detailed rebuttal of these kinds of arguments would become impossibly lengthy and repetitious.

In the final analysis, all of these kinds of arguments—when applied to profit-oriented market socialism—are based on the same dubious proposition: "there can be nothing new under the sun." That is to say, more precisely, "there can be no new forms of socialism under the sun." But the entire history of human civilization demonstrates that there *can* be new social forms and institutions under the sun. Humanity has gradually proceeded from a condition of primitive barbarism, under which the invariable guiding principle was "might makes right," to a highly evolved civilization, governed to a substantial extent by the rule of law and upholding high standards of individual rights, worth, and dignity.

For example, modern history has witnessed the dramatic rise to prominence of mass democracies: large and prosperous nation-states in which the highest authorities are periodically held accountable to the general population in free and open elections. Three hundred years ago, during the heyday of absolute monarchy in Europe, conservatives would have dismissed the concept of the mass democracy as totally preposterous. Such a polity, they would have argued, would inevitably degenerate into mediocrity and stagnation owing to the social leveling carried out by irresponsible demagogues elected by the rabble. Either that, or the polity would quickly become engulfed in a brutal civil war as the better classes fought to retain their advantages. The conservatives of three hundred years ago were eventually proved wrong by events. Events proved that it is possible to have a viable, functioning, genuine democratic political system within a large and stratified nation without social leveling and without civil war.

Of course, representative democracy as practiced in the modern mass democracies is not the hypothetical ideal of democracy. Social policies are not determined directly by the people, but are rather determined by a small group of elected officials. And these elected officials are not continuously accountable to the people, but are only accountable at relatively widely spaced elections. Moreover, during the election process, the wealthier element of society has a disproportionate impact on the outcome by means of financial support of candidates. Would-be rabble-rousing demagogues are kept out of the picture by their inability to attract significant campaign contributions from the wealthy. Another factor which has been essential to the success of representative democracy in recent times has been the growth of a large middle class which provides a buffer between rich and poor and which inhibits political instability owing to socioeconomic polarization. Three hundred years ago, the middle class was a much smaller proportion of the total population.

Conservatives today who argue that a socialist polity would inevitably degenerate into mediocrity and stagnation are following in the footsteps of conservatives three hundred years ago who argued that a democratic polity would inevitably degenerate into mediocrity and stagnation. It would be rash to predict that today's conservatives will be proved wrong on the issue of socialism in the same way that yesterday's conservatives were proved wrong on the issue of democracy. But there is at least a reasonable possibility of this. Today's conservatives are failing to recognize the possibility of new forms of socialism, and they are also failing to appreciate the developing social realities which are making these new forms of socialism increasingly attractive. When yesterday's conservatives dismissed the possibility of democracy, they had in mind the ideal concept of democracy and failed to recognize the institutional forms of representative democracy, as practiced today, which were capable of translating the democratic ideal into a practical and workable political system. When today's conservatives dismiss the possibility of socialism, they have in mind the ideal concept of socialism, and they fail to recognize the institutional forms of profit-oriented market socialism which are capable of translating the socialist ideal into a practical and workable economic system. Yesterday's conservatives failed to perceive how the development of a substantial middle class could make representative democracy more and more feasible and desirable. Similarly, today's conservatives fail to perceive how the developing realities of contemporary capitalism (the extreme inequality of capital wealth ownership, the separation of ownership and control, the institutionalization of capital markets, and so on) are making profit-oriented market socialism more and more feasible and desirable.

Dogmatic assertions that profit-oriented market socialism would be heir to all the same problems, real and imagined, ever associated with socialism—either as a real-world institution in the Communist nations, or as a hypothetical proposal infused with utopian delusions—are merely an effort to beg the question, to shut down the ordinary processes of critical thinking, to terminate the debate through direct appeal to prejudice and preconception. The concept of market socialism in general, including all forms from Langian to profit-oriented, is a dramatic new development in the intellectual history of socialism. It represents an informed, thoughtful, reflective effort to learn from the mistakes of Communistic socialism, social democratic socialism and utopian socialism, to find a genuinely new direction for socialism, to develop a practical and workable form of socialism to replace the misguided and half-baked proposals of the past. The concept of profit-oriented market socialism goes a step further in this direction: it refines the general idea of market socialism, and makes it even more precise, practical, and workable. The fact that some advocates of socialism in the past have been totally unrealistic dreamers and crackpots is not a legitimate argument against profit-oriented market socialism—any more than it is a legitimate argument against representative democracy that some unrealistic advocates of democracy in the past seemed to have thought that it would be possible to govern a large, complex nation along the same puristically democratic lines as a New England town meeting.

While much of what currently passes for the "case against socialism" is irrelevant or virtually irrelevant when applied to profit-oriented market socialism, there certainly does exist a logically sound and reasonably plausible case to be made against this proposed economic system. The purpose of this chapter is to enunciate and respond to that case. But before enumerating the main elements of the "con" case, I would like to briefly enumerate and discuss the main elements of the "pro" case. Some of these elements will be elucidated further and elaborated at appropriate points in the following discussion. The potential benefits of profit-oriented market socialism fall into three basic categories: (1) economic equity, (2) economic efficiency, (3) political democracy.

Economic equity. The central problem with contemporary capitalism is that it perpetuates extreme inequality in the distribution of unearned capital property income. Whatever may have been the case in the earlier history of capitalism, it is now becoming increasingly evident that the institutional evolution of capitalism has rendered capital property income (dividends, interest, capital gains, and so on) an unearned, rentier-type income. No appreciable effort or sacrifice is required from the capital owner in order to earn this return: it accrues to the financial capital itself rather than to the efforts or sacrifices of the owner. Entrepreneurship, risk-taking, time preference, and other familiar terms from the lexicon of capitalist apologetics are merely specious ex post facto rationalizations for a state of affairs mistakenly regarded by many as necessary and inevitable. The fact is that the present extreme inequality in the distribution of capital property income is almost entirely attributable to the workings of inheritance and chance. Entrepreneurship, risk-taking, or time preference have little or nothing to do with it.

Highly unequal distribution of unearned return is not only contrary to the financial interests of the large majority of the population, it is also ethically offensive in terms of universally accepted social standards. If there is some available material benefit which is not the consequence of the specific efforts and sacrifices of any particular individual in society, then all members in good standing of the society possess a natural right to it. Capital property return is basically an economic return to the marginal productivity of inanimate physical capital in production. Business firms must be obliged to pay this return to providers of financial capital in order that capital be efficiently allocated and utilized in the economy. But there is no reason why these providers must be private households. Financial capital can be provided to business firms just as efficiently and effectively by socially owned financial intermediaries. The present capitalist system distributes the return to inanimate capital in proportion to the financial capital assets of households. Owing to inheritance and chance, financial capital ownership is extremely unequal. The proposed profit-oriented market socialist system would distribute the return to inanimate capital in proportion to the earned labor income of households. Labor income is far more equally distributed among households than is financial capital. As a result, the large majority of the population, probably well over 90 percent, would receive more social dividend income under profit-oriented market socialism than they currently receive capital property income under capitalism.

In clarification of the ethical superiority of the social dividend distribution principle, it must once again be emphasized that the capital property return produced by business firms is the direct consequence of the productivity of physical capital. But since physical capital is inanimate, it does not lay claim to this return. This presents society with a distribution problem: On what basis should the return to physical capital be distributed among the households? The traditional pro-capitalist argument is that it should be distributed on the basis of household financial capital—among other reasons because it is the household sacrifices of saving which provide the financial capital which business firms transform into physical capital for use in production. The problem with this argument is that the distribution of household financial capital is determined primarily by inheritance and chance, rather than by the sacrifices of saving, etc. The alternative pro-socialist argument is that it should be distributed on the basis of household labor income—because labor income is the tangible manifestation of how much labor value is being provided to the economy by the household, and human labor is the primary *indirect* cause of the productivity of capital. After all, it is the labor effort of human beings which breathes life into capital, which makes capital productive. A gigantic capital stock would be absolutely sterile if it were not fertilized by human labor. Since labor is the most proximate cause of capital property return aside from inanimate capital itself, it makes sense to distribute capital property return, which is unclaimed by inanimate capital, to households on the basis of their labor contributions to the economy—as measured by their respective labor incomes.

No doubt this argument might be criticized as excessively abstract and speculative. But uncertainties regarding ethical principles are not resolved by strict logic alone. In fact, if they were so resolvable, they would not be "uncertainties" in the first place. This argument should be viewed in terms of what is best for the majority of the population. What is best for the majority of the population—in fact, what is best for the *large majority* of the population—is social dividend distribution of the capital property return (dividends, interest, etc.) produced by business enterprises. No doubt it will be very difficult for the tiny minority of wealthy capitalists, accustomed as they are to luxurious living standards financed by capital property income, to appreciate this argument. But the argument *will* be appreciated by the rest of the population, if and when the rest of the population becomes enlightened to the existence of an available socialist alternative—the profit-oriented market socialist alternative—which would not suffer from the efficiency flaws and liabilities associated with traditional concepts of socialism.

Economic efficiency. Owing to the equity advantage of socialism over capitalism in terms of a more equal distribution of capital property return, the superiority of socialism over capitalism is established if a socialist economic system could be implemented which would possess an efficiency level at least comparable to that of capitalism. The profit-oriented market socialist system proposed here is just such a system.

Owing to the close similarity between the institutions and operations of this system and those of capitalism, a strong prima facie case exists that it would enjoy an efficiency level comparable to that of capitalism. But beyond that, it may be plausibly argued that the efficiency of profit-oriented market socialism would be actually somewhat higher than that of contemporary capitalism. It is important to be circumspect in stating this argument. First of all, this is a secondary argument for socialism of very much smaller consequence relative to the primary argument which consists of the equity advantage of socialism. Second, it is not alleged that the efficiency advantage of profit-oriented market socialism over capitalism would be extremely large. The thunderous denunciations of the wanton waste of capitalistic business depressions by Karl Marx and other proponents of socialism suggested that they imagined that socialism would open a veritable cornucopia of production, banishing all scarcity and satisfying all wants. We can now see that this was a totally unrealistic vision. While the dictum of some economists that "human wants are infinite" may be an exaggeration, it is safe to say that human wants are sufficiently expandable, that regardless of the production level there will always be scarcity—in the sense that the total of human wants will exceed the level of production. Or at least there will be scarcity in this sense into the foreseeable future. While a case may be made that production would be somewhat higher under profit-oriented market socialism than it is presently under capitalism, the improvement would probably be modest, and almost certainly would not impact significantly on perceived scarcity.

There are three principal sources of a potentially higher production level under profit-oriented market socialism. First, the transformation of capital property return produced by business firms into a social dividend payment proportional to household labor income means that households would experience a higher effective wage on their labor. Since labor produces more income than it did before, presumably households would have an incentive to provide more labor. Higher labor provision by households translates into higher aggregate production. Second, the relative concentration of the outside ownership interest in the typical business firm would make high corporate executives more accountable than they are at present. The separation of ownership and control under contemporary capitalism has proceeded to such a point that the profit performance of a particular business firm has to be drastically deficient for its top managers to be in any immediate danger of dismissal. The public ownership authority under profit-oriented market socialism could be exercised in such a way as to put more pressure on corporation executives (in terms of a higher probability of dismissal for low profitability) to maintain a high rate of profitability. A higher effort level in the executive suites would favorably affect efficiency and productivity throughout the economy. Third, the profit-oriented market socialist economy might be willing to finance a higher rate of investment in business capital than is the capitalist economy. High executives and wealthy capitalists under capitalism are concerned not with the total output level but with the profit level, and they are perpetually concerned that "excessive" investment might "over-exploit the market" and lead to a low rate of profit. Under profit-oriented market socialism, the national government would have the option, if desired, of "forcing" a larger amount of business capital investment into the economy via special appropriations to the publicly owned financial intermediaries, funded out of tax revenue. This would yield a higher rate of economic expansion and a higher future production level. We will return to each of these three possibilities at appropriate points below in the response provided to the "con" case against profit-oriented market socialism.

Political democracy. To some extent, the distribution of political power, even in a fully democratic nation, follows the distribution of wealth and income. Individuals with higher wealth and income have greater influence on public decisionmaking than do individuals with lower wealth and income. Individuals with higher wealth and income are typically better educated and thus better equipped to be opinion leaders. They are more likely to take an active part in the political process, either by running for office themselves or by supporting the campaigns of others who are running for office. Short of socioeconomic levelling (which is hardly the intention of profit-oriented market socialism), there is no way to completely eliminate the disproportionate influence of wealthier people on the political process—nor would this necessarily be desirable in any case. But it may indeed be suggested that under contemporary capitalism the distribution of political power and influence is *excessively* unequal because the distribution of wealth and income is *excessively* unequal, and that the rectification of income distribution implied by profit-oriented market socialism would also produce, as a subsidiary effect, a rectification of the distribution of political power and influence.

Contemporary capitalism fosters and perpetuates the existence of a tiny minority of the population endowed with unseemly amounts of capital wealth. This tiny minority not only enjoys unduly luxurious living standards, it also exercises undue influence on the political processes of the nation. Profit-oriented market socialism would take the substantial proportion of national income represented by capital property return and distribute it to households as a social dividend supplement to labor income. Instead of following the highly unequal distribution of financial wealth, this income flow would instead follow the much less unequally distributed flow of labor income. This would entail a significant equalization of the distribution of household total income, and it would eliminate the extravagant incomes of the tiny minority of wealthy capitalists. No longer would this handful of plutocrats play such an important part in the campaign financing of aspirants to elective political office. The quality of democracy would be significantly enhanced.

Turning now to the arguments *against* profit-oriented market socialism and in favor of the capitalist status quo, these may be considered as denials of the three subsidiary propositions contained within the overall proposition which provides the primary rationale for profit-oriented market socialism: that highly unequal distribution of unearned capital property income is inequitable. The three subsidiary propositions within this overall proposition are as follows: (1) capital property income is unearned; (2) the distribution of capital property income is highly unequal; (3) this situation is inequitable. From a logical point of view, the most fundamental argument against socialism, whether of the market form or any other form, denies the first subsidiary proposition (that capital property income is unearned). There are two principal contrary arguments: (i) that capital property return is an earned return to the capital management effort of the capital owners; (ii) that capital property return is an earned return to the sacrifices of saving. If either one or both of these arguments is valid, then the receipt of capital property income by private households is economically and ethically justified, and there is no merit in the socialist critique of capitalism. The denial of the second subsidiary proposition (that the distribution of capital property income is highly unequal) is embodied within what has been described as the "people's capitalism thesis." This thesis states that "when properly interpreted," the distribution of capital property income is *not* all that unequal. People's capitalism was carefully discussed above in Chapter 2, and that discussion will not be reiterated in this chapter. Finally, there is the denial of the third subsidiary proposition (that this situation is seriously inequitable) on various noneconomic grounds not relating to productive efficiency. For example, a justification for the capitalist status quo might be sought in the philosophical notion of "natural rights of ownership." Or it might be sought in the political proposition that the proposed socialist cure for the inequity of capitalism would endanger personal freedom and political democracy. Pro-capitalism arguments of this variety might concede the *appearance* of inequity in capitalism—and they might even go so far as to admit the *reality* of a certain amount of inequity in capitalism—but they go on to assert that the proposed socialist cure for this inequity would entail problems far more serious than the inequity itself. The extreme inequality of capital property income is thus implicitly or explicitly asserted to be a "necessary evil."

Of course, the most obvious reason why the extreme inequality in capital property income distribution prevalent under contemporary capitalism might be a "necessary evil" is that the proposed socialist cure would impose serious economic efficiency costs on society. These alleged costs stem from the notion that under socialism, no payment would be made for the legitimate economic contributions of private households in terms of capital management effort and/or saving, and thus the supply of these factors of production would wither away—households would no longer provide them. This brings us around to the denial of the first subsidiary proposition, the proposition that capital property income is unearned. For the denial of the third subsidiary proposition to be logically independent of the denial of the first subsidiary proposition, it is necessary that the alleged problems of socialism be of a noneconomic nature (political, philosophical, psychological, etc.).

The effort made herein to enunciate a logical and orderly statement of capitalist apologetics might seem rather strange to some readers because it is so dissimilar to what they ordinarily imagine to be the "case for capitalism." Actual capitalist apologetics, both historical and contemporary, tends to be an amorphous blend of disparate ideas and propositions, heavily influenced by the real and imagined defects of Communistic socialism and proclaimed in overblown, evangelical, quasi-mystical rhetoric. In fairness, it should be noted that the disorderly and tendentious nature of most capitalist apologetics reflects the disorderly and tendentious nature of most of the socialist critique to which it responds. Another point is that the "case for capitalism," as generally known today, is a response to the entire range of socialist proposals, rather than to the specific profit-oriented market socialist proposal with which we are presently concerned.

The following three sections of this chapter will deal respectively with the capital management objection to socialism (that socialism would provide inadequate incentives to capital management effort—to the detriment of economic efficiency), the saving objection to socialism (that socialism would provide inadequate incentives to saving—to the detriment of economic growth), and the political objection to socialism (that socialism would threaten freedom and democracy). These objections will be examined in the light of the previously described proposal for profit-oriented market socialism. Finally, the last section of the chapter will summarize the discussion, and offer some general observations on capitalist apologetics as applied against the profit-oriented market socialist proposal put forward in this book.

VARIATIONS ON CAPITAL MANAGEMENT

Probably the single most widely perceived basic economic problem with socialism is an alleged absence of adequate financial incentives to effort. People would find that there is no appreciable monetary return to working hard or to other economically beneficial behavior such as the founding of new firms (i.e., engaging in entrepreneurship). Therefore they would decline to engage in this economically beneficial behavior: they would fail to work hard, they would fail to found new firms, and so on. As a consequence, economic efficiency and productivity would sag and decline. The economy would stagnate and decay. Quite possibly it would eventually collapse completely.

It so happens that this author agrees that the most serious potential problem of profit-oriented market socialism is indeed the possibility that financial incentives to effort would be inadequate. However, the "effort" referred to here is of a very specific variety and certainly does not encompass the broad range of "economically beneficial behavior." The profit-oriented market socialist proposal is designed explicitly to maintain exactly the same, or at least closely comparable, financial incentives to effort over each and every category of economically beneficial behavior—with one important exception. That one exception is what will be termed herein "capital management effort." If incentive problems would be significant under profit-oriented market socialism, they would be confined to this particular category. Thus it is very important that the reader fully understand what capital management effort is, and what it is not.

Capital management effort is defined herein as any and all active effort aimed at achieving a high rate of return on financial capital. Capital management effort, as thus defined, falls into two major subcategories: (1) corporate supervision (as opposed to corporate management); and (2) investment analysis. This definition will be duly refined and elaborated as we proceed, but it will be helpful to enumerate, at the outset, what capital management effort is *not*.

First and foremost, capital management effort is not labor as defined in standard economic analysis. In standard economic analysis, labor is any sort of activity by a person which is directly compensated (paid for) by a second party, whether that second party is another person or an organization, such as a business firm or a nonprofit agency. Labor income accounts for approximately 80 percent of total national income in advanced industrial nations such as the United States. The great majority of the adult, working-age population is dependent upon labor income in order to sustain life. The two exceptions consist of a small minority at the low end of the income spectrum who are physically or mentally incapable of work and who subsist on welfare doles, and a still smaller minority at the high end of the income spectrum who possess a sufficiently large amount of financial capital wealth that the income on this wealth provides at least a comfortable living—in other words, individuals who are, by definition, "capitalists."

A widespread misconception about socialism is that the concept itself demands a great deal of equality in the distribution of total disposable income among households—that is, of all income after taxes and transfers. A major input into this misconception has been the traditional program of social democracy, which envisions a very high degree of progressivity in the taxation of *all* forms of income, labor income as well as property income, and which calls for extremely generous welfare benefits to be distributed to the less advantaged elements of society. Of course, as has already been emphasized, social democracy has nothing to do with "socialism" as puristically and precisely defined in terms of public ownership of the capital stock. In fact, by the strict definition applied herein, social democratic "socialism" is not socialism at all. As a matter of fact, there is nothing whatever in the profit-oriented market socialist proposal, either explicit or implicit, which would entail greater progressivity in the taxation of labor income or more generous welfare benefits. There is no intention whatever to subject even very high labor incomes, such as those earned by successful doctors, lawyers, and executives, to a higher rate of taxation. A handful of labor incomes in the modern economy, especially those earned by "superstars" in popular culture and sports, achieve extraordinary heights—in some cases, many millions of dollars per year. Under profit-oriented market socialism, these incomes would be taxed no more and no less than they are under contemporary capitalism. Similarly, welfare benefits would be no larger or smaller than they are under contemporary capitalism. Thus the financial incentive to all types of labor would remain precisely the same as it is presently under contemporary capitalism.

There might be a case for making one important exception to this general rule. That exception would apply to the top tier of corporation executives. It is reasonably plausible that owing to the separation of ownership and control under contemporary capitalism, these top executives are at the present time directly appropriating to themselves a certain proportion of what would have been the total flow of capital property income. In other words, the attenuated accountability of the top tier of corporation executives under conditions of separation of ownership and control means that their rate of remuneration exceeds the marginal productivity of their managerial labor. According to standard economic theory, the legitimate economic and ethical entitlement of any person is to the marginal productivity of his/her labor—not to anything beyond that. I hasten to add, however, that any income reduction among high corporation executives would be relatively modest. A high level of performance among the top tier of corporation executives is vital to the success of the economy, which means that the marginal productivity of this type of labor is very high, and its remuneration must accordingly be quite generous. To use hypothetical figures, if the average rate of remuneration among high corporation executives under contemporary capitalism is, say, $750,000 per annum, then the appropriate average rate of annual remuneration under profit-oriented market socialism might be $500,000.

Whatever the amount paid for it, managerial effort provided by corporation executives is a form of labor and is not capital management effort as defined herein. The capital management effort argument for capitalism would be far more persuasive than it actually is if this were *not* the case. When we consider the totality of human effort which goes into trying to achieve a high rate of return on capital, common sense, together with a rudimentary understanding of the way the modern corporate economy works, suggests that most if not all of this effort is provided by corporation executives. Whatever might be thought of the current remuneration of corporation executives, most people recognize corporate management to be a technically demanding and psychologically stressful type of work. If the rhetoric, which is utilized in capitalist apologetics to assert that capital property income is an earned return to the capital management effort of the capital owners, could be legitimately applied to corporation executives, then this assertion would be far more believable. But it may *not* be so applied. The remuneration of corporation executives, whether it is applied in the form of salaries, bonuses, or benefits, is deemed labor income in both national income accounting and individual firm accounting. This remuneration rewards a form of labor (managerial labor), which means that the net income of the firm after managerial labor expenses have been met—that amount which is paid out in the form of dividends and interest—cannot be legitimately represented as a reward to managerial labor.

No doubt the most highly favored of all the buzzwords of capitalist apologetics is "entrepreneurship." This concept is cited more frequently than any other as a justification for the contemporary capitalistic status quo. The possibility of accumulating a vast capital fortune is (it is alleged) an absolutely indispensable incentive to entrepreneurial endeavor. The benefits of entrepreneurship (it is alleged) fully justify an extremely unequal distribution of financial capital wealth and thereby of capital property income. An important question is therefore: Is capital management effort to be identified with entrepreneurship? Such an identification is *not* warranted, since there is not a one-to-one correspondence between the two concepts. There is, however, some degree of overlap between the two concepts, as explained in the following.

The two basic subcategories of capital management effort have been described as corporate supervision and investment analysis. The typical entrepreneur engages in both of these: he or she first engages in investment analysis in order to ascertain what type of new firm might be profitably established, and then, after the firm has been established, he or she, in the capacity of owner, engages in corporate supervision. But also essential to the overall concept of entrepreneurship is personal involvement in firm management (as opposed to firm supervision). Firm management means that one spends long working days at the office studying specific marketing and production problems and issues, and making tough decisions as between competing courses of action. Firm supervision, on the other hand, means occasional perusal of audited financial statements to determine how profitable one particular firm is in relation to the average. With respect to any one firm, the time/energy requirements of firm management are vastly larger than the time/energy requirements of firm supervision. A true and genuine entrepreneur is not an outside investor, a silent partner, a rentier who merely puts up investment capital but remains otherwise uninvolved. In other words, he/she does not merely engage in firm supervision. Rather he or she actually and personally *manages* the new firm. This means that some part of the total remuneration of an entrepreneurial owner-manager is actually a return to managerial labor, rather than to entrepreneurship per se.

Unfortunately, there are no statistics available by which it can be precisely determined what percentage of the total flow of capital property income goes to individuals who have, at some point in their lives, personally established and managed an entrepreneurial business firm. In all likelihood, this percentage is quite low, perhaps in the order of 5 to 10 percent. This would mean that 90 to 95 percent of capital property income goes to individuals who established their entitlement to this income by means other than personal entrepreneurship—by such means as inheritance and financial speculation. The representation of capital property income, in capitalist apologetics, as an earned return to the noble enterprise of entrepreneurship, is no doubt the single most blatant and egregious departure from reality and honesty in an area heavily burdened by such departures.

It should be well noted, in relation to entrepreneurship, that the profit-oriented market socialist proposal put forward herein calls the bluff of those who assert that capital property income is primarily a return to personal entrepreneurship. Recall that a central feature of the proposal is for private ownership of entrepreneurial enterprises, so long as the founder-owner remains personally involved in the management of the firm. Upon voluntarily relinquishing management, the founder-owner would sell his/her ownership share for its full capitalized value to some other firm, most probably a publicly owned firm operating under the authority of the Bureau of Public Ownership. If there is any truth in the proposition that capital property income is mostly a return to personal entrepreneurship, then it would soon be found out under profit-oriented market socialism that very little capital property return was being received by the Bureau of Public Ownership from the population of large, established publicly owned business firms. Rather capital property return would be going mostly to the founder-owners of privately owned entrepreneurial enterprises. Of course, it would require an exceptionally naive defender of contemporary capitalism to seriously expect this situation to actually transpire under market socialism.

Entrepreneurship is by far the primary variation to be found in capitalist apologetics on the capital management effort theme—but it is only one of several important variations. It is important to see these variations for what they are: as simply repetitions and rewordings of the same basic argument. If the commonality of these arguments against market socialism is *not* perceived, then it might be thought that there is a multitude of separate and independent arguments to be made against profit-oriented market socialism. The conclusion might then all too easily be reached that surely all of these many different arguments cannot be invalid, surely one of them must be legitimate, surely socialism—even in this refined and updated form—must be rejected.

As far as the basic purpose of capitalist apologetics is concerned, there is really no need to keep cloning this basic argument, because the basic argument, stated simply and without rhetorical adornment or quasi-mystical embellishment, is indeed a very plausible and serious argument against the workability of profit-oriented market socialism. It applies both to the current (or "static") performance of the system, and to its long-term (or "dynamic") performance. In the opinion of this author, any sensible advocate of socialism who confronts this argument directly, and who takes the trouble to fully understand and appreciate it, will be forced to concede that there is a not insignificant possibility that even a socialist system so similar to contemporary capitalism as profit-oriented market socialism might in fact prove disappointing if put into operation. This sensible advocate should then be willing to admit that if, after a reasonable trial period, profit-oriented market socialism were found to be deficient, then society should make haste to restore capitalism.

The capital management argument commences with the unarguable, a priori proposition that capital, being inanimate, nonsentient, and devoid of intelligence and volition, cannot through its own effort apply itself effectively in production—as a human worker would do simply by seeking out his/her highest-paid job. This proposition applies both to physical capital currently being used by firms in production and to financial capital—funds which are to be allocated to physical capital investment in the future. This means that human beings must "manage" both physical and financial capital, much as a theatrical agent manages an actor or an actress. In order to motivate these managers to manage capital effectively, they must be paid the marginal productivity of their capital management effort.

Under capitalism, private individuals *own* their respective shares of the total capital stock. This ownership right entitles them to payments made for the use of capital by business firms. These individuals thus have a strong financial incentive to see to it that the capital earns a high rate of return—which will only be the case if the capital is effectively utilized (if it is physical capital) or effectively allocated (if it is financial capital). Thus the rational self-interest of the capital owners leads to the efficient use of capital in the economy.

Under socialism, the physical capital stock, as well as the capital investment fund, is legally owned by the general population, rather than by individual capital owners. Clearly, the general population has an interest in the effective use of its collectively owned capital. But equally as clearly, the general population cannot directly provide capital management effort to ensure the effective use of its capital. Instead, the general public must delegate its ownership authority to various individuals who are expected to provide the capital management effort which was previously provided by individual capital owners. Under the profit-oriented market socialist proposal developed here, for example, these individuals would be the personnel of the Bureau of Public Ownership (BPO), National Investment Banking System (NIBS), and National Entrepreneurial Investment Board (NEIB). In particular, they would be the line agents of the BPO, and the line investment officers of the NIBS and NEIB. Recall that these individuals would be allowed to retain as personal income only a very small percentage, in the realm of 1 or 2 percent, of the total amount of capital property return received by their respective public ownership agencies from business firms (dividends on stock shares in the case of the BPO, and interest on bonds and loans in the case of the NIBS and NEIB).

In other words, capital owners under capitalism who receive 100 percent of the return on their owned capital (less income taxes) would be replaced by public ownership personnel who would receive a mere 1 or 2 percent of the return on their capital responsibilities. The inference may be immediately drawn that since the financial incentive to capital management effort under socialism would be only a small fraction of what it is under capitalism, then the supply of capital management effort under socialism would be only a small fraction of what it is under capitalism, and hence the efficiency of capital utilization and overall economic performance under socialism would be only a small fraction of what they are under capitalism.

This chain of reasoning extends a very widely accepted concept in modern economics, that of the upward-sloping supply curve of labor, to capital management effort. According to the upward-sloping supply curve of labor, increases in wages and salaries increase labor quantity (or, possibly, labor intensity), while decreases in wages and salaries decrease labor quantity and/or intensity. If the typical wage or salary earner considers his/her probable reaction to a cut in his/her wage or salary to 1 or 2 percent of its present level, it is easy to imagine a total cessation of labor. As a matter of fact, at a rate of pay 1 to 2 percent of the current level, many if not most people would cease providing labor simply because they had died of starvation or exposure to the elements. Assuming, however, that 1 to 2 percent of the current rate of pay would be sufficient to sustain life and to provide a physical basis for labor, the situation might not be so clear. Refusal to provide labor under those circumstances would mean (for most people) that they would indeed die of starvation or exposure. A person might object that he or she would prefer to go on the public dole than to work for such a ridiculously low rate of pay. But what if there were no public dole? And what if there were also no private charities or family members to whom to appeal?

Despite its widespread acceptance and application in modern economics, the hypothesis of an upward-sloping supply curve of labor is not in fact founded on extremely solid ground, either conceptually, theoretically, or empirically. But we should not worry about that, because it is *not* a significant part of the pro-socialist counter-argument to the capital management effort argument for capitalism that the supply curve of labor is not upward-sloping, and hence (by extension) the supply curve of capital management effort is not upward-sloping. For the sake of argument, let us imagine that the supply curve of labor is in fact upward-sloping: higher payment for labor generates more labor, lower payment for labor generates less labor. Does it not follow, therefore, that the supply curve of capital management effort is also upward-sloping, so that the much lower payment for capital management effort to the non-owning capital managers under socialism would generate much less capital management effort than is provided by the capital owner-managers under capitalism?

It does *not* necessarily follow. To begin with, there are fundamental, qualitative differences between the labor income earned by individuals and the capital property income received by individuals. Labor income results from the multiplication of a fixed wage or salary rate by the amount of time worked. There is thus a proportional (or linear) relationship between labor income and time worked: a graph of labor income against time worked would show a straight line. Capital property income, on the other hand, results from the multiplication of a variable rate of return on capital against the amount of capital owned by the capital owner. The capital management effort provided by the capital owner affects only the rate of return on capital; it does not affect the amount of capital on which that rate of return is received. The relationship between capital management effort and rate of return on capital is a form of production function: the input of capital management effort generates the output of rate of return on capital. Now it is a universally accepted proposition of contemporary economics that production functions are characterized by diminishing returns to a factor of production: equal increments in the factor of production will generate steadily decreasing increments in the output. This means that the relationship between capital management effort and the rate of return on capital (and, by extension, the amount of capital property income received) is not a straight line as it is in the case of the relationship between labor time and labor income. Rather it is "bowed over": more precisely, it is concave upward-sloping, it increases at a decreasing rate.

Let us consider the relationship between capital management effort and the amount of capital property income received by the capital owner under capitalism. The question may be (should be) asked: How much of that capital property income is a marginal productivity return to the capital management effort of the capital owner, and how much of it is a marginal productivity return to the capital itself? The socialist position is that all or most of this capital property income is a return to capital itself, and that little or none of it is a return to capital management effort.

For more than 100 years, neoclassical economics has been hammering away at the idea that capital contributes *independently* to production. To some unknown extent, this emphasis was a reaction to the Marxian critique of capitalism, based on the classical labor theory of value, which asserted that capital derives its value entirely from labor, and that capital value represents only "embodied labor value." I do not wish to become entangled in a philosophical disputation regarding the "ultimate" source of value. As mentioned above, labor is in fact a viable candidate for this honor, based on the simple truism that even a gigantic stock of state-of-the-art capital would be completely unproductive if there were no labor there to operate it. But as a matter of fact, I have no problem whatever with the neoclassical proposition that capital contributes independently to production. This proposition simply implies that capital should be a priced commodity—that business firms (as well as government agencies and nonprofit organizations) should have to pay for its use. It does not necessarily imply that what is paid by business firms and other organizations for the use of capital should be distributed to private capital owners on the basis of their personally owned financial assets.

Capital property return paid out by organizations which use capital ought, on the basis of both economic and ethical principles, to be paid, in the form of capital property income (dividends, interest, etc.), to private capital owners *only to the extent* that it is a marginal product return to the capital management effort of the owners, and not a marginal product return to the capital itself. In light of more than a century of strong, not to

say strident, emphasis in neoclassical economics on the independent productivity of capital, one might naturally surmise that what we have here,
in capital property income, is a return to capital itself, and not a return to
capital management effort. In fact, in the more than 100 years since neoclassical economics discovered the independent productivity of capital,
there has never been a single mention made of the alleged capital management effort of the capital owner. As utilized in capitalist apologetics,
the neoclassical proposition that capital possesses independent productivity translates directly into "the capitalist is worthy of his capital property
income." Capitalist apologetics, in other words, simply ignores the distinction between capital itself and the capital owner. It blends the two together, endowing the human capital owner with the productivity, worth,
and social value of the nonhuman capital. Capitalist apologetics has gotten away with this crude deception for a very long time, but the possibility always exists that eventually enlightenment will descend upon the
population. In the words of Abraham Lincoln, "You can't fool all the
people all the time."

A strict application of the independent productivity of capital principle would leave no room whatever for capital management effort. In this
view, there is no such relationship, of the sort described above, between
capital management effort and the rate of return on capital. Rather the
rate of return on capital would be a fixed amount set by the interaction of
supply and demand in the market for capital, just as the wage on a certain
type of labor is a fixed amount set by the interaction of supply and demand in the market for that type of labor. The capital management effort
of the capital owner would be zero, and the amount of capital property
income received would be the product of the market-determined rate of
return on capital and the amount of financial capital held by the owner. If
this were the case, there would be no need to provide financial incentives
to the BPO agents and NIBS/NEIB investment officers under profit-
oriented market socialism in the form of personal retention of a proportion of the capital property return received by their agencies from their
particular capital responsibilities. Rather these individuals could merely
be salaried employees, and their job would essentially be no different
from any other type of salaried job.

As a matter of fact, it is fully possible that making all personnel of the
public ownership agencies under market socialism, including agents of
the BPO and investment officers of the NIBS and NEIB, simply salaried
employees, would in fact work quite well in practice. As is the case with
any other kind of salaried job, of course, BPO agents and NIBS/NEIB

investment officers would have to be subject to at least some minimum threat of dismissal for incompetence or uncooperativeness. Even though it has not yet been meaningfully incorporated into economic theory, it is obvious that a critical incentive to effort in any kind of job is the possibility of being fired if the job is being performed too shoddily. But given a reasonable probability of dismissal, it might well result in a satisfactory outcome if BPO agents and NIBS/NEIB investment officers were salaried employees.

On the basis of my own extended reflective study of profit-oriented market socialism, however, I have concluded that it would be rash to completely discount the possibility of a positive relationship between capital management effort and the rate of return on capital, and to assume that the rate of return on capital is completely independent of any effort provided by the capital owner. It might be a very simple matter to compare the profit rate of one firm with the average rate of profit, and to dismiss the top manager of the firm if the comparison is too unfavorable, or, if dismissal is either impractical or too drastic, to sell the stocks and bonds of that firm. It might also be a very simple matter to buy the stocks and bonds of a certain firm because it exhibits a higher-than-average profit rate. Still, these things do require a certain amount of attention, application, and effort on the part of human beings. There is certainly a possibility that capital management effort is indeed a significant factor in the economic equation, and we would not want to create a situation in which there would be no capital management effort at all provided under market socialism. The profit-oriented market socialist proposal put forward herein does envision capital management effort being provided by BPO agents and NIBS/NEIB investment officers. The sole purpose of the public ownership agencies would not merely be to take capital property return from publicly owned firms and distribute it to private households as social dividend income. Its more important purpose would be to take over the active economic role of capital owners under capitalism—to provide to the economy the primary factor of production capital management effort.

In my own theoretical work on profit-oriented market socialism, I have argued that the abstract essence of the primary socialist rebuttal to be made to the capital management effort argument against market socialism, resides in a concept which I have labeled the "plateau production function." Simply stated, this is the proposition that a very small amount of capital management effort (as provided by capital owners under capitalism or public ownership personnel under profit-oriented market socialism) suffices to achieve very close to the maximum rate of return on capital. That is, at very low levels of capital management effort, capital management effort has a very strong increasing effect on rate of return, but that strong effect soon dissipates, so that at higher levels of capital management effort, this effort has very little increasing effect on rate of return. A graph of rate of return against capital management effort shows a rapid rise toward an asymptotic upper limit. The appearance of this graph suggests one side of a plateau—thus the name.

There are three especially important implications of a plateau configuration in the production function relating capital management effort to the rate of return on capital. First, this function means that while capital management effort is important to the success of the economy, the economy does not need very much of it in order to be successful. Second, from the point of view of the individual capital owner under capitalism, it means that most of his or her observed capital property income is of a "producer's surplus" nature: that is, the utility value of this income far exceeds the disutility of the very small amount of capital management effort required to obtain it. Finally, it means that a profit-oriented market socialist economy, which paid the capital managers of the BPO, NIBS, and NEIB only a very small fraction of the capital property return, which was previously paid to private capital owners under capitalism, would nevertheless experience a level of capital management effort approximately equal to that experienced under capitalism, and hence a level of overall economic efficiency and productivity approximately equal to that of capitalism.

Among the two most important "coefficients" relevant to the potential performance of a profit-oriented market socialist system, relative to that of the market capitalist economic system, are the "retention coefficient" and the "effectiveness coefficient." The "retention coefficient" refers to the proportion of capital property return which is retained as personal income by the capital managers. The "effectiveness coefficient" refers to a parameter, which could be attached either to the rate of return function or to the aggregate production function, which determines the economic productivity of any given level of capital management effort, whether that level be high or low. The value of the effectiveness coefficient is determined by other economic and institutional factors—apart from the retention coefficient—which would affect the overall performance of the economic system.

The retention coefficient under profit-oriented market socialism would be dramatically smaller than it is under capitalism: the capital owners of capitalism retain 100 percent of capital property return (implying a retention coefficient of 1), while the public ownership personnel under profit-oriented market socialism would retain only 1 to 2 percent of this return (implying a retention coefficient of .01 to .02). This reduction in the retention coefficient might well, at first glance, suggest a severe deficiency of capital management effort under market socialism. But in light of the possibility of a "plateau production function" relating capital management effort to rate of return on capital, the matter is perceived to be not so straightforward. The salient implication of the plateau production function is that already under capitalism, there is a very small amount of capital management effort provided by the capital owners, and thus even a very drastic reduction in the retention coefficient would not have a noticeable reducing effect on the total supply of capital management effort.

The "retention coefficient" would clearly be much smaller under market socialism than it is presently under capitalism. Whether this would or would not mean a much smaller supply of capital management effort depends largely on whether or not the plateau production function is a good approximation to the actual real-world function relating capital management effort to rate of return on capital. Now as to the "effectiveness coefficient," critics of socialism would allege that this too would be much smaller than it is under capitalism. In fact, not wanting to accept that the validity of capitalism might depend on such a mundane-seeming concept as "capital management effort," they are quite likely to assert (assuming they can be induced to utilize terminology which has been developed by a proponent of socialism such as myself) that the "real problems of socialism" lie not so much in a low retention coefficient, as they do in a low effectiveness coefficient. When asked to justify this assertion, they will make reference to such factors as the following: the soft enterprise budget constraint under socialism; comprehensive central planning of the economy under socialism; the proliferation of intrusive social regulation of individual behavior and business enterprise under socialism; pervasive political intervention in the running of individual business enterprises under socialism; extreme social egalitarianism under socialism, as implemented through highly progressive taxation and a massive welfare state. All this, it is alleged, will make a terrible mess of the economy, so that it could be said that the "effectiveness coefficient" under market socialism would be a small fraction of what it is under market capitalism.

The basic problem with this assertion is that the factors just listed as determinants of socialist inefficiency are factors from which the profit-oriented market socialist proposal has been explicitly disassociated. The profit-oriented market socialist proposal does not call for central planning, it does not call for an expansion of business regulation, it does not call for a bigger welfare state—in fact, it calls for none of the things just listed. To cite these kinds of things as reasons for a lower effectiveness coefficient under market socialism is to engage in the question-begging tactic discussed earlier: the tactic of asserting that the real and perceived flaws of Communistic socialism and social democratic socialism must inevitably apply to *any* socialist system—including the proposed profit-oriented market socialist system. This basic argument may be described as the "there can be nothing new under the sun" argument. It need not be belabored that this is a fallacious argument. This is not to deny the possibility that the effectiveness coefficient of profit-oriented market socialism would in fact be smaller than that of capitalism, based on sound and sensible factors which really do apply to the proposed system. But it is to say that a simple recitation of the familiar litany of traditional anti-socialist propositions will not suffice as these "sound and sensible factors." It is going to take more thought than that.

On the pro-socialist side of the ledger, meanwhile, there are indeed several "sound and sensible factors" which suggest that the effectiveness coefficient would in fact be higher under profit-oriented market socialism than it is currently under capitalism. This possibility supplements the possibility of a plateau production function in the relationship between capital management effort and rate of return on capital. Conceivably the actual relationship might not be of the plateau configuration, so that actually a substantial amount of capital management is currently being provided under capitalism, and indeed a substantially smaller amount of it would tend to be provided under market socialism. The negative effect of this on economic performance might be offset by a higher effectiveness coefficient under market socialism. There are at least four factors that could improve the economic effectiveness coefficient as a result of the implementation of profit-oriented market socialism: (1) the translation of capital property income into social dividend income (distributed to households on the basis of household labor income) would increase the effective wage and salary payment to labor, and (presuming an upward-sloping supply curve of labor) lead to an increase in labor supply and consequently an increase in economic output; (2) the concentration of the outside ownership interest in a particular firm in the hands of a relatively small number of BPO agents would counteract the separation of ownership and control condition under contemporary capitalism, impose a higher degree of accountability on the top executives, and thus enhance their effort incentives; (3) the capital managers under profit-oriented market socialism, as a group, are likely to be more capable than the capital owners under capitalism, as a group; (4) the capital responsibility of the typical public ownership agency agent or investment officer could be set at a level to maximize his/her incentive to provide capital management effort. The first two of these four factors have already been discussed in the context of the "economic efficiency" component of the "pro" case on profit-oriented market socialism; therefore the discussion here will be confined to the latter two.

Capital manager capability. Capitalist apologetics routinely portrays the "typical capitalist" as that most admirable specimen of humanity: the brilliant, courageous, and resourceful entrepreneur. This portrayal is mythical, in that the actual "typical capitalist" under contemporary capitalism is either a rentier or a financial speculator, the origin of whose capital wealth lay in inheritance. Of the total amount of capital wealth in the capitalist economy, very little is in fact currently owned by active entrepreneurs. On the other hand, a great deal of it is owned by superannuated retirees, superannuated surviving spouses of wealthy capitalists, and various more or less unworthy sons, daughters, nephews, and nieces of wealthy capitalists. In other words, a great deal of it is owned by individuals whose personal capabilities in the area of capital management are not of the highest order. In contrast, under profit-oriented market socialism, most capital wealth would be managed by BPO agents and NIBS/NEIB investment officers in their prime working years who have demonstrated personal competence in the skills associated with capital management. For example, the primary function of the BPO agents would be more along the lines of corporate supervision, as opposed to investment analysis. Recall that these agents would be selected from a pool containing only those with high-level managerial experience in business enterprise. They would not—as is mostly the case under capitalism—be selected by the blind hand of inheritance. Moreover, not having an ownership right to their capital responsibilities, BPO agents and NIBS/NEIB investment officers would not be insulated from the possibility of dismissal in the event of demonstrable incompetence. The average personal competence and ability among those directly involved in capital management would therefore be higher under profit-oriented market socialism than it is under capitalism.

Capital responsibility. Under contemporary capitalism, a great deal of capital is owned (and therefore managed) by a very small number of extremely wealthy capitalist plutocrats, while a smaller but still substantial amount is owned and managed by a large number of middle-class individuals, each one of whom possesses a modest amount of capital wealth. Neither of these groups is likely to provide very much capital management effort. The wealthy plutocrats have so much wealth and income that they are nearing the point of satiation—to them the marginal utility of additional wealth and income is very low. Thus they have a low incentive to provide capital management effort. At the other end of the capital wealthholding spectrum are middle-class people whose capital wealth is too small to provide an appreciable income supplement, even if it is earning a high rate of return. They are therefore obliged to procure regular employment in order to earn the labor income necessary to sustain a comfortable standard of living. These people have little incentive to provide capital management effort because their limited capital wealth means that they will not receive much capital property income even if the rate of return on their wealth is quite high, and at the same time they have little capability of providing capital management effort because most of their time/energy resources are used up by the labor required to earn the labor income on which they are financially dependent.

Under profit-oriented market socialism, on the other hand, it would be possible to adjust the size of the capital responsibility of the typical capital manager (i.e., BPO agent or NIBS/NEIB investment officer), in light of the specified retention coefficient, in such a way that if the capital responsibility is earning a good rate of return, the personal income of the capital manager will be at a good level for inducing capital management effort—neither so large that the capital manager is likely to become satiated, nor so small that the capital manager does not have a meaningful incentive to effort. In terms of economic theory, the idea would be to set the capital responsibility of each individual agent or investment officer of the public ownership agencies at a level such as to make the effective personal rate of return on capital (i.e., the rate of return actually received by the individual—the total rate of return multiplied by the retention coefficient) approximately the rate at which the supply curve of capital management effort bends back. To provide a basis for understanding this, some explanation is needed of the economic concept of the "backward-bending supply curve of labor" (as extended to capital management effort).

As mentioned above, contemporary economists mostly believe in the proposition of the upward-sloping supply curve of labor. It is generally agreed that if the rate of hourly pay of the typical individual were to rise from, say, $25 an hour to $50 an hour, that individual would be disposed to provide more hours of labor per week. In the jargon of economics, the substitution effect would outweigh the income effort, and the wage rise would therefore increase the supply of labor. In the often rather backhanded mode of thought favored in economics, the wage rate is deemed the "price of leisure." Allocating one more hour per week to leisure means that the individual "pays" the wage that could have been earned in that hour. Therefore if the wage rate rises, leisure becomes more "expensive" and the consumer "substitutes" away from leisure—takes more income and less leisure. Thus the "substitution effect" of a wage increase is to increase labor (by decreasing leisure). But there is also an "income effect" at work, and this effect goes the other way. An increase in the wage rate increases the individual's effective real income, making that individual richer, and thus capable of purchasing more of all goods—including the good leisure. Thus the income effect of a wage increase is to decrease labor. These two effects work in opposition, and the presumption of an upward-sloping supply curve of labor is based on the assumption that the substitution effect dominates the income effect.

Reductio ad absurdum reasoning suggests that at very high wage rates, the income effect will dominate the substitution effect. For example, ask yourself how many hours of labor you would be likely to provide each week if your hourly rate of pay were $25. Now, keeping that figure in mind, ask yourself how many hours of labor per week you would be likely to provide if your hourly rate of pay were $25,000,000. Unless you are preposterously materialistic, you will work far fewer hours per week at $25,000,000 per hour than at $25 an hour. After all, you would need the time in order to play with all the expensive toys that could be purchased with your fabulous income. This means that between a wage rate of $25 an hour and one of $25,000,000 an hour, the income effect would dominate the substitution effect, and the supply curve of labor (measured between these two points) would be downward-sloping rather than upward-sloping. Economists are fairly well agreed that while most, if not all, people are currently operating in the upward-sloping ranges of their supply curves of labor (because they confront relatively modest wages for their labor), there does exist for each person a sufficiently high wage, such that if their actual wage were to rise above this level, their labor provision would commence to fall. In other words, supply curves of labor may be described as "backward-bending" (or "bow-shaped"): as the wage rises to a critical point, labor supply rises, but as the wage rises past that point, labor supply falls.

This idea may be extended to the supply curve of capital management effort, where the analogue to the hourly wage rate would be the effective financial return to an hour of capital management effort. This effective rate of return is determined not only by the rate of return on capital managed, but also by the *amount* of capital managed. For a very wealthy capitalist plutocrat, owing to the large amount of capital wealth involved, the effective rate of return on capital management effort might well be so high as to put that individual in the backward-bending range of his/her supply curve of capital management effort. At the same time, middle-class owners of small amounts of capital wealth might be in the upward-sloping ranges of their supply curves of labor, but their amounts of capital wealth are so small that the low effective financial return to capital management effort would entail a low supply of capital management effort. On the other hand, the capital responsibility amounts assigned to the capital managers under profit-oriented market socialism could be set at the level that would tend to produce the critical effective rate of return at which the supply curve of capital management effort bends back. This would tend to maximize the amount of capital management effort provided by each one of these capital managers.

We may summarize by saying that there are two major conceptual rebuttals to the pro-capitalist proposition that inadequate capital management effort, owing to the low retention coefficient of the capital managers, would cripple the economic performance of profit-oriented market socialism. First, there is the possibility that the production function relating capital management effort to rate of return on capital is of the plateau configuration, meaning that the input of a very small amount of capital management effort suffices to raise the rate of return to its asymptotic upper limit. The implication of this type of function is that the level of capital management effort is already very low under capitalism, so the fact that it would be equally low under socialism would be no problem. Second, there is the possibility that the effectiveness coefficient under profit-oriented market socialism would be higher than it is under capitalism. A higher effectiveness coefficient would both increase the incentive to capital management effort of the capital managers and have beneficial effects on overall economic performance through other channels as well (e.g., by making high corporation executives more conscientious and assiduous in the performance of their duties).

One thing is clear about this controversy: it will almost certainly not be settled by a priori economic theory. The proposition that a deficient supply of capital management effort, owing to the very low retention coefficient of the capital managers, will cripple the economic perform-ance of profit-oriented market socialism, is a logically sound proposition consistent with accepted economic principles. But equally so the counter-proposition that profit-oriented market socialism would be at least as ef-ficient as capitalism and possibly more efficient (owing to the plateau production function and/or a higher effectiveness coefficient), is a logi-cally sound proposition consistent with accepted economic principles. When (as is normally the case) a priori logic cannot settle a controversy, we must make reference to empirical evidence. Here also, it must be rec-ognized that all the available empirical evidence on this particular con-troversy is partial, tangential, indirect evidence, and as such, it is far from being conclusive in any meaningful sense. The only way that more or less conclusive empirical evidence could be obtained on the economic performance of profit-oriented market socialism would be to establish profit-oriented market socialism in the real world, and then observe its economic performance.

In lieu of that, we are forced to settle for bits and pieces of circum-stantial evidence which may—or may not—have much bearing on the fundamental question. Four areas of circumstantial evidence may be cited as being of particular significance: (1) the separation of ownership and control; (2) the institutionalization of capital markets; (3) the respect-able economic performance of public enterprise under capitalism; (4) the respectable economic performance of Communistic socialism. Each of these is briefly discussed below.

Separation of ownership and control. When we think of the definition of capital management effort (activity aimed at increasing the rate of re-turn on capital), the first thing that comes naturally to mind is the mana-gerial effort of corporation executives. Even those who suspect that corporation executives are paid more than they are worth will usually concede that corporate management is tough, stressful, hard work. Cor-poration executives tend to arrive at their offices early and leave late, with the intervening hours filled to overflowing with reading and writing reports, talking with people, considering options, and making decisions. And as the central concern of these managers is with the profitability of the corporation (as well as its ability to meet ongoing interest obliga-tions), it is apparent that the purpose of their intensive work effort is to raise the rate of return on capital, or at least on that part of the total capi-tal stock which is owned by their particular corporation. If the top man-agers of corporations owned these corporations, and if the interest and dividends which are the fruits of their effort went exclusively to these managers, then it would be far more plausible that interest and dividends are an earned return to capital management effort. It would be far more plausible because capital management effort could then be identified with corporate *management*. But the critical distinction between corporate *management* and corporate *supervision* has been strongly emphasized throughout this discussion. The interest and dividends are paid mostly to outside owners who provide corporate supervision, rather than to corporate executives who provide corporate management. The contributions of the former, such as they are, must absolutely not be confused with the obvious and manifest contributions of the latter.

Relative to corporate management, corporate supervision is child's play. A tremendous amount of effort goes into the production, estimation and reporting (as opposed to the *evaluation*) of a given firm's profit rate. This effort is provided, in the first instance, by the rank-and-file employees of the corporation. Additional coordinative and decisionmaking effort is then provided by the firm's managers. Finally, there is the effort provided by outside auditors who must study the firm's financial statements to ascertain whether they fairly represent the firm's condition. All this effort is labor—it is not corporate supervision. Corporate supervision occurs when an outside owner looks at (evaluates) the firm's bottomline profitability in relation to average profitability among business firms. Ninety-nine times out of a hundred there is not all that much of a difference, so the owner does nothing. One time out of a hundred the firm's profitability will be substantially below average profitability. In that case, if the outside owner holds a controlling share in the firm, he can fire the CEO and tell the Vice-Presidents to find themselves another CEO. Of course, the vast majority of outside owners under contemporary capitalism do not possess a controlling share in any particular firm. The only course available to them, when they believe that a particular firm in which they hold an interest is doing poorly, is to sell the stocks or bonds of that firm. All in all, the difficulty level of this decision might be compared to that of a decision on whether or not to take an umbrella when one leaves home. If it is sunny and the weather report says it will remain sunny all day, then do not take the umbrella. If it is raining and the weather report says it will keep on raining all day, then take the umbrella. One does not have to be an expert meteorologist, or to know how to manufacture an umbrella, in order to make this decision. No doubt this semifacetious "umbrella" example is somewhat excessive, somewhat of an overstatement. But perhaps it is not all that excessive, not all that much of an overstatement.

Whether we consider capital management effort as corporate supervision or as investment analysis, there is some obvious—though generally unappreciated—evidence that it is neither a particularly demanding nor a particularly challenging occupation. Once we have made the distinction between corporate management as provided by executives, and corporate supervision as provided by outside owners, it is apparent that corporate supervision is provided, in the first instance, by corporate boards of directors. The common custom is for corporate boards of directors to meet perhaps once a month for a few hours, during which the board members alternate between making inane comments and nodding off to sleep, while the managers ply them with various selected bits and pieces of information designed to show the corporation's operations in a favorable light. For the directors, the monthly board meetings represent an opportunity to be fed an expensive lunch, to feel important, and to escape, for the time being, from the need for actual work. The board of directors is of course representing the interests of the outside owners—but such representation is clearly not particularly taxing. After all, if the firm is paying out a reasonable rate of return to the outside owners, that suffices to keep them happy. They are not particularly interested in *how* the firm is making its profits. Their interest is confined to the bottom line; it does not extend to the thousand-and-one lines above the bottom line.

It might be objected that while the prevailing customs with respect to corporate boards of directors do indeed suggest that there is probably not all that much to corporate supervision as typically practiced in the contemporary capitalist economy, nevertheless stockholders, as well as holders of all other types of financial instruments, fully earn their capital property income by means of their continuous, intensive investment analysis effort. It may be true (according to this line of argument) that the typical outside owner does not have any meaningful direct authority over the incumbent managers (i.e., the discretionary ability to dismiss them) and hence has little opportunity to engage in corporate supervision as such—but even so, he or she is compelled to carefully study each and every firm in which an investment is held, as well as many other firms in the economy, with the eternally vexing question in mind: Should I sell certain financial instruments which I presently hold and reinvest the proceeds somewhere else, or should I stand pat? The apparent implication of this scenario is that investors should be spending long working days carefully reading and pondering the *Wall Street Journal, Forbes, Fortune, Business Week, Barron's*, as well as numerous other sources of information and enlightenment on the current and potential future performance of the multitude of available investment opportunities in the economy. Do actual real-world private investors do this sort of thing? Certainly there are a few extremely wealthy activist capitalists out there, such as the much-publicized Donald Trump, whose rapid-fire buyings and sellings are attended to with great interest by the business press. But this sort of thing is by no means the typical pattern.

The typical pattern is that of the passive capitalist who diversifies his/her portfolio according to prescribed wisdom and practices the officially approved "buy and hold" strategy. This type of capitalist spends very little time indeed studying and pondering the range of available investment opportunities, but rather selects investments quite casually, and then proceeds virtually to ignore these investments unless they become dramatically unproductive. The typical capitalist knows better than to waste any consequential amount of time in trying to "outsmart the market." He or she is normally occupied in more fruitful and fulfilling pasttimes—whether they might include a normal professional career, the acquisition of luxuries, or simply social climbing.

That this is the fact of the matter will be attested to by most of those who either are or have personal acquaintance with wealthy capitalists. But in addition to "common knowledge," we have other, more objective forms of evidence. One of these was the 1971 Purdue University Survey of the Individual Investor, during which an extensive questionnaire was completed by a large number of clients of a major brokerage house. All of the respondents to the survey were active traders in the stock market, and a considerable number of them were retired people with a great deal of time on their hands. The average amount of time spent by the respondents on studying investments and making investment decisions was 9.18 hours *per month*. This amounts to approximately one working day per month. As the reader is probably aware, the average labor job entails something over twenty working days per month. This information suggests that the disutility of investment analysis effort expended in pursuit of capital property income is trivial in comparison with the disutility of ordinary labor effort expended in pursuit of labor income (wages and salaries).

Of course, it could be speculated that many of the respondents to the Purdue University survey were middle-class people with relatively small capital wealth holdings, so that their need for labor income precluded them from engaging in much investment analysis. But surely (continuing according to this speculation) wealthy capitalists not dependent on labor income would indeed spend substantial amounts of time engaging in investment analysis. Against this speculation may be cited another piece of objective empirical evidence, this one from tax data published by the U.S. Internal Revenue Service. One of the annual publications of the IRS is *Statistics of Income: Individual Income Tax Returns*. From any issue of this publication it may be ascertained that the income of the highest-bracket taxpayers is dominated by property income (dividends, interest, and capital gains). But what is also very significant is that the large majority of these taxpayers also receive labor income (wages and salaries). And even though the labor income of the average highest-bracket taxpayer is a very small percentage of his/her total income, the *amount* of labor income received by this taxpayer is very high in an absolute sense. Obviously, these people are engaged in full-time professional careers.

Now this information reflects considerable moral credit on these wealthy capitalists. They don't *need* the labor income since they receive such large quantities of property income. But even so, they are resisting the temptation, such as it might be, to subside into a purely parasitical existence of uninterrupted consumption. They are *working*. But at the same time that this information reflects considerable moral credit on these wealthy capitalists, it also casts serious doubt on the proposition that capital property income is an earned return to capital management effort in the form of investment analysis. It stretches credulity to the breaking point to propose that these individuals come home after spending long, tough days at their offices, and proceed to spend long, tough evenings studying their investment portfolios.

Incidentally, this indication that wealthy capitalists engage in labor despite the absence of any financial need for labor income suggests an inherent *need* in adult human beings for work, or at least for some sort of systematic, goal-oriented activity. Perhaps natural selection has weeded out most of those whose genetic endowment predisposes them to inactivity. This in turn suggests that generous pecuniary incentives to effort may not be quite so critical as most economists—as well as most defenders of the capitalist status quo—seem to think. But this point will not be pursued, since it is the explicit intention of profit-oriented market socialism to provide practically the same pecuniary incentives to most types of productive endeavor as does contemporary capitalism.

Institutionalization of capital markets. Although the available evidence, both informal and formal, suggests that private investors are not particularly active in the provision of investment analysis, a very considerable amount of it is nevertheless provided to the economy. It is provided by individuals who are not investing their own money, but rather "company money." These individuals are the investment analysts and loan officers of the financial intermediaries: commercial banks, investment banks, insurance companies, pension funds, mutual funds, and so on. Such institutional investors as these are no longer mere participants in the real-world capital markets—they are the *dominant* participants. In addition, we can certainly consider the very substantial proportion of total investment spending which is funded by the retained earnings of nonfinancial corporations as being allocated by salaried employees rather than by individual investors. Both the amount of retained earnings and how this amount is to be allocated are unilaterally determined by the managers of these corporations. As is the case with all other ordinary business decisions (production levels, prices, marketing expenditures, research and development, etc.), the individual investors comprising the firm's outside ownership interest make no worthwhile, meaningful contribution to this decision.

For the most part, investing financial institutions apparently regard the task of selecting investments to be a relatively routine matter. Many of them entrust the task to salaried employees who are compensated in basically the same way as any other salaried employee. (A naive observation would be that these employees will do a poor job of selecting investments because they have no personal interest in the outcome—after all, it is not their personal wealth which is being invested. This is a naive observation because these employees *do* have a personal interest in the retention of their employment—which would be jeopardized if the performance of their recommended investments were to be noticeably poor.) Some financial institutions contract with professional investment counselors to provide information and recommendations, but these outside counselors are not paid an appreciable proportion of the total capital property income generated by the investments they propose. Adding together the compensation of internal investment decisionmakers and the fees of external investment counselors, these expenses to the typical financial intermediary amount to far less than 5 percent of the total amount of investment income received. There is an obvious parallel between these expenses of the financial intermediaries under contemporary capitalism and the amount that would be "retained" by the public ownership agencies under the proposed system of profit-oriented market socialism. If the financial intermediaries of capitalism do not have to pay their "capital managers" more than a small percentage of the total capital property income received in order to have the capital management job performed effectively, then society need not pay the personnel of the public ownership agencies under profit-oriented market socialism any more than this in order to obtain the requisite amount of capital management effort to keep the economy functioning efficiently.

The limited amount of time applied to investment analysis by individual investors and the relatively casual approach to investment analysis taken by institutional investors under capitalism are both natural consequences of what has been termed the "efficient capital markets hypothesis." The efficient capital markets hypothesis states that any relevant information about the potential future return to a particular investment instrument (e.g., the stocks or bonds of a particular firm) is very quickly, indeed almost instantly, incorporated into that instrument's market price. The salient implication of this hypothesis is that it would be unproductive to spend any appreciable amount of time and effort trying to find "good" investments. What would have been "good" investments in light of new information—had the prices of these instruments stayed the same—almost immediately revert to the status of "average" investments since their prices almost immediately rise. Therefore, over the long term, even a very capable investor cannot expect to do better than the average rate of return on capital in the market. (Unless, of course, the investor is exploiting inside information for personal gain. If this is indeed the case, the investor—if apprehended—will likely be committed to a penitentiary.)

Of course, professional investment counselors, stockbrokers, and the like hotly dispute this particular implication of the efficient capital markets hypothesis. They continue to insist that an intelligent and perceptive investor who studies the market carefully will in fact do consistently better than the average rate of return over the long term. If they are investment counselors, they are interested in getting investors to purchase their services, whether these services consist of generic advice widely distributed via newsletter, or of actual handling of the investor's portfolio. If they are stockbrokers or dealers in other types of financial instruments, they are interested in getting investors to trade briskly, the better to collect brokerage fees. These people practice the same sort of commercially motivated deception as was practiced by the manufacturers and purveyors of patent medicines in the United States during the late nineteenth century, before the Food and Drug Administration was established in an effort to contain the cruel and rampant exploitation of the gullible which reached epic proportions during that period.

The normal implication drawn from the efficient capital markets hypothesis is that a relatively modest amount of investment analysis time and effort will achieve approximately the expected market rate of return on capital, but that the expenditure of very large amounts of investment analysis time and effort above this modest amount are not likely to achieve a rate of return significantly above the market rate of return. As a matter of fact, this happens to be exactly the proposition contained in the "plateau production function" discussed above. The efficient capital markets hypothesis is totally consistent with the proposition that the relationship between capital management effort (in the form of investment analysis) and the rate of return on capital is of the plateau configuration: a very small amount of capital management effort quickly pushes the rate of return on capital up to its upper asymptotic limit (this upper asymptotic limit being essentially the same as the expected market rate of return).

Just as the separation of ownership and control drastically undercuts the plausibility of the proposition that capital property income is an earned return to capital management effort in the form of corporate supervision (once the distinction between corporate supervision and corporate management has been fully recognized and appreciated), so too the institutionalization of the capital markets drastically undercuts the plausibility of the proposition that capital property income is an earned return to capital management effort in the form of investment analysis. A substantial amount of investment analysis is indeed provided to the economy by the salaried employees of the financial intermediaries (i.e., the institutional investors). This substantial amount is quite sufficient to push the rate of return on capital to its maximum level. The efforts of these salaried employees make capital markets efficient, meaning that the price of a certain investment instrument closely reflects its potential future yield. The private investors are therefore simply parasitical free riders on the efforts of the salaried employees of the institutional investors. The private investors may select their investments casually, even randomly, and yet they can expect to receive approximately the average rate of return on capital. The only way they will receive less than the average rate of return is if they make such veritably moronic investment errors as buying stock shares in the Brooklyn Bridge from street-corner venders named "Vito." In a word, the growing domination of the capital markets by institutional investors is making it more and more clear that private capital owners, as such, are merely rentiers who make no meaningful productive contribution of their own to the economy.

Public enterprise under capitalism. According to capitalist apologetics, private capital owners are the spark plugs of the entire economic system: the vital catalysts without which the economic system is doomed to stagnation and ultimate collapse. The implication of the rhetoric is that any sort of production without benefit of capitalists is bound to be inadequate—quite possibly disastrously inadequate. The fact of the matter is, however, that the world has indeed accumulated a goodly amount of experience with production without capitalists, and that experience has strongly suggested that capitalists are far from being essential to the production process. One major example lies in the abundant experience of public enterprise under capitalism, of which typical examples include the U.S. Postal Service, Amtrak, the British nationalized industries prior to the Thatcher-era privatizations, the French automaker Renault and the Italian automaker Alfa Romeo, as well as a host of other examples from around the world.

The privatization movement of the 1980s and 1990s has currently attained faddish proportions, meaning that the common consensus opinion on the overall efficiency of public enterprises is, for the moment, excessively low. Common sense seems to have become a casualty in the rush to condemn public enterprise. How else can we explain why such significance is attached to the result, laboriously established by numerous researchers, that public enterprises, on average, earn lower profit rates than private enterprises? This is in fact an expected situation, and it bears no necessary relationship to efficiency as measured by average cost of production, labor productivity, and so on. After all, the reason why these enterprises are publicly owned rather than privately owned is that there were perceived circumstances, such as monopoly power or external effects, according to which profit maximization would not be economically or socially acceptable. It would not be healthy from the standpoint of the larger society for these enterprises to maximize their profits, and hence by social preference they make lower profits than they are capable of making.

In fairness, it should be pointed that on the basis of more sensible efficiency measures than profit rates, the performance of publicly owned enterprises has often been found by researchers to be inferior to performance by privately owned enterprises. But the actual numerical difference in performance is often not that great, usually being under 10 percent. And the differential is not necessarily attributable to the inherent inefficiency of public ownership owing to the inadequate financial incentives to managerial effort. For example, public enterprises are often subjected to political pressure to maintain employment in certain regions. They thus employ more labor than they should from a purely commercial standpoint, which means lower labor productivity and higher average costs of production. One does not need to privatize these enterprises in order to alleviate this particular problem; it is sufficient simply to remove the political constraint imposed on them of maintaining employment in certain regions. As to the argument that public enterprises are "inevitably" subjected to political pressure to maintain employment, this argument is hardly very convincing. If it is indeed politically possible to de-emphasize the employment maintenance goal through privatization of public enterprises, then it is equally politically possible to de-emphasize this goal simply by instructing the public enterprises not to be so concerned about it. In fact, if public enterprises were simply instructed to maximize profits, they would be just as focused and insensitive about pursuing profits as are private enterprises.

It is not the intention of profit-oriented market socialism to change the goal of the typical business enterprise from profit maximization to social welfare maximization. The typical privately owned business enterprise maximizes profits under capitalism, and the typical publicly owned business enterprise would continue to maximize profits under profit-oriented market socialism. That the efficiency and profitability of the typical publicly owned business enterprise under profit-oriented market socialism would be comparable to that of the typical privately owned business enterprise under capitalism is strongly suggested by the relative success of public enterprise under capitalism. These public enterprises have been functioning quite well, in many cases for decades, even though they are not subject to an explicit motivation toward profits, and even though their managers have no formal responsibilities to outside private capital owners. Presumably public enterprises which *were* subject to an explicit motivation toward profit, established via the responsibility of the managers to agents of a public ownership agency with a strong interest in profits, would do even better. This presumption, in turn, suggests the expendability of private capital owners.

Communistic socialism. The point to be made with respect to Communistic socialism parallels that just made with respect to public enterprise under capitalism: it is just on a larger scale. Communistic socialism as practiced throughout most of the twentieth century has demonstrated that a very high and impressive level of economic success may be achieved by an entire economic system from which private capital owners have been completely eliminated. No doubt the weight and significance of this point will not be fully appreciated by some people. In the wake of the spectacular political collapse of the Soviet Union in the early

1990s, there has occurred a dramatic strengthening of the misconception that Communistic socialism was—and still is for those nations still laboring under this system—an economic house of cards. The fact is, however, that throughout most of its history, the Soviet Union maintained a huge and very formidable military machine armed with the most technologically advanced weaponry. This could not have been done by a nation whose economy was a "house of cards." Despite the excessive military burden and the self-imposed isolation from the world economy, the Soviet Union managed to achieve a respectable standard of living for its population—a standard of living far beyond that of most capitalistic nations in the Third World.

To the relief of the West, the Soviet Union ultimately proved itself to be a *political* house of cards. But psychological factors had far more to do with the political collapse of the U.S.S.R. in the early 1990s than did economic factors. The official state policy of opposition to worldwide capitalism was subjecting the Soviet people to the continuing psychological strain of possible nuclear annihilation. At the same time, the state officials had to live with the continuing psychological strain of not being able to honor their commitments to the Soviet people: they simply could not make good on their decades-old promise of living standards for the Soviet people superior to those in the advanced capitalist nations of the West. The combination of these two psychological factors eventually put more pressure on the political system than it could stand. The rest, as they say, is history.

In Chapter 1 above, several important contributory factors to Soviet weakness were discussed, none of them having anything to do with socialism versus capitalism. These factors, ranging from the central planning system to the military burden, had nothing to do with the absence of private capital owners in the U.S.S.R. If the absence of private capital owners was an important contributor to economic weakness, then given all the other burdens under which the U.S.S.R. labored for so many decades, the absence of private capital owners would have been the coup de grace, so to speak, condemning the nation to a quick, complete, and ignominious economic collapse back in the 1920s. The fact that the U.S.S.R. achieved a respectable level of economic performance throughout the 70-year period from the 1920s to the 1980s, in the face of this formidable array of disadvantageous factors, strongly suggests that private capital owners, in and of themselves, have little or nothing to do with the level of economic success achieved by a nation. They are, in a word, expendable.

A footnote to the Soviet economic experience is the economic experience of the People's Republic of China. The rigidly Communistic political system of the P.R.C. is still intact, although in light of the fate of the Soviet Union, one wonders how long it can persist. The Communist Party leaders of the P.R.C. have avoided some Soviet mistakes (e.g., their relatively early abandonment of collective farming), but on the other hand they have to contend with one economic problem of overwhelming proportions from which the Soviet leaders were spared: the tremendous burden of a huge population on a limited territorial and natural resource base. For the moment, the People's Republic of China is generally regarded as possessing—despite its problems—one of the most dynamic and progressive economies in the world. Over the last 15 years, there has been a dramatic improvement in the standard of life among the Chinese people. And this improvement has occurred without benefit of the alleged services and contributions of private capital owners. Once again, we have a serious challenge, in terms of real-world human experience, to the proposition that private capital owners are vital to a nation's economic success.

This then completes our mini-survey of circumstantial empirical evidence bearing skeptically on the purported economic contributions of private capital owners. Obviously a great deal more such evidence could be cited and discussed. In fact, a truly "comprehensive" discussion would become impossibly lengthy. Some of this evidence could be interpreted as casting doubt on the potential performance of profit-oriented market socialism, and some of it could be interpreted (as in the above discussion) as casting a favorable light on its potential performance. But whatever the interpretation put on the evidence, the interpreter should be prepared to concede that in actual fact none of this type of evidence is directly relevant and strongly determinative. Profit-oriented market socialism has not yet been tried in the real world, and until it is tried, any illumination cast by some other type of real-world experience must necessarily be rather weak.

As mentioned earlier, in this author's judgment, the most sensible economic incentives argument to be made against profit-oriented market socialism is that owing to the low retention coefficient of the public ownership agencies (since the large majority of capital property return would be redistributed to the general public as a social dividend supplement to labor income), the personnel of these agencies (i.e., those individuals personally responsible for capital management) would have inadequate monetary incentives to capital management effort, thus leading to a drastic decline in the supply of capital management effort provided to the economy, and hence a similarly drastic decline in economic performance. Against this proposition may be mustered both theoretical considerations (especially the plateau production function relating capital management effort to the rate of return on capital) and empirical considerations (the separation of ownership and control, the institutionalization of capital markets, and so on). But these considerations are far short of being conclusive that inadequate capital management effort would *not* be a problem under profit-oriented market socialism. The only more or less conclusive demonstration of this would be the satisfactory performance of profit-oriented market socialism following its implementation.

Despite the fact that the potentiality of inadequate capital management effort is the most powerful single economic argument against profit-oriented market socialism, or indeed against any and all forms of market socialism, the reader will find not one reference to the term "capital management effort" in the voluminous corpus of written and spoken defenses of the capitalist economic system. Aside from the fact that the term was invented by a proponent of socialism (myself), there is the rather down-to-earth, humdrum, and uninspiring flavor of the term. It does not have the requisite overtones of mysticism and mythology—as does that gloriously evocative term, that all-time favorite of capitalist apologetics: "entrepreneurship." Capitalist apologetics thrives best in a logically fuzzy and intellectually muddled realm in which various disparate misconceptions and half-truths are jumbled up into a veritably impenetrable morass and presented with veritably religious fervor. There is little room in this realm for such a clear-cut, precise, well-defined, and thoroughly operational notion as capital management effort. Be it well noted, however, that whatever may be the reluctance of capitalist apologetics to deal with this concept on its own terms, the substantive content of a very large proportion of capitalist apologetics does indeed come down to no more and no less than the allegation that capital management effort would be inadequate under any kind of socialist system—including a market socialist system. What capitalist apologetics does is to play endless variations on this same theme, using different terminology and different phraseology. If and when superficial issues of terminology and phraseology are penetrated, it is found that the basic argument reduces to the capital management argument currently under discussion.

By far the single most important proxy term for "capital management effort" in capitalist apologetics is "entrepreneurship." But as was pointed out earlier, utilization of the term "entrepreneur" as a synonym for "capitalist" is patently spurious and propagandistic—simply because so few of those who presently own sufficient capital wealth to live comfortably off the income (i.e., capitalists) are now, or ever have been in the past, entrepreneurs. Essential to the idea of entrepreneurship is not only the founding of a new firm, but also its management for a considerable period of time following its foundation. Just as "entrepreneur" is an unsatisfactory synonym for "capitalist," so too "entrepreneurship" is an unsatisfactory synonym for "capital management effort." Capital management effort is a more general concept which applies to whatever contribution is made by capital owners in general—as distinct from that small minority of capital owners who are currently engaging in entrepreneurship as properly defined.

Aside from "entrepreneurship," two other important variations on capital management effort in capitalist apologetics are "wealthbuilding" and "risk-taking." The first of these is particularly associated with the important Austrian school figures Ludwig von Mises and Friedrich Hayek. The second is particularly associated with the Chicago school figure Frank Knight.

As described in the previous chapter, the origin of the idea of market socialism may be traced back to a debate between Oskar Lange (the "father of market socialism") and Mises and Hayek. Unfortunately, the specific proposal offered by Lange himself is too much tainted by textbook economic theory to be practicable as a real-world alternative. The profit-oriented market socialist proposal put forward in this book as a practical possibility is quite distinct from Langian market socialism. As mentioned in the last chapter, however, the basic idea of profit-oriented market socialism, under the designation "the artificial market," was indeed described and criticized by Mises in a brief passage in *Socialism: An Economic and Sociological Analysis* (1951). More recently, certain American neoconservative economists (Karen Vaughn, Peter Murrell, and Don Lavoie) have argued that, despite the influential judgment of Abram Bergson to the contrary, Oskar Lange did not actually respond successfully to the essential Austrian school argument against socialism being put forward by Mises and Hayek. According to the neoconservative economists, the Langian proposal might look good in the context of the static and unchanging world of the economic textbooks, but its inadequacy becomes painfully evident when one considers the real world: a dynamic and ever-changing environment filled with growth, investment, innovation, entrepreneurship, creative destruction, discovery, and so on. Mises's critique of the "artificial market" concept proceeds along much the same lines: the idea might look promising from the standpoint of static theory, but it breaks down entirely in light of the dynamic nature of the real world.

Of the body of critical writing by Ludwig von Mises and Friedrich Hayek on socialism, the vast majority of it is directed not against public ownership of capital, in and of itself, but rather against central planning, regulatory control of business enterprise, the welfare state, and socially imposed egalitarianism. Very little of this writing applies directly to the pure concept of market socialism (which involves none of these things), whether in the Langian form, the profit-oriented form, or any other form. Of the Austrian school inspired critical writing by the neoconservative economists against Oskar Lange's market socialist plan, very little of it applies sensibly to profit-oriented market socialism. But from the tone and general approach of these writings, in conjunction with Mises's explicit critique of the "artificial market" in *Socialism*, we may formulate a potential critique of profit-oriented market socialism based on the notion of dynamically oriented "wealthbuilding."

The basic idea is that the typical capital owner is not so much interested in the *rate of return* on his/her financial capital wealth in the current period; rather the typical capital owner is mainly interested in the *market value* of his/her financial capital wealth, as determined by its potential profitability over an extended range of future periods. In other words, the key issue is not capital property income on existing capital wealth—it is rather *wealthbuilding*: the expansion of capital wealth into the indefinite future. According to Mises, if genuine economic efficiency could be achieved through the maximization of return on the current capital stock, then perhaps a reasonably convincing case could be made for the artificial market (i.e., profit-oriented market socialism). This is because the firm managers can deal easily enough with the routine, well-defined tasks of producing and marketing the presently existing range of commodities using the presently existing capital stock. But when it comes to *change* (the introduction of new and improved commodities, replacing and upgrading the capital stock, etc.), then it is the capital owners—as opposed to the firm managers—who become the critical agents in the economy. It is the capital owners, as opposed to the firm managers, who by their investment decisions decide what new goods and new production processses will be introduced. The financial incentive to making good investment decisions with respect to a certain portfolio of financial capital is not so much the current rate of return on that portfolio, but rather the increase in the portfolio's market value which is generated by good investment decisions. In this light (continues Mises), the unworkability of the "artificial market" becomes obvious. The individual under socialism who makes investment decisions with respect to a particular portfolio of financial capital does not *own* that portfolio, hence he or she cannot personally benefit from the increase in the portfolio's value stemming from his/her good investment decisions. This lack of direct monetary incentives to good investment decisions means that financial capital will be allocated carelessly and arbitrarily. As a result, the prices of various commodities will no longer reflect their true economic values. The basis for rational economic calculation (i.e., correct and accurate market prices) will be gradually undermined and destroyed. The end result will be economic stagnation, decay, and ultimate collapse.

Mises's argument against the artificial market is based on a seriously deficient perception of reality. To begin with, Mises's characterization of the "static" issues of production and marketing as "routine and well-defined" is very much off-target. Correct decisions on methods of production, sizes of production runs, and effective marketing of the resulting commodities are very difficult and demanding. Moreover, anyone adequately familiar with the functions of corporate management in the contemporary economy realizes that these functions are hardly confined to current production and marketing—they certainly extend to future investment and innovation. As a matter of fact, it is completely unrealistic to neatly compartmentalize managerial functions into those pertaining to the "static" issues of production and marketing and those pertaining to the "dynamic" issues of investment and innovation. It is the close examination and careful study of current production and marketing which suggest improvements in both products and processes. To implement these envisioned improvements requires investment and innovation. The decisionmaking time horizon of the typical corporation is indefinitely long—each one of its employees and managers hopes and expects that it will continue on at least until their own personally expected retirement dates. For the majority of employees and managers, their personally expected retirement dates are not for many years in the future. They are thus compelled to provide for the future, to plan for innovation and investment, to think "dynamically."

Under contemporary market capitalism, problems of investment and innovation are indeed scrutinized intensively with the purpose of raising the rate of return on invested capital. But most of this work is done by the managers of established corporations and the investment analysts of the institutional investors. The contribution made in this area by private capital owners is minimal. In the fantasy world put forward by Mises, corporations obtain almost all of their investment capital directly from private investors, and these private investors are therefore intimately involved in the evaluation of competing investment projects. In reality, corporations obtain the vast majority of their investment capital from a combination of retained earnings and dealings with institutional investors. Very little is obtained directly from private investors.

As to Mises's distinction between the current rate of return on capital and the market value of capital wealth and his contention that the capital owner's primary concern is with the latter rather than the former, this is no more sensible than his distinction between the static issues of production and marketing and the dynamic issues of investment and innovation, and his contention that the firm manager's primary concern is with the former rather than the latter. In fact, current rate of return and market value are very closely connected. Whether we are considering a business corporation or a financial wealth portfolio, the current rate of return is the overwhelmingly dominant determinant of estimated future return, as reflected by market value (i.e., market price). If the capital owner chooses to sell a capital instrument whose price has risen since its purchase, the gain in value is converted into current income, called "capital gains." Very high income households tend to receive a substantial amount of capital gains income in addition to substantial amounts of dividend income and interest income. However, even at the very highest income levels, capital gains income does not sufficiently exceed dividend and interest income to justify Mises's contention that capital owners are more concerned with market value of capital wealth than with current return on capital wealth. In any case, the "current return on capital" is typically defined to *include* rises in market value: for example, the current return on a share of stock is dividends on the share plus increase in share price, divided by initial share price.

Putting aside peripheral and semantic issues, the heart of Mises's argument is that capital managers under profit-oriented market socialism would not receive enough personal financial incentive to motivate them to do a good job of capital management. Although Mises couches the argument in terms of the lack of ownership rights of the capital manager to the capital portfolio which he/she manages, the argument is logically analogous to the capital management effort argument against profit-oriented market socialism discussed earlier in this section. The simplest and most direct interpretation of Mises's argument is that capital managers under profit-oriented market socialism could not receive any capital gains income at all, either because there is no market at all for capital instruments, or because capital managers are not permitted to sell those capital instruments in their personally managed portfolios whose prices have risen in the capital markets. Now the profit-oriented market socialist system proposed herein does indeed envision active capital markets in which institutional investors would buy and sell capital instruments. In this author's original proposal for "pragmatic market socialism," no trading in stock shares was envisioned among Bureau of Public Ownership agents. But in the slightly modified pragmatic market socialist proposal developed in the "New Synthesis" section of Chapter 3, there would be trading in stock shares among BPO agents. This means that these agents would indeed receive capital gains income as well as dividend income.

Of course, the central potential problem of profit-oriented market socialism is not fixed by letting the BPO agents trade among themselves in the capital markets, so that their capital responsibilities generate capital gains income as well as dividend income. The central potential problem stems from the fact that the BPO agents would be allowed to retain as personal income only a very small fraction (somewhere around 1 to 2 percent) of the total capital property income received on their capital responsibilities—whether that total amount includes dividends plus capital gains, or dividends only. Dividends could be viewed as the "current return" on capital, while capital gains could be viewed as something qualitatively different, as the realization of "market value increase." The potential problem of profit-oriented market socialism is not that it would necessarily deny the capital managers (such as the BPO agents) any share of "market value increase" and instead confine them to "current return." The potential problem of profit-oriented market socialism is instead inherent in the fact that these capital managers would get only 1 to 2 percent of the total return to their capital responsibilities. This problem would remain even if the capital managers under market socialism were allowed to buy and sell in the capital markets, so that their capital responsibilities would receive "realized market value increase" (capital gains income) as well as "current return" (dividend income). This statement of the problem is a logical, sensible, and coherent interpretation of the Mises critique of the artificial market enunciated in *Socialism*. As already stated, this problem *could* be sufficiently valid to eliminate the possibility of an efficient market socialist economy.

Before proceeding on, it might be good to emphasize the dubiousness of the proposition that capital gains income is indeed something qualitatively different from dividend income. This idea is related to Mises's untenable distinction between the presumably "routine and well-defined" areas of current-period (static) production and marketing, and the allegedly "ever-changing and genuinely challenging" areas of future-period (dynamic) investment and innovation. Current capital property income (dividends) is supposedly generated exclusively by the former, while realized capital value increase (capital gains) is supposedly generated exclusively by the latter. It has already been pointed out that: (1) "static" production and marketing are no more "routine and well-defined" than are "dynamic" investment and innovation; (2) in the contemporary industrial economy, the real effort in *both* of these areas is expended by corporation executives rather than private investors. The salient implication of this is that allowing BPO agents to trade in the capital markets and to receive capital gains income on their capital responsibilities probably would not add anything to the potential economic performance of profit-oriented market socialism.

It was earlier indicated that the overwhelmingly dominant determinant of the estimated future return to a certain capital instrument (and hence its market price) is the current rate of return on that instrument. It would be more precise to say that *changes* in market price are overwhelmingly determined by recent *changes* in current rate of return. It must now be added that this is true of the *deterministic* influences. The deterministic influences are the objectively observable and measurable influences. The other major influence on market prices of capital instruments is that of random chance—the stochastic influence. The standard econometric formulation of an economic relationship has the dependent variable determined by a deterministic linear function of a set of quantifiable independent variables, plus a random variable called the "disturbance term." The larger the variance in the disturbance term, the larger the amount of unexplained variation in the dependent variable—that is, the less variation in the dependent variable that can be attributed to variation in the set of observable and measurable variables. This formulation, by the way, does not necessarily indicate acceptance of the notion of "pure" randomness, i.e., abandonment of the standard "cause and effect" principle. The usual interpretation of the disturbance term in economics is that it represents a set of currently unobservable and unmeasurable influences that, at least in principle, could possibly someday be observed and measured.

The prices of stock shares in particular, and capital instruments in general, are notorious for being extremely uncertain and highly unpredictable. Any capital market pundit worthy of his/her salt can take an observed price change in a certain capital instrument and manufacture several quasi-plausible reasons why the change occurred. The purported relationships underlying these reasons are, of course, virtually useless for forecasting purposes. Otherwise the pundits would themselves all have retired to lives of ease and luxury. Every so often individuals are quickly rendered quite wealthy by the drastic and unpredictable gyrations of stock share prices. These individuals—and defenders of the capitalistic economic system—want others to believe that these wealth increases were the result of exceptional investment prowess rather than blind chance. It also sometimes happens that wealthy individuals are suddenly impoverished by these same drastic and unpredictable gyrations. In these latter cases, the individuals involved are not likely to argue that they suffer from investment stupidity; they are obviously far more reconciled to the fact that chance has a lot to do with capital market outcomes. In reality, sudden capital market enrichments are not plausibly attributable to investment prowess, nor are sudden capital market impoverishments plausibly attributable to investment stupidity (unless it be the stupidity of inadequate portfolio diversification). Both the winners and the losers in the capital markets owe their situations almost entirely to chance.

The undeniable fact of a large amount of uncertainty with respect to the future prices of capital instruments brings us around to the "risk-taking" justification for capital property income. This notion was added to the intellectual armory of capitalist apologetics by Frank Knight (1885-1972), author of *Risk, Uncertainty and Profit* (1921). According to Knight, that indispensable contribution of the capitalist to the economic system, that contribution which fully justifies the capitalist's receipt of capital property income, is the contribution of "risk-taking." In purchasing and holding any sort of capital instrument, the capitalist is risking his/her wealth. This risk cannot be insured against, since it is inadequately measurable. For example, insurance companies do not issue policies against stock market losses simply because the probability of such losses cannot be precisely estimated. They cannot be precisely estimated because of the extreme variability of stock prices. This situation holds as well with respect to all other types of capital instruments (bonds, notes, etc.)—although perhaps not to the same degree as with stock shares. Therefore, holding any sort of capital instrument inevitably entails an uninsurable risk.

As a putative justification for the large capital property incomes of wealthy capitalists, risk-taking is subject to some serious problems. To begin with, risk-taking, in itself, is not a primary factor of production, such as physical capital, labor, and capital management effort. The capitalist could take risks by driving at 100 mph on a busy city street, and this risk-taking obviously would not assist economic production (unless it would be to spur the demand for funeral services). The risk-taking associated with capital ownership is rather a derivative condition generated by some kind of tangible behavior—whether it be the passive behavior of saving (to be discussed in the following section), or the active behavior of capital management effort expended in deciding upon the investments to be purchased with the saving. After all, if it were simply a matter of risk-taking, in and of itself, then clearly society as a whole could assume the risks of investment just as easily as private capitalists. In fact, society could handle these risks much more easily than individual capitalists, because the law of averages reduces the overall risk as the number of different investment projects increases, and society as a whole could undertake far more investment projects than any one capitalist.

The second problem is that risk-taking is an inevitable concomitant of *any* kind of human activity. For example, a working person takes a risk in driving to the office or factory, and a further risk in that the work done there might not be paid for (the employer may go bankrupt just prior to payday). It makes as much sense to argue that the workers need an additional payment over and above the normal wages and salaries paid for labor (say a social dividend supplement), in order to compensate them for the risks inherent in providing labor, as it does to argue that the capitalists need an additional payment over and above the normal capital property income paid for saving and/or capital management effort, in order to compensate them for the risks inherent in providing saving and/or capital management effort. That is to say, it does *not* make much sense.

The third and most serious problem for risk-taking as a justification for capital property income is that there is an inverse relationship between the amount of capital property income received and the risk level. Small-scale investors (i.e., middle-class people who have painfully accumulated a few thousand dollars out of their hard-earned wage and salary income), are taking a terrible risk when they put these savings into common stock or some other high return—but high variability—financial instrument. It is impractical for them to diversify significantly because of high brokerage fees and the relatively high prices of unit shares of most capital instruments. They are forced to keep their eggs in one basket—or at least in a very small number of baskets. Moreover, being painfully aware of the sacrifices that went into their small financial accumulations, they tend to be nervous and skittish investors. They follow the fortunes of their selected investments very closely, and when—as usually happens sooner or later—the prices of these investments begin to fall, they are very prone to panicking and selling at a loss. The fact that these small-scale investors are taking what for them is a large risk does not increase the capital property income they receive: the small amount they receive is based on the small value of their holdings. Consider, on the other hand, a wealthy capitalist who at some earlier date inherited a fortune worth, say, 50 million dollars. The fortune, which may now be worth 75 million dollars owing to normal appreciation, is kept safely diversified in a large portfolio containing 50 or 60 different investments. The law of averages practically guarantees that the average return on this portfolio will remain quite strong, even if a small number of individual investments go sour. It is much easier for this kind of investor to follow the usual "buy and hold" prescription proffered by the majority of personal investment gurus. Not having worked to accumulate the original fortune, the investor is not conscious of any appreciable sacrifice in having obtained it. Moreover, the law of averages protects his or her wealth from serious loss. The risk factor in the case of the wealthy, large-scale investor is negligible—and yet this investor receives large sums of capital property income. This income, of course, is based not on the assumption of risk, but rather on the amount of capital wealth owned. Quite obviously there is no little or no connection between the "disutility of risk-taking," such as it is, and the amount of capital property income received. Therefore, risk-taking does not suffice as a morally legitimate justification for capital property income.

One of the reasons why risk-taking has become such a popular justification for capital property income is that the development of the contemporary economy is making it more and more obvious that capital owners are mere rentiers who do not provide any significant amount of capital management effort, either in the form of corporate supervision or in the form of investment analysis. Since there is little or no tangible, observable effort involved for this income, justification is sought in the intuitively plausible but conceptually vapid construct of risk-taking. As will be discussed below in the context of the return to saving justification for capital property return, risk-taking is very analogous to the time preference construct. Risk-taking is automatically generated by either capital management effort or saving, in basically the same way that risk-taking is automatically generated by living (a living person runs the risk of dying). But capital property return cannot be sensibly justified as a return to risk-taking, because risk-taking is not a factor of production. If it is a return to anything, capital property return is a return either to capital management effort in some form, or to the sacrifices of saving.

Risk-taking may be viewed as a variant on capital management effort (just as it could be viewed as a variant on the sacrifices of saving) because the basic argument devolves to the assertion that there would be an inadequate incentive provided to the human providers of a valuable input to economic production. From a strict logical point of view, the argument is senseless because risk-taking is not a factor of production. But in a less strictly logical sense, risk-taking, which is generated by capital management effort, can be casually identified with the capital management effort itself. The argument that market socialism would fail to provide adequate incentives to risk-taking is then formally analogous to the argument that market socialism would fail to provide adequate incentives to capital management effort. The entire pro and con analysis of this proposition in the foregoing could then be repeated, with very little alteration except for substitution of the term "risk-taking" for the term "capital management effort," and it would remain just as sensible. In other words, risk-taking is not a new and independent defense of capitalism—it is merely a rewording of the capital management defense which we have carefully considered in this section. It shares this characteristic with "wealthbuilding," "entrepreneurship," and several other catchwords from the official lexicon of capitalist apologetics.

THE SAVING ISSUE

By far the most logically sound, economically sensible, and empirically plausible argument against profit-oriented market socialism is the potentially inadequate supply of capital management effort under the system, owing to the possibility that capital property return is in fact, either wholly or primarily, an earned return to capital management effort—either in the form of corporate supervision, investment analysis, or some combination of the two. If profit-oriented market socialism were to falter in practice, the most likely reason is that there would be inadequate capital management effort provided to the economy. After capital management effort, the second most important argument that capital property income is an earned return is the sacrifices of saving argument: that capital property income is a reward for saving, a reward which must be paid if an adequate amount of saving is to be done by private households. This saving, of course, is critical to the economy because it is the source of the investment fund used to finance research, development, innovation, and capital expansion. Without an adequate supply of saving, the economy would be doomed to stagnation and decline.

Relative to the capital management effort defense of capitalism, the sacrifices of saving defense has one major advantage and one major disadvantage. The major advantage is that it makes intuitive sense to a broad range of the population, from super-wealthy capitalists down to lower-middle-class and working-class people of very modest means. Super-wealthy capitalists are to some extent better able than are ordinary people to appreciate the dubiousness of the capital management defense of capital property income, because they know from personal experience how minimal is the time and effort they devote to corporate supervision and/or investment analysis, in relation to the large amount of capital property income which they receive. But being human beings, they of course want to feel morally justified about this large amount of income. They are thus drawn naturally to the thought that by preserving their wealth, by *not* liquidating their financial assets and engaging in an orgy of consumption (buying a bigger mansion, a better yacht, more fur coats and diamond necklaces, spending even more time and money in Monte Carlo casinos, and so on), they are allowing the resources that would have gone into their own augmented personal consumption to instead be used more productively to build factories and schools, to finance research and development, and to assist generally in the economic development of human civilization.

Of course, the super-wealthy capitalists are likely to already be enjoying a lavish standard of life, and so the "sacrificial" aspect of saving, such as it is, is for them less intense. At the other end of the income scale, working-class or middle-class households of modest means might not be in a position to appreciate the dubiousness of capital management effort as a defense of capital property income, since they have such minimal experience with this type of income. On the other hand, because their standard of living is so modest, they are naturally extremely conscious of the "sacrifices of saving." There are any number of very desirable commodities, not necessarily in the "luxury" category, that might be purchased with their small caches of savings, and thus it is a constant, severe temptation not to go ahead and liquidate these caches in order to buy some of these commodities. In light of the constant effort required to fight off temptations to spend savings accumulations, the interest income on these accumulations seems to working-class and middle-class households certainly to be a fair and legitimate return—it makes the effort to preserve savings accumulations at least a little bit more palatable. And so, at both ends of the income spectrum, although for somewhat different reasons at each end, there is a good level of basic intuitive plausibility in the proposition that capital property income is an earned return to the sacrifices of saving.

The major disadvantage of the sacrifices of saving defense of capital property income, relative to the capital management effort defense, is that when one goes beyond superficial intuitive first impressions to a careful, comprehensive, critical consideration of this defense, it becomes obvious that it possesses far less substantive content and apparent merit than does the capital management effort defense. Wheras capital management is an active behavior, saving is a passive behavior. This means that while capital management effort must be provided by individuals (e.g., BPO agents) and cannot be provided by "society as a whole," saving can indeed be provided by "society as a whole." More precisely, a part of national government tax revenues may be allocated to capital investment, thus accomplishing both saving itself, and transformation of the saving into investment, in one step. Therefore, if an adequate amount of saving is not being provided by private households under socialism, then—if society desires it—additional saving can be provided socially out of tax revenue. The sacrifices of saving, such as they are, need not be assumed individually by private households; they may also be assumed by all households acting in concert, that is to say, they may be assumed socially. Capital management effort is a better defense of capital property income than sacrifices of saving, because capital management effort clearly cannot be provided out of tax revenue. Capital management effort is active rather than passive, and therefore it requires a positive incentive (although, in all probability, not nearly as large a positive incentive as is provided to the capital owners under contemporary capitalism).

The obvious and elementary possibility of social provision of saving for investment purposes is the primary flaw in using the sacrifices of saving as a justification for capital property income. A secondary but still very serious flaw is that it is by no means clear that private household saving would indeed be lower under market socialism. If private household saving were as high (or higher) under profit-oriented market socialism as it is currently under capitalism, then there would be no need for further provision of saving resources out of tax revenue. Based on the evidence currently at hand, there is indeed a very substantial probability that this would in fact be the case. In the skin-deep thinking about these matters which is typical under contemporary capitalism, there is a great

deal of uncritical acceptance of the following closely related propositions: (1) interest (and other forms of property return) are a reward for
saving; (2) a zero rate of interest under socialism (reflecting a zero rate of
return on financial wealth in general under socialism) would reduce saving either to zero, or at least to a very low level. As to proposition (1),
there are other rewards to saving aside from interest, so that the effect of
the interest rate on saving may be very small, even negligible. As to
proposition (2), even if it were accepted, for the sake of argument, that
reducing the rate of interest to zero would tend, all other things being
equal, to substantially reduce saving by private households, this does not
necessarily imply that saving would in fact be less under socialism.
There would be other changes associated with a transition to profit-
oriented market socialism, and these other changes might completely
nullify the adverse effect on private household saving of eliminating
capital property return on financial wealth. In any case, as already noted,
a decline in private household saving does not necessarily imply a decline in aggregate saving: social saving out of tax revenue could be used
to eliminate the shortfall caused by lower private household saving.

The idea that capital property income is a return to the sacrifices of
saving dates back to the beginnings of capitalist apologetics in the early
nineteenth century. During that time the English economist Nassau Senior (1790-1864) came up with the memorable term "abstinence" to refer
to these sacrifices. This term was fiercely lambasted and ridiculed by
Karl Marx, in one of the more colorful and effective passages in *Das
Kapital* (Vol. I, Chap. XXIV, Section 3), on grounds that wealthy capitalists enjoying luxurious living standards cannot be sensibly represented
as practicing "abstinence," since this term connotes the excessively spartan living standards associated with some of the more fervent monastic
orders of the Middle Ages. Later on in the nineteenth century, the Austrian economist Eugen von Böhm-Bawerk (1851-1914), probably the
most important critic of Marxist economics of his era, came up with the
notion of "time preference." Böhm-Bawerk's time preference argument
is substantively the same as Senior's abstinence argument—it simply
does not use the questionable term "abstinence." Senior had argued that
saving is akin to abstinence, and therefore property return must be paid
to individuals in order to induce them to undertake this highly unpleasant
abstinence. Böhm-Bawerk argued that saving is saving, and does not imply, in the case of wealthy people, that they are experiencing spartan living standards—but all the same, property return *must* be paid, even to
wealthy people, in order to induce them to continue saving. The reason

for this is given as "time preference": the alleged inherent preference in all human beings, at all times and in all places, for consumption now rather than consumption later. If there were not a property return paid on savings accumulations, according to Böhm-Bawerk, then wealthy people would liquidate their capital assets and use the proceeds to buy even larger estates, still bigger yachts, and so on and so forth. In his famous dictum: The marginal productivity of physical capital explains why a rate of return *can* be paid to owners of financial capital; and time preference explains why it *must* be paid to these owners.

The proposition that consumption now is invariably preferred to consumption later is a naive—and invalid—extrapolation from the proposition that income *now* is invariably preferred to income later. The latter proposition is in fact almost certainly true, at least in a capitalist economy, because a certain amount of money received now can be—if the recipient does not wish to devote it currently to consumption—put into a financial instrument yielding a rate of interest (or some other form of property return). Thus the recipient will be able to consume the amount of money, plus accrued interest, later on. But it is a logical and empirical fallacy to conclude, from the invariable preference for income now to income later, that consumption now is invariably preferred to consumption later. Consumption is qualitatively different from income. Consumption always involves some sort of physical experience, and it is also inherently instantaneous. That is to say, consumption cannot be saved in the same way that income is saved. If an individual were to receive his or her income in the form of one lump sum payment per year of, say, $50,000, there would be no problem. The payment could be deposited in a bank account and drawn upon throughout the course of the year. But if the person received, to cover his or her food needs for the year, a large pile of perishable foodstuffs, which would remain edible for only one or two days, this pile being equivalent to what he or she normally consumes in one year—then there certainly *would* be a problem. A person cannot eat enough food to last for a year in one or two days, and in the absence of replenishment of the pile, that person would soon starve to death. In the jargon of economics, this indicates a limited amount of "intertemporal substitutability" with respect to consumption. On the other hand, income enjoys the maximum degree of intertemporal substitutability: a dollar's worth of income can be spent today, tomorrow, a year from now, ten years from now—all with equal ease.

The idea of time preference has a great deal in common with the idea of risk-taking, which was discussed in the previous section. Both ideas are superficially plausible defenses of capital property return which appeal to initial intuition, but which fail to hold up against a careful and critical examination. Neither idea emerged naturally from objective social scientific inquiry into the nature and functioning of society: rather both ideas were and remain transparent, ad hoc, ex post facto rationalizations for the receipt of capital property income by private individuals, ideas produced solely in response to the socialist intellectual challenge to the economic and ethical validity of capitalism. Both ideas are subject to the problem that that which is proposed as the justification for capital property income is not a primary factor of production: risk-taking clearly does not contribute directly to production, and so also neither does saving. Only after saving has been converted into investment does it contribute to production. According to the proverb, "there is many a slip 'twixt the cup and the lip"—similarly there is many a slip between saving and investment, and only a part of ex ante (before the fact) saving becomes actual ex post (after the fact) investment. As putative moral justifications for capital property income, both ideas suffer from the same fundamental flaw that there is an inverse relationship between the amount of capital property income received by the household, and that which is supposedly being compensated by capital property income. Wealthy capitalistic households receiving large amounts of capital property income are subject to *less* disutility from risk-taking owing to their greater ability to practice risk-spreading via portfolio diversification, and they also experience *less* disutility from saving (fending off time preference) because their current consumption standards are already so high. Finally, even if we were to grant that a certain measure of validity might attach to risk-taking and/or time preference, this would not necessarily justify the capitalistic mode of distributing capital property return produced by business enterprises to private households on the basis of household financial wealth. Just as the risk-taking of investment, such as it is, could be assumed socially, so too the sacrifices of saving, such as they are, could be borne by society as a whole.

Now it is factually true that under the profit-oriented market socialist system proposed herein, households would in general receive no property return, either in the form of interest or in any other form, on their financial assets. Such assets could be held only in the form of money (i.e., in cash and bank demand deposits). A certain household might be quite wealthy under this type of market socialism: for example, it might hold $10,000,000 in cash and bank demand deposits. The plan of market socialism being proposed herein envisions no restrictions being put on the amount of financial wealth which a given household may own. But it does, of course, envision the termination of property return payments on financial wealth. Under capitalism, on the other hand, a household owning $10,000,000 would invest it, and would receive during the course of the year, assuming a modest 5 percent rate of return, $500,000 in capital property income. Another household of more modest means, holding say $10,000 in financial assets, would receive, at the same rate of return, $500. Under market socialism, neither household would receive any property return on its financial wealth, since this wealth could not be held in the form of "investments." A household which started a year with $10,000,000 (in cash and demand deposits) would end the year with $10,000,000, and a household which started a year with $10,000 would end it with $10,000. Capitalist apologetics asserts that capital property income is a very important reason for holding accumulations of financial wealth—in fact, it may very well be the *sole* significant reason (as in the dictum: "people save in order to take advantage of the interest rate"). Therefore, capitalist apologetics would assert that under socialism, in which there would be no interest or other property return on investments available to private households, the hypothetical wealthy household with $10,000,000 would have no incentive to hold that $10,000,000, and the hypothetical modest household with $10,000 would have no incentive to hold that $10,000. Both households would go on a spending spree—the wealthy household might buy a 200-foot ocean-going yacht, while the modest household might buy a little motorboat for bass fishing.

Upon a little reflection, most readers will recognize the dubiousness of this prediction. Consider first the modest household. Upon a transition to socialism, small-scale holdings would be compensated 100 percent in cash. Thus if, for example, the household had been holding the $10,000 in certificates of deposit or an interest-bearing time deposit, this same amount would now be held in a simple demand deposit. Would the household, now deprived of $500 per year in interest income, rush out to spend the $10,000 which previously had produced that $500? Not necessarily. It could be that the $10,000 has been earmarked for retirement income purposes, or for providing a college education for the children, or for providing a bequest to the children, or just simply because the household feels more comfortable knowing that it has some "financial padding." Aside from the maintenance of existing savings accumulations, there is the question of further saving out of current income. This modest household will in all probability receive *more* current income under market socialism than it had been receiving under capitalism. It will lose the

$500 in capital property income which it had been receiving under capitalism, but it will gain some amount of social dividend income under market socialism. If it loses $500 in capital property income and gains $2,500 in social dividend income, it will have $2,000 more a year out of which to save. It may very well *increase* its level of saving.

Now consider the wealthy household, the one with $10,000,000 in financial assets under capitalism. The envisioned compensation plan would indeed be "fair and equitable"—but that does not imply full compensation of large-scale financial wealth based on a combination of inheritance and financial speculation. After socialization, this same household might be left with, say, $2,000,000 in demand deposits. Will the household rush out to spend the $2,000,000, since it will no longer bring in any capital property income? Not necessarily. Recall that under capitalism, the household had been accustomed to receiving $500,000 a year in capital property income on its $10,000,000 in investment assets. Most of that $500,000 a year was probably being spent on consumption—keeping up mortgage payments on the estate, paying the servants, etc. The household would have to confront the fact that it can no longer count on $500,000 a year in capital property income to sustain the style of life to which it was accustomed. In fact, if it went on spending $500,000 a year out of its current stock of $2,000,000 in financial assets, it could maintain this pattern for only four years. At $500,000 a year in consumption expenses, and no further property income, it would take four years to exhaust a $2,000,000 demand deposit. It need not be belabored that the household quite probably would *not* go on a spending spree. Quite probably it would instead start pondering ways to reduce expenses. For example, maybe the time has come to sell the estate and move into a modest mansion in town. Perhaps the time has also come to reduce the household staff. In actual fact, the annual consumption spending of this wealthy household is likely to be considerably less after socialization than it was before.

These stories are intended to suggest that there is a lot more to saving than the interest rate. Just as in the last section, I did not develop a formal economic theory of capital management effort, so too I do not intend to develop in this section a formal economic theory of saving. That would become far too technical. Some fairly general comments will have to suffice. It so happens that the existing economic theory of saving is not as comprehensive and well defined as one might expect of such an important economic category. In fact, the only model of saving which might be described as "standard textbook material" is a rather simplistic two-period model in which the household uses saving (or borrowing) as an instrument to allocate the total amount of income it receives over the two periods as between period-1 consumption and period-2 consumption. This model provides some insight into the effect of the interest rate and income (both in period 1 and period 2) on the level of saving. A basic result from this model is that the effect of the interest rate on saving is indeterminate. A rise (or fall) in the interest rate has competing substitution and income effects, and there is no a priori basis for presuming which effect will dominate. This indeterminacy exists even if time preference is incorporated into the model by specifying that period-1 consumption has a greater impact on intertemporal utility than period-2 consumption. This result parallels the result discussed in the last section that the effect of the wage rate on the supply of labor is indeterminate in general—and so also is the effect of the effective rate of return on capital management effort on the supply of capital management effort provided by the capital manager.

A fundamental postulate of the sacrifices of saving defense of capital property income is the "upward-sloping supply curve of saving as a function of the interest rate": the higher the interest rate, the higher the level of saving provided by private households. That this postulate is actually nothing more than a conjecture is demonstrated even by the rudimentary two-period model of saving discussed in practically every standard textbook of microeconomic theory. An upward-sloping supply curve of saving with respect to the interest rate would mean that the substitution effect of an interest rate change dominates the income effect. But there is nothing contrary to standard economic presumptions in the alternative conjecture that the substitution effect and income effect cancel each other out and the interest rate has *no* effect on saving, or in the alternative conjecture that the income effect dominates the substitution effect and the supply curve of saving is *downward-sloping* with respect to the interest rate. Naturally the level of indeterminacy increases as we proceed to more complicated models. A more realistic model of household saving would cover an indefinite number of periods rather than just two periods. It would take into account the fact that households typically expect to retire at some point in the future, and so they must make provision for sustaining consumption during the retirement years. An increasingly popular assumption in the models of saving currently under development in contemporary economic research is that household utility depends not only on consumption of commodities, but also on the amount of financial assets owned: in other words, financial wealth is valued "for its own sake."

There is also the complication of aggregation and general equilibrium: the relationship between the interest rate and aggregate saving, taking into account the production side of the economy, may be qualitatively different from the relationship between the interest rate and the saving of one particular household, prescinding from the production side of the economy. And then there is the dynamic element: the long-term relationship between interest rate and saving may be quite different from the short-run relationship between the two.

As the reader might well imagine, it can all become very complicated. It becomes even *more* complicated when we try to imagine what the impact on aggregate private household saving would be of the establishment of the profit-oriented market socialist system proposed herein. Economists like to describe proposals such as the one under consideration here as "counterfactual": meaning that the proposed conditions would be so dissimilar to present conditions that they would be extremely difficult to assess on the basis of knowledge pertaining to present conditions. As used in economics, the term "counterfactual" carries a connotation of unrealism and even utopianism. Its application to profit-oriented market socialism is probably unfair in that this system would in actual fact be extremely similar to observed realities under contemporary market capitalism in most ways. Be that as it may, the following informal comments are provided, in lieu of a formal analysis of the problem, to suggest that a substantial decline in the aggregate rate of saving of private households under profit-oriented market socialism is not all that likely.

To begin with, there is the fact that the "upward-sloping supply curve of saving" (the so-called "classical" theory of saving) is purely speculative from a theoretical standpoint. This has already been adequately discussed, and it will not be further discussed in the following. I do not want to give the impression that it is an important part of the argument being presented that the supply curve of saving is *not* upward-sloping with respect to the interest rate. This is not actually an important part of the argument, since even if the supply curve of saving with respect to the interest rate were in fact upward-sloping, this would not imply a reduction in private household saving under profit-oriented market socialism, relative to capitalism, if one or both of the following is true: (1) the effect of the interest rate on private household saving, while positive, is numerically very weak; (2) the effect of the interest rate on private household saving would be swamped by other effects.

Most people do not consult data on interest rates when deciding on how much they will save. Saving is usually a long-term proposition, interest rates do not vary all that much over the long term, and what fluctuations in interest rates will occur in the future is unknown anyway. A much more important question for most people, in deciding on their saving, is: "How much can I *afford* to save?" The amount that they can afford to save is largely determined by their income level. It was on the basis of this simple observation that John Maynard Keynes, the initiator of contemporary macroeconomic theory and probably the most influential economist of the twentieth century, postulated that the influence of the interest rate on saving is numerically insignificant and is dwarfed by the influence of income on saving. It is therefore quite important to note that the vast majority of households under profit-oriented socialism will have incomes higher than those they have presently under capitalism. To begin with, the vast majority of them will receive more social dividend income than they currently receive capital property income. In addition, there is the possibility that owing to the fact that the social dividend distribution principle implies an increase in the effective wage or salary rate of every household, households will provide more labor, thus increasing aggregate output and total household income. Therefore, most households will have more income out of which to save. This will be the case, that is, unless a deficiency of capital management effort reduces economic output and household income—so that saving falls. Note, however, that this would not be a saving problem in and of itself, but rather a derivative problem stemming from inadequate capital management effort. As emphasized earlier, if there would be an economic performance problem under profit-oriented market socialism, most probably it would stem from inadequate incentives to capital management effort.

Returning to the saving issue per se, another important point to keep in mind is that the great majority of saving provided by working-class and middle-class households is in fact "life-cycle saving" earmarked for the provision of retirement income. Most households provide for their retirement either by participation in a government pension plan (such as Social Security in the United States), or by participation in a private pension plan, often partially underwritten by the employer. The profit-oriented market socialist plan proposed here envisions no change in the terms and conditions of retirement planning. In particular, retirement plans would incorporate compound interest just as they do today under capitalism. One of the major exceptions to the principle that capital property income would not be available to private households would be the compound interest paid on retirement accumulations by financial intermediaries. Thus there is no reason to expect this very important component of private household saving to be affected by a transition to profit-oriented market socialism.

One of the cruder themes in capitalist apologetics is that socialism would deprive people of the ability to provide for their retirement years by eliminating all private ownership of income-producing capital instruments such as stocks and bonds. The fact is that only a tiny proportion of the retired population receives substantial income from stocks, bonds, and the like. Most retired people live on pensions and annuities which terminate upon the death of the recipient and his/her spouse. For these people, retirement planning would be exactly the same under market socialism as it is under capitalism. A related, but slightly more sophisticated theme in capitalist apologetics is that life-cycle saving is an important contributor to overall capital wealth inequality: capital-poor people tend to be young people just setting forth on their working careers, while capital-rich people are those nearing the end of their working years. If this were the case, then in general people could expect to become capital-rich as they became older, and there would be nothing in capital wealth inequality to be concerned about. Once again, however, the facts refute this proposition. The actual numerical contribution made by life-cycle saving to overall capital wealth inequality is minimal.

The contribution made by inheritance to capital wealth inequality, on the other hand, is very substantial. Mainstream economics is acknowledging this contribution to a much greater extent now than it did in the past. In fact, the "bequest motive" has become quite a conventional part of contemporary economic theories of saving and wealthholding. The emergence of the bequest motive has largely been a response to recognition that life-cycle saving, in and of itself, cannot account for real-world capital wealth inequality. These theories propose that there are not one but two principal incentives to saving: to provide retirement income, and to provide bequests to heirs. Household utility is made a function of the consumption stream over time, and also of the amount which the household passes on to heirs (usually children). A closely related approach is to make household utility a function of consumption and financial wealth. In this approach, the motives for holding financial wealth are viewed more generally: they may indeed include concern for the welfare of heirs, but they may also include the psychological security of the wealthholder himself or herself. After all, there is inevitably a high degree of uncertainty regarding the length of life. A rational wealthholder will want to ensure that the assets do not run out before life runs out.

Just as the basic capital management effort argument against market socialism has a number of variants, so too the basic saving argument has its variants (though not as many). The primary argument is that the availability of a rate of return on financial accumulations is a major—if not *the* major—reason for holding such accumulations, and in the absence of this rate of return, private households will hold much smaller amounts of financial assets. They will thus save less out of current income, causing a dearth of capital investment resources. Owing to the prevalence of the "bequest motive" in the contemporary economic theory of saving, we may anticipate the following variant on this primary argument. Socialism will not only cut off the payment of capital property return on financial assets of private households, it will also virtually eliminate the institution of inheritance by subjecting the wealth of deceased persons to veritably confiscatory estate taxation. Deprived of the opportunity to leave any appreciable bequests to heirs, households will hold far less in the way of financial assets, and will correspondingly save far less out of current income. Not only does socialism cut off the source of investment spending, but it is also morally reprehensible to prevent loving parents from freely expressing, in a financially tangible manner, their pure and noble altruism toward their loving children.

To begin with, a question could be raised regarding the purity and nobility of parental altruism in this case: to some extent, the promise of bequests is a means by which wealthy parents try to ensure that their children remain attentive, subservient, and obsequious. But leaving that aside, it must be emphasized at this point that the profit-oriented market socialist proposal under consideration here does *not* necessarily imply any alteration in the present situation respecting inheritances. It does not imply increasing the level of progressivity in estate taxation, nor the imposition of progressive taxes upon inheritances. Owing to the fact that this book continues to harp on the role of inheritance in maintaining extreme inequality in capital wealth ownership under contemporary capitalism, it would be understandable if some readers inferred that inheritance would be strictly curtailed under market socialism. However, such an inference would not be correct. The fundamental problem with capitalism is the unearned nature of capital property income. Capital property income is unearned even when it is received by an owner who personally accumulated the capital wealth on which it is paid. This problem is immensely aggravated when, owing to inheritance, several generations separate the individual who originally accumulated the capital wealth and the individual who is currently enjoying the capital property income produced by that wealth. Inheritance *aggravates* the problem—it does not *create* the problem.

It may very well be sufficient, therefore, simply to eliminate the payment of capital property income on the financial assets of households; meaning that institutions regarding inheritance, per se, could be left as they are today. What this means, for example, is that if the financial wealth of a certain pair of parents, at their deaths, is $2,000,000, then they would be able to leave that $2,000,000 to their children. The children would then obtain the right to $2,000,000 in purchasing power—no more and no less. When the children had gone through $1,000,000 of it, they would have $1,000,000 left. That is, the children would *not* receive these assets in the form of a block of income-producing capital wealth which could go on paying out income for decades, thus reproducing itself many times over. This example gives the basic idea—although in practice the amount bequeathed would be reduced by the same proportion paid in estate taxes as is paid currently under capitalism. Therefore, a saving objection based on the notion that market socialism would necessarily subject estates of deceased persons to confiscatory taxation, or otherwise erect impassable barriers to any sort of appreciable inheritance, is simply unfounded.

To the extent that the possibility of leaving bequests to heirs is indeed an important motivation to the accumulation and maintenance of financial assets, this important motivation would persist under market socialism. There is still a question, of course, regarding the *strength* of this particular motivation to saving. But the analysis of the potential effect of eliminating property return on financial assets of households, on the amount of saving done by those households, is basically the same whether we are envisioning these assets being used by people purely in their own interest (to provide general financial security, and/or to facilitate future consumption), or whether we are envisioning the assets as primarily intended to benefit children or other heirs. There are still competing substitution and income effects which make the effect of eliminating interest on household saving uncertain, even when we postulate no other changes in the condition of the household. And then the situation becomes still more complicated when we take into account other changes aside from the elimination of interest. In short, the basic question of the effect of socialism on private household saving is not fundamentally modified in light of the bequest motive.

Any and all sensible advocates of socialism should be willing to concede that agnosticism regarding the effect of eliminating capital property return on private household saving, does not properly translate into a complacent attitude on the saving issue. All things considered, there is a non-negligible possibility that private household saving would indeed decline significantly under market socialism. This possibility must be taken into account in planning for profit-oriented market socialism. Private household saving would have to be closely monitored, and at the first sign of significant decline, taxes must quickly be adjusted upwards to ensure that the shortfall in private household saving does not translate into a deficiency of investment resources. In fact, it would probably be sensible to definitely add a new category of national government spending under market socialism: the category of business physical capital investment. The amount actually appropriated to business physical capital investment would then depend on developments in private household saving. If private household saving remains steady or increases, then this appropriation would be very modest. If private household saving decreases significantly, then this appropriation would be substantial.

The naive version of the saving argument against socialism is that the drastic decline of private household saving, owing to the elimination of capital property income on privately owned financial assets, would translate quickly and directly into capital starvation. Business enterprises would be unable to obtain adequate investment resources with which to maintain and improve the capital stock. The economy would be abruptly plunged into a catastrophic state. This dark, quasi-apocalyptic image is excellent for frightening children and exceptionally naive and credulous people—and it has been utilized to this end by capitalist apologetics since the earliest days of the socialist challenge. The more sophisticated version of the saving argument, which we now take up, stipulates that a rational civilization, having adopted socialism, would not allow itself to become capital starved. That is, the decline in private household saving under socialism would be replaced by social saving out of tax revenue. A certain amount of government tax revenue would be appropriated directly into business capital investment. The argument is then that government intervention in the saving-investment processes of the economy would lead to a nonoptimal level of saving/investment, and moreover, to the gross misallocation of whatever amount is saved/invested. In terms of its propagandistic effectiveness at the gut intuition level, this argument is but a pale reflection of the capital starvation image. But at least it does possess a modicum of substance and plausibility in a strictly intellectual sense. It is an argument which needs to be considered.

As a matter of fact, attention was drawn to this argument by Oskar

Lange himself, the "father of market socialism." In his seminal essay "On the Economic Theory of Socialism," Lange cited two major potential problems with market socialism: (1) bureaucratization of economic life; (2) arbitrary saving rate. Although these problems might constrain the performance of market socialism, Lange argued that the performance of market capitalism was actually being constrained to a far greater extent by the far more serious problems of extreme inequality in capital wealth holding, the prevalence of imperfect competition among business enterprises, and inherent propensities toward severe business depression. Our attention at this point will be focused on the "arbitrary saving rate" issue. Lange had been sufficiently influenced by the laissez faire precepts of orthodox mainstream economics to think of it as a disadvantage of market socialism that quite possibly the system would not be able to rely entirely upon private household saving for the provision of investment resources.

Of course, if there is social determination of any part of aggregate saving, then it may be said that the aggregate saving rate is "socially determined." This would be the case even if 90 percent of saving came from private households, and only 10 percent from government appropriation of tax revenues. But apart from the possibility that social intervention in the determination of saving might not be all that important in a numerical sense, Lange may have been conceding too much to the pro-capitalist side of the debate in using the term "arbitrary" to describe the socially determined saving rate. This term makes it sound as if the saving rate would be randomly picked out of a hat. Of course, in reality the amount of tax revenue devoted to business capital investment, and thereby the aggregate saving rate, would be determined by an informed and thoughtful decisionmaking process.

Lange no doubt had in mind, as a benchmark for the optimal determination of saving, a theoretical construct known as the "microeconomic efficient saving condition." According to this construct, saving is at its optimal level when each household in the economy is equating the marginal disutility of saving to the market rate of interest, while at the same time each firm in the economy is also equating the marginal productivity of capital investment to the market rate of interest. In this way, the marginal disutility of saving for each household is brought into equality with the marginal productivity of investment for each firm. The benefits of investment are brought into perfect harmony with the sacrifices of saving. This rosy little proposition sums up the inadequate saving objection to market socialism in a neat, handy, pseudo-scientific nutshell. By denying households an interest return on their savings accumulations, socialism would destroy the nexus between the disutility of saving to the households and the productivity of capital to the firms. The microeconomic efficient saving condition is violated, saving thus becomes "arbitrary," and presumably the economy suffers accordingly.

The weakness of this argument against market socialism resides in the weakness of the microeconomic efficient saving condition. Even as a criterion of efficiency in and of itself (i.e., ignoring distributional considerations), the condition fails to meet reasonable standards of practicality and applicability. This is because it depends on a series of excessively strong assumptions: absence of external effects, perfect competition throughout the economy, perfect foresight, and so on. If any of these assumptions breaks down, a case arises for social intervention in saving. A case also arises when we focus on the more general question of social optimality, as opposed to the specific question of efficiency—that is, when we do take distributional considerations into account. Owing to the extreme inequality of capital wealth holding under contemporary capitalism, any putative gains in efficiency from fulfillment of the microeconomic efficient saving condition are swamped by the adverse effects on overall social welfare of the overall contemporary capitalist socioeconomic system.

The microeconomic efficient saving condition is analogous to the proposition of the economic efficiency of marginal cost pricing. They are both simplistic formulations from economic theory textbooks which are useful for pedagogic purposes, but which need not be taken very seriously when it comes to real-world policy decisionmaking. The attitude taken by the mainstream economics profession toward Oskar Lange's market socialist proposal reveals the profession's disregard of theoretical principles such as these when they seem to come into opposition with "common sense." Lange's market socialist proposal is founded upon marginal cost pricing—a principle which is violated by an imperfectly competitive, profit-maximizing firm. In the not unlikely case that imperfect competition is highly prevalent in the real world, a Langian market socialist economy based on production rules involving marginal cost pricing will display a higher level of economic efficiency than the equivalent capitalist economy. The economics profession simply shrugged off this supposedly quite weighty advantage of Langian market socialism, on the basis of various half-baked qualms and quibbles, such as that of Abram Bergson that excessive monitoring costs would be required under Langian market socialism to enforce the production rules. But there exists no worthwhile, generally accepted economic theory of "monitoring costs"—while the marginal cost pricing principle is backed up by whole chapters full of handsome equations. This demonstrates how easily theoretical considerations may be outweighed by "common sense" considerations when the two come into apparent conflict. For the same reason that the mainstream economics profession does not regard the fulfillment of marginal cost pricing as a particularly significant argument in favor of Langian market socialism, the violation of the microeconomic efficient saving condition is not a particularly significant argument against profit-oriented market socialism.

The aggregate saving rate is actually quite a stable, slow-moving economic variable. One simple and commonsensical principle for determining the aggregate saving rate under profit-oriented market socialism is that it should be the same as—or perhaps somewhat above—the aggregate saving rate under contemporary capitalism. What has been adequate saving under capitalism should presumably be adequate saving under market socialism. Of course, one could question whether the aggregate saving rate has indeed been adequate under contemporary capitalism. For a very long time, conservative economists have bemoaned an alleged deficiency of saving resources with which to fund capital investment. As the political pendulum swung to the right during the Reagan-Bush era in U.S. politics, greater credence was accorded to this viewpoint. The tax burden on the wealthy has been significantly eased, ostensibly to encourage saving and promote investment. The one certain effect of this policy has been to put more disposable income into the pockets of wealthy capitalists. How much of this additional disposable income has found its way into additional capital investment is a very problematic question. No doubt a very substantial proportion of this additional income—quite possibly all of it—has simply gone into even more luxurious living standards for these wealthy capitalists.

If under profit-oriented market socialism society has established discretionary control over the aggregate saving rate, and a consensus exists that saving and investment are inadequate, then the problem could be handled directly by an increase in the amount of tax revenue appropriated to business capital investment. This appropriation would be distributed to the population of business firms on purely commercial criteria. In other words, it would go to the firms with the best proposed investment projects in terms of both amount of return and safety of return. Some of the appropriation might be put into newly established government accounts in regular financial intermediaries of the sort already operating under capitalism. And some of it could be distributed to the newly established national government financial intermediaries: the National Investment Banking System (NIBS) and the National Entrepreneurial Investment Board (NEIB). Both the existing financial intermediaries and the new financial intermediaries would allocate their investment funds basically on the commercial basis of maximization of expected rate of return on investment. No doubt some critics of socialism will assert that these funds would be allocated in a politically directed and economically arbitrary manner. But this is simply an invocation of the tried-and-true tactic of begging the question. There is simply no objective, systematic evidence to back up this allegation. It simply expresses the close-minded presumption that all the errors and deficiencies ever associated with socialism in the past must inevitably apply to all incarnations of socialism which may occur in the future—even those incarnations which have been carefully and explicitly designed to avoid past errors and deficiencies.

FREEDOM AND DEMOCRACY

To this point we have been concerned with the economic objections to profit-oriented market socialism. We have focused on the allegations that capital management effort would be inadequate under market socialism, and that saving would be inadequate under market socialism. Backing up these economic objections is a very important political objection: that socialism of any kind, market or otherwise, is antithetical to freedom and democracy. The term "democratic market socialism" has frequently been employed here as a substitute for "market socialism" or "profit-oriented market socialism." This alternative term implies the possibility of a market socialist system that would be politically democratic as well as economically efficient. But is this a legitimate presumption? Many people take the political objection to socialism very seriously—in some cases, even more seriously than the economic objections. Any comprehensive statement of the case for market socialism must therefore confront and respond to the political component of capitalist apologetics.

One possible response to the political objection is ruled out because of the type of socialism proposed herein. This is the response that through abundant experience democracy and socialism have been proven compatible with social democracy. There have been numerous social democratic political parties—parties which proudly designate themselves "socialist"—which have been in power at various times in various European countries (an important recent example being the Mitterand era in France), and these parties have always observed scrupulous respect for democracy. They have not endeavored to suppress democracy, and they have been fully willing to vacate office if directed to do so by the electorate. Empirical experience with social democracy does indeed strongly suggest the compatibility of social democratic socialism and political democracy. However, this compatibility does not constitute a response to the political objection to socialism from the standpoint of the market socialist proposal under consideration here. This is because social democratic socialism, in contrast to the profit-oriented market socialism proposed here, does not involve public ownership of capital as a general principle. At most, social democracy might endeavor to achieve (or retain) public ownership of a small number of "key" industries (such as electric power, railroads, steel, and so on). But it does not endeavor to extend public ownership to the preponderant majority of business enterprise. By the strict definition of "socialism" employed herein, "social democratic socialism" is in fact a misnomer.

Profit-oriented market socialism, on the other hand, envisions public ownership of almost all large, established corporations. Entrepreneurial corporations and nonprofit corporations would be exempted from public ownership, but among the population of large corporations, entrepreneurial and nonprofit corporations constitute a very small minority. In the modern industrial economy, large, established corporations account for the great majority of production and employment. According to the political objection to market socialism, public ownership of such a large proportion of corporate business enterprise would give the national government a tremendous amount of economic power. This power would be exploited by the party in office to undermine and suppress democracy. The approved formulation of the problem in capitalist apologetics may be summed up as follows: Capitalism separates political power from economic power; socialism, on the other hand, combines political power with economic power. This combination would very likely prove fatal to personal freedom and political democracy.

The political objection to socialism first gained significant credibility and widespread acceptance in the 1930s. At that time, capitalist apologetics was temporarily on the defensive owing to the painful contrast which had emerged between the Depression-prostrated capitalist nations and the booming Soviet Union, then in the early stages of its planned industrialization campaign. One argument of capitalist apologetics concerning the U.S.S.R. of that period was that although Soviet citizens did not have to worry about involuntary unemployment, their living standards were still intolerably spartan by Western standards. Another argument was that the

U.S.S.R. was totally undemocratic, and as a matter of fact no population with democratic control over its government would have permitted its already spartan living standards to be further straitened by an industrialization campaign designed to benefit future generations. According to this latter argument, the industrialization campaign in fact clearly demonstrated just how undemocratic the Soviet Union really was. This argument received a tremendous boost owing to the Communist Party purges of the latter 1930s. Tremendous numbers of Communist Party officials, many of them having made important contributions to the Bolshevik victory during the revolutionary and civil war periods, were executed or banished to slave labor camps, often after having been forced to "confess" mythical treasonous activity during the course of humiliating show trials. Prior to the purges of the latter 1930s, it might have been possible to interpret internal dissension within the U.S.S.R. primarily as a struggle between forward-looking progressives and backward-looking reactionaries. Such an interpretation became very difficult in light of the purges. The purges demonstrated that even 20 years after the Russian Revolution, there remained very significant potential internal resistance to the regime. They also demonstrated the awesome amount of personal power which had become concentrated in the hands of the dictator Joseph Stalin.

Stalinist tyranny in the Soviet Union did more to discredit the socialist alternative to capitalism than any other factor, either empirical or theoretical, throughout the entire history of socialism. To aggravate the harm, Stalinist tyranny was later on closely replicated in the People's Republic of China during the Mao era. Smaller-scale tyrannies have been prevalent throughout the Communist world: in East Germany, North Korea, Vietnam, Cuba, and so on. The dismal political record compiled by communism throughout its history has quite possibly been a fatal blow to the prospects of socialism, now and for all time. There is simply no way around the fact that the Communistic nations have, without exception, combined pure public ownership socialism with highly oligarchic and undemocratic political systems. The question is whether it will ever be possible for a sufficient number of people to understand that the empirical association of socialism with political oligarchy, as obvious and dramatic as it has been in the Communist countries, does not indicate a causative relationship between the two.

To begin to see that socialism does not necessarily beget political oligarchy and tyranny, it is first helpful to recognize that capitalism does not necessarily beget political democracy and personal freedom. The most horrendous totalitarian regime of the twentieth century was established in Germany with the accession of Adolf Hitler to power in 1933. The Nazi regime in Germany persisted until its military defeat by the Allied powers in 1945. During that brief but terrible period, the crimes against humanity committed by Hitler's Nazi regime significantly exceeded those committed by Stalin's Communist regime. The Soviet Union had a great burden on its historical conscience, but at least it was never guilty of anything so cruel and wanton as the murder of six million Jewish people simply on grounds of their religious affiliation. Moreover, to its credit Communism was imbued with a noble vision of social progress for all humanity. Nazism, on the other hand, aspired toward nothing more than a worldwide caste civilization in which the German people would be the highest caste—a base, selfish, and unworthy aspiration. Despite use of the term "socialism" in "National Socialism" (the official name of the Nazi political philosophy), capitalism remained unmolested in Nazi Germany. Wealthy capitalists had had a strong hand in bringing Hitler to power, because they perceived National Socialism to be preferable to various left-wing alternatives, including unalloyed communism. Once in power, Hitler repaid the favor by fully respecting private property in capital (except with respect to the minority of capitalists who happened to be Jewish). German business enterprise was subjected to close governmental regulation and direction during the Nazi era, but the personal wealth and luxurious living standards of non-Jewish German capitalists were not significantly infringed upon.

Although Hitler's Third Reich is by far the most dramatic example, there have been many other examples in modern history of nations which are capitalistic in their basic economic institutions, and at the same time are politically oligarchic and undemocratic—sometimes to the point where they are reasonably described as "totalitarian dictatorships." Owing to this situation, capitalist apologetics is not able to assert that capitalism is both necessary *and sufficient* for political democracy. However, because of the absence of any authentically democratic Communist nations, capitalist apologetics can and does assert that capitalism is *necessary* to political democracy. In other words (according to this argument), the combination of economic and political power under socialism sets up conditions inimical to political democracy, and sooner or later political democracy is indeed strangled.

Although this proposition is in fact consistent with crude empiricism, as soon as one begins to study the history of communism in the modern world with a certain degree of attention, the dubiousness of the proposition becomes apparent. The fact is that the absence of democracy under communism is far more plausibly attributed to historical factors than it is to public ownership socialism in and of itself. None of the nations in which communism became established, from Russia in 1918 to Cuba in 1959, had had firmly established democratic traditions prior to their respective revolutions. Apart from the absence of democratic traditions, there was the suddenness and traumatic extremity of the Communist social transformation. Under all Communist transitions, all privately owned capital wealth has been immediately expropriated with no compensation whatever. No consideration has been given to the fact that some small-scale capital owners had personally accumulated their capital holdings out of legitimate labor income. The attitude of the revolutionary leaders toward wealthy capitalists has been viciously hostile: these leaders have thought themselves generous to be willing to spare the lives of the capitalists, let alone giving them any compensation whatsoever for their erstwhile capital property.

Unalloyed hard-core Marxism of the sort which inspired Lenin and his associates at the time of the Russian revolution, and which inspired the leaders of other Communist revolutions, has always engendered a great deal of skepticism, not to mention fear and loathing—not only among the wealthy capitalistic elite, but also among a considerable proportion of middle-class and even working-class people. Therefore, only under the most extraordinary conditions has a Communist revolution become possible. In the case of the Eastern European satellites of the Soviet Union, their "Communist revolutions" were imposed by the invading Red Army, and were in fact very much against the popular will. In Russia, China, and a handful of other cases, Communist revolutions succeeded internally, but only amidst the extreme disruption and hardship engendered by warfare, and then only by the narrowest of margins. The extreme and uncompromising policy measures taken by the new Communist governments (of which uncompensated expropriation of all capital wealth is only the most obvious example) instantly alienated large proportions of their respective populations. Communist revolutions have also aroused a great deal of anxious concern in the rest of the world. From the earliest days of the Bolshevik revolution in Russia, for example, there were urgent calls for massive armed intervention to crush out the menace of radical socialism before it had a chance to spread. These calls were not heeded at the time, but they instilled deep dread in the Communist leaders of possible invasion by hostile capitalistic nations. The eventual invasion of the Soviet Union by Nazi Germany in 1941 lent additional weight to this dread. The fear of invasion has been a constant factor throughout the histories of the Communist nations, and it remains relevant even today.

One must also take into account the revolutionary and conspiratorial nature of the Communist parties prior to their assumption of power. As hunted outlaws in their own land, they could not afford the luxuries of leisurely open debate and fully democratic decisionmaking in deciding upon party policies and activities. Rather the emphasis was on tight organization, strict discipline, and unquestioning obedience. Had these parties been otherwise, it is unlikely that they would have been successful in seizing and retaining power amidst chaotic revolutionary conditions. It is unrealistic and unfair to expect parties such as these, confronted with bitter hostility both within and without, to have established genuine political democracy in nations which had never had any appreciable historical experience with genuine political democracy.

An important milestone in the consolidation and formalization of the political argument against socialism was Friedrich Hayek's highly influential *The Road to Serfdom*, published in 1944. Much of the book's impact was due to its timing. In 1944, with World War II still raging, the democratic nations felt besieged by totalitarianism from both the right and the left. Hitler had just tried to conquer the world in the name of right-wing totalitarianism, and following the war, Stalin was likely to try the same in the name of left-wing totalitarianism. It was an emotionally intense period for all of humanity, and Hayek's *Road to Serfdom* addressed the primeval anxieties of many people. In the calmer retrospect afforded by fifty years of relative peace, Hayek's statement of the political case against socialism is more readily perceived as exaggerated and indiscriminate, especially when considered in the light of the market socialist proposal being put forward in this book.

In *The Road to Serfdom*, Hayek uses the term "socialism" in a very broad sense to encompass any and all social infringements upon the laissez faire ideal, infringements such as public regulation of business, progressive taxation, and welfare programs. Hayek claimed that these infringements gradually weaken the independence, initiative, and self-reliance of the population. The population becomes passive and dependent, it becomes the human equivalent of a herd of cattle, it develops a "slave mentality." Once in such a psychologically debilitated state, the population becomes especially susceptible to the authoritative rhetoric of dictatorially inclined demagogues. It stands by quietly as these demagogues and their cronies destroy democracy and set up brutal totalitarian regimes. And by the time the population fully understands that the demagogue-turned-dictator does not have their best interests at heart, it is too late to resist. At the time he wrote *The Road to Serfdom*, Hayek was a political refugee from Nazism, and clearly the principal inspiration to the book was an emotional reaction against the horrifying Nazi social system in Germany and Austria. But the book was also fueled by Hayek's intense revulsion toward the Communist tyranny in the Soviet Union. Along with many other social commentators, both at that time and since, Hayek placed great emphasis upon the remarkable similarities between Nazi totalitarianism and Communist totalitarianism—even though the two systems ostensibly derived from opposite ends of the ideological spectrum.

Socialism in the strict public ownership sense obviously could not be blamed for the excesses of Nazi totalitarianism, since Nazi Germany, in contrast to the Soviet Union, had carefully preserved and protected its wealthy capitalist class. In actual fact, Hayek devoted very little attention in *The Road to Serfdom* to public ownership of business enterprise as a contributory factor to the slave mentality and political totalitarianism. On the other hand, he devoted a great deal of attention to the standard social democratic agenda of business regulation, welfare programs, and so on. The major weakness of Hayek's argument is the indiscriminate virulence of its denunciation of this program. Hayek clearly disapproved even of the watered-down social democracy of the Rooseveltian New Deal in the United States. He implied that the distance between Franklin D. Roosevelt and Adolf Hitler was not nearly as great as it might seem at first sight. To most people, this was going too far. *The Road to Serfdom*, when read carefully, is a book which appeals strongly only to the extreme libertarian fringe of the conservative movement. Of course, many people did not (and do not) bother to read the book carefully—to a considerable extent its popularity then (and now) is attributable simply to its bitter denunciation of both Joseph Stalin's communism and Adolf Hitler's Nazism. Most rational, informed people are strongly opposed to such social systems—and this would certainly include any proponent of profit-oriented market socialism.

In actual fact, a much more focused and effective statement of the political objection to public ownership socialism was provided by Milton Friedman in *Capitalism and Freedom*, published in 1962. By 1962, the threat of totalitarianism appeared much diminished, and Friedman's book is not imbued with the same spirit of urgency and dread which permeated Hayek's *Road to Serfdom*. In actual fact, only a very small part of

Friedman's book deals directly with the political objection to public ownership socialism: the objection that public ownership socialism combines political and economic power to the detriment of democracy. Most of *Capitalism and Freedom* consists of a conventional assault, based on standard laissez faire preconceptions, on various social interventions in the free market. Friedman expresses disapproval of such things as occupational licensure and minimum wages—although he does not follow Hayek's example in claiming that these kinds of things tend quickly to breed a slave mentality and thus create a strong predisposition toward totalitarian dictatorship of the Stalin or Hitler variety. In Friedman's view, things such as occupational licensure and minimum wages—while they do not generate an immediate threat of dictatorship—do indeed seriously curtail personal freedom, as well as significantly diminishing economic efficiency. As profit-oriented market socialism is inherently neutral toward occupational licensure, minimum wages, and the like, the great majority of *Capitalism and Freedom* is completely irrelevant to it.

However, as mentioned, in one relatively brief section of the book, Friedman does provide a clear, focused, and intelligent statement of the charge that any sort of public ownership socialism—market or otherwise—would endanger democracy. Friedman's argument is simply a mirror image of the conventional argument against "bourgeois democracy" developed by Communist ideologues during the Cold War propaganda struggle between the Communist East and the non-Communist West. According to this traditional Communist argument, the proudly-touted Western democracy is a sham and a delusion. Candidates for elective office are so similar as to be tweedledee and tweedledum. They all have exactly the same attitude on the one political issue with real substance: whether the economy should be capitalistic or socialistic. Specifically, they are all totally supportive of the capitalist status quo. Anyone who might have a preference for socialism never has a chance in the political arena. Anyone daring to express pro-socialist views will be quickly dismissed from his or her employment on the instructions of the capitalists who own the firm. Thus reduced to poverty, the individual will be unable to engage in effective political activity. The media of communications are almost entirely privately owned, profit-maximizing business enterprises. The capitalists who own these enterprises see to it that little or no sensible pro-socialist material is published or otherwise disseminated. Finally, there is the direct control over the political process exercised by wealthy capitalists. Capital wealth provides some of these wealthy capitalists with both the leisure time and monetary resources necessary to run for and serve in elective government offices. A much larger number of wealthy capitalists do not become directly involved in the political process, but they use the tool of campaign contributions to ensure that only those candidates with what they consider "appropriate" (i.e., anti-socialist) attitudes have any reasonable chance of being elected to office.

One could take any typical expression of this argument penned by a Communist ideologue from the Cold War era, replace the term "wealthy capitalists" everywhere it occurs with "high party officials," and one would have a reasonable facsimile of Friedman's political argument against socialism in *Capitalism and Freedom*. According to Friedman, the party in power under socialism will use its economic authority to suppress opposition political parties and dissidents in general. It will utilize this authority with special energy and enthusiasm against political dissidents wanting the restoration of capitalism. Such individuals will be dismissed from their employment with publicly owned corporations, and will thus become ineffectual owing to poverty. The publicly owned media of communications will be required to prejudicially misrepresent the statements and viewpoints of political dissidents, and to uncover and expose their personal sins, faults, errors, and liabilities. As a result of all this, the incumbent political party will gain an insuperable advantage over the opposition. Elections might be held at the appointed times, but their outcomes will be predetermined by the dominant party. The political system will degenerate to a self-perpetuating oligarchy. Friedman is aware of the fact that this argument is simply an inversion of the traditional argument used by Communist ideologues to assault Western democracy. But he claims that under capitalism, the capitalist class is not in fact sufficiently aware of its own self-interest, nor sufficiently well-organized, to have the kind of control over political processes alleged by the Communist ideologues. On the other hand, says Friedman, under socialism the party in power actually *would* behave in exactly the manner envisioned of the capitalist class in the Communist argument.

Although there has been a tendency among pro-socialists to dismiss this kind of argument out of hand, in actual fact it is sufficiently weighty to require serious consideration. Let us then examine the argument in the context of the market socialist alternative to capitalism. Let us assume that we are considering a market socialist system established in a nation with a strong and viable democratic tradition, such as the United States or the United Kingdom. Let us also assume that there is no change in the formal, established political institutions of society: e.g., the government would still be divided into legislative, executive, and judicial branches, there would still be regularly scheduled elections, and so on.

The danger to democracy perceived by Milton Friedman lies in national government control both of business enterprise in general, and of those specific business enterprises concerned with communications (newspapers, book and magazine publishers, radio and television stations and networks, and so on). Control of business enterprise in general would be used by the party in power to deny gainful employment to political opponents; and control of the media of communications would be used to destroy the reputations and credibility of these opponents. The mechanism for exercising this control would be the issuance of instructions to the relevant firm managers, these instructions backed up by the threat of dismissal for disobedience. One possible solution to both of these problems lies in cooperative market socialism. Under this form of market socialism, the national government would have no authority to hire and dismiss managers of corporations: rather these managers would be elected internally by the employees. This, of course, would immediately pull the plug on the scenario envisioned by Friedman. Another solution would be the municipal ownership market socialist proposal of Leland Stauber. Under this form of market socialism, firm managers would be responsible to public ownership personnel appointed not by the national government, but by a host of local governments. It seems doubtful that a large number of more or less autonomous local governments could get sufficiently well organized to represent a serious threat to democracy through misuse of the public ownership authority.

Of course, the profit-oriented market socialist proposal recommended in this book is something different from both cooperative market socialism and municipal ownership market socialism. It does indeed envision an important role for the national government in the exercise of the public ownership authority. However, certain modifications may be proposed in the basic design to mitigate any possible threat to democracy implicit in public ownership of most large-scale business corporations. One of these modifications has already been mentioned in the foregoing: instead of the directors of the local offices of the Bureau of Public Ownership being appointed by the national BPO office, they might be appointed by local government officials of the municipality in which the office is located. In actual fact, this particular modification might result in a somewhat messy situation, and it may not regarded as necessary or desirable, in view of the other safeguards of democracy contained in the overall socioeconomic system—such as the one proposed in the following paragraph.

A second modification has not as yet been suggested, but it is now put forward as a definite part of the overall profit-oriented market socialist proposal. This is to make all or most media corporations (newspapers, book and magazine publishers, radio and television stations and networks, and so on) into labor-managed, cooperative enterprises. This would eliminate any BPO control over their high-level managers: these managers would instead be elected by the employees in regularly scheduled, open elections. On the basis of presently available evidence, it seems to this author that a profit-maximization incentive enforced by an outside ownership authority will tend to result in a higher level of overall economic efficiency within the firm than will labor self-management. But owing to the critical importance of an independent media of communications in preserving political democracy, I think that in this case the economic efficiency consideration should give way to the political safety consideration. So from this point forward, the discussion will be based on the assumption that BPO agents would not be involved in the hiring and firing of media corporation executives. These particular executives would be responsible only to their employees.

The elimination of media corporations from the authority of the BPO would eliminate the possibility of direct instructions by incumbent national government officials to these corporations to prejudicially misrepresent the personalities, ideas, and policy proposals of opposition party members. Of course, indirect pressure might be brought via threats to withhold advertising by the regular publicly owned business corporations. But this is a very indirect means of control, and it only applies to that part of the media dependent upon advertising revenues. In addition to guaranteeing objective reporting of oppositionist viewpoints, the independence of the media corporations will enhance the likelihood that efforts by the incumbent national government officials to economically harass opposition party members by denying them employment with publicly owned corporations would be quickly and widely exposed.

It need hardly be emphasized that misuse of the public ownership authority by incumbent officials to gain political advantages would be a very serious criminal offense. It would be far worse than the taking of bribes, because it would directly threaten the integrity of the democratic process. This offense would indeed be a form of treason. Any government official found to have issued illicit instructions to managers of publicly owned corporations would be subject to immediate dismissal from office and lengthy imprisonment. It would be very dangerous for these officials to issue any such instructions. The chain of transmission would be quite long, and at every link there would be a strong possibility of whistle-blowing and exposure.

Let us imagine, for example, that a certain national government official, say the president of the United States, wants to see to it that a certain vociferous political opponent is dismissed from his/her employment with a publicly owned corporation. Let us ignore, for purposes of simplicity, secretaries, aides, assistants, messengers, and so on. To begin with, the president has to give an instruction to the director of the national office of the BPO to effect the dismissal. The director of the national office has to transmit that instruction to the BPO agent within whose authority the corporation falls. The BPO agent then has to transmit the instruction to the chief executive officer of the corporation. The chief executive officer then executes the instruction by dismissing the political opponent. None of the three people involved in carrying out this illicit order (the BPO national director, the BPO agent, and the corporate chief executive) has anything personal to gain from this dismissal. All of them have a certain amount of insulation against being illicitly dismissed themselves. For example, if the corporation involved happens to be quite profitable, by the rules its chief executive officer *cannot* be dismissed (see above, p. 168). If discovered to have participated in such a nefarious conspiracy, they would all be subject to severe penalties. And the likelihood of discovery is substantial: at a bare minimum, the political opponent dismissed from his/her employment for no legitimate reason will raise a fuss. And even if one such conspiracy were indeed successfully carried out, how much would it help the president? The president of the United States, under any imaginable set of circumstances, will have tens of thousands of "vociferous opponents." It would be impossible to neutralize any appreciable fraction of them by such means as specified above. Any president who tried it would, with shocking rapidity, meet the same ignoble fate encountered by Richard M. Nixon in 1974. Nixon was forced to resign from the presidency in disgrace for misdeeds far less serious than trying to hamper opposition political parties through misuse of the public ownership authority.

Throughout the history of human civilization, democratic governance has been the exception rather than the rule. Even in the contemporary era, an era in which the idea of democracy has achieved almost universal acceptance and support among both the mass of society and the educated intelligentsia, the actual practice of democracy seems to be a frail reed, easily bent and easily broken. The terrible experience of twentieth-century fascism is still fresh in our minds. Until very recently, all of the Communist nations have been political oligarchies, and the progress currently being made toward the establishment of genuine democracy in the ex-Soviet Union and the Eastern European nations seems rather halting and uncertain. Effective one-party states are commonplace throughout the Third World, even in nations which loudly proclaim democratic ideals. Under the circumstances, a high degree of concern, within those fortunate nations which are genuinely democratic at the present time, with the maintenance of conditions favorable to the preservation of democracy, is both understandable and appropriate. But at the same time, the preservation of democracy is not a serious argument against the market socialist system proposed in this book. The establishment of this type of market socialist economy in a nation such as the U.S. or the U.K., nations which have enjoyed a long, strong democratic tradition, would not significantly increase the threat to democracy.

The scenario set forth by Milton Friedman, a scenario of gradual corruption of democratic processes through abuse of the public ownership authority, has nothing in common with the historical absence of genuine democracy within the Communist nations. Stalin, for example, did not get at his political opponents by surreptitiously engineering their dismissals from the publicly owned enterprises—rather he ordered them arrested by the secret police, and either executed or imprisoned in Siberian slave labor camps. Communist dictatorships, in common with all other dictatorships past and present, have been based on naked, brute force, and not on subtle, sub rosa subterfuges. Naked, brute force can always be utilized to destroy democracy, whether business enterprise is publicly owned or privately owned. It can be done whether economic living standards are high or low. At this very moment, there is nothing of any degree of tangibility preventing the armed forces of the United States from taking over the government. If those who control the instruments of force in our society ever become determined to do so, they could easily sweep aside the opposition and assume the reins of power—at least for a while.

Conservative economists such as Milton Friedman tend to have a rather warped and unrealistic view of basic human nature. They tend to believe that people, always and everywhere, engage in a purely egotistical pursuit of their own short-run self-interest. But men and women are social creatures: a certain amount of altruistic concern for their fellow humanity has been bred into them by natural selection, and reinforced by moral education both at home and in schools. If the me-first, numero-uno attitude which Friedman attributes to the leaders of the "party in power" under socialism, and which induces them to exploit the public ownership authority to preserve their personal hold on power, were indeed a realistic depiction of actual attitudes among humanity, then the U.S. military would long since have taken over the government, as would have the military in every other nation in the world which is at present genuinely democratic.

Of course, any effort at the present time by high-ranking U.S. military officers to organize a conspiracy to overthrow the elected government and install a military dictator would quickly be exposed by other high-ranking military officers—or their subordinates—unwilling to participate in the conspiracy. The basic obstacle to such a conspiracy is the tremendous commitment among all segments of society, including the military, to the democratic principle of governance. Individuals proposing to contravene this principle for purposes of personal gain and/or power would be regarded with horror and contempt by the vast majority of the population. As a result, any high-ranking officer in the United States military who commenced discussions of a possible military coup with his colleagues would very quickly be arrested and hustled off to a psychiatric ward for observation. Even if some of these colleagues might be intrigued by the idea in an abstract sense, they would have to ask themselves how likely it is that moral qualms could be suppressed in every one of the thousands of military personnel who would have to be involved in the conspiracy in order for it to have any appreciable chance of success. Even one whistle-blower could terminate the conspiracy and create disastrous personal consequences for the conspirators. Under the circumstances, the safer course, for an officer asked to join a conspiracy, would be to blow the whistle and take the relatively modest rewards available to a "defender of democracy," than to risk everything for the remote possibility of being part of a ruling military oligarchy.

For the same reasons that it would be well-nigh impossible to organize a military conspiracy to take over the government in the United States at the present time, it would be well-nigh impossible for the party in power, under a potential system of market socialism in the future United States, to eliminate the political opposition by means of misuse of the public ownership authority. There would be too much moral revulsion against such a thing among the entire population; too many individuals would have to participate; there would be too great a probability of exposure for it to be a serious temptation to the leaders of the party in power.

The notion that socialism and democracy are incompatible proceeds basically from the same fundamental misconception as does the notion that socialism and competition (among publicly owned firms) are incompatible. This is the misconception that governments in general, and national governments in particular, are totally focused, monolithic, coordinated, and disciplined organizations which single-mindedly and obsessively pursue the personal self-interest of whatever human individual happens to occupy the pinnacle of the governmental power pyramid. In actual fact, governments are composed of many thousands of different persons, and each one of them has his/her individual interests and point of view. This conglomeration of diverse individuals cannot and does not behave like a column of army ants on the march. It is unduly pessimistic and cynical to imagine that there is a strong tendency in human society toward extremely totalitarian governments such as transpired during Hitler's rule in Germany and Stalin's rule in Russia. Actually, such horrific cases as these have been relatively rare exceptions to the rule throughout modern history. Normally, the degree of internal discipline and common purpose mustered by national governments has been relatively limited.

The two major contributors to the safety of democratic governance are absence of crisis and historical tradition. Crisis conditions, such as severe economic hardship in the aftermath of a lost war, tend to politically galvanize the population, to polarize it, to jeopardize democracy. Democracy flourishes best under conditions of peace, prosperity, and stability—conditions under which there are no major economic threats or military challenges immediately at hand, under which there is no urgent need to make important decisions which impact heavily on the private lives of citizens, under which most individuals are content to let things remain pretty much as they have been in the past. The profit-oriented market socialist economy proposed in this book is a very cautious and limited step beyond the current market capitalist economy. Most people would experience a modest but appreciable financial gain, and the small minority of financial losers (the wealthy capitalists) would be paid a sufficient amount of compensation for surrendered capital property to keep them from becoming enraged political activists. There is simply no reason to expect such a system, peacefully implemented by strictly legal and democratic processes, to generate a sufficient amount of opposition to seriously endanger our democratic institutions and processes.

The second major reason for optimism is that many of those nations for which the profit-oriented market socialist proposal is especially well-suited are currently democratic nations with strong democratic traditions. In the United States, for example, the fervor of democratic convictions among the entire population, from the top of the socioeconomic spectrum to its bottom, is fully comparable to the fervor of religious convictions among the faithful. Almost every citizen is ready and willing to risk life, limb, and possessions in defense of democracy. Democracy is regarded as the political sine qua non of individual happiness and social welfare, as an indispensable ingredient of any higher form of human civilization. Owing to the strength of this conviction, any public official under market socialism who might endeavor to undermine democracy by misusing the public ownership authority for personal benefit would very quickly encounter a harsh and humiliating fate.

To conclude this discussion of the political objection to market socialism, I will briefly reiterate the diametrically opposed proposition: that far from endangering democracy, market socialism would in fact be quite likely to significantly improve the quality of democracy in contemporary society. Mention has been made in the foregoing of the traditional Communist critique of "bourgeois democracy." According to this critique, the capitalist class exercises a veritable stranglehold over the political system and social decisionmaking—despite the ostensibly free and open elections—owing to its control of the media of communications and its ability to deny employment to proponents of socialism. Except to the Communist ideologues responsible for this critique, the proposition that the capitalist class "controls the government" and "rules society" is generally regarded as preposterously exaggerated. Nevertheless, upon sober reflection, most people will have to concede that there is at least some kernel of truth in the critique. It seems self-evident that wealthy capitalists have a disproportionate influence on political processes and social decisionmaking—although no consensus would probably be possible on precisely *how* disproportionate their influence is.

It need hardly be emphasized that wealthy capitalists are not typical citizens. Their great financial wealth makes them very different from the common run of middle-class and working-class citizens. There is not necessarily a perfect correlation between their interests and the interests of the general population. One would naturally expect wealthy capitalists to be unusually conservative, to be unusually skeptical of proposed changes in a status quo situation which they find highly comfortable. On the other hand, this natural tendency toward conservatism might be mitigated, at least to some extent, by the greater personal security of wealthy people—they might feel less threatened by changes (of the right sort) than are individuals of more modest means. Whatever the differences may consist of, it seems inescapable that there would be differences in attitudes and preferences as between wealthy capitalists and the rest of the population. Owing to the disproportionate political influence of wealthy capitalists, actual social decisionmaking and public policies are likely to diverge somewhat from the optimum that would be settled on in the absence of this class. While it would be difficult to predict what policy changes might actually take place under market socialism as a result of the elimination of the disproportionate political influence of wealthy capitalists, it seems likely that these changes would at least be in the right direction from the standpoint of the majority of the population. Quite likely there is a political gain to be had from market socialism, as well as an economic gain.

A SUMMATION

The principal problem with contemporary capitalism—a problem potentially curable by means of profit-oriented market socialism—is an equity problem. This is the problem of highly unequal distribution of unearned capital property income. This income is almost entirely a function of the productivity of inanimate capital, rather than of any effort or sacrifices, past or present, of the human capital owners. Owing principally to the workings of inheritance and chance, the capital wealth on which capital property income is received, is distributed very unequally among households. As a result of this high degree of inequality, a social dividend principle of distributing capital property return produced by business corporations, under which this return would go to households on the basis of their earned labor income rather than their financial wealth, would financially benefit a large majority of the population—a majority most likely in excess of 90 percent. It would also represent a moral advance to society to eliminate the economic parasitism associated with contemporary capitalism. In addition to the equity benefit, there might well be significant efficiency benefits: social dividend distribution of capital property return could increase labor supply, the public ownership authority could be exercised in such a way as to enhance the accountability of high corporation executives, and a market socialist economy might well sustain a higher rate of saving and investment than does contemporary capitalism. Finally, there might well be a significant political benefit: the elimination of the disproportionate influence of wealthy capitalists on political processes could result in a purer form of democracy.

The profit-oriented market socialist system under consideration in this book represents an updated and refined socialist challenge to the validity of capitalism. It is a more precise and sophisticated challenge than the traditional socialist challenge, because it abandons those aspects of the traditional socialist challenge which have fallen into disrepute with the passage of time. This new challenge is fully consistent with a number of key propositions from contemporary mainstream economics: the efficacy of free market allocation relative to central planning allocation, the independent productivity of capital, the desirability of an external ownership interest in the typical business enterprise, and the efficiency of profit maximization as the fundamental motivation of business enterprise. Moreover, the new challenge is not excessively egalitarian: it is neutral with respect to both the proper degree of progressivity in the tax system and the proper dimensions of the welfare state. Owing to its fundamental originality, this new socialist challenge is immune (at least in a logical sense) to a large part of the traditional pro-capitalist response to the traditional socialist challenge. However, there is enough depth and flexibility in capitalist apologetics to mount a fully comprehensive, reasonably plausible defense against the profit-oriented market socialist assault. This chapter has developed this defense and provided a response to it from the pro-socialist side of the debate.

Capitalism's first and foremost line of defense against the challenge of market socialism lies in denying that capital property income is unearned. Two specific justifications may be offered for capital property income: (1) that it is an earned return to the active behavior of capital management effort; (2) that it is an earned return to the sacrifices of saving. Capital management effort is defined as any sort of human activity designed to increase the rate of return on physical or financial capital. This effort is most sensibly identified with corporate supervision and investment analysis, although it may be more loosely identified with the related concept of entrepreneurship, and still more loosely identified with the derivative concept of risk-taking. The argument is simply that the public ownership personnel charged with providing capital management effort under market socialism will not provide very much of it, because the financial incentive to this effort (capital property return) is mostly distributed to the general population in the form of a social dividend supplement to labor income. The response to this argument involves both theoretical considerations (such as the possibility of a plateau production function relating capital management effort to rate of return on capital), and empirical considerations (such as the separation of ownership and control in large corporations, and the active role of institutional investors in the capital markets). The saving argument is analogous to the capital management argument: the difference is basically that saving, rather than

Economic Justice

capital management effort, is proposed as the primary factor of production compensated by capital property income. The single most effective response to this argument is that *if* private household saving were to decline under socialism (not a particularly likely event, all things considered), the saving shortfall could be made up by social saving out of tax revenue.

The second line of defense of capitalism against the profit-oriented market socialist alternative lies in denying that the distribution of capital property income is "highly" unequal. This line of defense was considered in Chapter 2. Just as there are several variations on the basic capital management effort theme in capitalist apologetics, so too there are several variations on the basic "people's capitalism" theme. The basic people's capitalism theme states that *when properly interpreted*, the distribution of capital wealth (and hence of capital property income) is not all that unequal. The people's capitalism line of argument has always been, and continues to be, extremely effective in a propagandistic sense, owing to its strong appeal to both the subject's greed and the subject's pride. But when confronted by hard evidence and subjected to reflective scrutiny, the people's capitalism line is seen to lack any appreciable substantive content. There is really no way to get around the extravagant inequality of capital wealth distribution under contemporary capitalism. If a substantive economic case is to be made for capitalism, it has to be made on the basis that capital property income is in some sensible way an earned income.

Finally, capitalism's third and last line of defense is composed of various noneconomic considerations: political, psychological, philosophical, and so on. As the emphasis herein has been on economic considerations (properly so since socialism is, first and foremost, an economic concept), and as the noneconomic considerations can assume a bewildering variety of generally vacuous propositions, attention herein has been confined to what is certainly the single most important noneconomic argument against socialism. This is the political objection that socialism combines political and economic power, and hence poses a serious threat to genuinely democratic institutions and processes. The effectiveness of this objection is largely based on the observed association of public ownership socialism with oligarchic political systems in the Communist nations. As significant as this association may have been (and still is, in the case of the remaining Communist nations), the absence of democracy under communism is more plausibly attributed to unfavorable historical circumstances than it is to public ownership of capital in and of itself. In a society with a strong and viable democratic tradition, it would be very difficult for the party in power to successfully misuse the public ownership authority to hobble opposition political parties. Any such conspiracy would be too liable to exposure for this to be a serious temptation to the party in power.

To reiterate once again an extremely important point, it cannot be scientifically proved, on the basis of currently available evidence, whether profit-oriented market socialism would be superior to contemporary capitalism or inferior to contemporary capitalism. The available evidence is simply too indirect, too circumstantial. Profit-oriented market socialism represents a fundamentally new departure in socialist thinking: it is too different from past socialist experiences and past socialist proposals for these past experiences and proposals to provide much insight into the potential performance of this type of socialist system. While this means that the various problems, flaws, and liabilities of past socialist experiences and proposals cannot provide definitive arguments against this new socialist proposal, at the same time there is always the possibility that the newly proposed socialist system, if put into practice, would display serious problems, flaws, and liabilities of its own. It is necessary for advocates of this system to recognize this and to concede the possibility that market socialism might be a disappointment in practice, thus necessitating a return to capitalism. Market socialism could be a disappointment in practice because one or more of the objections to socialism, with which we have been concerned in this chapter, might actually be valid, substantive objections.

To any reasonably fair-minded person, who is prepared to give serious, objective consideration to the market socialist alternative, it will be evident that what has been presented in this chapter as the "case against profit-oriented market socialism" is indeed the best, most logical, most coherent case to be made against profit-oriented market socialism. Unfortunately, many individuals at the present time are not reasonably fair-minded when it comes to socialism, and they are not willing to give serious and objective consideration to any socialist proposal whatsoever, whether it be market-based or otherwise. To such individuals, what has been presented here as the case against profit-oriented market socialism cannot actually be all there is to this matter—simply because, as amply demonstrated by the discussion, an intelligible, cogent, and coherent response may be made to this case. They assume (although they would not admit this assumption to others—and in some cases not even to themselves) that any statement of the "case against socialism," to which a reasonably sensible response may be made, simply cannot be the "true" case against socialism. The true case against socialism would presumably be impervious to refutation: it would reduce proponents of socialism to helpless silence or incoherent babbling. Completely close-minded individuals are incapable or unwilling to take instruction in capitalist apologetics from a proponent of socialism such as myself. They conclude that I must be missing something, that I simply fail to understand, either out of ignorance or mental incapacity, why it is that any and all socialist economies, including the profit-oriented market socialist economy, must inevitably fail.

Capitalist apologetics is remarkably adaptable, resilient, and fecund, and individuals whose judgmental faculties have been paralyzed (for the time being) by capitalist apologetics display remarkable ingenuity in the production of ad hoc, off the cuff, extemporaneous objections to market socialism, whether of the profit-oriented variety or any other. No sooner has the proponent of market socialism commenced formulating an informed and intelligent response to one particular objection, when the opponent announces that in actual fact that particular objection is not really the heart of the matter—rather the heart of the matter lies in some other more or less totally unrelated objection. Once enmeshed in this kind of debate with a fully close-minded opponent of socialism, there is no way the proponent of socialism can win the game. The supply of diverse, unrelated, and mostly off the wall objections to profit-oriented market socialism—not to mention any other type of socialism—is seemingly inexhaustible.

To the extent that some of the myriad possible objections to profit-oriented market socialism possess some degree of substance, it is because they represent reworkings and rewordings of the objections considered herein: the capital management issue, the saving issue, the people's capitalism issue, and the democracy issue. For example, the capital management problem can be reworked as the entrepreneurship problem, the wealth-building problem, or the risk-taking problem. Of course, capitalist apologetics would rather use loaded, emotive, sonorous, quasi-mystical terms such as "entrepreneurship," in preference to such dry, unemotional, technical-sounding terms as "capital management effort." But the problem of potentially inadequate capital management effort under profit-oriented market socialism does not become an objectively more serious problem because it is restated as the problem of potentially inadequate entrepreneurship. Leaving aside those objections to market socialism which are really just reworkings of the objections already examined, what other kinds of objections remain? The remaining objections, as multitudinous as they may be, fall mostly into just two categories: (1) indiscriminate application of all the problems of Communistic socialism and social democratic socialism, real and imagined, to market socialism: (2) thoughtless projections of the existing problems of contemporary capitalism, in aggravated form, unto market socialism.

At the outset of this chapter the first of these categories was discussed in some detail. It is simply a matter of begging the question to attribute the perceived problems of communism and social democracy to a market socialist system designed specifically to avoid those problems. The fact that in the U.S.S.R. of the past, the government was reluctant to close down production enterprises, even though they were extremely unprofitable, does not mean that the government would intervene with the natural processes of bankruptcy in a potential market socialist economy in the future. The fact that in the Scandinavian countries of the past (and present?), income taxation of individuals was (is?) excessively progressive, does not mean that income taxation of individuals would be excessively progressive in a potential market socialist country of the future. The attribution to socialism of "inherent" tendencies toward excessive political intervention in the economic market and excessive egalitarianism is simply unfounded. It has no basis in logic, and it has no basis in fact. Socialism, properly defined, is nothing more and nothing less than public ownership of the majority of physical capital utilized by large, established business enterprises. Public ownership of capital does not necessarily imply excessive political intervention in the market, and it does not necessarily imply excessive egalitarianism. Those who aver that it does imply these things—as well as many other negative features—are committing the fundamental fallacy of assuming that "there can be nothing new under the sun." They are allowing their prejudice against socialism to seriously impair their logical and judgmental faculties and their ability to engage in critical thinking.

The second major category into which the nonsubstantive objections to profit-oriented market socialism fall is that of thoughtless projection of the existing problems of contemporary capitalism, in aggravated form, unto market socialism. The skeptic simply seizes upon some existing problem of contemporary capitalism (in some cases the problem applies to any human civilization at all, past or present, capitalistic or otherwise) and applies that problem to socialism. In many cases, the skeptic is at first oblivious to the fact that the problem seized upon is in fact a general problem, and is not confined to market socialism. When reminded of this, the skeptic simply asserts, without substantiation, that the problem would be "worse" under market socialism.

A typical example of this kind of objection applies to the relationship between BPO agents and corporation executives. Under the profit-oriented market socialist proposal, BPO agents would have the authority (under certain conditions) to dismiss the chief executive officers of unprofitable publicly owned business enterprises. It could be objected: But how could the BPO agents ever know for sure whether incompetence on the part of the CEO was a major contributor to low profitability? After all, the CEO might be a really excellent person, doing the best job humanly possible, and the problems of the corporation might be owing to external developments over which the CEO had no control whatsoever. In order to eliminate the possibility of external factors being responsible for the unsatisfactory profits, the BPO agents would have to possess a tremendous amount of information about the firm and its environment. Clearly it is not possible for limited, fallible human beings to have all this information. The conclusion is reached (by the skeptic) that under profit-oriented market socialism, there would be numerous unjustified dismissals, the morale of the corporation executives would be correspondingly abysmal, and the performance of the economy would suffer accordingly.

Upon a moment's reflection, it is recognized that the very same problem is already fully operative under capitalism. The board of directors of a corporation under capitalism is in exactly the same position as the BPO agents under market socialism. Under conditions of unsatisfactory profitability, it has to determine whether incompetence on the part of the CEO might be an important contributory factor. To make a flawless determination of this, it would need to possess a tremendous amount of information about the firm and its environment. The boards of directors of contemporary capitalism are staffed by human beings no less limited and fallible than the BPO agents under market socialism. Unjustified dismissals are therefore just as likely under contemporary capitalism as they would be under profit-oriented market socialism. Contemporary capitalism manages to survive and thrive despite this problem, and profit-oriented market socialism would do the same.

As to the allegation that this particular problem would be worse under market socialism than it is under capitalism, there is only one substantive reason that could be advanced for this. It could be alleged that under capitalism, members of boards of directors, on the whole, receive more capital property income than would the BPO agents of market socialism.

Therefore the latter would have less incentive to work hard and dig deep for information relating to the question of whether or not CEO incompetence is a serious contributor to a situation of unsatisfactory profitability. Under market socialism, therefore, unjustified dismissals would be a larger problem, there would be greater morale problems among the corporation executives, and the economy's performance would be adversely affected. This, of course, is indeed a logical possibility. Nevertheless, it is probably not an *actual* problem. Many things which are logically possible (e.g., a horse with a horn—a unicorn) do not exist in the real world. But note that if this *were* a problem under market socialism, it would simply be another manifestation of the capital management problem. Capital management effort includes as a subcategory corporate supervision, and corporate supervision involves collecting information on which to base a decision on whether or not CEO incompetence is a serious contributor to observed profitability problems. If BPO agents would not work as hard as members of boards of directors to obtain this kind of information because they would not receive a sufficient financial incentive to do so, this is simply another way of saying that the BPO agents would not provide an adequate amount of capital management effort, relative to that which is currently provided by capital owners under capitalism.

Clearly, space constraints—not to mention the constraints imposed by limited reader time and patience—preclude a comprehensive discussion of the overwhelming quantity of restated, reworded, irrelevant, and fallacious potential objections to the profit-oriented market socialist proposal put forward herein. Hopefully the open-minded reader will understand this, and will realize that the fact that some particular objection is not dealt with in this book does not mean that no satisfactory response exists to this objection. Hopefully enough discussion of capitalist apologetics, as applied specifically to the profit-oriented market socialist proposal, has been provided in this book to enable an informed reader to extrapolate an appropriate response to a purportedly "new" objection.

5

A NEW BEGINNING?

Does socialism have a future in the twenty-first century? Understandably enough, most people in the world today would answer this question, quite confidently, in the negative—especially if they understand the term "socialism" in its pure and original sense: public ownership of the capital stock. Throughout the twentieth century, the cause of public ownership socialism has been aggressively championed by the Communist nations. The dramatic collapse of the Soviet Union in the early 1990s broke the backbone of world communism, and it seems only a matter of time before the remaining Communist nations renounce the Communist social system. Although public ownership of capital (socialism) is only one part of the Communist social system, it is a very important part, and the renunciation of communism by the ex-Communist nations might well involve the renunciation of socialism as well. The reversion of all or most business enterprise in the ex-Communist nations to private ownership would close the book on the major twentieth century experiment in public ownership socialism initiated by the Russian Revolution of 1917.

Aside from the impending prospect of wholesale privatization of business firms in the ex-Communist nations, for the last two decades there has been a powerful trend toward privatization of formerly public enterprises in the Western non-Communist nations. The proportion of the aggregate capital stock operated by government-owned businesses has been significantly reduced. And even if we broaden the meaning of the term "socialism" to include the social democratic program (generic social egali- tarianism, extensive regulation of business enterprise, the welfare state, and so on), socialism is still perceived to be in a condition of rapid retreat throughout the world. It would probably be necessary to go back to the nineteenth century to find a period in which the overall level of faith in laissez faire was as strong as it is at the present time.

In light of these important indications, the large majority of people at the present time have concluded that socialism has been completely, definitively, and irrevocably defeated by capitalism. These people believe that within a short period of time, perhaps only a decade or two, the last vestiges of socialism—and faith in socialism—will have been expunged from the earth: that socialism will be recognized by all as being no less extinct than dinosaurs and mammoths. This belief may well be vindicated. At the moment, it would certainly be foolish to make a confident prediction to the contrary. Nevertheless, this book has shown the possibility of a socialist socioeconomic system that would be economically efficient, ethically fair, and politically democratic. It has shown the possibility of a socialist social system that would be significantly superior to the capitalist social system of today. In light of this possibility, socialism should not be written off. Socialism is still a viable option, and there remains an appreciable possibility that someday it will be widely recognized as such. As foolish as it would be to predict confidently that socialism is *not* finished, it would be only slightly less foolish to predict confidently that socialism *is* finished.

Socialism *may* have a future in the twenty-first century—but if there is to be any appreciable possibility of this, it *must* be a revised and modernized socialism which has been thoroughly purged of the grievous errors and misunderstandings of the past. At this point in history, the only kind of socialist system which merits serious consideration by humanity is a socialist system along the lines proposed in this book: a democratic market socialist system. Such a system would combine public ownership of that part of the capital stock which is owned and operated by large-scale, established business corporations, with a high degree of reliance on free-market allocation, and a democratic political system along the lines already well established in the United States, the United Kingdom, and the other advanced, industrialized nations. Of the three central components of communism (public ownership socialism, central planning, and political oligarchy), the latter two must be utterly rejected—they must be completely disassociated from socialism now and for all time. Socialism has already been badly—perhaps irreparably—stigmatized by its association with central planning and political oligarchy in the Communist nations. Socialism can only possibly have a future in human affairs if this disastrous stigma can be transcended.

In addition, socialism must sever its historic links with social democracy. Socialism must be recognized as a distinct and specific social reform, complete and entire unto itself. It must not be associated with proposals for the furtherance of generic social egalitarianism, extensive business regulation, the welfare state, and so on. Be it well noted, however, that this does *not* imply conflict between market socialism and social democracy. Rather it simply implies that the two concepts should be recognized as separate and independent of each other. Certainly there might be a predisposition among those strongly influenced by social democratic thinking toward interest in profit-oriented market socialism, because of the inherent egalitarianism of this proposal with respect to capital property income. But at the same time there is nothing contradictory about a proponent of profit-oriented market socialism who would be opposed to further implementations of the social democratic program beyond what has already become established in the advanced capitalist nations of today. Indeed, there is nothing contradictory about a proponent of profit-oriented market socialism who would like to see some degree of reduction and curtailment of the already established social democratic program.

The idea of a typical conservative Republican in the United States today favoring market socialism over contemporary capitalism will strike many people as nothing less than absurd. The fact is, however, that the typical conservative Republican in the United States today has a warped perception of socialism: he or she identifies socialism with the central planning excesses and the totalitarian political system of communism, as well as with the excessive social interventionism and radical egalitarianism of social democracy. True, these things have unfortunate historical associations with socialism—but they are not logically implied by socialism, defined simply, accurately, and correctly as public ownership of capital utilized by large-scale, established business corporations. The profit-oriented market socialist economy advocated by this book would most definitely be a socialist system according to the standard dictionary definition of socialism—but it would still operate almost identically to the present market capitalist economy with which we are familiar. The principal difference would simply be the distribution of capital property return produced by large, established business corporations to households on the basis of earned labor income rather than financial assets.

Most conservative Republicans in the present-day United States are middle-class people with a strong work ethic and a strong sense of individual responsibility. They tend to be incensed by mental images of indolent and undeserving welfare recipients living comfortably, without need of labor, at public expense. The fact is that the capitalist class is highly analogous to the class of undeserving welfare recipients. It too receives unearned income, and is thus rendered exempt from the need for labor. The main difference is that welfare recipients live at best comfortably, while capitalists tend to live quite luxuriously. The vast majority of conservative middle-class Republicans in the United States today would receive more social dividend income under profit-oriented market socialism than they are currently receiving capital property income under capitalism. The implied financial burden on them of preserving the unearned and undeserved financial privileges of the capitalist class is in fact considerably heavier than the tax burden on them to provide undeserving welfare recipients with a quasi-subsistence standard of living. Will the middle class of the United States, Republican and otherwise, remain forever blind to its own financial self-interest in market socialism? Will it remain forever blind to the inequity of extremely unequal distribution of a substantial flow of capital property income which is essentially unearned by capital owners? It would be unwise to bet on this.

If socialism can shed its unfortunate historical associations of straitjacket planning, political totalitarianism, and radical egalitarianism, and instead be identified with some sort of sensibly conservative proposal for democratic market socialism—such as the proposal which has been put forward in this book—then the socialist movement might well experience a rebirth in the twenty-first century. And this time the movement might well be successful in transforming the economies of all or most of the advanced industrialized nations of the world. Only time will tell if these possibilities will actually come to pass. As already stated, it would be foolish at this point to predict that they will in fact come to pass. Nevertheless, these possibilities are certainly more likely to come about than is generally recognized at the present time. As we look toward the twenty-first century, what factors might be discerned which are favorable to reawakened interest in and support for socialism?

One important factor has been the development of a fairly extensive and detailed economic literature on market socialism. Initiated by the seminal contribution of Oskar Lange in the 1930s ("On the Economic Theory of Socialism"), this literature has slowly but steadily grown and developed. By now the possibility not only of market socialism in general, but of a substantial array of distinct varieties of market socialism, is widely recognized within the economics profession. In addition to the original marginal cost pricing proposal of Oskar Lange, there are at least three other important market socialist possibilities: (1) service market socialism; (2) cooperative market socialism; (3) profit-oriented market socialism. Of these three, the emphasis herein has been on profit-oriented market socialism, since this system would represent the most cautious and conservative advance beyond the market capitalist economic system of today. But any market socialist system at all would no doubt represent a substantial improvement over the central planning socialism associated with twentieth-century communism. And it is also important to be aware of the fact that the economic performance of central planning socialism in the ex-U.S.S.R. was not at all as negligible as was made out by the jaundiced, propagandistic assessments in the West during the Cold War period of "Soviet economic weakness." The major weakness of the Soviet system was in fact political rather than economic. A market socialist economy capable of significantly outperforming the Soviet planned socialist economy would attain a very impressive level of performance indeed. It is more than likely that such an economy would outperform the market capitalist economy of today.

The case for democratic market socialism has already been carefully developed, and from this point forward only sketchy references will be made to it. Since there is no tangible example of democratic market socialism presently operating in the real world, at this point the case for democratic market socialism is inevitably of a "conceptual, theoretical, and intellectual" nature, rather than of a "factual" nature. The existence of a weighty conceptual, theoretical, and intellectual case for democratic market socialism will be of no consequence if this system is never given a chance to prove itself factually in the real world. So let us proceed past the observation that a good hypothetical case can be made for democratic market socialism, in order to ask what factors might incline humanity in the future to lend sufficient credence to this hypothetical case to enable the implementation of democratic market socialism in the real world.

Three such factors will be discussed in the following three sections of this final chapter. First, there is the post-Communist perspective. At this point in time, there is still a reasonable probability that the fundamental economic transitions now transpiring in the ex-Communist nations will result in a reasonable facsimile of some type of market socialist system. If this happens, and these economies commence to flourish and prosper, a powerful argument, an argument based on fact and not on theory, will be added to the pro-socialist side of the ledger. Second, there is the social democratic perspective. Although social democracy and market socialism are conceptually distinct reforms, those interested in social democracy should nevertheless support market socialism as a means to an end. It is plausibly arguable that the extreme conservatism of the small minority of plutocratic capitalists is a serious obstacle to extensions of the social democratic program. Market socialism would by its nature severely curtail the financial wealth and political power of this small minority, and hence it would remove this obstacle. Whether or not a major expansion of the social democratic program in the real world is desirable is another question, and I personally do not think it would be. But the removal of this particular political obstacle to the furtherance of the social democratic program ought to be enough to persuade most reasonable social democrats that market socialism would be a positive development.

Finally, there is the perspective from the capitalist heartland—by that meaning the wealthy industrialized capitalist nations of the West. Within these nations the distribution of the stock of financial capital wealth, and hence of the flow of capital property income paid to owners of financial capital wealth, is and remains extremely, extravagantly unequal. Contrary to abundant "people's capitalism" propaganda, there are no indications whatever that this extreme and extravagant inequality is declining over time. Rather it appears to be completely stable. This extreme and extravagant inequality is not merely an offense against universally accepted ethical standards of fairness and equity. It also implies—perhaps even more importantly—that the large majority of the population has a direct, personal, financial self-interest in the implementation of market socialism. Social dividend distribution of capital property return produced by publicly owned business corporations would benefit over 90 percent of the population. It would benefit not merely all working-class people, but also all middle-class people as well. It has been very difficult for capitalist apologetics to obscure and obfuscate this critical fact in the past—and it may become even more difficult for it to do so in the future.

THE POST-COMMUNIST PERSPECTIVE

The demise of the Cold War has been the most wondrously optimistic historic event since the defeat of fascism in 1945. No rational human being can fail to be profoundly enheartened by this epochal event. For the better part of half a century, the human race, having armed itself with nuclear weaponry and riven by bitter ideological conflict, danced on the edge of a volcano. We do not know with any degree of certainty how close we came to a nuclear holocaust. Some would assert that the threat was never all that large, since mankind is not so stupid as to go to war when the survival of the species might be at stake. Others, taking note of the powerful predisposition in mankind toward internecine hostility and violence—as clearly manifested by never-ending conflict and warfare throughout all of human history—would assert that the threat was indeed very tangible and significant. Nor do we know with any degree of certainty what would have happened had a nuclear war actually broken out. Possibly it would have been controlled after a small number of nuclear detonations over military targets. Or possibly it would have quickly escalated to maximum intensity, involving thousands of nuclear detonations, most of them over population centers. Had the unthinkable actually taken place, human civilization might have recovered—or humanity might instead have been started down a slippery slope leading to final extinction of the species.

During the Cold War years, most of us coped with the grim possibility of nuclear war simply by ignoring it as much as possible, by putting it out of our minds to the greatest feasible extent. On the whole, people took the threat of nuclear annihilation in stride. After all, every human individual has always had to confront the ominous reality of individual mortality. Whether the instrumentality be accident, disease, old age, or nuclear war, eventually all of us are fated to succumb. The end of the Cold War does not imply the end of human mortality—at least at the individual level. It does, however, increase the probability that each individual will live a normal lifespan, and will be spared a particularly brutal demise amidst conditions of unimaginably gigantic catastrophe. This in itself is certainly cause for celebration.

Although cautionary notes are somewhat unfashionable amidst the generally euphoric spirit of the times, it has to be recognized that while the immediate threat of all-out nuclear war has been greatly reduced, the threat has not been completely eliminated, especially in long-run terms. Unlike the Axis powers in 1945, the Soviet Union has not been militarily defeated and placed under foreign occupation. Especially now that it has been stripped of its buffer zone of Warsaw Pact satellite states, and moreover deprived of its phalanx of peripheral republics, the Russian nation cannot be expected to divest itself entirely of nuclear weaponry. Even in its truncated present status, it is still by far the largest nation in the world in terms of territory, it is relatively sparsely inhabited, and it is very richly endowed with natural resources. Russia has been invaded many times throughout its history, and the same temptations which attracted foreign invaders in the past will continue to operate in the future. However, any nation armed with even a relatively small number of nuclear missiles will not be a viable prospect for military invasion into the foreseeable future. Therefore, Russia will almost certainly retain some appreciable fraction of its nuclear arsenal.

The United States will also hang on to an appreciable part of its nuclear arsenal into the foreseeable future. The United States is a rich nation in a populous and generally poor world. The rich are always envied by the poor, and under the right circumstances, simmering resentment can burst forth into open hostility. Some nuclear missiles in reserve will guarantee that in the future there will not be a sudden wave into the United States of "illegal immigrants" preceded by tanks. The United States must also maintain a nuclear deterrent to forestall any possible future temptations among the Russian leadership to utilize its "defensive" nuclear missiles in an offensive manner. During the Cold War, there were those who insisted that the ideological conflict between communism and noncommunism was a very minor contributor to hostility and tension, and that instead what was being witnessed was basically just a classic geopolitical conflict between two superpowers, the United States and the Soviet Union. Most informed people would summarily dismiss the proposition that ideological conflict was a "minor" contributor to the Cold War. But at the same time there were undoubtedly some elements of classic geopolitical conflict involved in the situation. Ideological disengagement therefore does not necessarily imply total disengagement. What this means is that full-scale disarmament, nuclear and conventional, cannot be expected on either side anytime in the immediate future. Some of the arsenal will remain, and so also will some possibility that the arsenal will be used in anger.

During the Cold War years, democratic market socialism might have provided an ideological bridge between East and West. In fact, a very large part of my own interest in market socialism was motivated by this very possibility. The basic concept was (and remains) quite elementary. The three central characteristics of Eastern Communism are public ownership socialism, central planning of the economy, and political oligarchy. The three central characteristics of Western non-Communism are private ownership capitalism, market orientation of the economy, and political democracy. Many years ago (in the early 1960s, to be precise), I reached the conclusion that while Western non-Communism was a superior social system to Eastern Communism (owing to the very substantial superiority of market orientation to central planning, and of political democracy to political oligarchy), nevertheless it so happens that public ownership socialism is, in and of itself, substantially superior to private ownership capitalism. This latter proposition is based on two key considerations: (1) the development of extreme and extravagant inequality in the distribution of unearned capital property income under contemporary capitalism; (2) the availability of democratic market socialist alternatives to contemporary capitalism. Some system of democratic market social-ism, preferably of the profit-oriented variety, could have provided—and indeed might still provide (as suggested below)—a model for ideological convergence between the Communist East and the non-Communist West. This system would take the best features of the Western non-Communist social system (market reliance and political democracy) and combine them with public ownership socialism, which has been a central feature of the Eastern Communist social system—and a feature which, when iso-lated from central planning and political oligarchy, is in fact desirable in its own right. In this way, each side could take something from the other side, and it would not be necessary for either side to admit complete er-ror. This is the model of ideological *convergence*—as opposed to the model of ideological *capitulation*.

Given that the objective is the avoidance of nuclear war in the future and a peaceful and beneficent course of future human history, the ques-tion may be asked whether ideological convergence, both in terms of ac-tual social systems and psychological perceptions and attitudes, would foster this objective. It was a fairly common viewpoint in the West dur-ing the height of the Cold War that "anti-social" Soviet behavior was much more the result of traditional nationalistic self-aggrandizement than the result of genuine ideological conviction. A more defensible view-point is that ideological disagreement is one contributory factor among several to nationalistic antagonisms. The question is then just how im-portant this particular contributory factor is. Those who could perceive no means whatever through which the West could profitably emulate the East, and who therefore anticipated no convergence whatever of the West toward the East, had a psychological incentive to minimize this factor. This is because they conceived of the ideological gap as unbridgeable, at least from the Western side, and consequently they shied away from rec-ognizing the strong contribution that this gap was making to the prob-ability of nuclear holocaust. But to those, such as myself, who recog-nized in democratic market socialism a means of bridging the ideological gap between East and West from the Western side, the gap was not seen as so impermeable, and there was less need to flinch from recognizing the gap as the important contributor to the threat of nuclear holocaust that it actually was.

From the early 1960s, it has been the author's firm belief that signifi-cant ideological convergence between East and West would lead very rapidly and naturally to a reduction in war risk and substantial disarma-ment by both sides in both nuclear and conventional forces. This is not to say that I have expected total and complete disarmament on the basis of total and complete trust to arise simply from ideological convergence by East and West toward a common pattern of democratic market socialism. There are several other sources of war risk aside from the ideological conflict between Communism and its alternatives: in particular the existence of extremely large gaps between living standards in the rich and poor nations, as well as the sovereign nation-state system itself. But I have expected that very substantial progress could be made within a relatively short period of time were ideological conflict to be largely removed from the picture.

Current developments seem to be supporting this expectation. Even though the political and economic reform movement in Russia is far from complete, owing principally to the tremendous disruption caused by massive political changes, including the collapse of the Communist Party and the dissolution of the U.S.S.R., the Russian leadership is apparently sincerely interested in continuing substantial disarmament, and prospects seem favorable for further major arms reduction agreements as time proceeds. As mentioned above, in all probability Russia intends to maintain a minimum nuclear arsenal to provide last-resort deterrence—but that minimum arsenal is no doubt much smaller than the current arsenal. Of course, other reasons aside from ideological convergence can be discerned for Russian interest in disarmament. For one thing, the military burden is no doubt substantially reducing long-term economic growth: thus a smaller military capacity in the short term could be a means of augmenting long-term military capacity. There is also the obvious consideration that even if neither side envisioned any sort of ideological convergence, either real-world or attitudinal, within the foreseeable future (in other words, permanent "coexistence" between substantially different social systems), there would still be an incentive for both sides to seek disarmament as a means of reducing the threat of nuclear holocaust. But even granting these latter considerations, it is still difficult to avoid the impression that at least some of the current impetus toward disarmament is coming from the Eastern reform movement which is reducing the ideological gap between the Communist and non-Communist nations.

It has been the contention of this book that the West—regardless of what does or does not happen in the East—would be well advised to implement a reform movement of its own in the direction of democratic market socialism. Democratic market socialism, preferably of the profit-oriented variety, would be a modest but appreciable advance beyond contemporary capitalism. Purely on grounds of their own internal self-interest, the populations of the Western non-Communist nations should implement democratic market socialism. In the past, at the height of the Cold War, there was also a compelling *external* motivation for democratic market socialism. It could have provided a bridge between the competing ideological systems, enabling a mutually beneficial ideological convergence toward a higher social form. Nor should the past tense be used exclusively in this regard. Democratic market socialism might *still* provide a bridge between competing ideological systems; it might *still* enable a mutually beneficial convergence toward a higher social form.

Thus far the Eastern reform movement has made significant headway. Nevertheless, a substantial distance between East and West still remains. Only when both of the two superpowers in the ex-Communist world, namely Russia and China, have become fully, unambiguously, and indisputably democratic market capitalist nations along the lines of the United States and the Western European nations—only then will there be no external motivation whatsoever for democratic market socialism, and only then will there be absolutely no potential role for democratic market socialism as an ideological bridge between East and West. This has not happened yet, and despite the significant progress which has been made over the last few years, it may not happen for quite a long while into the future—if ever. China, the world's most populous nation, remains at this point still firmly committed to Communism. In Russia and the other republics of the ex-U.S.S.R., Communist Party domination of the social system has been repudiated, a fledgling democracy has been established, and considerable progress has been made toward removal of central government control over the economic system.

Privatization of business enterprise, on the other hand, is another story. The heart and soul of Marxist ideology has always been, and remains to this day, public ownership of capital utilized by large-scale productive enterprises. The other central aspects of the Communist social system, including central planning of the economy and tight control of the sociopolitical system by the Communist Party, find very little support in the basic texts of the Marxist faith. The Soviet people were aggressively indoctrinated in Marxist ideology for the better part of a century. It is no wonder, then, that the privatization component of the overall reform movement—especially in the case of large firms—has been slow and halting. For purposes of gaining some insight into the future prospects of privatization in the ex-U.S.S.R., it is helpful to go back in history a bit to consider the direction in which the U.S.S.R. was headed prior to the profound transformations of 1991-1992. Upon the accession of Mikhail Gorbachev to the position of Party First Secretary in March 1985, he called for a continuation and intensification of the debate over the future of the economy which had been developing since the death of Brezhnev in 1982. In June 1987, the Central Committee Plenum approved a remarkable document entitled "Basic theses for the radical restructuring of the management of the economy." The theses were a statement of intention rather than a finished policy proclamation. At the time they were issued, most Western analysts considered them very unlikely to be fully implemented. Events since then have demonstrated that the Soviet Union was indeed ready and willing to undertake drastic changes. Clearly if the substance and spirit of this document were eventually implemented, the Russian economy would indeed be radically transformed. Although the Communist Party no longer controls Russia, the line of thinking represented by the "Basic theses" is doubtlessly still very influential.

The "Basic theses" set forth in 1987, as undoubtedly radical as they were, did not envision an abandonment of public ownership socialism in the case of large-scale firms. If the theses as originally formulated were fully implemented, this would indeed represent a giant step away from central planning and toward market determination of economic outcomes, and also a giant step away from economic security and equality and toward free competition and material incentives to effort. The theses envisioned the restriction of central planning to the determination of a few macroeconomic variables such as the rate of investment. They envisioned almost all enterprises operating in a financially self-sufficient manner: subsidies would not be available even to forestall bankruptcies of major enterprises. They envisioned enterprise managers being able to hire and fire laborers at will. They envisioned top enterprise managers elected democratically by the workforce of the enterprise. Prices would be adjusted to equate supply and demand even if this meant drastic increases in the prices of consumer necessities and basic industrial commodities. Profits would reflect the perspicacity of enterprise managers in locating markets, and the diligence and industry of the workforce in producing goods for these markets. Private individuals would be free to set up small- to medium-scale business enterprises without bureaucratic restrictions or intrusions.

All this would certainly represent monumental change away from the old paternalistic, regulated, central planning system—but it does not, as envisioned, involve a renunciation of socialism per se. There would be no outside owners of large-scale business enterprises, no stockholders and bondholders of the sort which are customary under capitalism: individuals who take no part in the productive operations of the enterprise, either as employees or managers, but who nevertheless claim the profits, interest, and other forms of property return generated by the enterprise's productive operations. In a capitalist economy, the enterprise's managers are subject to approval by private stockholders, and bondholders and stockholders possess primary rights to residual income (profits) earned by the enterprise. Prior to its distribution to bondholders and stockholders, residual income is in principle subject to socially imposed taxation, but by custom a relatively small proportion of residual income is claimed by taxation. Some proportion of the enterprise's stocks and bonds may be held by managers and employees of the enterprise, but in practice in the large majority of enterprises, only a relatively small proportion of the enterprise's stocks and bonds are so held. These conditions constitute the practical meaning of "private ownership of the means of production" under modern capitalism. None of these conditions are necessarily and directly implied by the original proposed perestroika reforms contained in the "Basic theses." Any residual income earned by large business enterprises and not taken by taxation or other state claims and specifications would under those reforms be distributed wholly to the employees and managers of the enterprise. This would clearly avoid capitalistic exploitation as perceived by Karl Marx. It would in fact constitute a form of cooperative market socialism, such as described above in Chapter 3.

Although the Communist Party was ousted from power in the Soviet Union in 1991-1992, and the Union itself shortly thereafter disintegrated, much of the program adumbrated by the 1987 "Basic theses" has in fact been implemented. Central planning of physical production has been abandoned, prices for the most part have been liberated to determination by the forces of supply and demand, and enterprise managers have become almost as independent and autonomous as their counterparts under Western market capitalism. The situation with respect to "privatization" is still very obscure. A major complication is that the operative meaning of this term varies dramatically as between the various Eastern European ex-satellite nations and the various republics of the ex-U.S.S.R. In Russia itself, the main thrust of privatization at the moment seems to be in the direction envisioned by the "Basic theses": toward employee ownership, otherwise known as labor management or cooperative market socialism. A common pattern is that of distribution of ownership shares in enterprises to the respective managers and employees of these enterprises. Thus initially the enterprises are employee owned. A series of questions then arises: First, will managers and employees be allowed to sell their personal ownership shares to outside owners? Second, if such sales are permitted, will managers and employees in fact sell their shares to outside owners to a substantial extent? Finally, will the outside owners possess the effective authority to dismiss managers considered to be paying an inadequate rate of return on the outside owners' shares? If the answer to all these questions is in the affirmative, then the economy will indeed evolve toward the private ownership norm under Western capitalism. At this point, however, such an evolution is by no means certain.

The Eastern reform movement and the dramatic collapse of Soviet Communism have of course been widely interpreted throughout the world as the death knell of socialism. This interpretation may indeed ultimately be vindicated. However, it would be premature at this point to make a firm prediction that it will be. In some ways, the Eastern reform movement and the demise of Soviet Communism might actually assist the future prospects for a system of democratic market socialism along the lines proposed in this book. At least four such possibilities may be perceived. First, there is a possibility that economic reform in the Communist and ex-Communist nations might produce a reasonable facsimile of some form of market socialism, and if this economic system is successful, it will provide a tangible demonstration of the viability and attractiveness of market socialism in general. Second, the Eastern reform movement has demonstrated the ability and willingness of the Communist and ex-Communist nations to undertake significant social changes, and this might inspire the non-Communist nations to consider reciprocal social changes of their own. Third, the successful establishment of democracy in ex-Communist nations might lessen the effectiveness of the familiar anti-socialist argument that socialism is to be avoided even if there is only a slight possibility that it will result in totalitarianism—because "there is no return from totalitarianism." Finally, the decline of the "menace of world Communism" might reduce the level of emotional intensity regarding ideological issues, and permit a calmer and more rational contemplation of the socialist alternative. Each of these four possibilities is briefly discussed in the following.

Demonstration effect of a successful form of market socialism. Even though there have never been any full-scale, unalloyed implementations in the real world of market socialism along the lines proposed in this book, there have been some reasonably close approaches to a recognizable analogue to market socialism. During the early 1920s, the Soviet Union prospered under the New Economic Plan (NEP). Throughout the

1980s and into the 1990s, the People's Republic of China has prospered
under a reform program spearheaded by the responsibility system in agriculture. Both the Soviet NEP system and the recent Chinese reform program have much in common with the basic concept of market socialism,
and both are considered economically successful. But one has to be realistic about the level of success. The living standards achieved under both
of these episodes are negligible relative to those prevailing in the advanced capitalist nations today. The Soviet Union in the early 1920s was
recovering from a devastating decade of international war and civil war,
while the People's Republic of China today is a Third World nation
struggling beneath the weight of its huge population. However, as a result of the reform movement in Russia at the present time, an opportunity
is emerging for a far more powerful test case on market socialism.

For the most part, the current "privatization" campaign in Russia, insofar as large-scale production enterprises are concerned, is creating
labor-managed firms: firms consistent with the pattern of cooperative
market socialism—a pattern which has long been under intensive theoretical scrutiny in the economic systems literature. It is by no means clear
at this point that these labor-managed firms will eventually evolve into
standard outside-ownership capitalist-style firms. If they remain labor-
managed firms, and the Russian economy commences to prosper, this
will provide dramatic evidence of the economic viability of cooperative
market socialism in particular, and of any sort of market socialism in
general. And there is a very good chance that the Russian economy will
in fact commence to prosper in the near future. The much-publicized
hardships in Russia and the other republics of the ex-U.S.S.R. have been
in the nature of temporary transitional problems caused by the enormous
confusion and disruption attendant upon drastic political change. So
drastic were these changes that civil war has been a very real possibility.
But the danger of civil war now seems to be ebbing. The Russian land is
vast and well endowed with natural resources, and the Russian people are
resourceful and well educated. It is quite possible that within a short period of time, the Russian economy will commence surging forward quite
impressively. If this happens, and if labor-managed large-scale firms are
still part of the picture, it will provide unmistakable evidence of the po-
tentialities inherent in market socialism.

Motivation toward reciprocal reform movement in the West. As the
populations of the Western nations watch with intense interest and fasci-
nation the efforts of various Eastern reformers, from Gorbachev in the recent past to Yeltsin today, to radically change the traditional social

system of the Communist and ex-Communist nations, they experience an urgent desire to aid these individuals and to assist the transformations they are endeavoring to bring about. But what can be done? One can "approve of" the reformers, and say and write complimentary things about them. But there is always the uncomfortable realization that too much in the way of Western approval can actually undercut the position of these people in their own countries, and make them even more vulnerable to accusations by their traditionalist opponents that they are basely and cravenly abandoning traditional national ideals and customs.

An obviously more effective way to assist the reform process in the East would be to commence a parallel reform process in the West. As the East moves forward toward the Western market system and Western political democracy, the West could move forward toward a market socialist economy. It would be tremendously important to all those in the ex-Communist world, across the spectrum from ultra-conservative traditionalists to radical reformers, to see the West adopt for itself at least something from the Communist social system. Of course the "something" in question here is far more than some relatively minor peripheral issue: the core of Communist ideology has always been, and still remains, the principle of socialism, the principle of public ownership of the capital means of production. Acceptance by the West of this fundamental principle, even if it is in the form of a market socialist system far different from anything ever witnessed within the Communist world, would be a tremendous consolation and encouragement to all those in the Communist and ex-Communist nations. It would be a tangible concession by the rest of the world that the development of communistic socialism has not been completely and entirely a malevolent aberration in world history, that the supporters of Communism from 1917 to the present day have not been completely and totally in grievous error.

Such a concession would make it psychologically much easier for these supporters to renounce and abandon other components of the communistic social system, in particular the one-party state and various forms of central planning. It is extremely difficult for people to admit error, either as individuals or as citizens of nations. It is even more difficult for individuals to admit total error. In light of this difficulty, it may be unfair—and unrealistic—to expect that the populations of the Communist world will casually cast aside every aspect of Communist ideology, and cheerfully endeavor to make themselves over into exact replicas of the United States population, even though this would be an admission of total and grievous error in the past. If the West stands by, figuratively speaking with its arms folded and a knowing smirk on its face, waiting for the East to follow its example in each and every respect, then it is quite possible that the current reform movement in the East, despite its apparently high level of promise at the present time, will not ultimately be successful. On the other hand, if the West were to engage in the tangible conciliatory gesture of moving forward toward democratic market socialism, this would provide a tremendous impetus to the Eastern reform movement. By moving toward socialism, the West would be conceding that on this one very important issue, the East had been right all along. This would make it much easier for the East to concede that the West had been right all along on other important issues, in particular the key issues of the one-party state versus genuine democracy, and market allocation versus central planning. This would represent a genuine form of convergence—a movement by both sides toward a compromise middle position. Such compromises are of course an essential component of most peaceful conflict resolution in the real world.

Tangible refutation of the "no return" argument against socialism. Another aspect of the Eastern reform movement which could assist the cause of democratic market socialism in the West is the tangible refutation it is providing of the well-known anti-socialist argument that any type of socialist economy tends to evolve by degrees into some dreadful form of totalitarianism, and that once it is established there is no internal means of return from totalitarianism. The twentieth century has witnessed a number of extremely momentous developments in human civilization: marvelous technological advances in every area of human endeavor and achievement; the introduction and dissemination of nuclear weapons and long-range delivery systems; two world wars generated in large part by the sovereign nation-state system; the Russian Revolution and the rise of communistic socialism; and two experiences, in the form of Hitler's Germany and Stalin's U.S.S.R., with frighteningly extreme cases of totalitarian dictatorship. Perhaps the most terrifying aspect of totalitarian dictatorship as experienced in the twentieth century is that despite the fact that these regimes engage in ferocious persecution of large subgroups within their own people and furthermore tend to entangle their people in devastating international wars, the regimes display tremendous stability. This stability is accomplished by the total suppression of political dissent combined with an intensive propaganda campaign mounted by the tightly controlled media of mass communications. The suffocating effect of such regimes not only on the physical welfare of the population, but on the essence of its humanity, has been powerfully depicted in

George Orwell's famous novel *1984.*

The Orwellian nightmare certainly constitutes a psychological impediment to the consideration even of moderate, liberal, and democratic forms of socialism, such as the proposal for profit-oriented market socialism put forward herein. This is not entirely logical in that of the two major sources of inspiration for the Orwellian nightmare, Hitler's Germany and Stalin's Russia, the former retained its capitalistic essence (i.e., private ownership of capital property) from beginning to end. Nevertheless, according to the standard anti-socialist argument, socialism combines economic and political power: this leads to the suppression of genuinely democratic processes, and with the disappearance of these processes the path is opened to totalitarian excesses—a path which will certainly be followed by a regime interested in its own self-preservation. Although Hitler's Germany demonstrated that capitalism is not a *sufficient* condition for genuine democracy and the avoidance of totalitarian dictatorship, it may still be argued, on the basis of experience up to the present time, that capitalism is a *necessary* condition to this end. Up to this time, only the Communist countries have fully implemented public ownership of the great majority of capital property (socialism per se), and these countries have indeed displayed a marked tendency toward harshly repressive dictatorships (Stalin in Russia, Mao in China, etc.). It may of course be counterargued that these harsh dictatorships were brought on not by socialism itself, but by the post-revolutionary suppression of tendencies toward forcible internal resistance against the regime's authority, combined with intense fear of invasion by hostile capitalistic nations. But regardless of its logical weaknesses, the argument remains very potent psychologically because of the emotional power of Orwell's masterful depiction of totalitarian tyranny. Understandably enough, rational people want to avoid even the slightest risk of such tyranny.

To anyone persuaded by the economic case for market socialism, but hesitant on political grounds of possible tendencies under socialism toward totalitarianism, the present movements in Russia, China, and the other Communist and ex-Communist nations toward Western-style democracy provide very reassuring evidence of the potency and persistence of social inclinations toward genuine democracy, in the face of very adverse historical circumstances. Of course, in the aggregate this movement is still quite recent and has not proceeded very far as yet. Even in those nations which have held elections, the situation seems fluid and unstable, and democratic institutions and attitudes are still far from being firmly established. On the other hand, auspices seem good for the solidification of democracy in the future. At the present time, most people in the West fully expect that not only will all of the Communist nations of the world eventually abandon the one-party state and embrace political democracy, but also that they will abandon the economic institution of public ownership socialism and embrace private ownership capitalism. So far in the heartland Communist nations of Russia and China there has been more progress made toward political democracy (especially in Russia) than toward capitalism in a strict private ownership sense.

But the very fact that such a transformation from socialism back to capitalism is seriously entertained as a possibility could, somewhat ironically, augment the possibility of a transformation in the West from capitalism to socialism. Because once it is recognized that such transformations back and forth are fully possible, the idea might catch hold of an experimental implementation of some form of market socialism, such as the profit-oriented proposed herein. If the system did not work well in practice, it would be abolished and capitalism restored. If the ex-Communist nations were able to throw off totalitarian undemocratic regimes which had been entrenched for many decades, then it would certainly be possible to rescind by democratic decision an incrementalist market socialist system (assuming it were not performing well) only slightly different from the market capitalist system of today.

Relaxation of judgmental rigidity caused by past Cold War tensions. Turning finally to the fourth reason why the Eastern reform movement may strengthen prospects for market socialism in the West, we take note of the veritably paralyzing effect which the conflict with world Communism has had on the intellect and judgment of almost all people in the West, ranging from the most sophisticated intellectuals to the most parochial men in the street, with respect to the specific issue of capitalism versus socialism. Throughout most of the twentieth century, socialism has been effectively condemned through its association with an extremely radical, self-righteously messianic, international movement toward the universal implementation of the Communist social system—a system regarded with horror and repugnance in the West owing to its politically totalitarian and excessively bureaucratic aspects. Socialism has been regarded as the core of a perverse and evil social system which our national enemies have been callously attempting to force upon us against our continuously and clearly stated will.

Thus capitalism has been able to wrap itself up in the flag, to enlist in the cause of its own self-preservation the awesome force of nationalistic pride and prejudice. The Communist East was not alone in developing a fortress mentality during the long decades of conflict: such a mentality also came about in the capitalist West. Advocacy of socialism in any form whatsoever came to be widely regarded as subversive and seditious—as giving aid and comfort to the barbarians who lay in wait just beyond the gates. With the simultaneous escalation of the strategic conflict between Communism and non-Communism and the introduction of nuclear weapons after World War II, the tendency in the West to reject any and all thoughts of socialism in the interest of national security became even more pronounced.

Cold War tensions muddied the water and muddled the judgmental faculties of people to such an extent that socialism was deprived of the opportunity for a fair consideration based on the ordinary processes of objective, critical reasoning. Now at last, Cold War hostility, antagonism, and mental rigidity seem to be ebbing significantly. As the ideological distance between East and West shrinks, both military and psychological disarmament is accelerating rapidly. All this will hopefully reduce the predisposition in the West toward thoughtless rejection of the socialist alternative—and thus give market socialism the chance it deserves. The case for democratic market socialism is inherently a solid, substantive case. If this case is seriously, thoughtfully considered by a sufficient number of people, capitalism's continued ascendency will be called into serious question.

THE SOCIAL DEMOCRATIC PERSPECTIVE

In looking forward to the prospects of democratic market socialism in the twenty-first century, we now ask whether any support might be forthcoming from the social democratic camp. Such support is not critical to the implementation of market socialism, and in some respects the endorsement of market socialism by social democrats would be harmful. This is because capitalist apologetics has long endeavored to identify "socialism" with an extreme and excessive form of social democracy, and support of market socialism by individuals associated with social democracy would lend more credibility to this identification. In the final analysis, the success of market socialism depends on breaking the stranglehold which capitalist apologetics has gotten on public opinion, and on winning over to the cause of market socialism large numbers of middle-class people who today consider themselves firmly anti-socialist. Be that as it may, the fact remains that the number of people in the Western nations today who deem themselves "social democratic socialists" is not inconsequential, and while there would be some disadvantages of these people proclaiming in favor of market socialism, on the whole it is likely to be helpful.

At first glance, many if not most social democrats will be highly dubious of the profit-oriented market socialism proposed in this book. Many will be skeptical of the public ownership aspect of the proposal, for basically the same reasons that any common garden-variety anti-socialist would be skeptical of it. Others will fault the proposal on grounds that it does not explicitly advance the social democratic vision of socialism. This entire book has endeavored to refute the common garden-variety anti-socialism familiar to us all. Therefore, it is the latter concern which I particularly wish to address in this section. What response may be offered, by a proponent of profit-oriented market socialism, to the charge that this economic system does nothing to advance the objectives of social democracy (greater progressivity in the tax system, tighter regulation of business enterprise, a more generous welfare system, and so forth)?

The first point to be emphasized is that the profit-oriented market socialist proposal *is in no way opposed* to the social democratic program. Rather it is completely neutral toward it. The second point to be emphasized is the distinct possibility that through its curtailment of the political influence of the erstwhile capitalist class, profit-oriented market socialism would pave the way toward an eventual significant extension of the social democratic program. The overall argument is that even though the economic characteristics of the profit-oriented market socialist system emphasized in the proposal will not be particularly attractive to most contemporary social democrats, they should nevertheless support the proposal partly because of the immediate benefits which it promises, and partly because it would produce a political environment which would be more favorable to the further pursuit of the social democratic vision. Although at first glance profit-oriented market socialism might appear to be opposed to the interests of social democracy in some ways and irrelevant to these interests in other ways, the fact remains that there should be a sympathetic and mutually supportive relationship between exponents of social democracy and exponents of profit-oriented market socialism.

Contemporary social democracy had its historical roots in the orthodox Marxist ideology of the nineteenth century. In its initial phases, the revisionist secession from mainline Marxism emphasized two principal points of divergence from the orthodox position: (1) that socialism could be brought about by means of peaceful democratic processes as opposed to violent revolution; (2) that substantial progress could be made toward the objectives of socialism prior to the attainment of public ownership of the capital means of production, through such institutions and programs as progressive taxation, social insurance, and so on. With respect to the second point, the consensus viewpoint within the social democratic movement toward public ownership of capital seems to have evolved gradually from "Public ownership is *infeasible* in the short run but desirable in the long run" through "Public ownership is *irrelevant* to the primary objectives of socialism" to "Public ownership is *undesirable* on economic efficiency grounds." I would submit that this progression is an illustration of the human tendency toward making a virtue of necessity. Confronted with the apparent impossibility of achieving public ownership of the capital means of production, it became psychologically intolerable to social democrats to continue clinging to the belief that public ownership was desirable. Another applicable folkloric principle is that of sour grapes. Unable to attain the goal of public ownership of capital, the social democratic movement comforted itself by gradually migrating to the belief that the goal was not desirable anyway.

But if contemporary social democrats have indeed, finally and irrevocably, given up on the public ownership of capital, questions arise as to the consistency and accuracy of retaining such designations as "socialist" and "Marxist." The core of Karl Marx's perception of society was that private ownership of capital (under modern productive conditions) creates serious social problems which may only be cured by public ownership of capital. Marx *defined* capitalism in terms of private ownership of capital and he *defined* socialism in terms of public ownership of capital. These definitions have become standard and conventional, as may be verified by consulting almost any contemporary dictionary. The conventional anti-Marxist, anti-socialist position is that: (1) the social problems about which Marx complained may be adequately addressed in the absence of public ownership of capital; (2) public ownership of capital generates serious and unavoidable economic efficiency problems. If a contemporary social democrat accepts both of these points, then the distinction between that person and the common garden-variety anti-socialist becomes rather tenuous and nebulous. True, the social democrat believes that *more* intervention in the market economy is required: a greater degree of progessivity in the tax system, larger and more generous social welfare programs, and so forth. But this is a matter of degree and not of substance. One must wonder if the self-designation of himself or herself as a "Marxist" or a "socialist" by a person who accepts the above points is more of an affectation than a serious statement of belief.

As a proponent of socialism in the original, traditional, public owner-ship sense—which is arguably the only semantically useful sense—it is my own firm belief that Karl Marx would have readily acknowledged that if the public ownership of capital principle is invalid (i.e., public ownership would adversely affect aggregate social welfare), then it could truthfully be said that "Marxism is in error" and/or that "socialism is in error." The central core of the Marxist ideological system is the surplus labor theory of exploitation, a theory which portrays capitalism as suffer-ing from a major moral liability: the capitalist class appropriates to itself property income in the form of profits, interest, and so on, and this ap-propriation is justified on neither economic nor ethical grounds. Al-though as an economist inculcated in orthodox theory I do not think that Marx's surplus labor theory is the best way to formulate the principle of unearned property income, nevertheless I believe that Marx's perception of this moral flaw of modern capitalism was basically accurate and re-mains as valid today as it was in his own time.

As is well known, Marx extrapolated heroically from his basic com-plaint concerning maldistribution of capital property income. Most if not all of these extrapolations now appear, from the vantage point of the late twentieth century, to have been wide of the mark. First and foremost, it does not appear as though capitalism will allow unchecked business de-pressions to destroy the social system. Marx's prognostications of the revolutionary overthrow of capitalism were founded not on the moral in-equity of the exploitation mechanism, but on the inherent propensity within the system toward recurrent, worsening business depressions. Marx did not believe that the capitalist class would ever attain the degree of enlightenment necessary to enable significant social action toward the amelioration of these depressions. The rise of Keynesian anticyclical pol-icy, and its apparent success in the post-World War II period, strongly suggest the inaccuracy of Marx's revolutionary prognostication.

Beyond business fluctuations, Marx perceived capitalism to be an ag-gravating factor in numerous social problems ranging from crime to im-perialism. This line of argument was enthusiastically developed by many of Marx's followers—probably overenthusiastically. There are some ma-jor problems with it, including the following: (1) most of the cited prob-lems long predated the rise of modern capitalism; (2) considerable progress has been made in the amelioration of some of these problems relative to the situation under "harsh early industrial era capitalism" in the absence of any fundamental institutional shift; (3) emphasis on these problems distracts attention from the basic issue of maldistribution of capital wealth and income. To make matters even worse for the socialist cause in the contemporary era, the experience of mankind with the Communistic form of socialism, in the Soviet Union and elsewhere, has been deeply disappointing and extremely sobering. As much as pro-socialists may argue that the dysfunctional aspects of communistic socialism, such as oligarchic governance to the point of totalitarianism and central planning to the point of bureaucratic strangulation, are the result of historical and political factors rather than the consequence of public ownership socialism in and of itself, there is no escaping the fact that the history of Communistic socialism in the twentieth century has done immense harm to the image and prospects of socialism.

But it is still possible that socialism in the classic public ownership sense will remain a factor in human affairs in the twenty-first century. Although the collapse of Soviet Communism is widely proclaimed by conservatives as evidence of the death of socialism, as pointed out in the previous section, there are some embers of hope to be found amid the rubble. Most importantly, the definitive termination of the Cold War could enable many individuals to adopt a more calm and rational approach to the issue of capitalism versus socialism. Throughout most of the twentieth century, capitalist apologetics has been able to portray socialism as an integral part of an evil and insidious social system which our deadly national enemies are endeavoring to force upon us against our will. This tactic has been very successful in veritably paralyzing the judgmental faculties even of leaders and intellectuals, to say nothing of the man in the street. Now that the Cold War is hopefully behind us, a cooler and more judicious appraisal of socialism might become possible, enabling a larger number of people to perceive its virtues.

These embers of hope might be exploited by the socialist movement in the future. But for there to be a reasonable hope of success, the socialist movement should focus on a very limited and incremental socialist reform. The terrible twentieth-century experiences of humanity with fascism and Communism have bred a deep distrust of the notion of revolutionary change. Both the intellectuals and the rest of humanity have arrived at a high degree of consensus on the principle that in the future, social change should be cautious and gradual—"evolutionary rather than revolutionary" is the customary phrase. Profit-oriented market socialism represents an effort to implement socialism on an evolutionary rather than a revolutionary basis. It is an effort to arrive at a sort of "lowest common denominator" socialism—inspired by nothing more or less than Marx's fundamental complaint about maldistribution of capital property income under capitalism—on which a high degree of consensus might possibly be reached not only among contemporary socialists, but more importantly, among the vast majority which is presently opposed to socialism.

The profit-oriented market socialist principle incorporates profit maximization as the primary incentive within business enterprise as well as external control of the firm because these are characteristics of contemporary market capitalism, an economic system which is evidently operating at a high level of efficiency in the advanced industrial nations. Now it is certainly conceivable that in a broader social sense, nonprofit production would be preferable to profit maximization, or that employee control of the firm (as under cooperative market socialism) rather than external control would be preferable. Once the public ownership principle has been established by profit-oriented market socialism, there might thereafter be cautious experimentation with nonprofit production and/or employee control, and the results of this experimentation might sustain extensions of these forms and principles. The fact that the immediate proposal features profit maximization and external control does not imply complete certainty that these principles are optimal for society now and for all time.

The same is true of various proposals for the extension of the social democratic program such as a higher degree of progressivity in the tax system, tighter business regulation, national planning, "socialized medicine," and so on. None of these proposals are part of the profit-oriented market socialist proposal—but this does not mean that espousal of profit-oriented market socialism necessarily implies opposition to these things. If success is to be attained, it must be one step at a time, one thing at a time. The attainment of public ownership of the capital stock through profit-oriented market socialism would be a notable advance, both in and of itself, and because it might broaden the avenue leading toward further social reform and improvement.

It is this final point which particularly needs to be emphasized to the social democratic constituency. If implemented, profit-oriented market socialism would terminate the political influence of the capitalist class in social decisionmaking. This termination would not be instantaneous: most erstwhile capitalists would be highly nostalgic for the old system, and the compensation program would guarantee their retention of substantial financial clout during the early years of profit-oriented market socialism. It can certainly be anticipated that a major effort will be made to discredit and repeal the new economic system—even if its performance on most objective criteria is quite good. Hopefully the effort will be thwarted, but only time will tell.

If it is thwarted, then the influence of capitalists and their heirs in the political process will gradually fade away to a negligible level. The possibility which social democrats should consider, in their evaluation of profit-oriented market socialism, is that many of their projects and proposals would then have a greater chance of success. The great wealth of capitalists tends to make them simultaneously very conservative and very influential. The elimination of capitalists from the political process would remove one very important conservative bias in this process. The argument is not that public opinion would become definitely more liberal under profit-oriented market socialism, so that the social democratic interventionist program would be dramatically advanced. At least some of the opposition to the interventionist agenda is generated by the legitimate self-interest of the middle class and even the working class. It is also true that to some extent, great wealth may enable a person to take a broader and more enlightened view of the social interest relative to self-interest. It is an empirical fact that at least a few wealthy capitalists have been notably liberal and even social democratic in their political philosophy.

Nevertheless, even with these qualifications, it would seem that under profit-oriented market socialism the population would be at least somewhat more liberal in its viewpoints and at least somewhat more receptive to various social democratic ideas and proposals. Thus some social democrats may view profit-oriented market socialism principally as a means to an end. But I would also hope that most social democrats would view profit-oriented market socialism as desirable in its own right: as providing a viable means of overcoming the inequity of highly unequal distribution of unearned capital property income without incurring significant economic efficiency disadvantages. It is not merely a means toward worthwhile ends—it is also a worthwhile end in itself.

PROSPECTS IN THE CAPITALIST HEARTLAND

What are the chances that the large majority of the population of the advanced capitalist nations can be awakened to the fact that their best interests lie with democratic market socialism? It is useless to deny that at first glance these chances appear to be negligible, insignificant, and virtually nonexistent. It is not merely the minority of wealthy capitalists who are gloating over the collapse of Soviet Communism and the apparent defeat of socialism in the ex-Soviet Union and Eastern Europe—the glee extends down through the middle class and the working class, right down to the indigent and the starving. No doubt destitute and homeless beggars trundling their shopping carts down city streets at this very moment are deriving some degree of consolation and joy from the thought that the "socialist peril" is no more.

The tremendous grip which capitalist apologetics has gotten on the entire population—political figures, intellectuals, journalists, executives, middle managers, clerical workers, factory hands and truck drivers—is nothing less than awesome. At every level of society, in every occupation and professional specialization, the various propositions of capitalist apologetics are regarded as self-evidently factual. They are automatically spouted out as needed without one heartbeat of hesitation. Depending on the educational attainment and intellectual pretensions of the spouter, these propositions sometimes come out in a conceptually rarefied and convoluted form. At the other end of the educational/intellectual spectrum, they are apt to come out in a logically crude and rhetorically muddled form. But in whatever form they come out, they are based on exactly the same basic ideas. In actual fact, the propositions of capitalist apologetics are not much called upon in daily life, since there are so few advocates of socialism around who are willing to challenge the capitalist status quo. The initial reaction of most people, when confronted by someone who does not accept capitalist apologetics, is stunned disbelief. But as soon as this reaction passes, the familiar litany of capitalist apologetics tumbles forth, coherently or incoherently as the case may be.

The vast majority of people who subscribe firmly to the pro-capitalist faith, and who are ready, willing, and able to recite it mechanically whenever called upon to do so, would in fact be personally benefited by a system of democratic market socialism along the profit-oriented lines set forth in this book. They would personally receive larger incomes, because whatever capital property income (dividends, etc.) they would lose owing to the abolition of capitalism would be outweighed by the social dividend income they would gain under market socialism. In addition, they would have the mental and emotional satisfaction of knowing that there is *not* in society a small minority of financially super-privileged capitalists who owe their luxurious living standards not to any personal effort or contributions, but rather to the vagaries of inheritance and financial speculation. No doubt there can be no such thing as *perfect* justice and fairness in the world—but there can be *improvements* in justice and fairness. Market socialism would be one such improvement—a significant improvement. In other words, most people who currently reject socialism actually have both a personal, egotistical, financial self-interest in profit-oriented market socialism—and also a social, moral, and ethical interest in it. Quite simply, most people at the present time are mistaken in their beliefs about socialism. This critical factor *may* save socialism from extinction in the twenty-first century.

What is needed is a "campaign of enlightenment." People need to be made aware of the maldistribution of capital wealth under contemporary capitalism, and of the existence of a viable democratic market socialist alternative to contemporary capitalism. They need to be made aware of these things not merely as conceptual abstractions such as "2 + 2 = 4," or as trivial empirical curiosities such as the migratory routes of gray whales, but as indications which potentially have a direct and significant bearing on their own lives. For most people, the addition to their personal annual income represented by social dividend income would not be a minute and insignificant amount of money. Most people would become very interested and highly aroused if they believed, or even suspected, that they were being unfairly deprived of sums of money of this magnitude. The fact that most people have a personal interest in becoming enlightened on this issue enhances the probability that they will in fact—eventually—become enlightened. What type of enlightenment campaign is most likely to be successful, given the currently unpromising conditions?

First and foremost, the campaign must be very conservative and low-keyed. Logically unfocused, rhetorically overblown, and emotionally hysterical assaults on capitalism must be consistently and studiously avoided. Contemporary capitalism must be given due credit for very impressive performance in most respects. This is not to say that modern human civilization does not have very serious problems, ranging from environmental degradation to rampant crime. But it is to say that any arguments to the effect that these problems have been and are being seriously aggravated by capitalism, in and of itself, are highly unpersuasive to most minds. It must be continuously and tirelessly reiterated both that profit-oriented market socialism would be a very modest, incremental, marginalist and evolutionary advance beyond capitalism, and that the implementation of profit-oriented market socialism would be in the nature of a tentative and experimental step, with every intention of returning to capitalism should the economic performance of the new system, after a fair trial, prove to be disappointing.

Of course, to some it will seem absurd to propose that a reform so profound as the establishment of socialism can be presented as an experimental step, and that the proponents of such a step could be capable of admitting that the case for this step is not completely solid and absolutely irrefutable. Looking to the historical record, they will say, all those who have committed themselves to fundamental change, from Washington to Robespierre to Lenin, have been absolutely convinced that the changes would be for the better. Or if they had any doubts of this, they kept these doubts to themselves. Thus surely no one who commits himself or herself to the cause of democratic market socialism could possibly have any doubts as to the desirability of democratic market socialism—or if any such doubts might be harbored internally, surely they could never be admitted to others, especially to skeptics and opponents.

Yet what I am saying is that proponents of democratic market socialism *should* have doubts about it, and that they *should* admit these doubts to others—especially to skeptics and opponents, as a means of lending credibility to promises that if democratic market socialism performs poorly, it will indeed be abandoned and capitalism restored. But I also say that this attitude is *not* unreasonable, and that it is a misreading of the "historical record" to hold that it is unreasonable. The historical record can be misleading because it concentrates heavily on drastic changes accomplished through violence and war. Washington is associated with the American Revolution, Robespierre with the French Revolution, and Lenin with the Russian Revolution. All three events were extremely violent. The political, economic, and social changes brought about by the American, French, and Russian Revolutions were huge in comparison to the purely economic and very limited changes that would be brought about by the establishment of profit-oriented market socialism of the sort recommended herein. It is almost impossible to imagine such limited changes leading to the degree of polarization required to generate serious civil strife and even civil war. If any serious possibility of this started to emerge, I for one would instantly abandon support for market socialism. The relatively limited benefits to be gained from market socialism could not possibly justify the tremendous costs of a potential civil war.

Not only are the benefits from market socialism relatively limited, but it behooves proponents of market socialism to recognize that these benefits are far from certain. The case for profit-oriented market socialism is a strong case both theoretically and empirically, but nevertheless the case cannot be "proved" in any sort of scientifically rigorous sense. The evidence raised and discussed in the foregoing is all circumstantial, tangential evidence with an imperfect bearing on the fundamental question at hand. Really strong and impressive evidence can only possibly be provided by the actual implementation of profit-oriented market socialism in the real world. In the final analysis, the potential performance of a profit-oriented market socialist economy is an empirical question and not a theoretical question. Only an actual experiment with this type of market socialism will provide truly definitive and compelling evidence on this empirical question.

The world in which we live is a probabilistic world, a world composed of shades of gray—as opposed to white (truth) versus black (falsehood). Or more accurately, what we *know* of the world is inevitably probabilistic. Some things are true, and some things are false, but for the most part we do not know with absolute certainty which is which. With respect to any particular proposition about the real world, each of us has a subjective estimate of the probability that the proposition is in fact true. As this subjective probability rises, the terminology used to describe the proposition (in scientific discourse) changes: we describe the proposition first as a "conjecture," then as a "hypothesis," then as a "theory," and finally as a "fact." But even with respect to many acknowledged "facts," our subjective estimate of the probability of truth is often less then 100 percent. Of course, in everyday discourse, we do not adhere to strictly correct terminology because it would become unduly cumbersome to do so. We often describe as "facts" propositions which do not actually fit a strong definition of "fact": that us, as something which virtually all knowledgeable people agree is almost certainly true.

For example, the opening sentence of this section reads as follows: "What are the chances that the large majority of the population of the advanced capitalist nations can be awakened to the fact that their best interests lie with democratic market socialism?" In a strict sense, the word "fact" in this sentence is misused, since it is not true (at the moment) that almost all knowledgeable people agree that it is almost certainly true that the best interests of the large majority of the population of the advanced capitalist nations lie with democratic market socialism. To meet strict standards of accuracy, the sentence in question should read as follows: "What are the chances that the large majority of the population of the advanced capitalist nations can be awakened to the high likelihood (in the judgment of the author) that their best interests lie with democratic market socialism?" The case for democratic market socialism which has been presented in this book will seem to many people extremely complex and convoluted. (It really is not all that complex and convoluted in a logical sense, but it seems so because it contradicts so many widely accepted purported "facts" adduced by capitalist apologetics.)   Had I adhered to strictly correct terminology, as illustrated by this example, throughout the book, the case would have been rendered even more seemingly complex and convoluted—perhaps impossibly so. A certain amount of rhetorical hyperbole is permissible without violating the prevailing standards of respectable controversial discourse, and hopefully these standards have not been violated herein. But it is essential for any proponent of democratic market socialism to properly understand the case which may be made for democratic market socialism (a strong case but not an intellectually overpowering case), and to be aware of (and cautious of) rhetorically hyperbolic statements of that case.

The enlightenment campaign must focus on a very specific and precise market socialist proposal. It would probably be best to formalize the proposal at an early stage in the form of draft legislation entitled "An Act for Economic Justice." The legislation would cover surrender of financial capital instruments by private households, compensation arrangements, the purposes, structure and procedures of the public ownership agencies (the Bureau of Public Ownership, the National Investment Banking System, and the National Entrepreneurial Investment Board), and the payment of social dividend income to private households. The emphasis on a specific proposal might seem to go against the political wisdom that candidates for public office maximize their chances of election by speaking in vague and glowing generalities, and remaining noncommittal on specifics. One difference, of course, is that we are referring here to an abstract institutional proposal rather than to a person running for office. The same rules do not apply to proposals as apply to persons. Beyond that, there is the fact that socialism has such a poor reputation at the present time that a vague proposal for "socialism" will suggest to many people changes to which they are opposed (e.g., a large-scale expansion of welfare benefits).

The reason why most candidates for public office can get away with being vague and noncommittal is that the voting public is confident that, by and large, candidates for public office are highly intelligent, basically competent, and reasonably honest persons. As we know, in a political democracy with high standards of freedom of speech, politicians in general and government officials in particular come in for a great deal of harsh kidding. But neither those who make the jokes nor those who laugh at them sincerely believe the negative viewpoint on politicians and government officials which they manifest. At heart, the people recognize that politicians and government officials come from the same mold as the rest of us, and that they are no worse than the rest of us. The barbed humor at the expense of politicians and government officials is just a harmless means of releasing our natural resentment at those in authority over us. Such natural resentment as the people feel toward their leaders is basically the same as the natural resentment that children feel toward their parents. Children are constantly being restrained, admonished, and disciplined by their parents. Of course, they resent this.

While people verbally abuse politicians and government leaders, they are quite well aware that all individuals who are serving in elective offices, as well as all those who are merely candidates for such offices, have passed through a rigorous screening process, and that they are very likely to be high-quality individuals. Thus while the typical voter might have a mild preference for candidate A over candidate B, he or she is not likely to regard it as a major setback if candidate B is elected. Confidence that the system will continue to function acceptably regardless of which candidate is elected enables voters to be apathetic or frivolous, as the case may be, without experiencing serious pangs of conscience or anxiety. The typical candidate for political office today is well advised to avoid specifics, because in the absence of further information, most voters will deem the candidate basically acceptable. In addition, voters tend to be far more conscious of what they do *not* like than what they *do* like. Taking a specific position on a specific issue is likely to be harmful to a candidate, because those who disapprove of that position are far more likely to let it influence their voting than those who approve of that same position.

In the case of trying to develop political support for socialism, however, it is necessary to be very specific, because in the absence of further information, most voters will deem socialism basically unacceptable. As emphasized throughout this discussion, socialism has been dragged down by a number of extremely adverse associations: political oligarchy, central planning, an unrestrained welfare state, confiscatory taxation, and so on. Unless socialism can be adequately disassociated from these things, it is doomed to failure and extinction. Unless this disassociation is made explicit through specification of a precise and limited proposal for a profit-oriented market socialist system such as outlined herein, then many voters will assume the worst of the proposal. They will assume that the proposed system would bring about policies, institutions, and circumstances to which they are firmly opposed. In addition to disassociating this proposal from the various negative characteristics traditionally identified with socialism (the one-party state, central planning, etc.), the movement should also avoid becoming entangled with the conventional liberal and social democratic issues of the moment. For example, such hot issues of the moment range from gay rights and abortion rights through preservation of rain forests and whales. No doubt some of these issues are substantive, and no doubt some advocates of market socialism will take the conventional left-wing attitude on these issues. But insofar as the formal organization and official orientation of the movement toward market socialism are concerned, they must remain absolutely neutral toward these kinds of issues. They are separate and distinct issues from market socialism, and taking any position on them whatsoever is not only needless and illogical, but it would do severe damage to the prospects for successful implementation of market socialism.

In developing the specific and precise proposal for market socialism, several aspects require especially strong emphasis. To begin with, the compensation plan would not only compensate all small and medium-scale financial capital owners from the working class and the middle class to the full value of their holdings, but it would also compensate wealthy capitalists adequately to maintain them at a high standard of living—if not a luxurious standard of living. Working-class and middle-class people must be reassured that their financial capital property will not be expropriated, and wealthy capitalists must be assured that they will not be suddenly reduced to what would be for them a penurious condition. Another feature of the market socialist proposal to be strongly stressed is that entrepreneurial firms would be exempted from public ownership, regardless of the level of success they achieve, as long as the entrepreneurial founder of the firm remains active in management. This means that those who accumulate personal fortunes via entrepreneurship presently under capitalism will be able to do the same under market socialism. This feature definitively undercuts what is probably the single most propagandistically potent defense of capitalism: the allegation that financial wealth is a reward for entrepreneurship. Still another feature to emphasize is the fact that the profits of publicly owned firms will not be treated as if they were equivalent to tax revenue. That is, they will not be allocated to the general support of public spending, but will rather be directly distributed to private households as social dividend income. This is essential for two reasons: (1) so that households will have a gain to directly offset the loss of capital property income; plus (2) the general level of prejudice against taxes and governments is presently at such a high level that the idea that revenues of publicly owned business firms would simply "feed government bureaucracies" will predispose many people against market socialism.

Of course, the most central feature of this market socialist proposal, that feature which must be constantly and emphatically reiterated, is its close similarity to the contemporary market capitalist economy with which we are familiar, and which is almost universally recognized as displaying a high level of economic performance. The proposal under consideration here envisions a market economy which would be virtually indistinguishable from the present economy in terms of daily economic life. Consumer sovereignty would be assured, prices would be set by the free interplay of supply and demand, business firms would continue to pursue profits under the authority of an external ownership interest, in every important respect financial incentives to effort would be equivalent to what they are today, and so on down the list. If one had to sum up the proposal in one sentence, it could be described as follows: "This profit-oriented market socialist economy would work almost exactly like the contemporary market capitalist economy, except that profits of business firms would be distributed equitably to private households on the basis of their earned wage and salary income."

The tremendous amount of overlap between the proposed profit-oriented market socialist economy and the present capitalist market economy brings up the issue of nomenclature. Specifically, it brings up the question of whether it might not be sensible to find another name for the proposal—a name not involving the word "socialism." After all, it is evident that the proposal has little or nothing in common with the common conception of "socialism." Moreover, this common conception is overwhelmingly negative, involving as it does political totalitarianism, central planning, suffocating paternalism, rampant bureaucratization, crude egalitarianism, and so on. Over the years, this author has received innumerable well-intentioned recommendations to "find another name for it." There have even been a few suggestions as to what that name might be. Probably the best alternative name suggested to me is "public capitalism." The notion of transforming all members in good standing of the general public into "capitalists" catches the essence of the idea, and "public capitalism" is moreover considerably pithier and catchier than "profit-oriented market socialism." However, after considerable reflection on the matter, and with some misgivings, I have concluded that all things considered, the designation "socialism" should continue to be applied to this proposal. In terms of the standard and conventional dictionary definition of socialism (public ownership of the capital means of production), the proposal as it stands is definitely socialistic. More importantly, any effort to get around this basic fact via euphemistic circumlocution would be pounced upon by opponents of the proposal, and employed loudly—and probably effectively—as clear evidence of the basic dishonesty and chicanery of the proponents of the proposal. Therefore the term "socialism" should be retained. To counteract, as much as possible, the inherent tendency of the term "socialism" to elicit the wrong associations, the term should frequently—in fact almost invariably—be preceded (as has been done throughout this book) by the descriptors "democratic market" or "profit-oriented market."

Just as the close similarity between profit-oriented market socialism and contemporary market capitalism suggests the possibility of finding another name for the system not involving the word "socialism," so too it suggests the notion of "virtual socialism through taxation." The first and foremost objective of profit-oriented market socialism is to bring about a more equal and equitable distribution of unearned capital property return. The "find another name" idea is that this objective can be attained simply by finding a name for the proposal which does not use the word "socialism," because this particular word is heavily saddled by extremely negative connotations. The "virtual socialism through taxation" idea is that this objective can be attained by dropping the public ownership aspect of the proposal and instead subjecting capital property income to virtually confiscatory taxation, with the proceeds of this tax (for example) distributed to the population as a social dividend supplement to labor income. As discussed earlier, the fundamental flaw with "virtual socialism through taxation" is that it would leave the corporate executive elite inadequately accountable. The separation of ownership and control under contemporary capitalism has already created a situation in which high corporation executives are both overpaid and overly insulated against the threat of dismissal for poor performance. "Virtual socialism through taxation" would further aggravate the already seriously adverse consequences of the separation of ownership and control.

In addition to that, virtual socialism through taxation is no more practical a means of attaining the objectives of profit-oriented market socialism than is finding another name for the system not tainted by the word "socialism." The watchdogs of the capitalistic status quo are not so easily fooled. Just as they would pounce on any effort to implement profit-oriented market socialism under another name as a devious and dishonest attempt to slip the *literal* essence of socialism past an unsuspecting public, so too they would pounce on any effort to implement virtual socialism through taxation as a devious and dishonest attempt to slip the *conceptual* essence of socialism past an unsuspecting public. As a matter of fact, in the present era of rampant conservatism, the watchdogs over the financial privileges of wealthy capitalists are especially alert and aggressive. Under the circumstances, even the most tentative moves which threaten entrenched wealth—such as increasing the rate of estate taxation or replacing estate taxation with highly progressive taxation of inheritances—have virtually no chance of implementation. In the United States today, the guardians of the plutocrats are working hard to get taxation of capital gains income either greatly reduced or eliminated entirely. This dream of the plutocrats could indeed be realized in the near future. In light of this situation, it is highly unrealistic and borderline absurd to propose that either "socialism under another name" or "virtual socialism through taxation" *could* be achieved—but that "profit-oriented market socialism" *could not* be achieved.

The day that "socialism under another name" or "virtual socialism through taxation" become practical possibilities, then so too will "profit-oriented market socialism," as named and described in this book, become a practical possibility. That day will come about when the veritable strait-jacket in which capitalist apologetics has encased the rational and judgmental faculties of the population has been ripped off and destroyed. This can only be accomplished through a frontal assault on the various myths through which capitalism justifies itself: the myth that capital wealth is primarily a reward to entrepreneurship and other forms of capital management effort; the myth that capital property income is primarily a reward for the sacrifices of saving or the pressures of risk-taking; the people's capitalism myth that people not expecting substantial inheritances have a fair and significant opportunity to become capitalists themselves; the myth that socialism would jeopardize freedom and democracy. The assault on these myths must be low-keyed, easy-going, unhurried, and gentle—but it must all the same be a frontal assault. There is no real hope of overturning the many falsehoods and misconceptions propagated by capitalist apologetics by any sort of cleverly disingenuous subterfuge. One cannot "trick" the population on this matter—even if the intention is honorable and the goal worthwhile. One must rather win over the population though fair, frank, candid, honest, and straightforward persuasion. A majority of the population must be made to understand both that its own financial interests lie with market socialism, and that the social goals of economic justice and fairness are best served by market socialism. The only feasible means of accomplishing this is through observance of the strictest standards of openness and honesty in conducting the debate and advocating the proposal.

Some encouragement may be derived from the observation that unanimous approval is not needed for implementation of market socialism. If unanimity were required, then given the disputatious nature of humanity, this proposed reform would be well and truly impossible. But in a democratic polity, the majority will is determinative—unless it is a question of violating the natural rights of the individual. No doubt many capitalists will argue that their natural rights to property would be violated by the socialization of their capital wealth. However, given that a fair and reasonable amount of compensation is to be paid for surrendered capital wealth, they will probably not get too far with this line of argument. It can easily be countered by the argument that it is the working population, rather than the class of capital wealth owners, which has a natural right to capital property return which is produced not by human beings but by the inherent economic productivity of inanimate machines. This is because the current productivity of capital is more closely and directly related to the amount of current labor applied in production than it is to the past saving behavior which generated the capital stock. That saving would probably have been undertaken by households even in the absence of payment of capital property return on savings. In any event, if private households were indeed generating inadequate saving, additional saving could be provided from public tax revenues. It is not necessary for the full amount of saving to be provided by private households, and it is not necessary to pay households for the alleged "sacrifices of saving." These sacrifices, such as they may be, can be borne to some extent publicly rather than privately. In the final analysis, the large majority of households would be financially benefited if they were paid social dividend income on their earned labor income rather than capital property income on their savings. It is not in fact saving which imposes a serious sacrifice on this large majority of households—it is rather the continued preservation of capitalism.

Profit-oriented market socialism is fundamentally an economic concept, rather than a political, social, or philosophical concept. Therefore the judgment of the economics profession will be a critical factor in determining its likelihood of implementation. As does any other profession, economics gets its fair share of bad press. Economists are ridiculed for their inability to agree on much of anything. (As in: "If you laid all the economists on earth end to end, they wouldn't reach a conclusion.") They are also derided for their generally poor record of forecasting. (In defense of economics on this issue, I would point out that the only profession which does a really impressive job of forecasting is astronomy.

Unfortunately, knowing the exact time at which the sun will rise on the morning of December 25, 2250 A.D., is of limited usefulness to most people.) Finally, economists are lambasted for being ivory tower theoreticians whose complicated mathematical models have little apparent bearing on reality as most of us know it. (Again in defense of economics, many of these theoretical speculations might have a closer bearing on reality than can be proved at the present time. After all, Einstein's $E = mc^2$ was "only a theory" prior to its verification by means of, among other things, nuclear explosions.) Economics is similar to other much-maligned professions such as law, accounting, medicine, psychiatry, and politics. Despite all the quasi-humorous slurs and aspersions cast their way by the general population, specialists in economics—as in the case of specialists in law, accounting, etc.—are consulted attentively as and when the need arises. Therefore the judgment of professional economists on the viability and potential performance of profit-oriented market socialism will be solicited and, to a considerable extent, heeded. What, then, can this proposal expect from the profession of economics?

Having been an academic economist for more than 25 years, I can speak with some authority on the character, attitudes, and foibles of professional economists. One of the greatest strengths of contemporary economists is their strong and sincere devotion to completely fair, objective, impartial, and scientific inquiry in the investigation of all questions of interest, whether "positive" (concerning that which *is*) or "normative" (concerning that which *should be*). On the other hand, one of the greatest weaknesses of modern economists is that in general they are insufficiently aware of how far short their actual patterns of thought and investigative methods fall relative to the ideal standards which they so loudly and self-righteously proclaim. Adam Smith (1723-1790), the Scottish political economist and philosopher whose *Wealth of Nations* (1776) is credited with being the seminal document of contemporary economics, was a superb scholar and a brilliant writer. Moreover, his thinking was generally quite lucid, fair-minded, and balanced. But at the same time, Smith was definitely not purely a disinterested seeker after abstract scientific truth. His masterwork, *The Wealth of Nations*, has a pronounced politico-ideological agenda: the tome is basically an extended, elaborate polemic in favor of laissez faire. Smith argued for relatively modest government intervention in the workings of society generally and the economy in particular, on grounds that very often interventionist government policy, even though well intentioned, generates unanticipated and highly adverse consequences. When Ronald Reagan campaigned successfully for the United States presidency in 1980 on the basis of the slogan: "Let's get the federal government off the backs of the American people," he was invoking, albeit crudely, the laissez faire principle first firmly established in intellectual history by the work of Adam Smith in the eighteenth century.

Contemporary economics is still very much under the influence of the ideological predisposition of its founder, Adam Smith. By and large, contemporary economists are still skeptical of government intervention in the workings of the economy, and they are still much inclined toward laissez faire. However, as did Adam Smith himself, they will reluctantly allow that in some cases intervention is indeed justified. But they tend to put a heavy burden of proof on the proposers of intervention, and they are normally unenthusiastic about socially mandated reforms and innovations. On the other hand, they have considerable faith in the fundamental rationality of mankind, and thus they tend to gravitate toward the view that if something has become well-established in human civilization, even if it *does* constitute government intervention in the economy, then there is probably a very good reason for it. Also, as a general rule, economists tend to be rather academically oriented and passive in personal outlook. In a word, economists tend to be in favor of the status quo, whatever the status quo might consist of. These conventional prejudices, preconceptions, and predispositions of economists tend to hamper their scientific objectivity, especially when it comes to the analysis of anything to do with significant change. To a large extent, however, they remain blissfully unaware of the substantial degree to which their judgment is being influenced and biased by these "unscientific" factors.

All this suggests that if and when profit-oriented market socialism becomes a serious issue in contemporary economics, the overall evaluation of the profession will be skeptical and unsupportive. Market socialism would be a change away from the status quo, and economists tend to be against changes away from the status quo. Market socialism would involve some government intervention in the economy, and economists tend to be against government intervention in the economy. Moreover, the ingrained prejudice among economists against what they imagine as "socialism" is hardly any less intense or more sophisticated than is the analogous ingrained prejudice among the general public.

On the other hand, there are some hopeful considerations. Owing to their specialized knowledge of both theoretical and empirical matters which are germane to the issue, economists are more likely than are members of the general public to be aware of the dubiousness of the various tenets of capitalist apologetics. They are more likely to be aware of how limited is the actual role of private entrepreneurship in the modern corporate economy. They are more likely to be aware of how much doubt has been cast on the allegation that capital property income is an earned return to capital management effort by the separation of ownership and control and by the growing role of institutional investors in the capital markets. They understand theoretical concepts such as the substitution effect and the income effect, and how these concepts imply the ambiguity, for example, of the effect of the interest rate on the level of private household saving. Thus they are more aware of the dubiousness of the simplistic notion that interest income is an earned reward to the "sacrifices of saving." Above all, they are more likely than are members of the general public to be aware of the fact that the extravagantly unequal distribution of financial capital wealth under contemporary capitalism makes a mockery of that favorite standby of capitalist apologetics: "people's capitalism."

The volume of material which has been published in professional economics journals on market socialism in general and profit-oriented market socialism in particular demonstrates that contemporary economics, despite its prejudice against socialism and its predisposition against government intervention, does not summarily dismiss the concept of market socialism. For example, in my case, over the last 20 years I have published approximately 15 articles in the professional economics journals on my own version of profit-oriented market socialism ("pragmatic" market socialism), plus two professional books on the subject. From the sheer volume of this published material, it is apparent that the economics profession as a whole, as represented by the referees who recommended these contributions for publication and the editors who accepted them for publication, is not prepared to label market socialism as an uninteresting, harebrained, crackpot idea. This is not to say that there is not a substantial number of *individual* economists who are indeed prepared to label it as such. On the whole it has been a difficult struggle getting my own work on market socialism into print. Over the years I have accumulated a large quantity of negative referee reports on this work, some of them virtually dripping with sarcastic contempt. But although it may take a considerable period to find a publisher for this work, and although the outlets are generally not as prestigious as I would prefer, most of my work on pragmatic market socialism has been, and continues to be, published. This in itself is a very significant indication.

My professional contributions on pragmatic market socialism follow the same principles exemplified in this book. I have placed great emphasis on the fact that this type of market socialism would be a modest, conservative, and evolutionary advance beyond contemporary capitalism. I have studiously avoided strong and colorful rhetoric which overstates the case for market socialism. Frank admission is made that the case for market socialism in general, and for profit-oriented market socialism in particular, cannot be proven in advance beyond a shadow of a doubt, as if it were a mathematical theorem or a logical syllogism. From the beginning I have stressed the point that the proposal is being put forward for tentative and provisional implementation, so that if the system does not perform in practice as well as hoped and intended, then it will be abandoned and capitalism restored. This concentration on the experimental nature of the market socialist proposal is no doubt particularly influential with economists, because of their heartfelt aspirations toward "scientific inquiry." Economists are quasi-religious about science and scientific method, and thus they are able to clearly perceive and well appreciate the fact that the only way to gain more or less definitive evidence on the potential performance of such a "counterfactual" proposal as profit-oriented market socialism is to implement the system on an experimental basis, and then observe what happens. Until such evidence is achieved, the debate will remain, for the most part, just so much speculative hot air.

My hope is that if and when the idea of market socialism becomes sufficiently well known to and well accepted by the general public to be a serious political possibility, and hence the judgment of the economics profession on the idea commences to be solicited earnestly, the verdict of the profession will be basically noncommittal and neutral. Hopefully the profession will support the argument which I have long been advancing in the professional literature: that there is nothing in the corpus of generally accepted economic principles of the present day which constitutes serious evidence that profit-oriented market socialism would *not* work as hoped and intended. These generally accepted principles, both theoretical and empirical, are consistent with profit-oriented market socialism being a *superior* economic system to contemporary capitalism, and they are also consistent with profit-oriented market socialism being an *inferior* economic system to contemporary capitalism. The performance of profit-oriented market socialism cannot be confidently predicted on the basis of information currently available. The only effective way to settle the issue would be to implement profit-oriented market socialism in the real world on an experimental basis. As to whether such an experimental implementation would be desirable, owing to the prevalent passivity within the

profession of economics, I am *not* very hopeful that many economists
will express a personal judgment that it would be. (It would be nice to be
proved wrong on this.) But I *am* hopeful that not many economists will
come out as being personally opposed to the experiment. Hopefully most
economists will hold simply that this is a matter for the intuitive judgment of each citizen, because the weight of presently available economic
knowledge inclines neither one way nor the other.

If the economics profession can be to a sufficient extent "neutral-
ized," so to speak, then there is a very good chance that the general public will be enabled to see the light. The central question is whether or not
capital property income (dividends, interest, capital gains, etc.) is earned
income. Despite the best efforts of capitalist apologetics over the decades, many if not most people's common sense tells them that it is *not*
earned income. Nearly all people have some degree of empirical experience, however incomplete and imperfect, with the practical realities of
life under capitalism—with "capitalism at work." They are aware of the
fact that most people possessing sufficient "independent income" not to
be obliged to work for a living came by this status by virtue of inheritance rather than personal effort. As for "risk-taking" and the "sacrifices
of saving" as justifications for property income, how often in real life
does one witness inheritors declining their inheritances because they
would be unable to bear the "risk-taking" and "sacrifices of saving"
which must be undertaken in order to receive property income on inherited capital? The gut instincts of most people reject these and other arguments of capitalist apologetics that capital property income is earned
income. People are also aware of the great stability of financial status in
the real world—of the fact that the rich tend to stay rich, the poor tend to
stay poor, and those in between tend to stay in between.

In general, therefore, people are aware of a permanent condition of
economic injustice in the capitalistic real world, and thus they have a
natural predisposition toward a sympathetic interest in socialism. But for
the moment, they have been persuaded that they must suppress this natural interest. They have been persuaded that for reasons which they cannot
fully fathom or understand, for reasons which blend the scientific principles of economics together with a sort of quasi-religious philosophical
mysticism into an opaque and incomprehensible brew, the powerful indications of their own common sense and direct observation of the world
must be rejected and disregarded. They have been persuaded that any
personal resentment against capitalists in particular, or the capitalistic
status quo in general, manifests merely a base and childish envy—an

envy which is fraught with peril, because if it ever leads to a socialistic transformation of society, then every individual in society, from the highest to the lowest, will encounter personal catastrophe. In short, the public has been misled, fooled, and bamboozled—it has been blinded to both its own financial self-interest and the higher social interest.

The perceptual blindness and judgmental paralysis currently inflicted upon the population of the advanced capitalist nations is an unnatural situation—it is something which economists would describe as a "disequilibrium condition." When a system is out of equilibrium, as every student in a college course in principles of economics learns, natural forces operate to return the system to equilibrium. In this case, one sign of a return to a rational equilibrium is the development by concerned economists of a new approach to socialism—the market socialist approach. This new concept of socialism successfully meets the many and varied objections to traditional concepts of socialism. It disassociates socialism from its adverse historical connections with central planning, the welfare state, radical egalitarianism, etc. It shows an avenue by which the essential socialist equity goal, which would be achieved by public ownership of capital operated by large, established corporations, can be combined with an efficient and dynamic market economy. It shows a socialist system which would be fully compatible with political democracy and personal freedom.

The next step toward rational equilibrium is the enlightenment of the general public with respect to the concept of market socialism—to wake the public up, to make it aware of the fact that democratic market socialism is a viable and attractive alternative to the contemporary capitalist status quo, both from the personal point of view and from the social point of view. If this next step can be accomplished, then democratic market socialism will emerge from its lowly present status as a purely speculative, hypothetical proposal of interest mainly to specialists in economic systems theory, to a force to be reckoned with in the real world of practical politics. This may not happen today, and it may not happen tomorrow. But it would be rash indeed to assert that the idea of market socialism will never achieve sufficient substance and support to become a serious candidate for real-world implementation. The idea has already come too far to be dismissed as an irrelevant, utopian delusion. There is every possibility that in due course, the idea of market socialism will arise out of the realm of intellectual history and proceed forward into the realm of real-world history.

A FUTURE FOR SOCIALISM

Contemporary capitalism is perpetuating the inequity of extremely unequal distribution of unearned capital property return. This is hardly an abstract, theoretical liability irrelevant to the practical concerns of daily life. On the contrary, the salient implication of this particular liability is that more than 90 percent of households in the advanced capitalist nations, including virtually all working-class and middle-class households, are receiving less personal, disposable income than they ought to be receiving. They ought to be receiving social dividend income instead of capital property income, because the large majority of these households would receive more social dividend income under socialism than they are currently receiving capital property income under capitalism. While the defenders of the capitalist status quo normally concede that the extreme inequality of capital wealth ownership is troubling and regrettable, they continue to insist that any equity advantages of socialism would be swamped by efficiency disadvantages. In other words, socialism would be a cure worse than the disease, and the extreme inequality of capital wealth ownership under contemporary capitalism must therefore be accepted as a necessary evil.

This conventional rationalization of capitalist apologetics is now being directly confronted and challenged by the idea of democratic market socialism. Market socialism proposes to combine public ownership of the capital stock (more precisely, of that part of the capital stock owned and operated by large, established corporations) with a market economy embodying decentralization of economic decision-making authority, the determination of prices by supply and demand, financial incentives to effort, and consumer sovereignty. A number of carefully considered proposals for market socialism have been developed in the professional literature on economic systems. These range from the initial 1930s proposal of Oskar Lange, through proposals for nonprofit production and labor management, to the profit-oriented proposals independently put forward by this author, Leland Stauber, and John Roemer. The primary emphasis in this book has been placed on profit-oriented market socialism because, in the author's judgment, this is the most practical and attractive form of market socialism on the basis of presently available information. Profit-oriented market socialism is distinguished from other forms of market socialism by its reliance upon a profit-maximization incentive imposed on the publicly owned business enterprises by an external authority in the form of one or more active public ownership agencies. This would create a situation exactly parallel to that under market capitalism, in which a profit-maximization incentive is imposed on privately owned business enterprises by boards of directors representing external owners.

Most of the standard body of capitalist apologetics is directed against characteristics and conditions traditionally associated with socialism, such as central planning, the welfare state, confiscatory taxation and so on, which are not logically implied by the public ownership essence of socialism. Market socialist proposals have been firmly and explicitly disassociated from these adverse characteristics and conditions. Therefore, the invocation of most of the traditional critique of socialism (tendencies toward bureaucratization, socioeconomic leveling, etc.) against market socialism—although frequently done more or less automatically by those whose minds are completely closed against socialism—constitutes mere begging of the question. While this is often an effective debating tactic, it is wholly indefensible from an intellectual standpoint.

However, as has been duly emphasized herein, even when the extraneous and irrelevant elements have been completely purged from it, there remains a core of capitalist apologetics which is indeed plausibly applicable even to profit-oriented market socialism. It may be argued that capital property income is an earned return on two separate and independent bases: that it is a return to capital management effort in the form of entrepreneurship and other activities, and that it is a return to the disutility ("sacrifices") of saving. It may also be argued that the distribution of capital wealth—when properly interpreted—is not nearly as unequal as it appears to be at first glance (the "people's capitalism" thesis). Finally, it may be argued that socialism in any form, owing to its combination of economic and political power, represents an intolerable threat to political democracy and personal freedom.

When subjected to close and critical scrutiny in light of various indications from both economic theory and empirical reality, the case against profit-oriented market socialism mustered by capitalist apologetics is perceived to be dubious and unsatisfactory. Economic theory is basically ambiguous on the capital management argument, but there are certain empirical indications, in particular the separation and ownership and control and the role of institutional investors in capital markets, which cast grave doubt on it. Economic theory is similarly ambiguous on the saving argument, but this argument founders decisively in the face of an obvious possibility: public provision—if necessary—of saving resources out of tax revenue. The people's capitalism thesis also withers away when

confronted by hard, documented, statistical evidence. As for political democracy and personal freedom, these are determined by historical circumstances and cultural attitudes, and not by formal institutions
pertaining to the ownership of productive capital. Under favorable historical circumstances and cultural attitudes, a profit-oriented market socialist economy along the lines presented herein would not constitute a
significant threat to political democracy and personal freedom.

In sum, while the case against profit-oriented market socialism cannot
be disproved in a strict scientific sense, this case is sufficiently forced
and implausible-looking that this form of socialism ought to be given a
fair and adequate opportunity to prove itself. Profit-oriented market socialism should be implemented on an experimental basis for several
years, and the results carefully monitored and studied. If these results are
adverse, then society should, could, and would restore the capitalist
status quo ante. But if the results are favorable, then the change would be
deemed permanent. The idea of a "return to capitalism" (if necessary)
might strike some as unrealistic and impractical. Such a conclusion, however, proceeds from a misconception of profit-oriented market socialism
as a radical departure from the capitalist status quo. In actual fact, profit-
oriented market socialism would be a very marginal and incremental step
beyond capitalism, both in terms of ideology and institutions. Hence the
actual obstacles to a return to capitalism (if necessary) would be minor
and easily surmounted.

There exists one final argument against market socialism to which no
reference has hitherto been made. This is the argument that regardless of
the power and plausibility of the logical, objective case which may be
made in favor of market socialism (in the profit-oriented form or any
other form)—nevertheless this case will remain forever null, void, and
irrelevant because of the eternal, unshakable, and irrevocable bias in the
population against socialism per se, in whatever guise, shape, or form it
might be presented. According to this argument, *even if* the case for
profit-oriented market socialism were clearly valid by any reasonable and
objective standard, it would still not matter one whit, because owing to
ingrained prejudice, neither the intelligentsia nor the general population
will ever be able to perceive the validity of this case. In other words, socialism is impossible on psychological grounds even though it might be
desirable on objective grounds. Therefore, concludes the argument, it is a
waste of time even to think about socialism, let alone to go to the trouble
of seriously studying socialism and advocating it.

Given that I personally have devoted a large part of my professional career to thinking about, studying, and advocating socialism (in the form of profit-oriented market socialism), it is understandable that I would regard this particular argument as not only unpersuasive but totally odious. It bespeaks a particularly unhealthy amalgam of personal passivity and snobbish contempt for others. It is also unduly cynical and unbearably pessimistic. If humanity were as immutably dense and obstinate as this argument makes out, it would be impossible to explain the enormous strides which human civilization has made throughout recorded history. While humanity is obviously not always and invariably receptive to reasonable persuasion, over a sufficient period of time it is sufficiently receptive to reasonable persuasion to give hope to advocates of market socialism such as myself.

A variant on the theme of "it is useless even to think about socialism at this time" is the notion that profound social changes can only emerge out of crisis conditions, and since such desperate conditions are not presently existent under contemporary capitalism, there is not a chance that the population could be induced to consider such a profound social change as the abolition of capitalism and the inauguration of socialism. One basic flaw in this proposition is that the particular socialist form under consideration here, that of profit-oriented market socialism, is sufficiently similar to market capitalism that its inauguration would hardly constitute a "profound social change." Another basic flaw is the assumption that profound social changes are invariably precipitated by crisis conditions in which famine, pestilence, intolerable hardship, and death are rampant throughout the land. Some profound social changes have indeed been brought about by such conditions—but others have occurred in the absence of such conditions. The Russian Revolution of 1917, for example, was certainly precipitated by crisis conditions. But neither the American Revolution of 1776 nor the French Revolution of 1789 were precipitated by crisis conditions. The American people who made the Revolution of 1776 and the French people who made the Revolution of 1789 were not suffering from famine or pestilence, intolerable hardship, or the fear of death. On the whole, the American people of 1776 and the French people of 1789 were relatively comfortable and secure. As a matter of fact, in some ways comfortable and secure conditions are more conducive to major social changes than crisis conditions. Under genuine, full-fledged, literal crisis conditions, the people are usually too fearful, exhausted, and demoralized to seriously contemplate social changes. They may not like the status quo, but they are too weak to do anything about it.

Another more recent example of profound change in the absence of crisis has been the rapid and dramatic transformation of the Soviet Union and Eastern Europe. Ten years ago, there was not an inkling that such amazing changes were in the offing. True enough, ten years ago some of the more rhetorically intemperate critics of Soviet Communism were insisting that the system was in a state of crisis. But this kind of propagandistic cant had been spouted for decades, and not even the spouters (most of them anyway) really believed that Soviet Communism was actually on the brink of total collapse and dissolution. Ten years ago, famine, pestilence, intolerable hardship, and death were hardly rampant throughout the Soviet Union and Eastern Europe. The people in those nations were relatively comfortable and secure. Living standards were as high or higher than those in many Third World capitalist nations which have experienced no perceptible social upheaval over the last ten years. It was not a literal crisis which precipitated the radical transformation of the Soviet world, but rather a crisis of confidence among the high leadership. After decades of exposing their people to the risk of nuclear annihilation in the interest of a socioeconomic system which stubbornly refused—despite their repeated promises—to deliver living standards superior to, or even comparable to, those in the advanced capitalist nations, the high leadership, quite simply and understandably, suffered an unbearable attack of conscience. In despair, they finally loosened their grip on power. The rest is history.

The peaceful, bloodless overthrow of Soviet Communism in the East, an overthrow which occurred without significant heralding but with stunning rapidity, could be an omen of an analogous eventuality in the West: the peaceful, bloodless overthrow of capitalism. No doubt "overthrow" is too colorful an expression. The evolutionary progression from contemporary capitalism to market socialism would be better described as a "replacement" or as a "transition." But regardless of terminology, the point remains: since the highly rigid and undemocratic social system of Soviet Communism proved itself capable of dramatic transformation in a remarkably brief period of time, clearly the open and democratic societies of the Western capitalist world possess an analogous capability. It is not merely through a potential demonstration effect that the transformation of the communistic East might augur an analogous transformation of the capitalistic West. One of the most potent forces throughout the twentieth century toward the stability and preservation of the capitalistic status quo has been the association of the concept of socialism with a dreaded national enemy: the world Communist movement. It has been extremely difficult for people in the West to look calmly and objectively at the pure concept of socialism, when it has been such an integral part of a socio-economic system generally regarded as hideously totalitarian. The perception of the Communist leadership as a band of fanatical would-be messiahs maniacally determined to force socialism down our throats, has been an insuperable obstacle to a fair and balanced evaluation of socialism in and of itself. But now, as the Cold War recedes and the Western people relax, the possibilities for clear-eyed, rational, and objective evaluation of the socialist alternative to capitalism are being greatly enhanced. The models of democratic market socialism discussed in this book provide a fair and reasonable basis for comparison. A strong case may be made for these models. Indeed, these models may enable a rebirth of the socialist cause and a reinvigoration of the socialist movement in the twenty-first century.

Even aside from the passing of the Cold War, there are many positive signs as the twenty-first century approaches. Social and environmental problems abound all around the world, but despite all the difficulties, human civilization in on the advance. Never before in human history have so many people enjoyed such high standards of prosperity and security. Even in the Third World, there is a slow but steady trend toward improvement, and auspices for the future are favorable. The wonders of science and technology continue apace, and mankind is actively exploring the environment from the depths of the oceans to the depths of outer space. Human civilization may well be poised on the edge of a golden age of unparalleled progress. Democratic market socialism should be, and could be, part of that golden age of progress.

REFERENCE NOTES

The viewpoint on market socialism expressed in this book is a judgmental distillation based on several literatures, some of them very general and extensive, and others quite focused and limited. In order to facilitate the interested reader's access to these literatures, the references provided here will be grouped by topics. In the case of very general topics (e.g., I. A. General History and Evaluation of Socialism), the literature is extremely voluminous, and therefore only a more or less random sampling of representative references will be provided. In the case of more focused and limited topics which bear directly on the proposal for market socialism put forward herein (e.g., II. C. Profit-Oriented Market Socialism), an effort has been made to provide a relatively exhaustive reference list. References are arranged according to the following list of topics:

I. Background: Historical Socialism and Social Intervention
A. General History and Evaluation of Socialism
B. Marxist Political Economy
C. Revisionism and Social Democracy
D. Soviet and Eastern European Socialism: Historical Perspective
E. Soviet and Eastern European Socialism: Recent Developments
F. Chinese Socialism: Historical Perspective
G. Chinese Socialism: Recent Developments
H. Regulation and Public Ownership: Historical Perspective
I. Regulation and Public Ownership: Recent Developments
J. Illustrative General Capitalist Apologetics

II. Market Socialism: Proposals and Appraisals
A. Langian Market Socialism
B. Cooperative Market Socialism
C. Profit-Oriented Market Socialism
D. Relevant Evidence: Distribution of Capital Wealth
E. Relevant Evidence: Separation of Ownership and Control
F. Relevant Evidence: Institutional Investors and Capital Markets
G. Specialized Capitalist Apologetics re Market Socialism

I. Background: Historical Socialism and Social Intervention

I. A. General History and Evaluation of Socialism

There is a tremendous popular, professional, and polemical literature which traces the complex real-world and intellectual history of Marxism and socialism. The range of style and treatment is very wide, from popular surveys such as Max Beer (1957) and Edward Hyams (1974), through college textbooks such as Ben Aggar (1979), to scholarly treatises such as George D. H. Cole's five volumes (1953-1960) and Carl Landauer's two volumes (1960). There are also several documentary compilations available, such as those edited by Alec Nove and D. M. Nuti (1972), Irving Howe (1976), Dan Jacobs (1979), and Emile Burns (1982). As the present work is not an analysis of historical socialist thought but rather a contemporary reformulation and advocacy of socialism, little reference has been made to the general historical literature, and only a very small sampling from this voluminous literature is listed below.

Aggar, Ben, ed. *Western Marxism: An Introduction.* Santa Monica, Cal.: Goodyear Pub. Co., 1979.

Beer, Max. *The General History of Socialism and Social Struggles.* London: Russel and Russel, 1957.

Berki, R. N. *Socialism.* New York: St. Martin's Press, 1975.

Berlin, Isaiah. *Karl Marx: His Life and Environment.* Oxford: Oxford University Press, 1948.

Burns, Emile, ed. *The Marxist Reader.* New York: Avenel, 1982.

Cole, George D. H. *A History of Socialist Thought,* five volumes. London: Macmillan, 1953-1960.

Del Vayo, J. Alvarez. *The March of Socialism.* New York: Hill and Wang, 1974.

Eddy, W. H. C. *Understanding Marxism: An Approach through Dialogue.* Totowa, N.J.: Barnes and Noble, 1979.

Feinstein, C. H. *Socialism, Capitalism, and Economic Growth: Essays Presented to Maurice Dobb.* Cambridge: Cambridge University Press, 1967.

Gray, Alexander. *The Socialist Tradition.* London: Longmans, 1963.

Hunt, E. K. *Property and Prophets: The Evolution of Economic Institutions and Idologies,* second edition. New York: Harper and Row, 1975.

Hyams, Edward. *The Millennium Postponed: Socialism from Sir Thomas More to Mao Tse-tung.* New York: Taplinger, 1974.

Jacobs, Dan N., ed. *From Marx to Mao and Marchais: Documents on the*

Development of Communist Variations. New York: Longman, 1979.

Kilroy, Silk, Robert. *Socialism since Marx*. New York: Taplinger, 1972.

Landauer, Carl. *European Socialism*, two volumes. Berkeley: University of California Press, 1960.

Leonhard, Wolfgang. *Three Faces of Marxism: The Political Concepts of Soviet Ideology, Maoism, and Humanist Marxism*. New York: Paragon Books, 1979.

Lindsay, Jack. *The Crisis in Marxism*. Totowa, N.J.: Barnes and Noble, 1981.

Martin, Joseph. *A Guide to Marxism*. New York: St. Martin's Press, 1980.

McLellan, David. *Marxism after Marx: An Introduction*. New York: Harper and Row, 1979.

Mehring, Franz. *Karl Marx*. London: George Allen and Unwin, 1948.

Meyer, Alfred G. *Marxism: The Unity of Theory and Practice*, revised edition. Cambridge, Mass.: Harvard University Press, 1970.

Nove, Alec, and D. M. Nuti. *Socialist Economics: Selected Readings*. Harmondsworth, U.K.: Penguin Books, 1972.

Raddatz, Fritz J. *Karl Marx: A Political Biography*. Boston: Little, Brown, 1979.

Rexroth, Kenneth. *Communalism: From Its Origins to the Twentieth Century*. New York: Seabury, 1974.

Ulam, Adam B. *Ideologies and Illusions: Revolutionary Thought from Herzen to Solzhenitsyn*. Cambridge, Mass.: Harvard University Press, 1976.

———. *The Unfinished Revolution: Marxism and Communism in the Modern World*, revised edition. Boulder, Col.: Westview Press, 1979.

I. B. Marxist Political Economy

The work of Karl Marx (1818-1883) provided a hard intellectual core for the socialist critique of capitalism, and thereby greatly strengthened the socialist movement in the nineteenth century. Marx's magnum opus *Das Kapital* (three volumes published between 1867 and 1894) is very lengthy and notoriously unreadable—although it does contain numerous brilliantly written passages. Most modern readers prefer to get their Marx from edited compilations such as Freedman (1962), rather than directly from *Das Kapital*. Also, Marx's lifelong collaborator Friedrich Engels (1820-1895), in his rather strangely titled polemic *Anti-Dühring* (1894—a refutation of the "unsound" socialist thinking of a certain

Professor Eugen Dühring), provided an exposition of classical Marxism which is relatively accessible to the typical modern reader, and which also has the advantage of a late nineteenth-century perspective (*Das Kapital*'s perspective is basically mid-nineteenth century).

The standard contemporary Western assessment of Marxist political economy, as represented by Joan Robinson (1942), Herbert Mayo (1960), Murray Wolfson (1968), Paul Samuelson (1971), and so on, is respectful but basically skeptical. For more stridently critical assessments of Marxist political economy, see section I. J. below ("Illustrative General Capitalist Apologetics"). Many of the references in the present section are quite favorable to Marxist political economy. Included in this category is a small sampling from the voluminous output of Progress Publishers (Moscow) during the Cold War era: Leontyev (1968), Menshikov (1969, 1975), Kozlov (1977), Afanasyev (1983), and so on. In addition, a handful of twentieth-century Western scholars sympathetic to Marxism have endeavored to refine and update the original Marxist critique of capitalism in light of more recent theoretical and empirical developments: e.g., Paul Sweezy (1942), Ronald Meek (1956), Ernest Mandel (1970), and John E. Roemer (1981, 1982, 1986, 1988).

The last of these, John E. Roemer, is the foremost exponent of analytical Marxism (i.e., the mathematical analysis of Marxist concepts) in the United States, and is also notable for his recent development of the "bank-centric" form of profit-oriented market socialism. Roemer's substantial published work on analytical Marxism and market socialism clearly demonstrates the basic compatibility of market socialism with Marx's fundamental critique of capitalism—even though Marx's own strident denunciations of the "anarchy of the market" certainly tend to obscure this compatibility.

Afanasyev, V. *Bourgeois Economic Thought, 1930s-70s*. Moscow: Progress Publishers, 1983.

Desai, Meghnad. *Marxian Economics*. Totowa, N.J.: Rowman & Littlefield, 1979.

Engels, Frederick. *Anti-Dühring: Herr Eugen Dühring's Revolution in Science*, third edition. Moscow: Progress Publishers, 1969. Originally published in 1894.

Freedman, Robert, ed. *Marx on Economics*. New York: Penguin, 1962.

Gottheil, Fred M. *Marx's Economic Predictions*. Evanston, Ill.: Northwestern University Press, 1966.

Gouverneur, Jacques. *Contemporary Capitalism and Marxist Economics*. Totowa, N.J.: Barnes and Noble, 1983.

Inozemtsev, N. *Contemporary Capitalism: New Developments and Contradictions*. Moscow: Progress Publishers, 1974.

Kozlov, G. A., ed. *Political Economy: Capitalism*. Moscow: Progress Publishers, 1977.

Leontyev, L. *A Short Course of Political Economy*. Moscow: Progress Publishers, 1968.

Mandel, Ernest. *Marxist Economic Theory*, two volumes. New York: Monthly Review Press, 1970.

Marx, Karl. *Capital: A Critique of Political Economy*, three volumes. New York: International Publishers, 1967. Originally published in German, three volumes, 1867-1894.

Mayo, Henry B. *Introduction to Marxist Theory*. New York: Oxford University Press, 1960.

Meek, Ronald L. *Studies in the Labour Theory of Value*, second edition. New York: Monthly Review Press, 1976. First published in 1956.

Menshikov, S. *Millionaires and Managers: Structure of the U.S. Financial Oligarchy*. Moscow: Progress Publishers, 1969.

———. *The Economic Cycle: Postwar Developments*. Moscow: Progress Publishers, 1975.

Morishima, Michio. *Marx's Economics: A Dual Theory of Value and Growth*. Cambridge: Cambridge University Press, 1973.

Oakley, Allen. *Marx's Critique of Political Economy*, two volumes. Boston: Routledge and Kegan Paul, 1984, 1985.

Osadchaya, Irina. *From Keynes to Neoclassical Synthesis: A Critical Analysis*. Moscow: Progress Publishers, 1974.

Pevsner, Ya. *State-Monopoly Capitalism and the Labour Theory of Value*. Moscow: Progress Publishers, 1982.

Robinson, Joan. *An Essay on Marxian Economics*, second edition. New York: St. Martin's, 1963. First edition published in 1942.

Roemer, John E. *Analytical Foundations of Marxian Economic Theory*. Cambridge: Cambridge University Press, 1981.

———. *A General Theory of Exploitation and Class*. Cambridge, Mass.: Harvard University Press, 1982.

———, ed. *Analytical Marxism*. Cambridge: Cambridge University Press, 1986.

———. *Free to Lose*. Cambridge, Mass.: Harvard University Press, 1988.

Samuelson, Paul. "Understanding the Marxian Notion of Exploitation: A Summary of the So-Called Transformation Problem," *Journal of Economic Literature* 9(2): 399-431, June 1971.

Shemyatenkov, V. *The Enigma of Capital: A Marxist Viewpoint.* Moscow: Progress Publishers, 1981.

Smirnov, A. D., V. V. Golosov, and V. F. Maximova, eds. *The Teaching of Political Economy: A Critique of Non-Marxian Theories.* Moscow: Progress Publishers, 1984.

Sweezy, Paul M. *The Theory of Capitalist Development.* New York: Oxford University Press, 1942.

Varga, Y. *Politico-Economic Problems of Capitalism.* Moscow: Progress Publishers, 1968.

Wolfson, Murray. *A Reappraisal of Marxian Economics.* New York: Columbia University Press, 1968.

Yakovlev, A. N., ed. *Capitalism at the End of the Century.* Moscow: Progress Publishers, 1987.

I. C. Revisionism and Social Democracy

Founded on the seminal contribution of Eduard Bernstein (1899), social democratic socialism (a.k.a. revisionist socialism, social democracy, etc.) quickly developed a large literature which has continued down to the present day. The scornful attitude of hardline Marxists toward social democratic socialism is typified by the compilation of V. I. Lenin's polemical essays and articles issued by Progress Publishers (Moscow) in 1966. A later example in this vein is Fedoseyev et al. (1980).

The list provided below consists mostly of works in English by British and American authors which are quite sympathetic to social democratic socialism. Examples from the tradition of British democratic socialism include works by the famous literary luminaries affiliated with the Fabian Society: George Bernard Shaw (1928) and H. G. Wells (1931). Later contributions in this tradition include E. F. M. Durbin (1940), C. A. R. Crosland (1963), and John Gyford and Stephen Haseler (1971). During the early part of the twentieth century, social democratic socialism was pursued unsuccessfully in the United States by the perennial presidental candidate Norman Thomas (1884-1968). Current adherents to the tradition of what is generally known as "American socialism" include the bestselling author Michael Harrington (1962, 1980, 1989), and the "radical economists" Samuel Bowles (1973, 1983, 1986, 1990), and Howard Sherman (1972, 1987).

Bernstein, Eduard. *Evolutionary Socialism.* New York: Schocken Books, 1961. Originally published in German in 1899.

Bottomore, Tom. *The Socialist Economy: Theory and Practice.* New York: Guilford Press, 1990.

Bowles, Samuel, and Herbert Gintis. *Schooling in Capitalist America.* New York: Basic Books, 1973.

―――. *Democracy and Capitalism: Property, Community, and the Contradictions of Modern Social Thought.* New York: Basic Books, 1986.

Bowles, Samuel, David M. Gordon, and Thomas E. Weisskopf. *Beyond the Waste Land: A Democratic Alternative to Economic Decline.* New York: Basic Books, 1983.

―――. *After the Waste Land: A Democratic Economics for the Year 2000.* Armonk, N.Y.: M. E. Sharpe, 1990.

Castles, Francis G. *The Social Democratic Image of Society: A Study of the Achievement and Origins of Scandinavian Social Democracy in Comparative Perspective.* Boston: Routledge and Kegan Paul, 1978.

Chalmers, Douglas A. *The Social Democratic Party of Germany: From Working Class Movement to Modern Political Party.* New Haven, Conn.: Yale University Press, 1964.

Crosland, C. A. R. *The Future of Socialism.* New York: Schocken, 1963.

Dominick, Raymond H. *Wilhelm Liebknecht and the Founding of the German Social Democratic Party.* Chapel Hill: University of North Carolina Press, 1982.

Durbin, E. F. M. *The Politics of Democratic Socialism: An Essay on Social Policy.* London: D. Routledge and Sons, 1940.

Einhorn, Eric S., and John Logue. *Modern Welfare States: Politics and Policies in Social Democratic Scandinavia.* New York: Praeger, 1989.

Esping-Anderson, Gosta. *Politics against Markets: The Social Democratic Road to Power.* Princeton, N.J.: Princeton University Press, 1985.

Fedoseyev, P. N., ed. *What is "Democratic Socialism"?* Moscow: Progress Publishers, 1980.

Greene, Nathanael, ed. *European Socialism since World War I.* Chicago: Quadrangle Books, 1971.

Gyford, John, and Stephen Haseler. *Social Democracy: Beyond Revisionism.* London: Fabian Society, 1971.

Harrington, Michael. *The Other America: Poverty in the United States.* New York: Macmillan, 1962.

―――. *The Twilight of Capitalism.* New York: Basic Books, 1980.

―――. *Socialism: Past and Future.* New York: Arcade (Little, Brown and Co.), 1989.

Labedz, Leopold, ed. *Revisionism: Essays on the History of Marxist*

Ideas. Plainview, New York: Books for Libraries Press, 1974.

Lenin, Vladimir Ilich. *Against Revisionism*, second revised edition. Moscow: Progress Publishers, 1966.

Macmillan, Harold. *The Middle Way: A Study of the Problem of Economic and Social Progress in a Free and Democratic Society*. New York: St. Martin's Press, 1966. Originally published in 1938.

Padgett, Stephen, and William E. Paterson. *A History of Social Democracy in Postwar Europe*. New York: Longman, 1991.

Paterson, William E., and Alistair H. Thomas. *The Future of Social Democracy: Problems and Prospects of Social Democratic Parties in Western Europe*. New York: Oxford University Press, 1986.

Pelinka, Anton. *Social Democratic Parties in Europe*. New York: Praeger, 1983.

Radice, Giles. *Democratic Socialism: A Short Survey*. New York: Longmans, 1965.

Roberts, Bruce, and Susan Feiner, eds. *Radical Economics*. Boston: Kluwer Academic Publishers, 1992.

Shaw, George Bernard. *The Intelligent Woman's Guide to Socialism and Capitalism*. New York: Brentano's, 1928.

Sherman, Howard. *Radical Political Economy*. New York: Basic Books, 1972.

———. *Foundations of Radical Political Economy*. Armonk, N.Y.: M. E. Sharpe, 1987.

Swanberg, W. A. *Norman Thomas: The Last Idealist*. New York: Scribners, 1976.

Sykes, Patricia Lee. *Losing from the Inside: The Cost of Conflict in the British Social Democratic Party*. New Brunswick, N.J.: Transaction Books, 1988.

Thomas, Norman Mattoon. *America's Way Out: A Program for Democracy*. New York: Macmillan, 1931.

———. *Democratic Socialism: A New Appraisal*. New York: League for Industrial Democracy, 1953.

Webb, Sidney, and Beatrice Webb. *A Constitution for the Socialist Commonwealth of Great Britain*. New York: Longmans, Green and Co., 1920.

———. *The Decay of Capitalist Civilization*. Westminster, U.K.: Fabian Society, 1923.

Weldon, John C. *On the Political Economy of Social Democracy: Selected Papers*. Montreal: McGill-Queen's University Press, 1991.

Wells, H. G. *The Work, Wealth and Happiness of Mankind*. Garden City,

N.Y.: Doubleday, Doran and Co., 1931.
Yorburg, Betty. *Utopia and Reality: A Collective Portrait of American Socialists.* New York: Columbia University Press, 1969.

I. D. Soviet and Eastern European Socialism: Historical Perspective

As befits what has been perhaps the most sweeping experiment in social engineering in all of human history, there is a tremendous literature on the ex-Soviet Union and its erstwhile Eastern European satellite states. The following list of references is oriented mostly to Western descriptions and assessments of the Soviet-style planned socialist economy, but a relatively small sample is also provided of works on the history and political system of Soviet and Eastern European communism. While Western assessments of the Soviet-style economic system have been merely skeptical, assessments of the Soviet-style political system have been outrightly condemnatory. A few examples of Soviet Communism's apologetic literature have also been provided in the form of books published by Progress Publishers (Moscow).

Afanasyev, V. G. *The Scientific Management of Society.* Moscow: Progress Publishers, 1971.

Ames, Edward. *Soviet Economic Processes.* Homewood, Ill.: Irwin, 1965.

Antonov-Ovseyenko, Anton. *The Time of Stalin: Portrait of a Tyranny.* New York: Harper and Row, 1981.

Aragon, Louis. *A History of the USSR: From Lenin to Khrushchev.* London: Weidenfeld and Nicolson, 1964.

Balassa, Bela. "The Dynamic Efficiency of the Soviet Economy," *American Economic Review* 54 (Sup.): 490-505, May 1964.

Bergson, Abram. *The Economics of Soviet Planning.* New Haven: Yale University Press, 1964.

———. *Productivity and the Social System: The USSR and the West.* Cambridge, Mass.: Harvard University Press, 1978.

———. *Planning and Performance in Socialist Countries: The USSR and Eastern Europe.* Boston: Unwin Hyman, 1989.

Bergson, Abram, and Herbert S. Levine, eds. *The Soviet Economy: Toward the Year 2000.* London: George Allen and Unwin, 1983.

Berliner, Joseph S. *Factory and Manager in the U.S.S.R.* Cambridge, Mass.: Harvard University Press, 1957.

———. "The Static Efficiency of the Soviet Economy," *American Economic Review* 54(2): 480-489, May 1964.

Bornstein, Morris, and Daniel Fusfeld, eds. *The Soviet Economy: A Book of Readings*, fourth edition. Homewood, Ill.: Irwin, 1974.

Brzezinski, Zbigniew K. *The Soviet Bloc: Unity and Conflict*, revised edition. Cambridge, Mass.: Harvard University Press, 1967.

Carr, E. H., and R. W. Davies. *Foundations of a Planned Economy*. London: Macmillan, 1969.

Cave, Martin, Alistair McAuley, and Judith Thornton, eds. *New Trends in Soviet Economics*. Armonk, N.Y.: M. E. Sharpe, 1982.

Chamberlin, William Henry. *The Soviet Planned Economic Order*. New York: Greenwood, 1969. First published in 1931.

Clark, Ronald W. *Lenin: A Biography*. New York: Harper and Row, 1988.

Cole, John, and Trevor Buck. *Modern Soviet Economic Performance*. New York: Basil Blackwell, 1987.

Conquest, Robert. *The Great Terror: A Reassessment*. New York: Oxford University Press, 1990.

Desai, Padma. *The Soviet Economy in Decline: Problems and Prospects*. New York: Basil Blackwell, 1987.

Desai, Padma, and Ricardo Martin. "Efficiency Loss from Resource Misallocation in Soviet Industry," *Quarterly Journal of Economics* 98(3): 441-456, August 1983.

Dyker, David A. *The Soviet Economy*. New York: St. Martin's, 1976.

Erlich, Alexander. *The Soviet Industrialization Debate, 1924-1928*. Cambridge, Mass.: Harvard University Press, 1960.

Feiwel, George. *The Soviet Quest for Economic Efficiency: Issues, Controversies, and Reforms*, revised edition. New York: Praeger, 1972.

Gaucher, Roland. *Opposition in the U.S.S.R.: 1917-1967*. New York: Funk and Wagnalls, 1969.

Gisser, Micha, and Paul Jonas. "Soviet Growth in the Absence of Planning: A Hypothetical Alternative." *Journal of Political Economy* 82(2): 333-347, March 1974.

Goldman, Marshall I. *U.S.S.R. in Crisis: The Failure of an Economic System*. New York: Norton, 1983.

Granick, David. *Management of the Industrial Firm in the U.S.S.R.* New York: Columbia University Press, 1954.

———. *The Red Executive*. London: Macmillan and Co., 1960.

———. *Job Rights in the Soviet Union: Their Consequences*. New York: Cambridge University Press, 1987.

Gregory, Paul R., and Robert C. Stuart. *Soviet Economic Structure and Performance*, second edition. New York: Harper and Row, 1981.

Grey, Ian. *Stalin: Man of History*. Garden City, N.Y.: Doubleday, 1979.

Heller, Michel, and Aleksandr Nekrich. *Utopia in Power: A History of the USSR from 1917 to the Present.* London: Hutchinson, 1985.

Hingley, Ronald. *Joseph Stalin: Man and Legend.* New York: Konecky and Konecky, 1974.

Holzman, Franklyn D., ed. *Readings on the Soviet Economy.* Chicago: Rand McNally, 1962.

Inkeles, Alex. *Public Opinion in Soviet Russia: A Study in Mass Persuasion.* Cambridge, Mass.: Harvard University Press, 1958.

———. *Social Change in Soviet Russia.* Cambridge, Mass.: Harvard University Press, 1968.

Jaworskyj, Michael, ed. *Soviet Political Thought, 1917-1961: An Anthology.* Baltimore, Md.: Johns Hopkins University Press, 1967.

Kaser, Michael. *Soviet Economics.* New York: McGraw-Hill, 1970.

Keep, John L. H. *The Russian Revolution: A Study in Mass Mobilization.* New York: Norton, 1976.

Kotkoff, Vladimir. *Soviet Economy, 1940-1965.* Baltimore, Md.: Dangary Publishing Co., 1961.

Kozlov, G. A., ed. *Political Economy: Socialism.* Moscow: Progress Publishers, 1977.

Krutogolov, M. A. *Talks on Soviet Democracy.* Moscow: Progress Publishers, 1980.

Lavigne, Marie. *The Socialist Economies of the Soviet Union and Europe.* White Plains, N.Y.: International Arts and Sciences Press, 1970.

Liberman, Evsey G. *Economic Methods and the Effectiveness of Production.* White Plains, N.Y.: International Arts and Sciences Press, 1971.

Millar, James R. *The Soviet Economic Experiment.* Urbana, Ill.: University of Illinois Press, 1990.

Moore, Barrington, Jr. *Terror and Progess—USSR: Some Sources of Change and Stability in the Soviet Dictatorship.* Cambridge, Mass.: Harvard University Press, 1954.

Nove, Alec. *The Soviet Economy.* New York: Praeger, 1961.

Ofer, Gur. "Soviet Economic Growth: 1928-1985," *Journal of Economic Literature* 25(4): 1767-1833, December 1987.

Perfilyev, M. *Soviet Democracy and Bourgeois Sovietology.* Moscow: Progress Publishers, n.d.

Pipes, Richard, ed. *Revolutionary Russia.* Cambridge, Mass.: Harvard University Press, 1968.

Rush, Myron. *Political Succession in the USSR.* New York: Columbia University Press, 1965.

Salisbury, Harrison. *Black Night, White Snow: Russia's Revolutions, 1905-1917.* New York: Doubleday, 1978.

Schroeder, Gertrude E. "The Soviet Economy on a Treadmill of 'Reforms.'" In Joint Economic Committee, U.S. Congress, *Soviet Economy in a Time of Change,* Washington, D.C.: U.S. Government Printing Office, 1979.

Shaffer, Harry G., ed. *The Soviet System in Theory and Practice: Western and Soviet Views.* New York: Frederick Ungar, 1984.

Shahnazarov, G. *Socialist Democracy.* Moscow: Progress Publishers, 1974.

Shanor, Donald R. *Soviet Europe.* New York: Harper and Row, 1975.

Sharpe, Myron E., ed. *Planning, Profit and Incentives in the U.S.S.R.,* two volumes. White Plains, N.Y.: International Arts and Sciences Press, 1966.

Shvyrkov, Yu M. *Centralized Planning of the Economy.* Moscow: Progress Publishers, 1980.

Simis, Konstantin. *USSR—The Corrupt Society: The Secret World of Soviet Capitalism.* New York: Simon and Schuster, 1982.

Smith, Hedrick. *The Russians.* New York: Quadrangle, 1976.

Spulber, Nicholas. *The Soviet Economy: Structure, Principles and Problems.* New York: Norton, 1962.

————, ed. *Foundations of Soviet Strategy for Economic Growth.* Bloomington: Indiana University Press, 1964.

Towster, Julian. *Political Power in the U.S.S.R., 1917-1947.* New York: Oxford University Press, 1948.

Tucker, Robert C., ed. *Stalinism: Essays in Historical Interpretation.* New York: Norton, 1977.

Voslensky, Michael. *Nomenklatura: The Soviet Ruling Class—An Insider's Report.* Garden City, N.Y.: Doubleday, 1984.

Wilczynski, J. *Socialist Economic Development and Reforms.* London: Macmillan, 1972.

Wiles, Peter J. D. *The Political Economy of Communism.* Cambridge, Mass.: Harvard University Press, 1962.

Yanowitch, Murray, comp. *Contemporary Soviet Economics: A Collection of Readings from Soviet Sources,* two volumes. White Plains, N.Y.: International Arts and Sciences Press, 1969.

Yun, Oleg. *Improvement of Soviet Economic Planning.* Moscow: Progress Publishers, 1988.

Zauberman, Alfred. *Aspects of Planometrics.* New Haven: Yale University Press, 1967.

I. E. Soviet and Eastern European Socialism: Recent Developments

The pace of political and economic change in the former U.S.S.R. and Eastern Europe over the last decade has been dizzying, and what will finally emerge out of this turbulent and difficult period is still highly uncertain. The journalistic literature on the subject, although up to date, tends to be anecdotal and inconclusive—while the professional literature tends to be quite dated by the time it finally appears in print. But despite these shortcomings, there is certainly no shortage of either journalistic or professional literature—as the following list suggests. This list of illustrative references is confined entirely to the economic transitions, as opposed to the political transitions.

Adam, Jan. *Economic Reform in the Soviet Union and Eastern Europe Since the 1960s.* New York: St. Martin's Press, 1989.

Aganbegyan, Abel. *Inside Perestroika: The Future of the Soviet Economy.* New York: Harper, 1989.

Arkhipov, R. V., et al. "The Path to Privatization," *Problems of Economics* 34(8): 23-34, December 1991.

Aslund, Anders. *How Russia Became a Market Economy.* Washington: Brookings, 1995.

———, ed. *Market Socialism or the Restoration of Capitalism?* New York: Cambridge University Press, 1992.

Aslund, Anders, and Richard Layard, eds. *Changing the Economic System in Russia.* New York: St. Martin's Press, 1993.

Baldassarri, Mario, Luigi Paganetto, and Edmund S. Phelps, eds. *Privatization Processes in Eastern Europe: Theoretical Foundations and Empirical Results.* New York: St. Martin's Press, 1993.

Bergson, Abram. "The USSR Before the Fall: How Poor and Why," *Journal of Economic Perspectives* 5(4): 29-44, Fall 1991.

Bim, Alexander S., Derek C. Jones, and Thomas Weisskopf. "Hybrid Forms of Enterprise Organization in the Former USSR and Russian Federation," *Comparative Economic Studies* 35(1): 1-38, Spring 1993.

Bird, Graham, ed. *Economic Reform in Eastern Europe.* Brookfield, Vt.: Ashgate, 1992.

Blanchard, Olivier, et al. *Post-Communist Reform: Pain and Progress.* Cambridge, Mass.: MIT Press, 1993.

Boycko, Maxim, Andrei Shleifer, and Robert Vishny. *Privatizing Russia.* Cambridge, Mass.: MIT Press, 1995.

Brus, Wlodzimierz. *From Marx to the Market: Socialism in Search of an Economic System.* New York: Oxford University Press, 1989.

Buck, Trevor, Igor Filatotchev, and Mike Wright. "Employee Buyouts and the Transformation of Russian Industry," *Comparative Economic Studies* 36(2): 1-16, Summer 1994.

Campbell, Robert W. *The Socialist Economies in Transition: A Primer on Semi-Reformed Systems*. Bloomington, Indiana: Indiana University Press, 1991.

Clague, Christopher, and Gordon C. Rausser, eds. *The Emergence of Market Economies in Eastern Europe*. Cambridge, Mass.: Blackwell, 1992.

Claudon, Michael P., and Tamar Gutner, eds. *Comrades Go Private: Strategies for Eastern European Privatization*. New York: New York University Press, 1992.

Desai, Padma. *Perestroika in Perspective*. Princeton, N.J.: Princeton University Press, 1989.

Earle, John S., Roman Frydman, and Andrzej Rapaczynski, eds. *Privatization in the Transition to a Market Economy: Studies of Preconditions and Policies in Eastern Europe*. New York: St. Martin's Press, 1993.

Ellman, Michael, ed. "System Change in Eastern Europe: Lessons of the First Four Years," *Journal of Comparative Economics* 19(1): 1-116, August 1994.

Farrell, John P., ed. "The Economic Transition in Eastern Europe," *Comparative Economic Studies* 33(2): 1-177, Summer 1991.

Frydman, Roman, and Andrzej Rapaczynski. "Privatization in Eastern Europe: Is the State Withering Away?" *Finance and Development* 30(2): 10-13, June 1993.

Gabrisch, Hubert, ed. *Economic Reforms in Eastern Europe and the Soviet Union*. Boulder, Col.: Westview Press, 1989.

Gregory, Paul R., and Robert C. Stuart. *Soviet Economic Structure and Performance*, fourth edition. New York: Harper and Row, 1990.

Hewett, Edward A. *Reforming the Soviet Economy: Equality Versus Efficiency*. Washington, D.C.: Brookings Institution, 1988.

Johnson, Simon, and Heidi Kroll. "Managerial Strategies for Spontaneous Privatization," *Soviet Economy* 7(4): 281-316, October-December 1991.

Jones, Anthony. *Perestroika and the Economy: New Thinking in Soviet Economics*. Armonk, N.Y.: M. E. Sharpe, 1989.

Jones, Anthony, and William Moskoff, eds. *The Great Market Debate in Soviet Economics: An Anthology*. Armonk, N.Y.: M. E. Sharpe, 1991.

Keren, Michael, and Gur Ofer, eds. *Trials of Transition: Economic Reform in the Former Communist Bloc*. Boulder, Col.: Westview, 1992.

Linz, Susan J., ed. "A Symposium on Reorganization and Reform in the Soviet Economy." *Comparative Economic Studies* 29(4): 1-172, Winter 1987.

Mezhenkov, Vladimir, and Eva Skelley, ed. *Perestroika in Action: A Collection of Press Articles and Reviews*. Moscow: Progress Publishers, 1988.

Mikiforov, L., and T. Kuznetsova. "Conceptual Foundations of Destatization and Privatization," *Problems of Economics* 34(7): 6-24, November 1991.

Milor, Vedat, ed. *Changing Political Economies: Privatization in Post-Communist and Reforming Communist States*. Boulder, Col.: Rienner, 1994.

Murrell, Peter, ed. "Symposium on Economic Transition in the Soviet Union and Eastern Europe." *Journal of Economic Perspectives* 5(4): 3-227, Fall 1991.

Murrell, Peter, and Yijiang Wang. "When Privatization Should Be Delayed: The Effect of Communist Legacies on Organizational and Institutional Reforms," *Journal of Comparative Economics* 17(2): 385-406, June 1993.

Nelson, Lynn D., and Irina Y. Kuzes. "Evaluating the Russian Voucher Privatization Program," *Comparative Economic Studies* 36(1): 55-68, Spring 1994.

Peck, Merton J, and Thomas J. Richardson, eds. *What Is To Be Done? Proposals for the Soviet Transition to the Market*. New Haven: Yale University Press, 1991.

Roland, Gerard. "The Political Economy of Restructuring and Privatization in Eastern Europe," *European Economic Review* 37(2-3): 533-540, April 1993.

Sachs, Jeffrey D. "Privatization in Russia: Some Lessons from Eastern Europe," *American Economic Review* 82(2): 43-48, May 1992.

Shlapentokh, Vladimir. "Privatization Debates in Russia: 1989-1992," *Comparative Economic Studies* 35(2): 19-32, Summer 1993.

Smith, Hedrick. *The New Russians*. New York: Random House, 1990.

Tedstrom, John E., ed. *Socialism, Perestroika, and the Dilemmas of Soviet Economic Reform*. Boulder, Col.: Westview, 1990.

Van Brabant, Jozef M. *Privatizing Eastern Europe: The Role of Markets and Ownership in the Transition*. Norwell, Mass.: Kluwer Academic Press, 1992.

Van Brabant, Jozef M. "Lessons from the Wholesale Transformations in the East," *Comparative Economic Studies* 35(4): 73-102, Winter 1993.

Vasiliev, D. "The Russian Privatization Program," *Problems of Economic Transition* 36(4): 15-26, August 1993.

Weisskopf, Thomas E. "Russia in Transition: Perils of the Fast Track to Capitalism," *Challenge* 35(6): 28-37, Nov.-Dec. 1992.

Wessel, Robert H. "Privatization in the Former Soviet Union—One Year Later," *Business Economics* 28(1): 31-34, January 1993.

Winiecki, Jan. *Post-Soviet-Type Economies in Transition.* Brookfield, Vt.: Ashgate, 1993.

I. F. Chinese Socialism: Historical Perspective

The references in this section pertain mostly to the "classical socialist period" in modern Chinese economic history (approximately 1950 to 1975). A few illustrative references are also provided on history and the political situation. Of course, such a traumatic experience of radical social leveling as the Cultural Revolution of the 1960s had a tremendously adverse effect on economic performance.

Axilrod, Eric. *The Political Economy of the Chinese Revolution.* Hong Kong: Union Research Institute, 1972.

Barnett, A. Doak. *Cadres, Bureaucracy and Political Power in Communist China.* New York: Columbia University Press, 1967.

Barnouin, Barbara. *Ten Years of Turbulence: The Chinese Cultural Revolution.* New York: Kegan Paul International, 1993.

Chen, Nai-Ruenn, and Walter Galenson. *The Chinese Economy under Communism.* Chicago: Aldine, 1969.

Chow, Gregory C. *The Chinese Economy.* New York: Harper and Row, 1985.

Delayne, Jan. *The Chinese Economy.* New York: Harper and Row, 1973.

Hoffman, Charles. *Work Incentive Practices and Policies in the People's Republic of China, 1953-1965.* Albany: State University of New York Press, 1967.

Howard, Roger. *Mao Tse-Tung and the Chinese People.* New York: Monthly Review Press, 1977.

Howe, Christopher, and Kenneth R. Walker, eds. *The Foundations of the Chinese Planned Economy: A Documentary Survey, 1953-1965.* Basingstoke, U.K.: Macmillan, 1989.

Karol, K. S. *The Second Chinese Revolution.* New York: Hill and Wang, 1974.

Luo, Zi-ping. *A Generation Lost: China under the Cultural Revolution.* New York: Avon, 1991.

MacFarquhar, Roderick. *The Origins of the Cultural Revolution. 1. Contradictions among the People, 1956-57.* New York: Columbia University Press, 1974.

————. *The Origins of the Cultural Revolution. 2. The Great Leap Forward, 1958-1960.* New York: Columbia University Press, 1983.

————, ed. *The Politics of China, 1949-1989.* New York: Cambridge University Press, 1993.

Myers, Ramon H. *The Chinese Economy: Past and Present.* Belmont, Cal.: Wadsworth, 1980.

Prybyla, Jan S. *The Chinese Economy: Problems and Policies,* second revised edition. Columbia: University of South Carolina Press, 1981.

Rice, Edward E. *Mao's Way.* Berkeley, Cal.: University of California Press, 1972.

Robottom, John. *Twentieth Century China.* New York: G. P. Putnam's Sons, 1971.

Selden, Mark. *The Political Economy of Chinese Socialism.* Armonk, N.Y.: M. E. Sharpe, 1988.

————. *The Political Economy of Chinese Development.* Armonk, N.Y.: M. E. Sharpe, 1993.

Wei, Yung, ed. *Communist China: A System-Functional Reader.* Columbus, Oh.: Charles E. Merrill, 1972.

I. G. Chinese Socialism: Recent Developments

Over the past 15 years, the socialist economic system of the People's Republic of China has undergone a dramatic transformation, as documented by the following list of illustrative references. In many ways, the reformed Chinese socialist system resembles a market socialist system roughly along the lines proposed in this book. In addition, at the moment the Chinese economy is generally considered to be "dynamic." Unfortunately, China cannot be held up as an exemplar of profit-oriented market socialism for at least three reasons: (1) its economic performance will be lackluster into the foreseeable future owing simply to the drag of its huge population; (2) its political system remains highly undemocratic; (3) there are numerous specific divergences between the Chinese market socialist system and the profit-oriented market socialist system proposed herein (e.g., in China, the net revenues of publicly owned enterprises are not distributed to the population as a social dividend supplement to labor income, as they would be under profit-oriented market socialism).

Byrd, William A. *The Market Mechanism and Economic Reforms in China.* Armonk, N.Y.: Sharpe, 1991.

————, ed. *Chinese Industrial Firms under Reform.* New York: Oxford University Press, 1992.

Byrd, William A., and Qingsong Lin, eds. *China's Rural Industry: Structure, Development, and Reform.* New York: Oxford University Press, 1990.

Chang, David W. *China under Deng Xiaoping: Political and Economic Reform.* New York: St. Martin's Press, 1988.

Chen, Kang, Gary H. Jefferson, and Inderjit Singh. "Lessons from China's Economic Reform," *Journal of Comparative Economics* 16(2): 201-225, June 1992.

Dorn, James A. and Xi Wang, eds. *Economic Reform in China: Problems and Prospects.* Chicago: University of Chicago Press, 1990.

Fan, Qimiao, and Peter Nolan, eds. *China's Economic Reforms: The Costs and Benefits of Incrementalism.* New York: St. Martin's Press, 1994.

Gordon, Myron J. "China's Path to Market Socialism," *Challenge* 35(1): 53-56, Jan.-Feb. 1992.

Guo, Jiann-Jong. *Price Reform in China, 1979-86.* New York: St. Martin's Press, 1992.

Jefferson, Gary W., and Wenyi Xu. "The Impact of Reform on Socialist Enterprises in Transition: Structure, Conduct, and Performance in Chinese Industry," *Journal of Comparative Economics* 15(1): 45-64, March 1991.

Jefferson, Gary W., and Thomas G. Rawski. "Enterprise Reform in Chinese Industry," *Journal of Economic Perspectives* 8(2): 47-70, Spring 1994.

Nolan, Peter. *The Political Economy of Collective Farms: An Analysis of Chinese Post-Mao Reforms.* Boulder, Col.: Westview, 1988.

Nolan, Peter, and Fureng Dong, eds. *The Chinese Economy and Its Future: Achievements and Problems in Post-Mao Reform.* Cambridge, Mass.: Blackwell, 1990.

Perkins, Dwight. "Completing China's Move to the Market," *Journal of Economic Perspectives* 8(2): 23-46, Spring 1994.

————. "Reforming China's Economic System," *Journal of Economic Literature* 26(2): 601-645, June 1988.

Putterman, Louis. *Continuity and Change in China's Rural Development: Collective and Reform Eras in Perspective.* New York: Oxford University Press, 1993.

Putterman, Louis, and Bingyuang Hsiung. "Pre- and Post-reform Income Distribution in a Chinese Commune: The Case of Dahe Township in Hebei Province," *Journal of Comparative Economics* 13(3): 406-445, September 1989.

Reynolds, Bruce L., ed. *Chinese Economic Reform: How Far, How Fast?* San Diego: Academic Press, 1988.

World Bank. *Macroeconomic Stability and Industrial Growth under Decentralized Socialism.* Washington: Author, 1990.

————. *China: Reform and the Role of the Plan in the 1990s.* Washington: Author, 1992.

I. H. Regulation and Public Ownership: Historical Perspective

The following list of references pertains to the nature and traditionally perceived purposes of public regulation or ownership of production enterprises within economies that remain "mostly" capitalistic—by that meaning that the great majority of production enterprises remain privately owned, are operated for profit, and are subjected to a relatively limited amount of regulation by public agencies.

Aharoni, Yair. *The Evolution and Management of State-Owned Enterprises.* Cambridge, Mass.: Ballinger, 1986.

Bailey, Elizabeth E. *Economic Theory of Regulatory Constraint.* Lexington, Mass.: Lexington Books, 1973.

Baumol, William J., ed. *Public and Private Enterprise in a Mixed Economy.* New York: St. Martin's Press, 1980.

Bös, Dieter. *Public Enterprise Economics: Theory and Application.* Amsterdam: North-Holland, 1986.

Crew, M. A., and Paul R. Kleindorfer. *Public Utility Economics.* New York: St. Martin's, 1979.

Lewis, Ben. *British Planning and Nationalization.* New York: Twentieth Century Fund, 1952.

Kelf-Cohen, Rolf. *British Nationalization: 1945-1973.* New York: St. Martin's, 1973.

Nove, Alec. *Efficiency Criteria for Nationalized Industries.* Toronto: University of Toronto Press, 1973.

Pegrum, Dudley F. *Public Regulation of Business,* revised edition. Homewood, Ill.: Irwin, 1965.

Pryke, Richard. *Public Enterprise in Practice.* New York: St. Martin's Press, 1971.

————. *The Nationalized Industries: Policies and Performance Since 1968.* Oxford: Martin Robertson, 1981.

Reid, Graham, and Kevin Allen. *Nationalized Industries*. Harmondsworth, U.K.: Penguin, 1970.

Robson, William A. *Nationalized Industry and Public Ownership*, second edition. London: Allen and Unwin, 1962.

Shepherd, William G. *Economic Performance Under Public Ownership*. New Haven: Yale University Press, 1965.

————. *Public Enterprise: Economic Analysis of Theory and Practice*. Lexington, Mass.: Lexington Books, 1976.

Weiss, Leonard W. "State Regulation of Public Utilities and Marginal-Cost Pricing." In Leonard Weiss and Michael Klass, eds., *Case Studies in Regulation: Revolution and Reform*, Boston: Little, Brown, 1981.

Wilcox, Clair. *Public Policies Toward Business*, second (revised) edition. Homewood, Ill.: Irwin, 1960.

Wiseman, Jack. "Guidelines for Public Enterprise: A British Experiment," *Southern Economic Journal* 30(1): 39-48, July 1963.

I. I. Regulation and Public Ownership: Recent Developments

The renaissance of laissez faire over the last two decades is documented by the following list of illustrative references. In addition to description and assessment of real-world deregulation and privatization, the list includes some important intellectual milestones in the rightward swing of the pendulum of social opinion. These include the negative appraisals of regulation by George Stigler (1971), Richard Posner (1974), and Sam Peltzman (1976), as well as a survey by Thomas Borcherding et al. of numerous studies on the performance of public enterprise (1982), most of which suggested the relative inefficiency of public enterprise relative to private enterprise. With respect to the Borcherding et al. survey, it is interesting to note that despite the apparent preponderance of evidence, the authors were reluctant to conclude that public enterprise is actually as inefficient as suggested by most of these studies, and that privatization is actually a desirable course of action in terms of social welfare. Be that as it may, privatization, as well as deregulation, are currently rolling forward like veritable juggernauts.

Bailey, Elizabeth E., David R. Graham, and Daniel P. Kaplan. *Deregulating the Airlines*. Cambridge, Mass.: MIT Press, 1985.

Beesley, Michael E. *Privatization, Regulation and Deregulation*. New York: Routledge, 1992.

Borcherding, Thomas E., Werner W. Pommerehne, and Friedrich Schneider. "Comparing the Efficiency of Private and Public Production:

The Evidence from Five Countries." *Zeitshrift für Nationalökonomie*, Sup. 2: 127-156, 1982.

Bös, Dieter. *Privatization: A Theoretical Treatment*. New York: Oxford University Press, 1991.

Button, Kenneth, ed. *Airline Deregulation: International Experiences*. New York: New York University Press, 1991.

Button, Kenneth, and Dennis Swann, eds. *The Age of Regulatory Reform*. New York: Oxford University Press, 1989.

Carbajo, Jose, ed. *Regulatory Reform in Transport: Some Recent Experiences*. Washington: World Bank, 1993.

Dempsey, Paul Stephen. *The Social and Economic Consequences of Deregulation: The Transportation Industry in Transition*. Westport, Ct.: Quorum Books, 1989.

Dempsey, Paul Stephen, and Andrew R. Goetz. *Airline Deregulation and Laissez-Faire Mythology*. Westport, Ct.: Quorum Books, 1992.

DiIulio, John J., Jr., ed. *Deregulating the Public Service: Can Government Be Improved?* Washington: Brookings Institution, 1994.

Donahue, John D. *The Privatization Decision: Public Ends, Private Means*. New York: Basic Books, 1989.

Foster, Christopher D. *Privatization, Public Ownership and the Regulation of Natural Monopoly*. Cambridge: Blackwell, 1992.

Gayle, Dennis, J. and Jonathan N. Goodrich, eds. *Privatization and Deregulation in Global Perspective*. Westport, Ct.: Quorum Books, 1990.

Gomez-Ibanez, Jose A., and John R. Meyer. *Going Private: The International Experience with Transport Privatization*. Washington: Brookings Institution, 1993.

Martin, Brendan. *In the Public Interest? Privatization and Public Sector Reform*. Atlantic Highlands, N.J.: Zed Books, 1993.

Ott, Attiat F., and Keith Hartley, eds. *Privatization and Economic Efficiency: A Comparative Analysis of Developed and Developing Countries*. Brookfield, Vermont: Elgar, 1991.

Peltzman, Sam. "Toward a More General Theory of Regulation." *Journal of Law and Economics* 19(2): 211-240, August 1976.

Posner, Richard A. "Theories of Economic Regulation." *Bell Journal of Economics and Management Science* 4(2): 335-358, Fall 1974.

Ramanadham, V. V. *The Economics of Public Enterprise*. New York: Routledge, 1991.

———. *Constraints and Impacts of Privatization*. New York: Routledge, 1993.

Rose-Ackerman, Susan. *Rethinking the Progressive Agenda: The Reform of the American Regulatory State*. New York: Free Press, 1992.

Shirley, Mary, and John Nellis. *Public Enterprise Reform: The Lessons of Experience*. Washington: World Bank, 1991.

Stigler, George. "The Theory of Economic Regulation." *Bell Journal of Economics and Management Science* 2(1): 3-21, Spring 1971.

Suleiman, Ezra N., and John Waterbury, eds. *The Political Economy of Public Sector Reform and Privatization*. Boulder, Col.: Westview, 1990.

Tye, William B. *The Transition to Deregulation: Developing Economic Standards for Public Policies*. Westport, Ct.: Quorum Books, 1991.

Vickers, John, and George Yarrow. "Economic Perspectives on Privatization," *Journal of Economic Perspectives* 5(2): 111-132, Spring 1991.

Whitfield, Dexter. *The Welfare State: Privatization, Deregulation, Commercialization of Public Services*. Boulder, Col.: Westview Press, 1992.

World Bank. *Bureaucrats in Business: The Economics and Politics of Government Ownership*. Washington: Author, 1995.

I. J. Illustrative General Capitalist Apologetics

Much of the material listed in the foregoing sections is implicitly apologetic of capitalism, because it dwells upon dysfunctional social conditions (e.g., Soviet totalitarianism during the Stalinist period) that are associated in some way with socialism. But while the readers immersed in these dysfunctional conditions might understandably conclude that socialism is inferior to capitalism, there is no open and explicit effort made by the authors to foster this conclusion. The present section lists some references which are different in being more openly and directly apologetic of capitalism. Included herein are such classic nineteenth- and early twentieth-century assaults on Marxist political economy as Eugen von Böhm-Bawerk (1884, 1889, 1896, 1921), John Bates Clark (1899), and William Hurrell Mallock (1908). Efforts by contemporary Marxists such as John E. Roemer to update and rectify the Marxist critique of capitalism have been met by updated and rectified refutations of the Marxist critique by contemporary anti-Marxists such as N. Scott Arnold (1990) and David Gordon (1990).

In some ways, the earlier critiques of Marxism in particular and socialism in general are more logical and focused than later critiques, because the waters had not yet been muddied by the real and perceived problems of real-world Communistic socialism and real-world social democratic socialism. For example, the twentieth century condemnations of socialism by the Austrian school luminaries Ludwig von Mises (1920, 1943, 1944, 1951, 1956) and Friedrich Hayek (1935, 1944, 1988) are strongly influenced by the Soviet central planning effort, and are therefore mostly off-target as far as market socialism is concerned. Closely aligned with the classic Austrian school critique of socialism provided by Mises and Hayek is the explicitly anti-Communist literature exemplified by Harry and Bonaro Overstreet (1958), Roy Cadwell (1962), and William Ebenstein (1964). This literature makes much of an alleged (or implied) causative relationship between capitalism on the one hand and freedom and democracy on the other. On this particular relationship, see also Joseph Schumpeter (1942) and Milton Friedman (1962).

Also included in the following list are some examples of "implicit" capitalist apologetics—works which do not comment directly on the capitalism versus socialism question, but which by some manner or means suggest or imply that capitalism has essential virtues which socialism could not possibly emulate. The most important of these virtues is entrepreneurship. The modern cult of the discovering, innovating, risk-taking, and generally heroic entrepreneur was commenced by Frank Knight (1921), and has been carried forward in the contemporary period most notably by Israel Kirzner (1973, 1979, 1985, 1989). For an example of how the cult of the entrepreneur plays out "on the street," see Scott Witt (1979). A second example is provided by the property rights literature, exemplified by Furubotn and Pejovich (1972, 1974): capitalism respects property rights but socialism would not. A third example is provided by the cautionary literature on saving, exemplied by Kotlikoff (1984, 1989) and Seidman (1989): capitalism provides essential incentives to saving but socialism would not. A fourth example is provided by the pejorative literature on bureaucracy, exemplified by Mises (1943, 1944) and Niskanen (1971, 1975): capitalism keeps bureaucracy to a tolerable level—but under socialism bureaucracy would presumably run rampant.

Arnold, N. Scott. *Marx's Radical Critique of Capitalist Society: A Reconstruction and Critical Evaluation.* New York: Oxford University Press, 1990.

Böhm-Bawerk, Eugen von. *Capital and Interest. I. History and Critique of Interest Theories. II. Positive Theory of Capital. III. Further Essays on Capital and Interest.* South Holland, Ill.: Libertarian Press, 1959. Originally published in German in 1884 (I), 1889 (II), and

1921 (III).

————. *Karl Marx and the Close of His System*. Edited with an introduction by Paul M. Sweezy. New York: Augustus M. Kelley, 1949. Reprinted Philadelphia: Orion Editions, 1984. Originally published in German in 1896.

Cadwell, Roy. *Communism in the Modern World*. New York: Dorrance, 1962.

Clark, John Bates. *The Distribution of Wealth: A Theory of Wages, Interest and Profits*. New York: Macmillan, 1899.

Ebenstein, William. *Two Ways of Life: The Communist Challenge to Democracy*. New York: Holt, Rinehart and Winston, 1964.

Friedman, Milton. *Capitalism and Freedom*. Chicago: University of Chicago Press, 1962.

Furubotn, Eirik, and Svetozar Pejovich. "Property Rights and Economic Theory: A Survey of Recent Literature." *Journal of Economic Literature* 10(4): 1137-1162, December 1972.

————, eds. *The Economics of Property Rights*. Cambridge, Mass.: Ballinger, 1974.

Gordon, David. *Resurrecting Marx: The Analytical Marxists on Freedom, Exploitation and Justice*. New Brunswick, N.J.: Transaction Books, 1990.

Hayek, Friedrich, ed. *Collectivist Economic Planning: Critical Studies on the Possibilities of Socialism*. London: George Routledge and Sons, 1935. Reprinted New York: Augustus M. Kelley, 1975. (Hayek's contributions: "The Nature and History of the Problem" and "The Present State of the Debate.")

————. *The Road to Serfdom*. Chicago: University of Chicago Press, 1944.

————. *The Fatal Conceit: The Errors of Socialism*, edited by W. W. Bartley III. Chicago: University of Chicago Press, 1988.

Kirzner, Israel M. *Competition and Entrepreneurship*. Chicago: University of Chicago Press, 1973.

————. *Perception, Opportunity and Profit: Studies in the Theory of Entrepreneurship*. Chicago: University of Chicago Press, 1979.

————. *Discovery and the Capitalist Process*. Chicago: University of Chicago Press, 1985.

————. *Discovery, Capitalism, and Distributive Justice*. New York: Basil Blackwell, 1989.

Knight, Frank. *Risk, Uncertainty and Profit*. Boston: Houghton Mifflin, 1921.

Kotlikoff, Lawrence J. "Taxation and Savings: A Neoclassical Perspective." *Journal of Economic Literature* 22(4): 1576-1629, December 1984.

———. *What Determines Savings?* Cambridge, Mass.: MIT Press, 1989.

Mallock, William Hurrell. *A Critical Examination of Socialism.* New Brunswick, N.J.: Transaction Publishers, 1989. Originally published in 1908.

Mises, Ludwig von. "Economic Calculation in the Socialist Commonwealth." In Friedrich Hayek, ed., *Collectivist Economic Planning*, London: George Routledge and Sons, 1935. Originally published in German in 1920.

———. *Bureaucracy.* New Haven: Yale University Press, 1943.

———. *Omnipotent Government.* New Haven: Yale University Press, 1944.

———. *Socialism: An Economic and Sociological Analysis*, revised English edition. London: Jonathan Cape, 1951.

———. *The Anti-Capitalist Mentality.* New York: Van Nostrand, 1956.

———. *Human Action: A Treatise on Economics*, third revised edition. Chicago: Henry Regnery, 1966.

Niskanen, William A., Jr. *Bureaucracy and Representative Government.* Chicago: Aldine-Atherton, 1971.

———. "Bureaucrats and Politicians," *Journal of Law and Economics* 18(3): 617-643, December 1975.

Overstreet, Harry, and Bonaro Overstreet. *What We Must Know about Communism.* New York: Norton, 1958.

Schumpeter, Joseph. *Capitalism, Socialism and Democracy.* New York: Harper and Bros., 1942.

Seidman, Laurence S. *Saving for America's Economic Future: Parables and Policies.* Armonk, N.Y.: M. E. Sharpe, 1989.

Sims, Edwin C. *Capitalism: In Spite of It All.* New York: Gordon and Breach, 1989.

Witt, Scott. *How Self-Made Millionaires Build Their Fortunes.* West Nyack, N.Y.: Parker Pub. Co., 1979.

II. Market Socialism: Proposals and Appraisals

II. A. Langian Market Socialism
The significance of Oskar Lange's contribution may be gauged from the fact that almost all college textbooks for courses in comparative

economic systems contain at least several pages of explicit discussion of the concept of market socialism, covering at a minimum Lange's seminal contribution. Several representative textbooks are included in the following list: George Halm (1960), Richard Carson (1973), Egon Neuberger and William Duffy (1976), Allan Gruchy (1977), Wayne Leeman (1977), Vaclav Holesovsky (1977), Andrew Zimbalist and Howard Sherman (1984), Gary Pickersgill and Joyce Pickersgill (1985), Morris Bornstein (1985), John Elliott (1985), Paul Gregory and Robert Stuart (1985), and H. Stephen Gardner (1988). Although there has never developed a flourishing professional journal literature on the Langian proposal such as that on the pure theory of the cooperative, commentaries or analyses more or less closely focused on the original Lange proposal continue to appear sporadically. Some examples include Abram Bergson (1948, 1967), James Yunker (1971, 1973), Paul Craig Roberts (1971), Nicholas Spulber (1972), George Feiwel (1972), Egon Neuberger (1973), Deborah Milenkovitch (1984), Tadeusz Kowalik (1991), and Joseph Persky (1991). Much more abundant is the literature which has been tangentially affected by Lange. Some studies in the pure theory of welfare economics or public enterprise economics have appropriated Langian nomenclature: Abba Lerner's 1944 treatise on welfare economics falls into this category. And many contributions to the economics of socialism published since the latter 1930s, while not particularly oriented to Lange, nevertheless manifest some of his influence, more or less, as the case may be. Examples include Henry Dickinson (1939), Burnham Beckwith (1949, 1974, 1978), Trygve Hoff (1949), and Henry Smith (1962).

Beckwith, Burnham P. *The Economic Theory of a Socialist Economy.* Stanford, Cal.: Stanford University Press, 1949.

———. *Liberal Socialism: The Pure Welfare Economics of a Liberal Socialist Economy.* New York: Exposition Press, 1974.

———. *Liberal Socialism Applied: The Applied Welfare Economics of a Liberal Socialist Economy.* Palo Alto, Cal.: Author, 1978.

Bergson, Abram. "Socialist Economics." In Howard Ellis, ed., *A Survey of Contemporary Economics,* Philadelphia: Blakiston, 1948.

———. "Market Socialism Revisited," *Journal of Political Economy* 75(5): 655-673, October 1967.

Bornstein, Morris, ed. Part II: "Socialist Market Economy." In *Comparative Economic Systems: Models and Cases*, fifth edition. Homewood, Ill.: Irwin, 1985.

Carson, Richard L. Chapter 19: "Traditional Market Socialism: Structure and Functioning." In *Comparative Economic Systems.* New York:

Macmillan, 1973.

Dickinson, Henry D. *Economics of Socialism*. London: Oxford University Press, 1939.

Elliott, John E. Chapter 15: "The Economic Theory of Decentralized Socialism." In *Comparative Economic Systems*, second edition. Belmont, Cal.: Wadsworth, 1985.

Feiwel, George R. "On the Economic Theory of Socialism: Some Reflections on Lange's Contribution," *Kyklos* 25(3): 601-618, 1972.

Gardner, H. Stephen. Chapter 10 section: "Lange's Theory of Market Socialism." In *Comparative Economic Systems*. Chicago: Dryden Press, 1988.

Gregory, Paul R., and Robert C. Stuart. Chapter 5 section: "Market Socialism: Theoretical Foundations." In *Comparative Economic Systems*, second edition. Boston: Houghton Mifflin, 1985.

Halm, George N. Part 5: "The Economic Theory of Liberal Socialism." In *Economic Systems: A Comparative Analysis*. New York: Holt, Rinehart and Winston, 1960.

Hoff, Trygve J. B. *Economic Calculation in the Socialist Society*. London: William Hodge, 1949.

Holesovsky, Vaclav. Chapter 6 section: "The Lange Model." In *Economic Systems: Analysis and Comparison*. New York: McGraw-Hill, 1977.

Kowalik, Tadeusz. "Oskar Lange's Market Socialism," *Dissent*, 86-95, Winter 1991.

Lange, Oskar. "On the Economic Theory of Socialism," *Review of Economic Studies* 4(1): 53-71, October 1936, and 4(2): 123-142, February 1937. Published in book form with contributions by Benjamin Lippincott, ed., and Fred M. Taylor: University of Minnesota Press, 1938. Reprinted by McGraw-Hill, 1964.

Leeman, Wayne A. Part II: "Market Socialism." In *Centralized and Decentralized Economic Systems*. Chicago: Rand McNally, 1977.

Lerner, Abba. *The Economics of Control*. New York: Macmillan, 1944.

Milenkovitch, Deborah D. "Is Market Socialism Efficient?" In Andrew Zimbalist, ed., *Comparative Economic Systems: An Assessment of Knowledge, Theory and Method*, Boston: Kluwer-Nijhoff, 1984.

Neuberger, Egon. "The Plan and the Market: The Models of Oskar Lange." *American Economist* 17(2): 153-158, Fall 1973.

Neuberger, Egon, and William J. Duffy. Chapter 8: "The Plan and the Market: The Models of Oskar Lange." In *Comparative Economic Systems: A Decision-Making Approach*. Boston: Allyn and Bacon,

1976.

Persky, Joseph. "Lange and von Mises: Large-Scale Enterprises, and the Economic Case for Socialism," *Journal of Economic Perspectives* 5(4): 229-236, Fall 1991.

Pickersgill, Gary M., and Joyce E. Pickersgill. Chapter 19: "Traditional Market Socialism: Structure and Functioning." In *Contemporary Economic Systems: A Comparative View*, second edition. St. Paul, Minn.: West Pub. Co., 1985.

Roberts, Paul Craig. "On Oskar Lange's Theory of Planning." *Journal of Political Economy* 79(3): 577-583, May-June 1971.

Spulber, Nicholas. "On Some Issues in the Theory of the Socialist Economy," *Kyklos* 25(4): 715-735, 1972.

Smith, Henry. *The Economics of Socialism Reconsidered*. London: Oxford University Press, 1962.

Yunker, James A. "The Administrative Costs of Langian Socialism." Ph.D. dissertation, Northwestern University, 1971.

———. "An Appraisal of Langian Socialism," *Indian Economic Journal* 20(3): 383-413, January-March 1973.

Zimbalist, Andrew, and Howard J. Sherman. Chapter 14: "The Theory of Market Socialism." In *Comparing Economic Systems: A Political-Economic Approach*. Orlando, Fla.: Academic Press, 1984.

II. B. Cooperative Market Socialism

Benjamin Ward initiated a large technical literature on the economic theory of the production cooperative with a simple model of employee income-maximization in his 1958 *American Economic Review* article, a model later developed in his 1967 textbook on socialist economic theory. The revelation that the basic notion of a cooperative was reasonably amenable to the standard mathematical tools of neoclassical economic theory inspired a snowballing wave of work. Early contributions include Amartya Sen (1966), Evsey Domar (1966), Walter Oi and Elizabeth Clayton (1968), and James Meade (1972). By the late 1970s the technical literature had become sufficiently extensive to support major surveys: Alfred Steinherr (1978), Norman Ireland (1982), and Frederick Pryor (1983). The theoretical literature has continued to flourish and proliferate throughout the 1980s and into the 1990s, as exemplified by the recent symposium on the subject in the *Journal of Comparative Economics* edited by Yehuda Don et al. (1992).

There has also been an extensive empirical literature inspired by the predissolution Yugoslavian economy, plywood companies in the U.S.

Pacific Northwest, Mondragon in the Basque region of Spain, and so on. Examples include Deborah Milenkovitch (1971), Howard Wachtel (1973), Ellen Comisso (1979), Saul Estrin (1983), Stephen R. Sacks (1983), Katrina Berman (1967), Carl Bellas (1971), Ana Johnson and William Whyte (1977), Terry Molner (1984), and Melissa Moye (1993). For additional empirical assessments of labor self-management, see Derek Jones and Jan Svejnar (1982), Frank H. Stephen (1982), and John P. Bonin et al. (1993).

Although the majority of the theoretical and empirical literature on the economic performance of the production cooperative might be described as lukewarm at best, there are indeed a number of important scholars, both economists and otherwise, who have vigorously defended and advocated the concept. Examples include Jacques Drèze (1989, 1993), David Miller (1989, 1991), Alec Nove (1983, 1991), David Schweickart (1987, 1992, 1993), Jaroslav Vanek (1969, 1970, 1971, 1977), and Thomas Weisskopf (1992, 1993).

Bellas, Carl J. *Industrial Democracy and the Worker-Owned Firm: A Study of Twenty-One Plywood Companies in the Pacific Northwest.* New York: Praeger Publishers, 1971.

Berman, Katrina. *Worker-Owned Plywood Firms: An Economic Analysis.* Pullman: Washington State University Press, 1967.

Bonin, John P., Derek C. Jones, and Louis Putterman. "Theoretical and Empirical Studies of Producer Cooperatives: Will the Twain Ever Meet?" *Journal of Economic Literature* 31(3): 1290-1320, September 1993.

Comisso, Ellen T. *Workers' Control Under Plan and Market.* New Haven: Yale University Press, 1979.

Domar, Evsey D. "The Soviet Collective Farm as a Producer Cooperative," *American Economic Review* 56(4): 734-757, September 1966.

Don, Yehuda, Nava Kahana, and Avi Weiss, eds. "Theoretical and Applied Aspects of Labor-Managed Firms," *Journal of Comparative Economics* 16(4): 567-764, December 1992.

Drèze, Jacques H. *Labour Management, Contracts and Capital Markets.* New York: Basil Blackwell, 1989.

———. "Self-Management and Economic Theory: Efficiency, Funding, and Employment," in John Roemer and Pranab Bardhan, eds., *Market Socialism: The Current Debate,* New York: Oxford University Press, 1993.

Estrin, Saul. *Self-Management: Economic Theory and Yugoslav Practice.* Cambridge: Cambridge University Press, 1983.

Horvat, Branko, Mihailo Markovic, and Rusi Supek, eds. *Self-Governing Socialism*. New York: International Arts and Sciences Press, 1975.

Ireland, Norman J. *The Economics of Labor-Managed Enterprises*. New York: St. Martin's Press, 1982.

Johnson, Ana Gutierrez, and William F. Whyte. "The Mondragon System of Worker Production Cooperatives," *Industrial and Labor Relations Review* 31(1): 18-30, October 1977.

Jones, Derek C., and Jan Svejnar, eds. *Participatory and Self-Managed Firms*. Lexington, Mass.: Lexington Books, 1982.

Meade, James E. "The Theory of Labour-Managed Firms and Profit Sharing." *Economic Journal* 83(325): 402-428, March 1972.

Milenkovitch, Deborah D. *Plan and Market in Yugoslav Economic Thought*. New Haven: Yale University Press, 1971.

Miller, David. *Market, State and Community: Theoretical Foundations of Market Socialism*. Oxford: Clarenden Press, 1989.

———. "A Vision of Market Socialism," *Dissent*, 406-414, Summer 1991.

Molner, Terry. "Mondragon: A Third Way," *Review of Social Economy* 42(3): 260-271, December 1984.

Moye, A. Melissa. "Mondragon: Adapting Co-operative Structures to Meet the Demands of a Changing Environment," *Economic and Industrial Democracy* 14(2): 251-276, May 1993.

Nove, Alec. *The Economics of Feasible Socialism*. London: George Allen and Unwin, 1983.

———. *The Economics of Feasible Socialism Revisited*. New York: Harper Collins Academic, 1991.

Oi, Walter Y., and E. M. Clayton. "A Peasant's View of a Soviet Collective Farm," *American Economic Review* 58(1): 37-59, March 1968.

Pryor, Frederick L. "The Economics of Production Cooperatives," *Annals of Public and Cooperative Economy* 54(2): 133-173, June 1983.

Sacks, Stephen R. *Self-Management and Efficiency: Large Corporations in Yugoslavia*. London: Allen and Unwin, 1983.

Schweickart, David. *Capitalism or Worker Control: An Ethical and Economic Appraisal*. New York: Praeger, 1980.

———. "Market Socialist Capitalist Roaders: A Comment on Arnold," *Economics and Philosophy* 3(2): 308-319, October 1987.

———. "A Reply to Arnold's Reply," *Economics and Philosophy* 3(2): 331-334, October 1987.

———. "Socialism, Democracy, Market, Planning: Putting the Pieces Together," *Review of Radical Political Economics* 24(3-4): 29-45,

Fall-Winter 1992.

———. "Economic Democracy: Worthy Socialism That Would Really Work," *Science and Society* 56(1): 9-38, Spring 1992.

———. *Against Capitalism.* New York: Cambridge University Press, 1993.

Sen, Amartya S. "Labour Allocation in a Cooperative Enterprise." *Review of Economic Studies* 33(4): 361-371, October 1966.

Sperry, Charles W. "What Makes Mondragon Work?" *Review of Social Economy* 43(3): 345-356, December 1985.

Steinherr, Alfred. "The Labor-Managed Firm: A Survey of the Economics Literature," *Annals of Public and Cooperative Economy* 49(2): 129-148, April-June 1978.

Stephen, Frank H., ed. *The Performance of Labor-Managed Firms.* New York: St. Martin's Press, 1982.

Vanek, Jaroslav. "Decentralization and Workers' Management: A Theoretical Appraisal." *American Economic Review* 59(5): 1006-1014, December 1969.

———. *The General Theory of Labor-Managed Market Economics.* Ithaca: N.Y.: Cornell University Press, 1970.

———. *The Participatory Economy.* Ithaca, N.Y.: Cornell University Press, 1971.

———. *The Labor-Managed Economy: Essays.* Ithaca, N.Y.: Cornell University Press, 1977.

Wachtel, Howard M. *Workers' Management and Workers' Wages in Yugoslavia.* Ithaca, N.Y.: Cornell University Press, 1973.

Ward, Benjamin. "The Firm in Illyria: Market Syndicalism." *American Economic Review* 48(3): 566-589, September 1958.

———. Part III: "Decentralized Socialism." *The Socialist Economy: A Study of Organizational Alternatives.* New York: Random House, 1967.

Weisskopf, Thomas E. "Challenges to Market Socialism: A Response to Critics." *Dissent*, 250-261, Spring 1992.

———. "Toward a Socialism for the Future, in the Wake of the Demise of the Socialism of the Past," *Review of Radical Political Economy* 24(3-4): 1-28, Fall-Winter 1992.

———. "The Case for Market Socialism," *Economic Review* (Keizai Kenkyu) 43(4): 305-319, October 1992.

———. "A Democratic Enterprise-Based Market Socialism," in John Roemer and Pranab Bardhan, eds., *Market Socialism: The Current Debate,* New York: Oxford University Press, 1993.

II. C. Profit-Oriented Market Socialism

This section of references contains the work of James A. Yunker (the author) on pragmatic market socialism, of Leland G. Stauber on municipal ownership market socialism, and of John E. Roemer and coauthors (chiefly Pranab Bardhan) on bank-centric market socialism. Since the major input into this book has obviously been my own prior work on market socialism, I will provide here some indication of the intents and purposes of each of my own contributions. Every one of the several articles on pragmatic market socialism contains a thumbnail institutional description of the system, but for a more extended institutional description see my 1992 book *Socialism Revised and Modernized: The Case for Pragmatic Market Socialism*, Chapter 2. The 1992 book covers much the same ground as the present book, but the presentation is oriented more to the professional economist than to the general reader. The 1993 book (*Capitalism versus Pragmatic Market Socialism: A General Equilibrium Evaluation*) is intended as a technical appendix to the 1992 book, an appendix directed to the specialist in economic systems theory.

See Yunker (1975) for a comparison of Langian, service, cooperative, and pragmatic market socialism; and see Yunker (1995) for a combined evaluation of the three models of profit-oriented market socialism: pragmatic, municipal ownership, and bank-centric. For a response to the capital management effort defense of capitalism from the perspective of pragmatic market socialism, see Yunker (1974, 1976, 1988, 1992 Chapter 4, 1993, 1996). For empirical evidence supportive of the plateau production function in capital management effort (which challenges the validity of the capital management effort justification for capital property income), see Yunker and Krehbiel (1988). For a technical critique of risk-taking as a justification for capital property income, see Yunker (1988). For a response to the saving defense of capitalism from the perspective of pragmatic market socialism, see Yunker (1976, 1988, 1992 Chapter 5, 1993). For a technical critique of the time preference justification for interest income (as a reward to saving), see Yunker (1992).

For a response to the people's capital thesis, see Yunker (1977, 1982, 1992 Chapter 7). For defense of the potential dynamic performance of pragmatic market socialism, see Yunker (1978, 1986, 1992 Chapter 6). For defense of pragmatic market socialism's compatibility with democracy, see Yunker (1986, 1992 Chapter 8). For analysis of possible international implications of adoption of pragmatic market socialism by the leading Western nations, see Yunker (1982, 1985, 1992 Chapter 9, 1993). For an extended response to potential assaults on profit-oriented market socialism based on agency theory, property rights, and other new and unintegrated branches of economic theory, see Yunker (1994). For argument to the effect that economic output would be higher under pragmatic market socialism than under capitalism owing to higher labor supply, see Yunker (1991, 1993). For argument to the effect that economic output would be higher under pragmatic market socialism than under capitalism owing to more assiduous effort among high-level corporation executives exposed to a larger threat of dismissal, see Yunker (1979, 1981, 1992 Chapter 4).

Bardhan, Pranab, "On Tackling the Soft Budget Constraint in Market Socialism," in John Roemer and Pranab Bardhan, eds., *Market Socialism: The Current Debate*, New York: Oxford University Press, 1993.

Bardhan, Pranab, and John Roemer. "On the Workability of Market Socialism," *Journal of Economic Perspectives* 8(2): 177-182, Spring 1994.

Roemer, John E. "Market Socialism—A Blueprint: How Such an Economy Might Work," *Dissent*, 562-575, Fall 1991.

———. *A Future for Socialism.* Cambridge, Mass.: Harvard University Press, 1994.

Roemer, John E., and Pranab Bardhan. "Market Socialism: A Case for Rejuvenation," *Journal of Economic Perspectives* 6(3): 101-116, Summer 1992.

———."Introduction," in John E. Roemer and Pranab Bardhan. *Market Socialism: The Current Debate*, New York: Oxford University Press, 1993.

Roemer, John E., and Joaquim Silvestre. "Investment Policy in Market Socialism," in John Roemer and Pranab Bardhan, eds., *Market Socialism: The Current Debate*, New York: Oxford University Press, 1993.

Stauber, Leland G. "The Implications of Market Socialism in the United States," *Polity* 8(1): 38-62, Fall 1975.

———. "A Proposal for a Democratic Market Economy," *Journal of Comparative Economics* 1(3): 235-258, September 1977.

———. "A Democratic Market Economy: A Response," *Journal of Comparative Economics* 2(4): 382-389, December 1978.

———. *A New Program for Democratic Socialism.* Carbondale, Ill.: Four Willows Press, 1987.

———. "A Concrete Proposal for Market Socialism for Large Enterprises: Reactions from West and East and Further Discussion," *Coexistence* 30(3): 213-235, September 1993.

Yunker, James A. "Capital Management Under Market Socialism," *Review of Social Economy* 32(2): 196-210, October 1974.

————. "A Survey of Market Socialist Forms," *Annals of Public and Cooperative Economy* 46(2): 131-162, April-June 1975.

————. "On the Potential Efficiency of Market Socialism," *ACES Bulletin* 18(2): 25-52, Summer 1976.

————. "The Social Dividend Under Market Socialism," *Annals of Public and Cooperative Economy* 48(1): 91-133, January-March 1977.

————. "Investment Propensities Under Capitalism and Market Socialism," *Rivista di Scienze Economiche e Commerciali* 25(10): 842-855, October 1978.

————. "The Microeconomic Efficiency Argument for Socialism Revisited," *Journal of Economic Issues* 13(1): 73-112, March 1979.

————. "The Microeconomic Efficiency of Socialism: Reply," *Journal of Economic Issues* 15(1): 220-227, March 1981.

————. "Ideological Harmonization as a Means of Promoting Authentic Detente: A False Hope?" *Co-Existence* 19(2): 158-176, October 1982.

————. "The People's Capitalism Thesis: A Skeptical Evaluation," *ACES Bulletin* 24(4): 1-47, Winter 1982.

————. "Practical Considerations in Designing a Supernational Federation," *World Futures* 21(3/4): 159-218, 1985.

————. "A Market Socialist Critique of Capitalism's Dynamic Performance," *Journal of Economic Issues* 20(1): 63-86, March 1986.

————. "Would Democracy Survive Under Market Socialism?" *Polity* 18(4): 678-695, Summer 1986.

————. "Risk-Taking as a Justification for Property Income," *Journal of Comparative Economics* 12(1): 74-88, March 1988.

————. "On the Morality of Capitalism: In Light of the Market Socialist Alternative," *Forum for Social Economics* 17(2): 23-39, Spring 1988.

————. "A New Perspective on Market Socialism," *Comparative Economic Studies* 30(2): 69-116, Summer 1988.

————. "Ludwig von Mises on the 'Artificial Market,'" *Comparative Economic Studies* 32(1): 108-140, Spring 1990.

————. "The Equity-Efficiency Tradeoff under Capitalism and Market Socialism," *Eastern Economic Journal* 17(1): 31-44, January 1991.

————. "Relatively Stable Lifetime Consumption as Evidence of Positive Time Preference," *Journal of Post-Keynesian Economics* 14(3): 347-366, Spring 1992.

———. *Socialism Revised and Modernized: The Case for Pragmatic Market Socialism*. New York: Praeger, 1992.

———. *Capitalism versus Pragmatic Market Socialism: A General Equilibrium Evaluation*. Norwell, Mass.: Kluwer Academic Publishers, 1993.

———. "New Prospects for East-West Ideological Convergence: A Market Socialist Viewpoint," *Coexistence* 30(3): 237-267, September 1993.

———. "Agency Issues and Managerial Incentives: Contemporary Capitalism versus Market Socialism," in Paul Zarembka, ed., *Research in Political Economy*, Vol. 14, Greenwich, Conn.: JAI Press, 1994.

———. "Evaluating Changes in the Distribution of Capital Wealth," *Economic Inquiry* 32(4): 597-615, October 1994.

———. "Post-Lange Market Socialism: An Evaluation of Profit-Oriented Proposals," *Journal of Economic Issues* 29(3): 683-717, September 1995.

———. "Capital Management under Profit-Oriented Market Socialism: An Explicit Function Approach," *Southern Economic Journal* 63(1): 18-35, July 1996.

Yunker, James A., and Timothy Krehbiel. "Investment Analysis by the Individual Investor," *Quarterly Review of Economics and Business* 28(4): 90-101, Winter 1988.

II. D. Relevant Evidence: Distribution of Capital Wealth

Only a relatively small proportion of the overall literature on wealth and income inequality has to do with capital wealth inequality. Many of the references on the following list are concerned with inequality in general, and are included merely to demonstrate that economic inequality is considered to be a social and ethical problem—a problem sufficiently serious to be worthy of effort toward amelioration (if the efficiency costs of such amelioration would not be too excessive). In this category are included several examples from the abundant concerned (not to say alarmist) literature on recent increases in overall inequality within the United States and the world: see Bishop et al. (1991), Denny Braun (1991), Fred Campano (1991), Camilo Dagum and Michele Zenga (1990), Folke Dovring (1991), Lynn Karoly (1993), Frank Levy et al. (1991, 1992), Frank Levy (1987), Nan Maxwell (1990), Lars Osberg (1984), and Andrew Winnick (1989).

With respect to the distribution of wealth (as opposed to income), most of the available material relates mainly to total wealth rather than to capital wealth. However, some information on capital wealth is often included in these studies and reports. For empirical information on the distribution of total wealth and/or capital wealth under contemporary capitalism in the U.S. and U.K., see Robert Lampman (1962), Dorothy Projector and Gertrude Weiss (1966), A. B. Atkinson (1972), James Smith and Stephen Franklin (1974), A. B. Atkinson and A. J. Harrison (1978), Melvin Oliver and Thomas Shapiro (1990), Daphne Greenwood and Edward Wolff (1992), and Edward Wolff (1987, 1989, 1992, 1994). Analysis of the various social problems and disadvantages of excessive wealth inequality is contained in C. Wright Mills (1956), Gabriel Kolko (1962), Ferdinand Lundberg (1968), Vance Packard (1989), Tom Bottomore and Robert Brym (1989), Sidney Carroll (1991), and Herbert Inhaber and Sidney Carroll (1991).

For references on the relatively minor contribution made by life cycle saving to overall wealth inequality, see A. B. Atkinson (1971) and J. S. Flemming (1979). For empirical and theoretical references on the major contribution made by inheritance to overall wealth inequality, see Josiah Wedgwood (1929), Colin Harbury (1962), Colin Harbury et al. (1973, 1977, 1979), Nicholas Oulton (1976), John A. Brittain (1977, 1978), Paul Menchik (1979, 1980), Paul Menchik and David Martin (1983), and Gerhard Orosel (1991).

Atkinson, Anthony B. "The Distribution of Wealth and the Individual Life Cycle," *Oxford Economic Papers* 23(2): 239-254, July 1971.
———. *Unequal Shares: Wealth in Britain.* London: Penguin, 1972.
———, ed. *Wealth, Income and Inequality*, second edition. New York: Oxford University Press, 1980.
Atkinson, Anthony B., and A. J. Harrison. *The Distribution of Personal Wealth in Britain.* Cambridge: Cambridge University Press, 1978.
Avery, Robert B., Gregory E. Elliehausen. "Financial Characteristics of High-Income Families," *Federal Reserve Bulletin* 72(3): 163-177, March 1986.
Avery, Robert B., Gregory E. Elliehausen, Glenn B. Canner, and Thomas A. Gustafson. "Survey of Consumer Finances, 1983," *Federal Reserve Bulletin* 70(9): 679-692, September 1984.
———. "Survey of Consumer Finances, 1983: Second Report," *Federal Reserve Bulletin* 70(12): 857-872, December 1984.
Barlow, Robin, Harvey Brazer, and James Morgan. *Economic Behavior of the Affluent.* Washington, D.C.: Brookings Institution, 1966.
Bishop, John A., John P. Formby, and W. James Smith. "Lorenz Dominance and Welfare: Changes in the U.S. Distribution of Income,

1967-1986," *Review of Economics and Statistics*, 134-139, February 1991.

Blitz, Rudolph C., and John J. Siegfried. "How Did the Wealthiest Americans Get So Rich?" *Quarterly Review of Economics and Finance*, 5-26, Spring 1992.

Bottomore, Tom, and Robert J. Brym. *The Capitalist Class: An International Study*. New York: New York University Press, 1989.

Braun, Denny. *The Rich Get Richer: The Rise of Income Inequality in the United States and the World*. Chicago: Nelson-Hall, 1991.

Brittain, John A. *The Inheritance of Economic Status*. Washington, D.C.: Brookings Institution, 1977.

―――. *Inheritance and the Inequality of Material Wealth*. Washington: Brookings Institution, 1978.

Bronfenbrenner, Martin. *Income Distribution Theory*. Chicago: Aldine-Atherton, 1971.

Campano, Fred. "Recent Trends in U.S. Family Income: A Comparison of All, White, and Black Families," *Journal of Post-Keynesian Economics*, 337-350, Spring 1991.

Carroll, Sidney L. "American Family Fortunes as Economic Deadweight," *Challenge*, 11-18, May-June 1991.

Dagum, Camilo, and Michele Zenga, eds. *Income and Wealth Distribution, Inequality and Poverty*. New York: Springer, 1990.

Dovring, Folke. *Inequality: The Political Economy of Income Distribution*. New York: Praeger, 1991.

Flemming, J. S. "The Effects of Earnings Inequality, Imperfect Capital Markets, and Dynastic Altruism on the Distribution of Wealth in Life Cycle Models," *Economica* 46(184): 363-380, November 1979.

Greenwood, Daphne, and Edward N. Wolff. "Changes in Wealth in the United States: Savings, Capital Gains, Inheritance, and Lifetime Transfers," *Journal of Population Economics* 5(4): 261-288, 1992.

Harbury, Colin D. "Inheritance and the Distribution of Personal Wealth in Britain," *Economic Journal* 72(228): 845-868, 1962.

Harbury, Colin D., and David M. Hitchens. *Inheritance and Wealth Inequality in Britain*. London: George Allen and Unwin, 1979.

Harbury, Colin D., David M. Hitchens, and Patrick C. McMahon. "On the Measurement of Inherited Wealth," *Review of Income and Wealth* 23(3): 309-314, September 1977.

Harbury, Colin D., and Patrick C. McMahon. "Inheritance and the Characteristics of Top Wealth Leavers in Britain," *Economic Journal* 83(331): 810-833, September 1973.

Inhaber, Herbert, and Sidney Carroll. *How Rich Is Too Rich? Economic Fairness and the Distribution of Income and Wealth in the United States.* New York: Praeger, 1991.

Juster, F. Thomas, and Kathleen A. Kuester. "Differences in the Measurement of Wealth, Wealth Inequality, and Wealth Consumption Obtained from Alternative U.S. Wealth Surveys," *Review of Income and Wealth,* 33-62, March 1991.

Karoly, Lynn. "The Trend in Inequality among Families, Individuals and Workers in the United States: A 25-Year Perspective," in *Uneven Tides: Rising Inequality in America,* Peter Gottschalk and Sheldon Danziger, eds. New York: Russell Sage Foundation, 1993.

Kennickell, Arthur, and Janice Shack-Marquez. "Changes in Family Finances from 1983 to 1989: Evidence from the Survey of Consumer Finances." *Federal Reserve Bulletin,* 1-18, January 1992.

Kessler, Denis, and Andre Masson, eds. *Modelling the Accumulation and Distribution of Wealth.* New York: Oxford University Press, 1988.

Kolko, Gabriel. *Wealth and Power in America.* New York: Praeger, 1962.

Lampman, Robert J. *The Share of the Top Wealth-Holders in National Wealth, 1922-1956.* Princeton, N.J.: Princeton University Press, 1962.

Levy, Frank S. *Dollars and Dreams: The Changing American Income Distribution.* New York: Russell Sage Foundation, 1987.

Levy, Frank S., and Richard C. Michel. *The Economic Future of America Families: Income and Wealth Trends.* Washington, D.C.: Urban Institute Press, 1991.

Levy, Frank S., and Richard J. Murnane. "U.S. Earnings Levels and Earnings Inequality: A Review of Recent Trends and Proposed Explanations," *Journal of Economic Literature* 30(3): 1333-1381, September 1992.

Lundberg, Ferdinand. *The Rich and the Super-Rich.* New York: Lyle Stuart, 1968.

Maxwell, Nan L. *Income Inequality in the United States, 1957-1985 .* Westport, Ct.: Greenwood, 1990.

Menchik, Paul L. "Inter-Generational Transmission of Inequality: An Empirical Study," *Economica* 46(184): 349-362, November 1979.

———. "The Importance of Material Inheritance: The Financial Link Between Generations," in James D. Smith, ed., *Modeling the Distribution and Intergenerational Transmission of Wealth.* Chicago: University of Chicago Press, 1980.

————. "Primogeniture, Equal Sharing, and the U.S. Distribution of Wealth," *Quarterly Journal of Economics* 94(2): 299-316, March 1980.

Menchik, Paul L., and David Martin. "Income Distribution, Lifetime Savings, and Bequests," *American Economic Review* 73(4): 672-690, September 1983.

Miller, Herman P. *Rich Man, Poor Man.* New York: Thomas Y. Crowell, 1971.

Mills, C. Wright. *The Power Elite.* New York: Oxford University Press, 1956.

Oliver, Melvin L., and Thomas M. Shapiro. "Wealth of a Nation: A Reassessment of Asset Inequality in America Shows at Least One Third of Households Are Asset-Poor," *American Journal of Economics and Sociology*, 129-151, April 1990.

Orosel, Gerhard O. "Inheritance and Inequality When Wealth Enters the Utility Function," *Journal of Economics (Zeitschrift für Nationalökonomie)* 53(2): 133-160, 1991.

Osberg, Lars. *Economic Inequality in the United States.* Armonk, N.Y.: M. E. Sharpe, 1984.

Oulton, Nicholas. "Inheritance and the Distribution of Wealth," *Oxford Economic Papers* 28(1): 86-101, March 1976.

Packard, Vance O. *The Ultra Rich: How Much Is Too Much?* Boston: Little, Brown, 1989.

Perlo, Victor. "'People's Capitalism' and Stock Ownership," *American Economic Review* 48(3): 333-347, June 1958.

Projector, Dorothy S. *Survey of Changes in Family Finances.* Washington, D.C.: Board of Governors of the Federal Reserve System, 1968.

Projector, Dorothy S., and Gertrude S. Weiss. *Survey of Financial Characteristics of Consumers.* Washington, D.C.: Board of Governors of the Federal Reserve System, 1966.

Ryscavage, Paul, and Peter Henle. "Earnings Inequality Accelerates in the 1980's," *Monthly Labor Review*, 3-16, December 1990.

Sahota, Gian Singh. "Theories of Personal Income Distribution: A Survey," *Journal of Economic Literature* 16(1): 1-55, March 1978.

Siegfried, John J., and Alison Roberts. "How Did the Wealthiest Britons Get So Rich?" *Review of Industrial Organization* 6(1): 19-32, 1991.

Smith, James D., ed. *The Personal Distribution of Income and Wealth.* New York: National Bureau of Economic Research, 1975.

Smith, James D., and Stephen D. Franklin. "The Concentration of Personal Wealth: 1922-1969," *American Economic Review* 64(2):

162-167, May 1974.

Thurow, Lester D. *Generating Inequality: Mechanisms of Distribution in the U.S. Economy.* New York: Basic Books, 1975.

Toshiyuki, Mizoguchi, ed. *Making Economies More Efficient and More Equitable: Factors Determining Income Distribution.* New York: Oxford University Press, 1991.

Tullock, Gordon. *Economics of Income Redistribution.* Boston: Kluwer-Nijhoff, 1983.

Wedgwood, Josiah. *The Economics of Inheritance.* London: Routledge and Kegan Paul, 1929.

Winnick, Andrew J. *Toward Two Societies: The Changing Distributions of Income and Wealth in the United States since 1960.* New York: Praeger, 1989.

Wolff, Edward N., ed. *International Comparisons of the Distribution of Household Wealth.* New York: Oxford University Press, 1987.

———. "Estimates of Household Wealth Inequality in the U.S., 1962-1983," *Review of Income and Wealth* 33(3): 231-256, September 1987.

———. "Long-Term Trends in U.S. Wealth Inequality: Methological Issues and Results," in Robert E. Lipsey and Helen Stone, eds., *The Measurement of Saving, Investment, and Wealth.* Chicago: University of Chicago Press, 1989.

———. "Changing Inequality of Wealth," *American Economic Review* 82(2): 552-558, May 1992.

———. "Trends in Household Wealth in the United States, 1962-83 and 1983-89," *Review of Income and Wealth* 40(2): 143-174, June 1994.

———. *Top Heavy: A Study of the Increasing Inequality of Wealth in America.* New York: Twentieth Century Fund Press, 1995.

II. E. Relevant Evidence: Separation of Ownership and Control

The seminal contribution of Adolf Berle and Gardiner Means (1932) on separation of ownership and control has inspired at least three related yet quite distinct literatures. First, there is an economic literature on the measurement of separation, and its impact (if any) on firm behavior. See, for example, Robert Gordon (1945), Robert J. Larner (1966, 1970), Joseph R. Monsen et al. (1968), David Kamerschen (1968, 1969, 1973), Brian Hindley (1970), John Palmer (1972, 1973, 1974), Kenneth Boudreaux (1973), Robert Sorenson (1974), Michael Lawriwsky (1984), Christos Pitelis and Roger Sugden (1986), Dennis Leech (1987), and Rexford Santerre and Stephen Neun (1989). Second, there has been a theoretical and empirical literature on managerial alternatives to the standard profit-maximization theory of the firm. See, for example, Joseph McQuire et al. (1962), Robin Marris (1964), Robert Marris and Dennis Mueller (1980), Oliver Williamson (1964, 1975, 1981), John Williamson (1966), William Baumol (1967), C. J. Hawkins (1970), Wilbur Lewellen (1970), Wilbur Lewellen and Blaine Huntsman (1970), M. A. Crew et al. (1971), J. R. Wildsmith (1974), David Ciscel (1974), and Gordon Tullock (1978). Third, there has been a large theoretical literature on the principal-agent situation. See, for example, Stanley Baiman (1980), Stanley Baiman and Joel Demski(1980), Joel Demski et al. (1978, 1980, 1984, 1989), Milton Harris and Arthur Raviv (1978, 1979), James Hess (1983), L. Peter Jennergren (1980), Rober B. Myerson (1982), Barry Nalebuff and Joseph Stiglitz (1983), Stephen Ross (1973), David Sappington (1983, 1991), Stephen Shavell (1979), and Ann Van Ackere (1993). Quite a lot of the principal-agent literature has appeared in accounting journals, which is not surprising in that the profession of accounting (particularly the public accounting branch) owes much of its size and importance to the separation of ownership and control. The "doctrine of irrelevance" (i.e., the proposition that the separation of ownership and control has *not* had an appreciable effect on firm performance) has been argued most notably by Eugene Fama (1980), Eugene Fama and Michael Jensen (1983), and Michael Jensen and William Meckling (1976).

Blair, Margaret M. *Ownership and Control: Rethinking Corporate Governance for the Twenty-First Century*. Washington: Brookings, 1995.

Baiman, Stanley. "Agency Research in Managerial Accounting: A Survey," *Journal of Accounting Literature* 1: 154-213, Spring 1982.

Baiman, Stanley, and Joel Demski. "Economically Optimal Performance Evaluation and Control Systems," *Journal of Accounting Research* 18 (Sup.): 184-220, 1980.

Baumol, William J. *Business Behavior, Value and Growth*, revised edition. New York: Harcourt, Brace and World, 1967. First ed.: 1959.

Berle, Adolf A. *Power Without Property*. New York: Harcourt Brace, 1959.

Berle, Adolf A., and Gardiner C. Means. *The Modern Corporation and Private Property*. New York: Macmillan, 1932.

Boudreaux, Kenneth J. "Managerialism and Risk-Return Performance," *Southern Economic Journal* 39(3): 366-373, January 1973.

Burnham, James. *The Managerial Revolution*. New York: John Day, 1941.

Ciscel, David H. "Determinants of Executive Compensation," *Southern Economic Journal* 40(4): 613-617, April 1974.

Copeland, Melvin Thomas, and Andrew Renwick Towl. *The Board of Directors and Business Management*. Boston: Division of Research, Graduate School of Business Administration, Harvard University, 1947.

Crew, M. A., M. W. Jones-Lee, and C. K. Rowley. "X-Theory Versus Management Discretion Theory," *Southern Economic Journal* 38(2): 173-184, October 1971.

Demski, Joel, and Gerald Feltham. "Economic Incentives in Budgetary Control Systems," *Accounting Review* 53(2): 336-359, April 1978.

Demski, Joel, and D. Kreps. "Models in Managerial Accounting," *Journal of Accounting Research* 20: Supplement, 1980.

Demski, Joel, and David E. M. Sappington. "Optimal Incentive Contracts with Multiple Agents," *Journal of Economic Theory* 17: 152-171, 1984.

———. "Hierarchical Structure and Responsibility Accounting," *Journal of Accounting Research* 27(1): 40-58, 1989.

Gordon, Robert A. *Business Leadership in the Large Corporation*. Washington: Brookings Institution, 1945.

Fama, Eugene F. "Agency Problems and the Theory of the Firm," *Journal of Political Economy* 88(2): 288-307, April 1980.

Fama, Eugene F., and Michael C. Jensen. "Separation of Ownership and Control," *Journal of Law and Economics* 26(2): 301-326, June 1983.

Harris, Milton, and Arthur Raviv. "Some Results on Incentive Contracts with Applications to Education, Health Insurance and Law Enforcement," *American Economic Review* 68(1): 20-30, March 1978.

———. "Optimal Incentive Contracts with Imperfect Information," *Journal of Economic Theory* 20(2): 231-259, April 1979.

Hawkins, C. J. "On the Sales Revenue Maximization Hypothesis," *Journal of Industrial Economics* 18(2): 129-140, April 1970.

Heller, Milton F., Jr. "The Board of Directors: Legalistic Anachronism or Vital Force?" *California Management Review* 14(3): 24-30, Spring 1972.

Hess, James D. Chapter 13: "Principals and Agents." In *The Economics of Organization*. Amsterdam: North-Holland, 1983.

Hindley, Brian. "Separation of Ownership and Control in the Modern Corporation," *Journal of Law and Economics* 13(1): 185-221, April 1970.

Jennergren, L. Peter. "On the Design of Incentives in Business Firms: A

Survey of Some Research," *Managerial Science* 26(2): 180-201, February 1980.

Jensen, Michael C., ed. "Symposium on the Market for Corporate Control: The Scientific Evidence," *Journal of Financial Economics* 11(1-4): 1-471, April 1983.

Jensen, Michael C., and William H. Meckling. "Theory of the Firm: Managerial Behavior, Agency Costs and Ownership Structure," *Journal of Financial Economics* 3(4): 305-360, October 1976.

Jensen, Michael C., and Jerold L. Zimmerman, eds. "Symposium on Management Compensation and the Managerial Labor Market," *Journal of Accounting and Economics* 7(1-3): 3-251, April 1985.

Kamerschen, David R. "The Influence of Ownership and Control on Profit Rates," *American Economic Review* 58(3): 432-447, June 1968.

―――. "The Effect of Separation of Ownership and Control on the Performance of the Large Firm in the U.S. Economy," *Revista di Scienze Economiche e Commerziali* 16(5): 489-493, May 1969.

―――. "Further Thoughts on the Separation of Ownership and Control," *Revista di Scienze Economiche e Commerziali* 20(2): 179-183, February 1973.

Larner, Robert J. "The 200 Largest Nonfinancial Corporations," *American Economic Review* 56(4): 777-787, September 1966.

―――. *Management Control and the Large Corporation.* New York: Dunellen, 1970.

Lawriwsky, Michael L. "A Critical View of Studies Examining the Performance Effects of the Separation of Ownership and Control," *Revista Internazionale di Scienze Economiche e Commerciali* 31(4): 312-328, April 1984.

Leech, Dennis. "Corporate Ownership and Control: A New Look at the Evidence of Berle and Means," *Oxford Economic Papers* N.S. 39(3): 534-551, September 1987.

Lewellen, Wilbur G. *The Ownership Income of Management.* Princeton, N.J.: National Bureau of Economic Research, 1971.

Lewellen, Wilbur G., and Blaine Huntsman. "Managerial Pay and Corporate Performance," *American Economic Review* 60(4): 710-720, September 1970.

Mace, Myles L. "The President and the Board of Directors," *Harvard Business Review* 50(2): 37-49, March-April 1972.

Marris, Robin. *The Economic Theory of Managerial Capitalism.* Glencoe, Ill.: Free Press, 1964.

Marris, Robin, and Dennis C. Mueller. "The Corporate Economy: Growth, Competition and the Invisible Hand," *Journal of Economic Literature* 18(1): 32-63, March 1980.

Marris, Robin, and Adrian Wood, eds. *The Corporate Economy: Growth, Competition and Innovative Potential.* Cambridge, Mass.: Harvard University Press, 1971.

McGuire, Joseph W., John S. Y. Chiu, and Alvar O. Elbring. "Executive Incomes, Sales and Profits," *American Economic Review* 52(3): 753-761, September 1962.

Monsen, R. Joseph, John S. Y. Chiu, and David E. Cooley. "The Effect of Separation of Ownership and Control on the Performance of a Large Firm," *Quarterly Journal of Economics* 83(2): 435-451, August 1968.

Myerson, Roger B. "Optimal Coordination Mechanisms in Generalized Principal-Agent Problems," *Journal of Mathematical Economics* 10(1): 67-81, June 1982.

Nalebuff, Barry J., and Joseph E. Stiglitz. "Prizes and Incentives: Towards a General Theory of Compensation and Competition," *Bell Journal of Economics* 14(1): 21-43, Spring 1983.

Palmer, John. "The Separation of Ownership from Control in Large US Industrial Corporations," *Quarterly Review of Economics and Business* 12(3): 55-62, Autumn 1972.

―――. "The Profit Performance Effects of the Separation of Ownership and Control in Large U.S. Industrial Corporations," *Bell Journal of Economics and Management Science* 3(1): 293-303: Spring 1973.

―――. "Interaction Effects and the Separation of Ownership from Control," *Revista Internazionale di Scienze Economiche e Commerziali* 21(2): 146-150, February 1974.

Pitelis, Christos N., and Roger Sugden. "The Separation of Ownership and Control in the Theory of the Firm: A Reappraisal," *International Journal of Industrial Organization* 4(1): 69-86, March 1986.

Pratt, John W., and Richard Zeckhauser. *Principals and Agents: The Structure of Business.* Boston: Harvard Business School, 1985.

Radice, H. K. "Control Type, Profitability and Growth in Large Firms: An Empirical Study," *Economic Journal* 81: 547-562, September 1971.

Ross, Stephen A. "The Economic Theory of Agency: The Principal's Problem," *American Economic Review* 63(2): 134-139, May 1973.

Santerre, Rexford E., and Stephen P. Neun. "Managerial Control and Executive Compensation in the 1930s: A Reexamination," *Quarterly*

Journal of Business and Economics 28(4): 100-118, Autumn 1989.

Sappington, David E. M. "Limited Liability Contracts between Principal and Agent," *Journal of Economic Theory* 29: 1-21, 1983.

————. "Incentives in Principal-Agent Relationships," *Journal of Economic Perspectives* 5(2): 45-66, Spring 1991.

Shavell, Stephen. "Risk Sharing and Incentives in the Principal and Agent Relationship," *Bell Journal of Economics* 10(1): 55-73, Spring 1979.

Sorensen, Robert. "The Separation of Ownership and Control and Firm Performance: An Empirical Analysis," *Southern Economic Journal* 41(1): 145-148, July 1974.

Tullock, Gordon. "Welfare Effects of Sales Maximization," *Economic Inquiry* 16(1): 113-118, January 1978.

Van Ackere, Ann. "The Principal/Agent Paradigm: Its Relevance to Various Functional Fields," *European Journal of Operational Research* 70: 83-103, 1993.

Vance, Jack O. "The Care and Feeding of the Board of Directors," *California Management Review* 21(4): 29-34, Summer 1979.

Wildsmith, J. R. *Managerial Theories of the Firm.* New York: Dunellen, 1973.

Williamson, John. "Profit, Growth and Sales Maximization," *Economica* New Series 33: 1-16, February 1966.

Williamson, Oliver E. *The Economics of Discretionary Behavior: Managerial Objectives in a Theory of the Firm.* Englewood Cliffs, N.J.: Prentice-Hall, 1964.

————. *Markets and Hierarchies.* New York: Free Press, 1975.

————. "The Modern Corporation: Origins, Evolution, Attributes," *Journal of Economic Literature* 19(4): 1537-1568, December 1981.

II. F. Relevant Evidence: Institutional Investors and Capital Markets

Included here is a sampling of references on the structure and operations of capital markets, with special emphasis on the important role of institutional investors in these markets, and on the efficiency of these markets. A compelling implication of the efficient markets hypothesis is that it is fruitless to try to "outsmart the market," and that in the absence of inside information the "buy and hold" strategy is optimal because it minimizes transactions costs. This implication is stated explicitly by Burton Malkiel (1973), Burton Malkiel and Paul Istenberg (1978), and Simon Keane (1980, 1983). Another reference of special interest is James Walter (1962), whose study of investment divisions of life insurance companies demonstrated that investment analysis and selection is considered to be a routine task not requiring special incentive schemes and payments for the employees who perform the task.

Agrawal, Anup, and Gershon Mandelker. "Shark Repellents and the Role of Institutional Investors in Corporate Governance," *Managerial and Decision Economics* 13(1): 15-22, January-February 1992.

Brown, Lawrence D. "Earnings Forecasting Research: Its Implications for Capital Markets Research," *International Journal of Forecasting* 9(3): 295-320, November 1993.

Berkman, Neil. "Institutional Investors and the Stock Market," *New England Economic Review*, November-December 1977.

Bernstein, Peter L. *Capital Ideas: The Improbable Origins of Modern Wall Street.* New York: Free Press, 1992.

Blume, Marshall E., Jeremy J. Siegel, and Dan Rottenberg. *Revolution on Wall Street: The Rise and Decline of the New York Stock Exchange.* New York: Norton, 1993.

Campbell, Tim S., and William A. Kracaw. *Financial Institutions and Capital Markets.* New York: HarperCollins, 1993.

Cootner, Paul H., ed. *The Random Character of Stock Market Prices.* Cambridge, Mass.: MIT Press, 1964.

Cosh, A. D., et al. "Institutional Investment, Mergers and the Market for Corporate Control," *International Journal of Industrial Organization* 7(1): 73-100, March 1989.

Dimsdale, Nicholas, and Martha Prevezer, eds. *Capital Markets and Corporate Governance.* New York: Oxford University Press, 1994.

Dimson, Elroy, ed. *Stock Market Anomalies.* New York: Cambridge University Press, 1988.

Dyckman, Thomas R. *Efficient Capital Markets and Accounting: A Critical Analysis,* second edition. Englewood Cliffs, N.J.: Prentice-Hall, 1986.

Eakins, Stan. "Institutional Investor Support of Managers: An Investigation of Tender Offers," *Quarterly Journal of Business and Economics* 32(3): 75-84, Summer 1993.

Emery, John T. "Efficient Capital Markets and the Information Content of Accounting Numbers," *Journal of Financial and Quantitative Analysis* 9(2): 139-149, March 1974.

Fabozzi, Frank J., and Franco Modigliani. *Capital Markets: Institutions and Instruments.* Englewood Cliffs, N.J.: Prentice-Hall, 1992.

Fama, Eugene F. "Efficient Capital Markets: A Review of Theory and Empirical Work," *Journal of Finance* 25(2): 383-417, May 1970.

————. "Efficient Capital Markets: II," *Journal of Finance* 46(5): 1575-1617, December 1991.

Fama, Eugene F., and Arthur B. Laffer. "Information and Capital Markets," *Journal of Business* 44(3): 289-298, July 1971.

Farrar, Donald E., and Lance Girton. "Institutional Investors and Concentration of Financial Power: Berle and Means Revisited," *Journal of Finance* 36(2): 369-381, May 1981.

Foley, Bernard J. *Capital Markets*. New York: St. Martin's Press, 1991.

Frederickson, E. Bruce, and Moon K. Kim. "Projections and Implications of Equity Holdings by Institutional Investors in the Year 2000," *Quarterly Journal of Business and Economics* 25(3): 34-54, Summer 1986.

Gonedes, Nicholas J. "Efficient Capital Markets and External Accounting," *Accounting Review* 47(1): 11-21, January 1972.

Jensen, Michael C., ed. *Studies in the Theory of Capital Markets*. New York: Praeger, 1972.

Keane, Simon M. *The Efficient Market Hypothesis and the Implications for Financial Reporting*. London: Gee and Co., 1980.

————. *Stock Market Efficiency: Theory, Evidence and Implications*. New York: Humanities Press, 1983.

Lee, Unro. "Do Stock Prices Follow Random Walk? Some International Evidence," *International Review of Economics and Finance* 1(4): 315-327, 1992.

Leroy, Stephen F. "Efficient Capital Markets and Martingales," *Journal of Economic Literature* 27(4): 1583-1621, December 1989.

Malkiel, Burton G. *A Random Walk down Wall Street*. New York: Norton, 1973.

Malkiel, Burton, and Paul B. Istenberg. "A Winning Strategy for an Efficient Market," *Journal of Portfolio Management* 4(4): 20-25, Summer 1978.

Mayer, Colin, and Xavier Vives, eds. *Capital Markets and Financial Intermediation*. New York: Cambridge University Press, 1992.

Peters, Edgar E. *Chaos and Order in the Capital Markets: A New View of Cycles, Prices amd Market Volatility*. New York: Wiley, 1991.

Prodano, Sylvio. *Pension Funds: Investment and Performance*. Brookfield, Vt.: Gower, 1987.

Schwartz, Robert A. "Institutionalization of the Equity Markets," *Journal of Portfolio Management* 17(2): 44-49, Winter 1991.

Schwert, G. William, and Clifford W. Smith, Jr., eds. *Empirical Research in Capital Markets*. New York: McGraw-Hill, 1992.

Sheffrin, Steven M. Chapter 4: "Efficient Markets and Rational Expectations." In *Rational Expectations*. Cambridge: Cambridge University Press, 1983.

Shiller, Robert J. *Market Volatility*. Cambridge, Mass.: MIT Press, 1989.

———. "Who's Minding the Store?" In *Report of the Twentieth Century Fund Task Force on Market Speculation and Corporate Governance*. New York: Twentieth Century Fund Press, 1992.

Strong, Norman, and Martin Walker. *Information and Capital Markets*. New York: Basil Blackwell, 1987.

Szewczyk, Samuel H., George P. Tsetsekos, and Raj Varma. "Institutional Ownership and the Liquidity of Common Stock Offerings," *Financial Review* 27(2): 211-225, May 1992.

Walter, James E. *The Investment Process: As Characterized by Leading Life Insurance Companies*. Boston: Division of Research, Graduate School of Business Administration, Harvard University, 1962.

Wessel, Robert H. "The Takeover Mania on World Capital Markets," *Revista Internazionale de Scienze Economiche e Commerziali* 37(7): 629-644, July 1990.

II. G. Specialized Capitalist Apologetics re Market Socialism

Owing both to the relative novelty of the market socialist concept, and to the fact that it has not as yet attracted sufficient attention, interest, and sympathy to represent a serious threat to the capitalist status quo, there is not yet a great deal in the way of capitalist apologetics aimed explicitly at market socialism. Some of the references listed above in Sections II.A. (on Langian market socialism) and II.B. (on cooperative market socialism) are lukewarm or even negative toward these variants of market socialism, but in this author's judgment none of them are sufficiently strident or tendentious to qualify as full-fledged capitalist apologetics. The references listed below, in contrast, probably do qualify as such.

Some critics of Marxist political economy, such as N. Scott Arnold (1987, 1992) and David McNally (1993), argue that the whole idea of market socialism is antithetical to Marxist doctrine. This argument has been vigorously disputed by David Schweickart, a proponent of cooperative market socialism (see the exchange between N. Scott Arnold and David Schweickart in the October 1987 issue of *Economics and Philosophy*). Even if the argument *were* valid, the reaction of most contemporary proponents of market socialism would probably be: "So much the worse for Marx!"

At the moment a widely employed argument against market socialism in general is that this system has already been tried in Eastern Europe (during the post-Stalin reform era), and it failed miserably—end of story. This argument is found, for example, in János Kornai (1986, 1992, 1993), Alberto Chilosi (1992), Michael Keren (1993), and Joseph Stiglitz (1993, 1994). It is also implied (perhaps unintentionally) by the title of William S. Kern's compilation on Eastern European reform: *From Socialism to Market Economy: The Transition Problem*—which suggests the fundamental incompatibility of socialism with the free market. The argument is dubious mainly because the Eastern European nations, despite decades of rhetoric and tinkering with "reforms," never came close to a genuine implementation of market socialism (Soviet central planning orthodoxy was too strong for that).

With respect to Langian market socialism, the list below includes Friedrich Hayek's well-known critique in *Economica* (1940). It also includes several more recent assaults on Langian market socialism: such as those by G. Warren Nutter (1974), Karen Vaughn (1980), Peter Murrell (1983), Don Lavoie (1985), and David Steele (1992). Inspired by Austrian school ideology, these critiques argue that whatever might be the virtues of Langian market socialism in terms of static neoclassical economic theory, the system would perform abysmally in the long run owing to inadequate entrepreneurship and dynamism. Of course, in the author's judgment, assaults on Langian market socialism are simply beating a dead horse. With respect to cooperative market socialism, the list below includes Michael Jensen and William Meckling's critique in the *Journal of Business* (1979), which is sufficiently dismissive toward its subject to qualify as full-fledged capitalist apologetics.

Contemporary critiques directed explicitly against variants of profit-oriented market socialism are, for the moment, fairly rare. But there are a few examples to be cited. The author's proposal for pragmatic market socialism has been criticized by Peter Murrell (1981, 1983) and Louis Putterman (in two articles, both published in 1993). My response to Peter Murrell's 1981 critique was contained in the same issue of the *Journal of Economic Issues* (March 1981) in which the critique appeared. My response to Murrell's 1983 critique is contained (implicitly) in my 1993 technical book on a general equilibrium evaluation of capital versus pragmatic market socialism. My response to Putterman is contained in my 1994 article in *Research in Political Economy*. This same article also replies to other, more general criticisms of market socialism, such as that by Louis Makowski and Joseph Ostroy (1993). Leland Stauber's municipal ownership market socialist proposal was criticized by Susan Rose-

Ackerman (1978) and Wayne Leeman (1978). Stauber responded to these critiques in the same issue of the *Journal of Comparative Economics* (March 1978). An exhange on bank-centric market socialism between John Roemer and Pranab Bardhan (on the pro side) and Andrei Shleifer and Robert Vishny (on the con side) is contained in the Spring 1994 issue of the *Journal of Economic Perspectives*.

Arnold, N. Scott. "Marx and Disequilibrium in Market Socialist Relations of Production," *Economics and Philosophy* 3(1): 23-47, April 1987.

―――. "Further Thoughts on the Degeneration of Market Socialism: A Reply to Schweickart," *Economics and Philosophy* 3(2): 320-330, October 1987.

―――. "Final Reply to Professor Schweickart," *Economics and Philosophy* 3(2): 335-338, October 1987.

―――. "Market Socialism," *Critical Review* 6(4): 517-557, Fall 1992.

Chilosi, Alberto. "Market Socialism: A Historical View and a Retrospective Assessment," *Economic Systems* 16: 171-185, April 1992.

Hayek, Friedrich. "Socialist Calculation: The 'Competitive Solution,'" *Economica* 7 (New Series): 125-149, May 1940.

Jensen, Michael C., and William H. Meckling. "Rights and Production Functions: An Application to Labor-Managed Firms and Co-Determination," *Journal of Business* 52(4): 469-506, October 1979.

Keren, Michael. "On the Impossibility of Market Socialism," *Eastern Economic Journal* 19(3): 333-344, Summer 1993.

Kern, William S., ed. *From Socialism to Market Economy: The Transition Problem.* Kalamazoo, Mich.: Upjohn Institute, 1992.

Kornai, János. "The Soft Budget Constraint," *Kyklos* 39(1): 3-30, 1986.

―――. *The Socialist System: The Political Economy of Communism.* Princeton, N.J.: Princeton University Press, 1992.

―――. "Market Socialism Revisited," in John Roemer and Pranab Bardhan, eds., *Market Socialism: The Current Debate.* New York: Oxford University Press, 1993.

Lavoie, Don. *Rivalry and Central Planning: The Socialist Calculation Debate Reconsidered.* New York: Cambridge University Press, 1985.

Leeman, Wayne A. "On Leland G. Stauber, 'A Proposal for a Democratic Market Economy,'" *Journal of Comparative Economics* 2(1): 71-72, March 1978.

Makowski, Louis, and Joseph M. Ostroy, "General Equilibrium and Market Socialism: Clarifying the Logic of Competitive Markets," in John

Roemer and Pranab Bardhan, eds., *Market Socialism: The Current Debate.* New York: Oxford University Press, 1993.

McNally, David. *Against the Market: Political Economy, Market Socialism and the Marxist Critique.* New York: Routledge, 1993.

Murrell, Peter. "The Microeconomic Efficiency Argument for Socialism Revisited: Comment," *Journal of Economic Issues* 15(1): 211-219, March 1981.

―――. "Did the Theory of Market Socialism Answer the Challenge of Ludwig von Mises? A Reinterpretation of the Socialist Controversy." *History of Political Economy* 15(1): 92-105, 1983.

―――. "Incentives and Income Under Market Socialism," *Journal of Comparative Economics* 8(3): 261-276, September 1984.

Nutter, G. Warren. "Markets Without Property: A Grand Illusion," in Eirik Furubotn and Svetozar Pejovich, eds., *The Economics of Property Rights*, Cambridge, Mass.: Ballinger, 1974.

Putterman, Louis. "The Public as Principal: Agency under Common Ownership Market Socialism," in John Roemer and Pranab Bardhan, eds., *Market Socialism: The Current Debate.* New York: Oxford University Press, 1993.

―――. "Exit, Voice, and Portfolio Choice: Agency and Public Ownership," *Economics and Politics* 5(3): 205-218, November 1993.

Rose-Ackerman, Susan. "Redistribution Policy and Local Government Behavior, Comment on L. Stauber, 'A Proposal for a Democratic Market Economy,'" *Journal of Comparative Economics* 2(1): 73-84, March 1978.

Shleifer, Andrei, and Robert Vishny. "Pervasive Shortages under Socialism," *Rand Journal of Economics* 23(2): 237-246, Summer 1992.

―――. "The Politics of Market Socialism," *Journal of Economic Perspectives* 8(2): 165-176, Spring 1994.

Steele, David Ramsey. *From Marx to Mises: Post-Capitalist Society and the Challenge of Economic Calculation.* LaSalle, Ill.: Open Court, 1992.

Stiglitz, Joseph E. "Market Socialism and Neoclassical Economics," in John Roemer and Pranab Bardhan, eds., *Market Socialism: The Current Debate.* New York: Oxford University Press, 1993.

―――. *Whither Socialism?* Cambridge, Mass.: MIT Press, 1994.

Vaughn, Karen. "Economic Calculation under Socialism: The Austrian Contribution," *Economic Inquiry* 18(4): 535-554, October 1980.

INDEX

ABOUT THE AUTHOR

James A. Yunker is Professor of Economics at Western Illinois University (Macomb, Illinois), where he teaches Economic Theory and Econometrics. His education was at Fordham University (B.A., 1965), the University of California at Berkeley (M.A., 1966), and Northwestern University (Ph.D., 1971). From the mid-1970s onward, his primary research interest has been market socialism, and he has published extensively on the subject. He has a home page on the World Wide Web at the following URL:

http://www.ECNet.Net/users/miecon/wiu/faculty/yunker/jyunker.htm